DANCE of DAYS

TWO DECADES OF PUNK IN THE NATION'S CAPITAL

Mark Andersen & Mark Jenkins

dance of days

"I thought my eyes would be dry
But now I see and know
This moment has a bitter taste
I will not have my statement
Spit back in my face

We all struggle
For our dreams to be realized
They end up objects of our own despise
Why?

The dance of days

How did I find myself
Standing in this place?
We have done so much

And now I find myself
Standing in this place again
We can do so much more . . ."

—Embrace, 1985

two decades of punk in the nation's capital

Mark Andersen & Mark Jenkins

Akashic Books
New York

Dance of Days

Two Decades of Punk in the Nation's Capital

All of Mark Andersen's royalties from the sale of this book will be donated to the Arthur S. Flemming Center, a cooperative project of Emmaus Services for the Aging, Positive Force DC, the Washington Peace Center, Brian MacKenzie Infoshop, Peter Maurin Center/Catholic Worker Bookstore, the Interfaith Conference of Metropolitan Washington, DC Independent Media Center, mutualaid.org, Gray Panthers of Metro DC, and DC Books to Prisoners Project. The Center is an outpost of radical arts, organizing, education, and service in the Shaw neighborhood. For more information, or to send a donation, contact Emmaus Services for the Aging, 1426 9th Street, NW, Washington, DC 20001, 202-745-1200, 202-745-1246 (fax), emmausservices.org, emmausdc@aol.com.

Design: David Janik, Jason Farrell, and Sohrab Habibion

Front Cover Photographs: HR of Bad Brains, Rock Against Racism show, Valley Green public housing project, September 1979 *(by Lucian Perkins)*; Ian MacKaye of Minor Threat, Wilson Center, 1983 *(by Jim Saah, www.jimsaah.com)*; Kathi Wilcox and Kathleen Hanna of Bikini Kill, with Laura Solitaire and Erika Reinstein of Riot Grrrl DC in front row, PF Filipino human rights benefit, St. Stephen's Church, October 1991 *(by Brad Sigal)*

Back Cover Photograph: Guy Picciotto and Brendan Canty of Fugazi, PF March on Washington Memorial Concert, Sylvan Theater, August 1993 *(by Pat Graham)*

All Photographs and Images: Courtesy of the artists

ISBN: 1-888451-44-0
Library of Congress Control Number: 2003102243
©2001, 2003 Mark Andersen and Mark Jenkins
Published by Akashic Books
Originally published by Soft Skull Press
Fourth printing (Second Akashic Books printing)
Printed in Canada

Akashic Books
PO Box 1456
New York, NY 10009
Akashic7@aol.com
www.akashicbooks.com

table of contents

for Tulin, Royce, and Beau

Mark Andersen thanks: my parents Anna Margaret Vik and Merlin Peter Andersen, my siblings Barbara and Dale, the Tischmak clan, Elizabeth Ellison, B. Wardlaw, David Steinberg, Brendan Hoar and his grandmother, Gladys Gallagher Hoart, Ian MacKaye, Jeff Nelson, Jenny Toomey, Cynthia Connolly, Claire O'Neal McBride and anyone who ever lived at PF House, Edison Street House, or who worked with me at Emmaus, Common Concerns, PETA, the Washington Peace Center, CARE, Arlington Food Co-op or Iona while I was wrestling with this book, my beloved Tulin, Johnny Temple and Johanna Ingalls at Akashic, Dan Sinker at Punk Planet, Lely Constantinople, Alec MacKaye, Rachel Lynn Anderson, Donna Wilson for taking care of Demo while I was in Montana, Sean Knight, Brad Sigal, Joy Simonson, Meridith Welch, my recovery comrades, everyone who shared of themselves in any way to make this possible, especially Jen Smith, Sharon Cheslow, Kim Kane, Tim Yo (R.I.P.), Martin Sprouse, Mark Jenkins, Richard Nash, Sander, David, Nick, Annika, Boomer, Chris, Danielle and all at Soft Skull, Charlie Moats, Kim Coletta, J. Robbins, Anderson Allen, Sid McCray, Leslie Clague, Sohrab Habibion, Ethelbert Miller, Joey Aronstamn, Wendel Blow, Maria Jones, Tomas Squip, Pete Murray, Danny Ingram, Lydia and Caroline Ely, Allison Chang, Allison Kuttner, Bryan Lehman, Mark Weills, Ananda La Vita, Claudia Von Vacano, Joe Hunter, Marty Gruss, Dave Redman, Malcolm Riviera, Jerry Williams, Don Smith, Erika Reinstein, Melissa, Michael, Amy, and Alec at Dischord Direct, Paul and Dead Inside for help with the UK tour, Niall, Charlotte, and all the other great people we met on the road, Adam, Stu, Helen, and all those who have helped me on my various tours, Lori Taylor, Mo Sussman, Wendy, Krishna (R.I.P.), and Moe, Robert Hilton, Isaac UK, Diana Beruff, Paul Bishow, Gini Muller, David Curtis, Eric and Todd Mason, Tony Countey and family for use of their couch, Dave, Michelle, Jay, Jason, Jen and all the Minot Cultural Collective Center punks, Irene Kachena Strauss, Jennifer Baumgardner and Amy Richards for inspiration past and present, Chuck Bettis, Richard Gibson and MFD, the one-and-only original Rammer, Pat Graham, Jim Saah, Chris Henderson, John Falls, Lucian Perkins, Glen Friedman, Jay Rabinowitz, Monica Gesue, Susie Josephson, Tiffany Pruitt, Lloyd Wolf, and any photog or other co-conspirator we failed to credit or thank (let me know and I'll make sure it gets in future editions!), and, finally, all my PF DC pals over the years.

Mark Andersen would also like to acknowledge all those interviewed for this book: Joey Aronstamn, Tommy Ashton, Randy Austin, Natalie Avery, Brian Baker, Chris Bald, Jeff Bale, Billy Banks, Charles Bennington, Tom Berard, Jello Biafra, Dug Birdzell, Paul Bishow, Wendel Blow, Anne Bonafede, Alec Bourgeois, Mark Bowen, Margo Buckley, Molly Burnham, Russell Braen, Myron Bretholz, Shawn Brown, David Byers, Keith Campbell, Brendan Canty, Rupert Chappelle, Sharon Cheslow, Leslie Clague, Eamon Clifford, Michelle Cochran, Cynthia Connolly, Lara Connolly, Neil Cooper, Paul Cornwell, Anthony Countey, Scott Crawford, Charlie Davis, Dana DeNike, Dave Dictor, Pierre DuVeuw, Lydia Ely, Nick English, Boyd Farrell, Mike Fellows, Dante Ferrando, Roddy Frantz, Robert Goldstein, Vivien Greene, Sab Grey, Geordie Grindle, Skip Groff, Dave Grohl, John Hagerhorst, Mark Haggerty, Kendall Hall, Mike Hampton, Kathleen Hanna, Xyra Harper, Chris Haskett, Mike Heath, HR, Susan Hudson, Lida Husik, Danny Ingram, Kenny Inouye, Eddie Janney, JC, Darryl Jenifer, Mark Jenkins, Calvin Johnson, Michael Johnston, Kim Kane, Larry Keitz, Tim Kerr, Jon Kirschsten, Steve Kiviat, Eric Lagdameo, Joe Lally, Steve Lorber, Mic Lowe, Tom Lyle, Alec MacKaye, Amanda MacKaye, Ian MacKaye, Lois Maffeo, Mike Markarian, Michael Marriotte, Seth Martin, Sid McCray, Gary Miller, Susan Mumford, Pete Murray, Jeff Nelson, Molly Neuman, Steve Niles, the NOU, Gordon Ornelas, Mitch Parker, Guy Picciotto, Amy Pickering, Lyle Preslar, Bert Queiroz, Jack Rabid, Michael Reidy, Barbara Anne Rice, Monica Richards, Jimi Riley, Malcolm Riviera, Henry Rollins, Joe Sasfy, Scooter, Colin Sears, Janelle Simmons, Erin Smith, Jen Smith, Steve Squint, Tomas Squip, Martin Sprouse, John Stabb, Franz Stahl, Pete Stahl, Kent Stax, Nathan Strejcek, Bobby Sullivan, Mark Sullivan, Mark & Joe/Supertouch, Chris Sussman, Mo Sussman, Johnny Temple, Skeeter Thompson, Chris Thomson, Jenny Toomey, Geoff Turner, Tesco Vee, Jerry Williams, Allison Wolfe, Howard Wuelfing, Tim Yohannon, and Don Zientara.

For advice, assistance, and forbearance, **Mark Jenkins** thanks Robin Diener, Larry Levine, Dave Nuttycombe, Brian Nelson, and Jim Gumm.

introduction

by Mark Jenkins

Dance of Days is overwhelmingly Mark Andersen's book. He conceived the idea, did extensive research, and wrote the first draft. My job was to focus and streamline the manuscript, emphasizing the narrative, pruning some of the digressions, and generally making it more accessible.

Yet I'm not simply the rewrite man. I've covered local music since 1976, so I was able to add details and analysis based on firsthand observations that Andersen—who didn't arrive in Washington until 1984—couldn't have made. In fact, some of the quotations and commentary that survive from the book's first draft are from features and reviews I wrote for the *Washington Post*, the *Washington City Paper*, and other periodicals.

One of my goals was to make the book more objective. Still, we didn't want to lose Andersen's voice altogether. Because he was intimately involved in many of the events recounted here, his first-person accounts couldn't be—and shouldn't be—eliminated. They are preserved in a series of asides in the latter chapters. There are also two asides in my voice, early in the book.

Andersen and I hold different views of some (but certainly not all) of the topics covered in this history. That's partially explained by our different experiences of Washington and its punk scene. We also sometimes differ about which particulars are important to the tale. To oversimplify, Andersen is more interested in the message, while I'd rather just tell the story. Still, we both agree that it's a story well worth telling. And I think we both agree that *Dance of Days* tells it better than any book either of us could have produced on our own.

My work on this book is dedicated to the memory of Libby Hatch.

preface 2003

by Mark Jenkins

This is the third printing of *Dance of Days*, which was first published in May 2001. It is not considerably different from the previous editions, although the graphic design has been updated and some corrections and additions have been made. But one significant thing has changed: the publisher.

Dance of Days was originally published by Soft Skull Press, and indeed began with an idea from Soft Skull founder Sander Hicks. He suggested that I write a biography of Ian MacKaye. I proposed instead that I help Mark Andersen revise and condense a book whose first draft he had already written, but had put aside.

Sander was the catalyst, but as *Dance of Days* approached completion he was not very involved. And when it came time to send the book to press, Sander announced that Soft Skull did not have the money to print it. Soft Skull couldn't even locate the guy it had hired to prepare the index. (I ended up compiling an index myself, which didn't appear until the second edition.)

We later learned, in a roundabout way, that Soft Skull had gotten in some costly trouble with *Fortunate Son*, a biography of George W. Bush. We still don't know every detail of that controversy, but it threatened to stop the publication of our book.

Postponing *Dance of Days* would have been the logical solution, except that excerpts from the book had already appeared in *Punk Planet* and *Washington City Paper*, reviews had been scheduled for publication, and promotional events had been organized. With such preliminaries underway, delaying the book would have been awkward.

So we decided to pay the cost of printing 4000 copies ourselves. This was possible only because I had inherited some money a few years before. Fittingly, the bequest came from Libby Hatch, who played in two of the bands mentioned early in the book.

While Soft Skull was in turmoil, Mark Andersen embarked on three self-financed publicity tours, including a three-week, 8000-mile solo jaunt that began with a cancelled flight to Minneapolis on September 11, 2001. In addition to that expedition, he did one tour with me and another with Dan Sinker, editor of *Punk Planet.* Dan's collection of interviews from his magazine was published by Akashic Books, a company run by Johnny Temple, another DC punk veteran. Mark A. was impressed by Akashic's support of the tour, and began to talk about taking *Dance of Days* to that publisher.

Demand for more books led us to stay with Soft Skull for a second printing, this time of 5000 copies in a sleeker format (and again funded by me). But when that one sold out—officially, at the end of 2002—we decided to go to Akashic.

Sander Hicks, who played a crucial role in the creation of this book, no longer runs Soft Skull. His successor, Richard Nash, seems to be doing a good job of unsnarling the company's finances, including gradually repaying the costs of the first two printings of this book and beginning to pay interest on the overdue royalties.

Our experiences with *Dance of Days,* Mark A. and I have joked more than once, showed us why bands sign with major labels. So we're happy to be with Akashic, which is not only an indie publisher, but one that has already demonstrated its interest in and dedication to this book.

*"There ain't no rock'n'roll no more
Just the sickly sound of greed . . ."*
—Ian Hunter, "Apathy 83"

MARK ANDERSEN WITH HIS DOG, CURLY, ON THE FAMILY FARM, SHERIDAN COUNTY, MONTANA, 1975 *(by Margaret Vik Andersen)*

punk beginnings

A prairie wind blew autumn's leaves down the streets of Plentywood, Montana. A longhaired kid in dusty jeans and cowboy boots, crouching against the frigid breeze, stepped through the doorway into a tiny record store.

The heat of the cramped room that was Garrick's Records and Tapes fogged the boy's wire-rimmed glasses. After taking off his work gloves and wiping the haze from the lenses, he shuffled through the bins, pausing to pick up one particular LP. The boy studied a stark black-and-white photograph of a woman with a defiant gaze and disheveled hair. As he did, excitement flickered in his eyes, and a faint smile crossed his face. It was the record he had been looking for.

The year was 1975. The album was Patti Smith's *Horses*. I was 16 years old, taking a break from hauling grain to the nearby Farmers' Union Elevator. The youngest child in a farm family, I lived out in the countryside on the Fort Peck Indian Reservation, 15 miles from the nearest town or paved road.

I had grown up immersed in conservative Christian pieties and love-it-or-leave-it patriotism. By the mid-'70s, I was estranged from those beliefs, feeling suffocated by the narrowness of my world. From what I knew, Patti Smith seemed like a kindred spirit. When I first played *Horses* on my plastic dime-store stereo, it took only Smith's deep, sandpaper voice and the lines "Jesus died for somebody's sins/But not mine" to know that I had been right.

I grew up feeling that nothing "fit," especially me. When I showed my treasured new album to a friend, he took one look and said crossly, "Doesn't she ever comb her hair?" I was hurt by his reaction but not that surprised. In music, as with most things, I was used to feeling at odds with my peers, my world.

My alienation went to alarming, inexplicable extremes. As strange as it may sound, sometimes I could hear the rage roaring in my head—a dark, screaming noise. At times, it blocked out everything else. More than once, I feared for my sanity.

Rock music was one of the few things that gave me hope. As a kid in the late '60s and early '70s, I would hear reassuring sparks of rage and melody on the radio—songs like the Rolling Stones' "(I Can't Get No) Satisfaction" or the Yardbirds' "Heart Full of Soul"—mixed in with body counts from a war in a far-off place called Vietnam, reports of student protests, famine in Biafra, and more—during the dusty bus trip home after school.

By the mid-'70s, my anthem was the Kinks' "I'm Not Like Everybody Else." I first read about the song in Greil Marcus's *Mystery Train*, one of two books—*Buried Alive*, Myra Friedman's biography of Janis Joplin, the other—that I stole from the Sheridan County Library, sure that I could never find them elsewhere.

Marcus's description alone convinced me this was my song: "A fearsome, ferocious bit of hard rock . . . singer Ray Davies opened the song as a sickly kid pushed up against the wall by a gang of thugs—that is, everybody else—then broke wide open with a rage that negated the whole world he wouldn't serve, that he wouldn't and couldn't change into. By the fiery last chorus, he was free . . ." Months later, I managed to find the song on an LP nestled in a Woolworth's cutout bin in Williston, North Dakota. I rushed home, played it, and was transported. It didn't matter that no one else I knew would even want to hear it. The song told me that I was not alone, that the pain I felt was real, that the world was insane, not me.

It's hard to overstate how important rock music became to me in those years. In the Doors' "When the Music's Over," Jim Morrison sang, "The music is your only friend." For all the song's morose self-absorption, those words expressed exactly how I then felt. There were entire summers when I basically stayed on the farm, going into town for only a couple hours every week or two. I didn't go to church, I didn't drink or smoke, I had no girlfriend, I wasn't an athlete. Thus, I wasn't really part of any of the existing teen social groups. My peers respected me as a good (if fairly lazy) student, but mostly I was alone.

My tastes tended to accentuate my isolation, for I disdained current music in favor of older, more obscure rock and blues artists. A small paperback, *Rock Revolution*, became my Bible, particularly sections entitled "The Heavy Metal Kids," "Glitter Rock," and "Rages to Come: Predictions of Rock's Future," all written by one loopy, lovable Lester Bangs.

Bangs's crazed but compelling descriptions of the MC5, New York Dolls, the Stooges, and more soon had me in hot pursuit of these underground heroes. At the time, the '60s were not yet a profitable nostalgia-commodity. Moreover, I lived in one of the most rural parts of America, hundreds of miles from any serious record store. Thus, my musical interests compelled me to rummage through cutout bins. The extra effort, however, made the discovery of gems like the MC5's *Kick Out the Jams*, or the Dolls' *Too Much Too Soon*, or the Stooges' first album even more sweet. From Melanie to Ted Nugent to Jefferson Airplane, '60s-related performers became my heroes. My love for rock of that era and subsequent excavation of its history provided a tenuous center to my life.

That search nurtured a budding awareness of a world beyond the one I knew. Rock music had been deeply intertwined with the political and cultural struggles of the 1950s and 1960s as well as with the ennui settling over America in the mid-'70s.

Although little of the original wave of rock was explicitly political, culturally it was revolutionary. Rock was the bastard child of black rhythm and blues and white country music, its rise coinciding with the Montgomery bus boycott and the *Brown vs. the Board of Education* Supreme Court decision that ordered school desegregation. Aware of this, conservatives denounced rock with racially charged terms like "jungle music."

Rock's irreverent lyrics were also filled with references to sexuality. In their time, songs like Little Richard's "Good Golly Miss Molly" ("you sure like to ball") were considered obscene by some. Even Elvis Presley's dancing was seen as too lewd for prime-time TV audiences. Although the limitations of the sexual revolution that would flow, in part, from this emerging new culture would become obvious, rock's refreshingly frank sexuality was a healthy tonic at the time.

Less obvious but just as real was the fact that the new music initially came largely from independent channels like Chicago's Chess Records and Sun Studios in Memphis. As Martin and Seagrave argue in their book *Anti-Rock: The Opposition to Rock'n'roll* the corporate powers of the day were concerned that the new music was out of its control and might undermine the appeal and profitability of its existing pop wares.

Soon enough, however, those powers had gained control over this new form. The raw music and lyrics were toned down. By the early '60s, much of what was termed "rock'n'roll" had more in common with the pop pablum that had predated rock than with bawdy originals like Chuck Berry, Little Richard, or Jerry Lee Lewis.

This sad state of affairs was reversed by a second wave of rock that began with the Beatles and the British Invasion. Soon, the rebirth of American rock followed, largely in countercultural enclaves. As the "baby boom" generation grew up, so did its music. Instead of bemoaning the "Summertime Blues" or celebrating "School Days," many songs spoke a disturbing, almost secret language championing drugs, sex, personal freedom, and a new culture in opposition to the old.

By the late 1960s, "rock" and "revolution" had become synonymous in the minds of many. The civil rights struggle together with the Vietnam War had produced committed youth activists who meshed more or less easily with a burgeoning counterculture. The rude rebel voice of '50s rock was now transformed into the radical challenge of artists like Jefferson Airplane, Bob Dylan, and Jimi Hendrix. Rock now seemed the voice of the new consciousness, the harbinger of a new age.

But money was still to be made. CBS Records—home of Joplin, Dylan, and other key '60s artists—boasted "The Man Can't Bust Our Music" in ads that ran in the tumultuous year of 1968. While it was amusing to see one of the world's largest entertainment corporations claiming to be antiestablishment, it wasn't convincing. Most efforts to co-opt '60s idealism weren't so clumsy. While many performers may have felt they could use the established structures to further the cause, clearly the labels were equally sure that profits, not revolution, would be the result.

With the immense turmoil created by the war, the spread of new forms of recreational drugs, and the artificial security of college life, there was plenty of fuel for countercultural illusions. In 1973, however, when the direct US troop involvement in Vietnam and the radicalizing threat of the draft finally ground to a halt, the equation shifted.

Much of the '60s ideology seemed, after all, to have been tainted by simple hedonism and self-interest. As the drug culture generated casualties and transformed once positive energy into crippling addictions, and the economic demands of career and family reared their heads, life didn't seem so open-ended. While the case of Jerry Rubin—from Yippie leader screaming "Do it!" to well-groomed Wall Street type—is extreme, it became clear to the rebel children of "Amerika" that talking about revolution is far easier than living it.

Rock took the fall too. In part, this was due to the untimely deaths of some of its creative leaders. Even before that, however, a gradual divorce of rock from the radical politics of the counterculture was underway. The interests of the rock star would hardly be advanced by the destruction of the machinery that made his or her lofty lifestyle possible. With little effort made to build an alternative to the industry, there were few institutions to turn '60s rock's idealism into lasting practice. The simple fruits of success combined with the demands of the business tended to propel rock rebels into the establishment.

An anecdote recounted in Abe Peck's book *Uncovering the Sixties: The Life and Times of the Underground Press* illustrates this tendency with painful acuity. Jeff Shero, a writer with a popular underground newspaper, *The Rat*, had known Janis Joplin since their college days together in the early 1960s. By 1968, though, Janis was a star, the most celebrated female rock singer in America. When Shero called to ask for an interview, she coyly replied, "Well, honey, I'm talkin' to *Time* and *Newsweek*. Why do I want to do an interview with a li'l ol' hippie publication?"

When Shero responded quickly with the obvious appeal to countercultural solidarity ("Because rock music is part of our culture"), Joplin replied with an equally apparent point of view: "Hell, millions of people read *Newsweek*. I'd rather do that." Though it must have been bitter for counterculturists like Shero, this was the cold reality of competing self-interests lying just beneath the illusion of rock/revolution solidarity.

As the dreams of the late '60s faded, rock again became mere popular entertainment. Some stars like Joplin, Hendrix, and Morrison became icons, saved from the embarrassment of faltering creativity and commerical debasement by their deaths. However, as artists like the Rolling Stones, the Who, and Dylan lived jet-set lifestyles, cushioned from the world by their wealth, their music lost its urgency. At the same time, mountains of money were being spent on recording, packaging, and marketing rock. By the mid-1970s, rock music was highly profitable, professional show business—and boring as hell.

The transformation was jarring. In 1969, at the height of the Vietnam War, the Rolling Stones toured the US with lead singer Mick Jagger wearing a mock Uncle Sam hat and the omega symbol, the sign of draft resistance. By 1975, the Stones were a show biz circus act, replete with a gigantic inflatable phallus. Jagger's increasingly affected vocals betrayed not a whit of sincere emotion or meaning. If that weren't enough, the sight of the Stones hobnobbing with the social elite (including Princess Margaret of England) was alone sufficient to send shivers down the spine of any unrepentant counterculturist.

Ian Hunter, the creative force behind the potent early-'70s rock band, Mott the Hoople, capsulized the moment perfectly in the song "Apathy 83." Written in 1975 after seeing a halfhearted Rolling Stones show, the song's chorus—with the line "and it's apathy for the devil"—parodied the

Stones' incendiary classic, "Sympathy For the Devil." It was a bitter eulogy, not only for the Stones as an artistic force, but for rock as a whole.

Over a sinuous, mournful bass line, Hunter sang with a hungry expectation ("I'm standing on the edge of Vesuvius/My mouth is running dry") that, by the song's end, had been replaced by horrified realization: "Nostalgia is starting to focus too late/Imagination is starting to itch/There ain't no rock'n'roll no more/Just the music of the rich . . . apathy's at a fever pitch." Such an attack on one of the reigning "gods" of rock was then unheard of—but it spoke the truth. "Apathy 83" was a believer's epitaph for a fallen faith.

Hunter's song helped me understand why so much rock seemed tame and uninteresting. At the time, I wrote a telling journal entry: "There has to be real emotion, that's why I listen to music, to be freed from my limited existence, to broaden my horizons . . . that's why I love the blues and the music derived from it, because they are so intense and emotionally involved. That's why the music of the '60s has such a great fascination for me. It was done in a time of ideals, high hopes, great expectations, and tremendous sincerity and intensity. That's the trouble with today's rock music, nobody believes enough and is willing to sacrifice, to stand up and be counted."

Patti Smith, of course, was an exception to my indictment. Her 1976 LP, *Radio Ethiopia*, struck me as even better than *Horses*. Beyond its more focused, aggressive music, I was transfixed by Patti's liner notes about artistic freedom, her struggle with a Christian upbringing, and the legacy of the 1960s. What Patti seemed to be saying was that the idealism all-too-neatly allocated to that rapidly receding moment could still exist in our own lives. I was captivated by her galvanizing version of "My Generation" on *Saturday Night Live*, and I bought every magazine that mentioned her, searching for her debut 45, "Hey Joe/Piss Factory," as well as bootlegs like *Teenage Perversity* and *Ships in the Night*.

In the process, I found a new magazine, *Rock Scene*, at Service Drug in Williston and fell in love. Although it was mostly a trashy photo-'zine, it had a good sense of humor and often featured Patti as well as other unknown New York performers like the Ramones, Talking Heads, Television, Heartbreakers, and Richard Hell. I also devoured its wacky "Dear Abby"-style column by transsexual Wayne (now Jayne) County. Admiring the courage of this fellow misfit, I even considered writing to ask for advice.

I was beginning to feel a need for more than mere advice, however. To survive my hostile environment psychologically, I had withdrawn to a romanticized past in my mind. In this imaginary place, everything made sense.

But my refuge was a lie, a fantasy. The past was gone and I was just an angry, confused teenager, caught out of place, out of time. I hated the present and saw no future. I didn't really live, I just existed. My life was spent in avoidance—hiding from people, from work, from my own emotions. For all of my condemnation of others, I was not "standing up" either. I was languishing in a vacuum, doing manual labor I hated, taking classes that didn't seem to matter. And this was as good as it would likely get, for sometime soon I would have to earn my own way. I felt trapped, even more lost and bitter than before.

Growing ever more fatalistic, I found myself drawn to the darker side of the 1960s: Charles Manson, Altamont. Although rock music had opened new doors in my mind, I didn't really believe in myself or in those possibilities. Indeed, they only made my existence more unbearable. I didn't see any way out—alive.

Like most suicidal kids, I didn't understand what was happening to me. I didn't know how to ask for help—not that I would have accepted it if offered, given my hair-trigger temper. My parents genuinely tried, to no avail. But they also would literally whip me when I got too far out of line. The punishment only made me feel more alone and self-destructive.

I don't remember the first time they hit me, but I do remember the last. As usual, I had been unruly and belligerent about something or other. At wit's end, my mother grabbed a flyswatter—as was her custom, my father tended to use his belt—and, driven by frustration, was preparing to whip me with the wire handle.

She did hit me. But, for once, I didn't just accept the blow. Instead, I took the impact with my hand. My fingers closed around the wire as it bit into the flesh of my palm. I wrenched the swatter from my mother's hands, mangling it beyond repair. With clenched fists, I confronted her, my lanky teenage body looming menacingly over my mother's small frame. My rage poured out, with gritted teeth cutting off each word harshly: "DON'T . . . EVER . . . HIT . . . ME . . . AGAIN."

The confrontation slid crazily toward a violent resolution . . . and pulled up just short. Seeing the fear in my mother's eyes, shame welled up inside of me, and my blind fury ebbed. Without another word, I threw down the flyswatter, turned, and walked away.

Though the moment was, in a way, a small triumph, it was also frightening, for I had been within a hairsbreadth of attacking my own mother. Now perched on the brink of an abyss, I felt barely above barbarism, with no real direction, no hope, nothing to live for. All I seemed to have was my fury and loneliness.

Shortly thereafter, in late 1976, I picked up a new issue of *Rock Scene* at Service Drug. Flipping through the pages, my eyes fell upon a small picture of a ragged teenager with spiky hair, screaming into a microphone. The featured band's motto was equally arresting: "We hate everything." I shuddered slightly, repulsed by the ugly image.

But there was an attraction as well. Suddenly, I found myself surprised, realizing "I feel that way, I hate everything, too." I hesitated and flipped the page, glancing at the photo one more time so I'd remember the name of the band. They were called the Sex Pistols.

That day was when my life began.

put a bullet
thru the jukebox

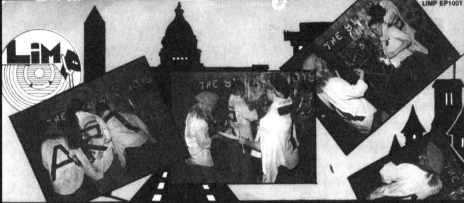

LIMP EP1001

THE SLICKEE BOYS
"MERSEY, MERSEY ME"

*"Put a bullet thru the jukebox
Blast it, Blow it, With a nuke!"*
—The Slickee Boys, "Put a Bullet Thru The Jukebox," 1977

COVER OF SLICKEE BOYS' "MERSEY, MERSEY ME" 45, 1977 *(design by Kim Kane, photos by Don Hammerman and David Howcroft; the Artettes are Xyra Harper, Patricia Ragan, Cathy Filbert; the Slickee Boys are Marshall Keith, Kim Kane, Martha Hull, Howard Weuling, Dan Palenski.)*

put a bullet thru the jukebox

The mood at the Keg, a hard-rock dive in the Glover Park neighborhood of Northwest Washington, had suddenly turned ugly.

It was a steamy night in July 1976. An unknown local band, Overkill, was midway through a set of offbeat originals and renditions of songs by the Velvet Underground, Roxy Music, and various obscure '60s garage bands. If Overkill's music and appearance—most of the members sported close-cropped hair and shades—weren't enough to show that this was not rock as usual, several television sets were chattering continuously onstage, beaming random images at the audience.

Expecting the usual cover versions of hard-rock standards, much of the Keg crowd was mystified by the band. One of Overkill's songs contained the good-natured chorus, "We can be weird together," but few listeners seemed interested in accepting the invitation.

One disgruntled, alcohol-fueled man with shoulder-length hair kept yelling for Overkill to play some Alice Cooper. The band ignored him and played on. Undeterred, the heckler continued. In a break between songs, bassist Harrison Sohmer took off his gaudy shades and stepped to the microphone: "Why don't you go fuck Alice Cooper?"

The longhair redoubled his commentary, now joined by two equally hairy buddies. Then Overkill singer Barney Jones, clad in tight-fitting black and white clothing and wraparound sunglasses, moved to the front of the stage. "Why don't you cut your hair?" he demanded.

A decade earlier, such taunts were barked by conservative elders at youths who defined themselves as members of a new counterculture. By the mid-1970s, however, long hair was common among men whose only connection to '60s youth culture was via its leftover hedonism. Jones's words—like Overkill's performance itself—served notice that the '60s were over and that something really needed to be done about the '70s.

One of the people in the audience that night was Myron Bretholz. A DJ on WGTB-FM at nearby Georgetown University and a writer for the DC music monthly *Unicorn Times*, he was well aware of rock's present doldrums. To him, the evening was invigorating. Once again, rock seemed to have danger, wit, and meaning.

In the next month's *Unicorn Times*, Bretholz applauded what he'd seen: "Overkill is doing something so radical, so avant that I fear committing such notions to print: Overkill is doing punk rock, and in a city where a Dan Fogelberg show would probably sell out a month in advance, punk rock, my friends, is radical."

x x x

In theory, punks disdained hippies, but the hostility was often that of different sects of the same faith. Thus it's not surprising that DC punk first announced itself in three neighborhoods that had been the centers of the city's counterculture in the '60s: upscale but student-heavy Georgetown, diverse and increasingly gay-oriented Dupont Circle, and polyglot, revolution-minded Adams-Morgan.

Although Georgetown University was a staunchly conservative Jesuit-run institution, its radio station became one of DC punk's early havens. Founded in 1960 by Francis B. Heyden, an eccentric priest who headed the astronomy department, WGTB had no direct academic purpose. Georgetown didn't have journalism or broadcasting departments, and so when Heyden left WGTB there was no departmental line of succession. The station fell into the hands of students, led by program director Peter Barry Chowka and chief engineer Ken Sleeman.

Under their leadership, a station that had featured sports news and light music was transformed into a center of campus radicalism, broadcasting the views of Maoist news reporters and radical feminist, lesbian, and gay commentators, as well as increasingly hard-edged or experimental rock. By the mid-'70s, WGTB staffer Ruth Stenstrom recalled, "the cultural explosions of the '60s had become institutionalized into a competently run, responsive, listener-supported radio station."

Not surprisingly, WGTB's new stance led to controversy. Chowka was forced to resign in 1972 after accusations that he was using the station to support George McGovern's presidential campaign. Sleeman took over the post, and for a time was able to satisfy both the administration and the station's staff. In late 1975, however, WGTB's continued activism prompted an attack from an unusually high-profile source: former Vice-President Spiro Agnew. "The voice of Third World communism is pervasive in academia," Agnew complained to the *New York Times*. "WGTB, a tiny radio station at Georgetown University, broadcasts what seems to be propaganda for the Third World and all but rejoiced over the fall of South Vietnam."

By the end of the year, Sleeman had been removed from his post. In March 1976, the university fired the entire staff and took the station off the air for three months. In the late spring of 1976, what Georgetown's administration hoped would be a more housebroken version of WGTB returned to the airwaves. One of the reinstated DJs was Georgetown student Steve Lorber, whose "Mystic Eyes" program had already begun to play some of the new music emerging from New York's CBGB's.

In an interview, Lorber joked that he first got on the air in October 1974 by "bribing the music director with a couple of tabs of acid." Lorber didn't have much sympathy for the station's "hippie" management, but he was happy that "WGTB allowed airplay of every type of music." Thanks to Lorber, Bretholz, John Paige, and other DJs who either survived the purge or arrived soon after it, WGTB would soon become perhaps the most important institution in the development of the early DC punk scene. The station had returned to the airwaves just in time to help launch a rock renaissance.

x x x

Washington wasn't on punk's touring circuit in 1976, but that was because punk didn't really have a touring circuit. Groups like the Modern Lovers, Television, and Talking Heads were rarely seen outside their hometowns. Still, *Punk* magazine and punk records were available in local music stores, and while the city's "free-form" commercial rock station WHFS favored Bruce Springsteen and Jackson Browne, WGTB played everything from obscure '60s proto-punks like the Monks to British art-rock like Henry Cow to the new crop of American art-garage bands like Pere Ubu.

Nineteen seventy-six was also the year that the Patti Smith Group and the Ramones, having finally released major-label albums, were welcomed at slightly incongruous DC venues: The former

played the Cellar Door, the Georgetown folk club where local pop-rocker Nils Lofgren first intro-
duced himself to Neil Young; the latter played three nights of their infamous 20-minute sets at the
Childe Harold, a Dupont Circle restaurant once known as Emmylou Harris's home base. These
bands were eventually followed by most of punk's other most significant exponents, although
Television never made it to Washington and the Sex Pistols' show at a roller rink in suburban
Alexandria was one of the four US gigs scrubbed by the band's immigration problems.

When Overkill began performing in the summer of '76, it was hailed as Washington's first punk
band. Still, the Catholic University-spawned quintet was not entirely unprecedented. Several years
earlier, the Dubonettes had begun offering their version of the New York Dolls' glitter-flecked roots-
rock. In 1976, renamed Charlie and the Pep Boys, they recorded an album for A&M; it was produced
by Lofgren, whose Grin was one of the first '70s DC bands to rediscover the appeal of the tuneful,
energetic three-minute song.

Around the same time the Dubonettes began playing, the Razz was forging its sound from
British-invasion-era blues-rock, the Flaming Groovies' *Teenage Head*, and Roxy Music. (They opened
for the latter band at the University of Maryland in 1974.) The Razz was on hiatus when Overkill
appeared, but the quintet soon started playing again, becoming one of the biggest local draws of the
late '70s. Joining these bands within a year were the Look, the Ritz, the Controls, and the Slickee
Boys.

Of these, the longest-running by far was the Slickee Boys, the creation of Kim Kane, a record
collector with a passion for '60s American and British garage bands. Like many of his DC-area suburban peers, he was from a State Department background and spent much of his early life overseas,
most notably in South Korea.

Although as a child Kane lived largely outside rock's sphere of influence, the music captured
his imagination at an early age. Upon his return to the US in 1968, his enthusiasm was confirmed
by seeing such bands as the Jimi Hendrix Experience and Alice Cooper. Once out of high school
and into the job market, Kane found solace as a collector of rock's past and in more contemporary
fringe luminaries like the Stooges.

In early 1976, Kane realized something was happening. Already intrigued by the CBGB's scene
in New York, Kane began "reading British music papers like *New Musical Express* and *Melody Maker*,
and starting to see little notices about these weird new bands like the Sex Pistols." Kane had

become friends with Lorber through his WGTB radio show, and the DJ pushed Kane to form a band of his own that combined '60s rock and punk. "The energy was the same," Kane says. "I had thought about forming a band since 1967 and punk gave me that last little kick."

Besides mixing rock with punk, Kane wanted to utilize the jarring cross-cultural images from his experiences as a youth in Korea. For the band-to-be, he chose the name "Slickee Boys," GI slang for the rockabilly-inspired Korean street toughs who sold knives, cigarettes, and other black market goods to American soldiers. With a concept and sound in mind, Kane picked up the guitar seriously for the first time and began looking for allies.

The original Slickees lineup was built around fledgling player Kane and more accomplished guitarist Marshall Keith, with some assistance from Kane's brother Tommy. Kane recruited a lead singer and rhythm section from an unlikely source: a struggling soft-rock/r'n'b group, Lone Oak, that was breaking up.

Tommy Kane had known one of the group's singers, Martha Hull, from high school in suburban Bethesda, Maryland. Hull's deep, supple voice and onstage charisma complemented Kane's outlandish costumes and showmanship, helping to stabilize the mix of punk, pop, and psychedelia that constituted the band's self-described "slickee-delic" sound.

Since Kane didn't believe there were any places the band could play, the Slickees initially formed simply to record a single. After six practice sessions, the Slickee Boys recorded their first 7" record in June 1976. Lorber, who had become a supporter of the band and the nearest thing it had to a manager, produced the record at Underground Sound, a studio in Largo, Maryland.

The EP featured one odd Kane original, "Manganese Android Puppies," and four eclectic covers: UK rockabilly king Vince Taylor's "Brand New Cadillac," the Yardbirds' "Psycho Daisies," '60s DC rock heroes the Hangmen's "What a Boy Can't Do," and an instrumental rave-up of the theme from "Exodus."

"We did the best we could do with what we had, but we didn't have any idea what we were doing," Kane said. "Unfortunately, we listened to the engineers. They would tell us what to do. That's why our sound was so 'twinkie' in the early days. The engineers were not punks and would just try to make nice, listenable, radio-friendly records."

Recording the songs was just the beginning of the challenge; the next step was to get the session out on vinyl. With typical enthusiasm, Kane formed his own label, Dacoit—named for South Asian bandits—and with Lorber's help put out the record himself. An exuberant Kane-penned mini-manifesto expressed the label's do-it-yourself ethic: "Dacoit is your usual classic 'We can do it our own damn selves' company. We simply put out our own music our own way for ourselves and the wave that would go for it. We even glue our own covers! . . . This is real live local new or 'old' wave sound, no hype, no super slickness, our own art, our own production, our own pushing."

True to Kane's idiosyncratic motifs, the record was called *Hot and Cool*, after a Korean Beatles cover band, and featured graphics heavily influenced by Japanese comic books. Although Kane would later dismiss the EP as a deeply flawed first effort, the record remains a testament to the infectious DIY energy of so much early punk.

After recording, pressing, and producing DC's first punk record, the next step was obvious: getting a gig. "It was a complete vacuum," Kane recalled. "Now we had a band, but where were we going to play? Who would we play with? By pure accident, we discovered this band, Overkill, who had done a couple of gigs. They let us get up and do a six-song set in between breaks in their set at My Friend's House," a crab and beer joint in the Maryland suburbs.

x x x

It was Lorber who made the connection. According to Overkill guitarist-songwriter Randy Austin, Lorber met the band's Harrison Sohmer at Georgetown's Discount Records around the same time that the Slickees were coming together.

Although most of Overkill had been practicing together since late 1975, the band had just been completed with the addition of lead singer Barney Jones, who returned from college in May 1976. As Austin remembered it, "After talking to Harrison, Steve came to one of our practices. I guess he liked us and ended up kind of managing us."

Overkill's set drew heavily on '60s garage-rock nuggets like the Seeds' "Pushin' Too Hard" and more recent items like Lou Reed's "Vicious," with only a few originals. Although acknowledging the Velvet Underground as a strong influence at the time, Austin noted, "We weren't really trying to pattern ourselves after anybody. We were just messing around with some old songs and trying to write a few, to make a sound of our own."

Unlike the Slickee Boys, Overkill was eager to play out. After some investigation, Lorber decided to approach the Keg, a run-down heavy-metal bar in Glover Park, just north of Georgetown (and barely a block from his own apartment). Overkill proved to be an extremely engaging live band, with lead singer Jones exuding unpredictable, caustic charisma. "Barney had real presence, he was a goofball acting out, using weird stage props," said Kane.

It was too much for some Keg patrons. "People would come expecting to hear a Zeppelin/Aerosmith cover band only to get us instead," Austin recalled. "Sometimes they'd get really hostile."

One of those who witnessed confrontations between Overkill and its audience was Michael Reidy, lead singer for the then-dormant Razz. "Barney was a real character," he said. "When people gave the band shit, he wasn't afraid to give it right back. You know, like 'We suck? OK, come on up here and I'll suck your cock.' Nobody else was doing that kind of thing at the time." Encouraged by Overkill's spirit, Reidy and guitarist Abaad Behram would soon convince their bandmates to bring the Razz out of retirement.

Overkill performed regularly at the Keg over the summer, and WGTB played the band's crudely recorded but compelling live version of Brute Force's "In Jim's Garage." By the fall of 1976, however, the group faced what would prove to be a perennial nemesis of DC punk bands: college. Jones decided to return to school to study conducting, effectively ending Overkill. Only a few live tapes exist of their performances, although the Slickee Boys would later cover the band's best-known original, "Heart Murmur."

x x x

Another Overkill fan who was soon to play on the Keg's stage was rock writer and musician Howard Wuelfing, a New Jersey native who moved to DC after graduating from Rutgers in 1975. "It seemed to be the stupidest time to move," Wuelfing recalled, "because I was just starting to hear about all the CBGB's bands. By contrast, there was nothing happening in DC."

Already a fan of the Dolls, the Dictators, and the Stooges, Wuelfing was inspired by the Ramones and, later, Richard Hell and the Voidoids. Before he could start his own band, however, Wuelfing was recruited by guitarist Robert Goldstein to play bass for his new group, the Look.

Goldstein laughingly described himself as "one of the million teenagers who bought an electric guitar after hearing the Beatles." He taught himself to play and performed with a few high school bands at home, a small town outside of Pittsburgh. In 1967, he moved to DC to attend Georgetown University's Foreign Service School.

While at Georgetown, Goldstein witnessed WGTB's metamorphosis into a countercultural beacon, and became an avid listener. He also developed a growing interest in the art world, and decided to try to form a band that would combine both of his passions.

After adding Bryan Ferry–acolyte Teaman Treadway on vocals and Chris Thompson (also a WGTB DJ) on drums, the Look played its first gig in early 1977. The quartet was pulling in two directions from the outset. "Goldstein was more into art-rock like Roxy Music and David Bowie, while I was into the Monkees, Ramones, Richard Hell—trash rock," said Wuelfing.

Briefly, the Look also included keyboardist Xyra Harper, yet another WGTB DJ and the singer in a pre–Barney Jones version of Overkill. (She cowrote "Heart Murmur.") A self-described "flower child," Harper found a similar energy in punk. Her radio show, "Revolt Into Style," championed artier (and often British) punk, balancing Lorber's taste for garage-rock.

The Look first played the Keg when the Slickee Boys' original rhythm section suddenly quit, causing Kane to ask the band to substitute for his on short notice. When all went well, the Look's impromptu show turned into a Monday night residency.

Thanks to this regular gig and the groundwork done by Overkill and the Slickees, a sense of community began to develop. "I didn't really notice it at the time but it's true. It was our version of a punk scene," Wuelfing observed years later. "People would come to the Keg with dog collars and ripped up shirts. At a certain point, you could look around at a Keg show and see a lot of other people not in groups yet but thinking about it."

x x x

In 1976, the city's embryonic punk scene was rooted mostly on downtown campuses, but WGTB sent the message to younger listeners in the suburbs. One convert was Mike Heath, a teenager lost in what he described as "suburban Babylon"—in his case, Burtonsville, Maryland.

Heath saw the Slickee Boys for the first time in the fall of 1976, after entering the University of Maryland. "It was exciting and scary all at the same time," he remembered. "Physically, the Slickees were a very foreboding-looking group, especially Kim Kane with his long dark hair, Fu Manchu mustache, and wild clothes. All the other guys in the band looked really tough too. Martha Hull seemed kind of like this gangster's moll with this really big voice."

To Heath, like many other punk partisans, "it was like fighting a war back then to get the stuff out, to find gig space, just to be heard, really—to kick out all the crap that was being foisted upon people." Heath tried to fight back by writing about the rising English scene for one of the University of Maryland student papers. After rejection by both the mainstream and "alternative" publications, Heath took the example of the UK punk fanzine *Sniffin' Glue* to heart and started the first local fanzine devoted exclusively to punk; he named it *Vintage Violence* after the first solo album by ex–Velvet Undergrounder John Cale.

"This is in the day before there were Kinko's stores on every corner," Heath recalled. "I wrote up all these articles—no photos, just writing—and then I typed them up on all these mimeograph sheets and snuck into one of the mimeograph rooms on campus and ran off a couple hundred copies." Later, Rob Kennedy and Caki Callas would join Heath in producing the fanzine, bringing Callas's graphics skills (and access to a Xerox machine) to the publication.

About eight months after Michael Reidy first saw Overkill face down hecklers at the Keg, the Razz returned to action. Although the Razz had existed in one form or another since the early '70s, the band had been hibernating since 1975. The Razz was more palatable to club audiences (and owners) because of its roots-rock material and accomplished musicianship. Robert Goldstein winced remembering a time when the Look played with the Razz at the Keg: "They just totally obliterated us."

Despite its mainstream-rock roots, the Razz had a punky spirit, embodied by flamboyant frontman Reidy. Like the Slickee Boys, the quintet was a record-collector band, but with a special flair. As Randy Austin put it, "Even though the Razz were very much playing '70s Stones hard rock, they did it with such a tremendous sense of style that they made it their own."

The Razz helped bridge the gap between the older rock crowd and the emerging scene, thus helping the latter survive. The revived band started at the Keg, but quickly outgrew it and began to frequent other venues, including the Psychedelly, a bar in the nearby suburb of Bethesda. Psychedelly owner Lou Sordo was not sympathetic toward punk, but was sufficiently impressed by the Razz that he began to allow similar bands into his club. Eventually, the Psychedelly became a regular stop for many new bands.

"What kept the Slickee Boys existing in the early days was the Razz," said Kane. "We couldn't play anywhere. The Razz was bigger and could play other places. They got us in."

The Razz's solidarity with other new bands was not unusual. Overkill had gotten the Slickee Boys their first show, and the Slickees had done likewise for the Look. This sense of common cause in a hostile environment tended to minimize competition. "Everybody was really nice, no bullshit," said another early convert to punk, Keith Campbell.

An American University student, Campbell had already been playing guitar for several years but was dissatisfied with '70s rock music. After various cover bands, he was looking to start something different, something original—but with a striking lack of success.

One day in April 1976, Campbell came upon an intense curly-haired student on the steps of the Student Center, smashing transistor radios and reading his poetry through a huge bullhorn. This display attracted more than a little ridicule, but Campbell was transfixed. "I just stood there and watched and said to myself, 'Man, this guy is alright!'"

The performer called himself Nicky Butane, but his real name was Roddy Frantz. He and Campbell became friends, swapping ideas about music and making plans. Frantz knew a great deal about the CBGB's scene; his brother Chris was in the then-unknown New York band Talking Heads. "I remember Roddy telling me that they were going to be big and I'd just go 'Sure. . .'" Campbell recalled, laughing.

Sparked by the first Ramones album, Campbell, Frantz, and two other musicians founded the Controls. Like most punk bands, the Controls opposed conventional rock wisdom. Their first show—at American University's pub in March 1977—began with solo poetry, shifting into Ramones-ish buzzsaw rock with Frantz's half-chanted/half-sung vocals over the top. This mixture of the raw and the arty mirrored the aesthetic of the Look.

The Controls soon dissolved amid personal differences, but the band satisfied Campbell in ways that his previous musical efforts never had. "Roddy couldn't sing but he was a very strong performer. So I said, why don't we just do it?" chuckled Campbell years later. "That was what was so good about punk. It was wide open, anything could happen."

x x x

Perhaps the most unlikely embodiment of that wide-open spirit in DC was White Boy. The band's founder, James Kowalski, was a '50s rock fan who had become a printing-company executive. On a business trip to New York, he had gone to see Suicide and the Cramps at Max's Kansas City. He walked away transformed. "It scared me! I thought there was a good chance that [Suicide lead singer] Alan Vega was crazy, I mean really crazy. He was throwing glass around, you know, acting completely bizarre."

The anarchy of the performance galvanized the 36-year-old former rebel. "When I came back from New York there was going to be a party next door in the basement," he recalled. "I told the band that was going to play that I could get a band together in four days to open for them."

ANTE PUNK
by Mark Jenkins

As a kid, I lived in various mid-Atlantic states, but mostly in Alexandria, Virginia, which is across the Potomac River from Washington. (In fact, the area where I lived was part of the original District of Columbia, before the Virginia portion was retroceded in 1846.) Thanks to the influence of my best friend, I became a Beatles fan at age nine. I stayed faithful to the Beatles for years, but gradually started listening to a broader range of music.

The first rock concert I attended was the Beatles at Shea Stadium in 1965. That was a singular event, but it didn't prove entirely exceptional: In my subsequent experience, most rock concerts were held in stadiums and sports facilities with lousy sound and very little connection between performer and audience. As a teenager, I saw a few shows at such Georgetown venues as the Emergency (an all-ages club that didn't serve alcohol) and the Cellar Door (which allowed under-18s accompanied by adults). More typical, however, was the Capital Centre, the new suburban basketball arena where most fans could really only see the show on the huge video screens above the stage. Going to a rock concert was virtually the same experience as watching late-night TV rock shows like *Midnight Special*.

That changed for me in 1974–75, years that I spent mostly in Boston and New York. I went to CBGB's, the Rat, and similar clubs, seeing such acts as Patti Smith, Television, the Ramones, the Heartbreakers, Talking Heads, Jonathan Richman, the Real Kids, and Willie Alexander (as well as many others that were less memorable). These performers not only restored my interest in rock, which had flagged in the early '70s; they also redefined live rock for me as something urgent, intimate, and unpredictable. Even though I was still a teenager when I first visited CBGB's, punk was the beginning of my second life as a rock fan.

In 1976, I moved to Washington, a city I knew fairly well but had never lived in. My reaction was very different than Mark Andersen's when he arrived a decade later. DC didn't have New York and Boston's

This impromptu performance proved memorable. "We performed for all these kids who came from Wilson High School to this party," said Kowalski. "We scared them shitless. They were sitting around in the basement and the band came out and just played this one chord over and over again. I came blasting in the back door with this old cape and every finger had dozens of rings, all these gold chains and makeup and this huge wig. I grabbed the mic and yelled 'Good evening and fuck you!' And all these kids are just going, 'Oh my God!'"

Kowalski soon took the stage name "Mr. Ott" and brought his teenage son Glen (renamed "Jake Whipp") into the group on guitar. His one-off project would evolve into White Boy, a band unlike any DC had seen before or since. Steve Lorber described White Boy at the time as "a weird father/son aggregation which combined a progressive heavy metal sound with a punky, maniacal edge." While this description was reasonably accurate, it hardly conveys the chaos the group would prove capable of generating.

No record company would have considered signing a band whose singer was a balding, middle-aged man given to wearing garish leisure suits, space-age sunglasses, and oddly colored wigs as he rolled around onstage, singing his best-known song, "I Could Puke." But Kowalski got inspiration and practical advice from David Thomas, then known as Crocus Behemoth, the oversized lead singer of Cleveland's Pere Ubu.

"I was a huge Pere Ubu fan," Kowalski remembered. "So I just

alternative newspapers or punk clubs, but as a city it seemed to work a lot better. In the mid-'70s, New York and Boston were both in disinvestment freefall, with transit systems that wouldn't have been tolerated in Bombay or Mexico City. Washington, however, was about to open a new rail system.

Washington was also less racially polarized than New York or Boston. Although Home Rule had just arrived a few years before, Washington held out the promise of enlightened, empowered African-American leadership. It was a relief after Boston, where I lived through the riots that greeted the court-ordered busing to finally integrate the school system. (As almost everyone knows, such local leaders as Marion Barry did not live up to their promise. Still, it's worth noting that, for all its problems, Washington is not Detroit or Newark. Among major American cities with an African-American majority, it has the highest education and income levels.)

I started sending reviews to rock magazines in the mid-'70s, and was occasionally published in venues such as *Creem* and *Fusion*. In Washington, I wrote for a string of undercapitalized alternative papers, most of which folded after a year or two. (My first piece about a local punk band was a short item on the Slickee Boys' *Hot and Cool* published in *Washington Newsworks*.) So from the first I attempted as a journalist to keep a certain detachment from the punk scene.

That didn't mean I wasn't friendly with lots of local musicians. After all, some of them (like Howard Wuelfing) were also rock writers, and many of them worked at the record stores where I shopped. The Shirkers were founded by my *Unicorn Times* coworker Steve Bialer and my girlfriend Libby Hatch, who later joined Tru Fax and the Insaniacs. I helped design posters, fliers, and record covers for the Shirkers, the Nurses, and the Insaniacs, among others, and first became friendly with Michael Reidy (who designed all the artwork for the Razz) because of my ability to make a drop-white halftone. As a part-time freelance writer, I endeavored to be fair when I wrote about these and other local bands. But in its early days, DC's punk scene was just too small for its players not to assume multiple roles.

called information in Cleveland and ran down some of the names that were on the Pere Ubu record and got his real name and phone number." Thomas proved to be an extremely friendly source of information and encouragement. With Thomas's advice, White Boy recorded and released its first EP in early 1977.

However puerile the lyrics, such records as "Spastic"—which *New Musical Express* claimed "made Iggy Pop sound like a church warden"—were impressive DIY endeavors. The band produced, recorded, and then released its records on its own label, Doodley Squat, based in the Kowalski family's house in a quiet neighborhood in upper Northwest DC. "We wrote them" was proudly printed on the record's lyric sheet—not an idle boast considering that, not long ago, the only route out of the basement had been to play covers.

x x x

Although the Keg still restricted punk bands to off-nights, the club provided a nucleus around which a larger community could coalesce. By 1978, a second generation of bands was emerging from basements and garages: The Young Turds, D'Chumps, Half Japanese, Nice Guise, the Rudements, the Puppets, and the Shirkers had a brash energy not seen in DC for years. As Kane recalled, "It was a boom period, so much enthusiasm and activity—bands just started popping up."

The audience was growing too, but the growing roster of bands still had few places to play. More established groups like the Slickee Boys could play enough to survive, but not to truly build a following. It was even more daunting for bands just starting out.

Various one-off gigs were organized at restaurants or bars, none of which were about to invite a band like White Boy to become a regular attraction. Shows were also arranged at such avant-garde art venues as the Washington Project for the Arts and the Museum of Temporary Art, which occupied shabby (and thus punk-safe) quarters in downtown buildings the DC government had scheduled for demolition. The same neighborhood was also the site of the Atlantis, a venue that would become a DC institution.

The discovery of the Atlantis was an accident. After the Look disbanded, Goldstein allied with former Controls singer Roddy Frantz to form what would become one of the city's most popular (if controversial) bands, the Urban Verbs. The new group needed a place to rehearse, and Goldstein found it in the Atlantic Building, where he rented an office for his work as an exhibition-design consultant. Goldstein made a deal to use the building's lightly patronized restaurant as a new wave club; the Verbs would play for free in exchange for practice space.

The first Atlantis punk show was January 27, 1978: The Urban Verbs played their entire repertoire, followed by the Slickees and White Boy. Soon punk dominated the club's schedule, although relations between the club's owners and its patrons were always strained. The Atlantis was the city's principal punk venue for only about a year, but the club was to reopen in 1980 with a new name derived from the building's address: 930 F Street NW.

x x x

Around the same time, the Verbs played a part in creating another local punk landmark: Don Zientara's Inner Ear Studio. Zientara was an anti–Vietnam-War activist, amateur recording engineer, and sometime musician who had played in a local band with Goldstein. Zientara had learned how to make amps and PA systems out of old televisions and stereos, and had a small mixer and recorder that made crude yet competent recordings. At Goldstein's request, Zientara made a number of live tapes of the Look and the Urban Verbs.

Recording shows at the Atlantis brought Zientara into contact with more area bands. Seeing what Zientara did for the Verbs, others began to approach him to record their bands as well. To better meet this small but growing demand, he set up a recording studio in the basement of his home in suburban Arlington, Virginia.

Another key element of the DC scene had fallen into place a few months before, with the September 1977 opening of Yesterday and Today, a record store in the Maryland suburb of Rockville. Owner Skip Groff had been a student disc jockey at University of Maryland radio station WMUC in the mid-'60s. Later, he did a stint at Rockville's Top 40 station, WINX, where he convinced the management to let him play less mainstream rock in a late-evening show called "Heavy Metal Thunder." Heath recalled that "back in 1973 and '74, Skip would play Roxy Music, Bowie, Blue Oyster Cult, Slade—more or less underground glam-rock stuff" on WINX.

Groff had initially envisioned his store as catering mostly to people who like himself were interested in rare '60s rock, rather than meeting demand for more recent punk music. However, Groff noted, "When you start selling 15 to 20 Buzzcocks or X-Ray Spex records and one Beatles record, your ideas get changed around pretty quickly."

Groff emphasized that the success of what soon became known as "Y and T" really "was all a matter of accident, not design." However unplanned, the appearance of a store that catered to the punk community was crucial. For local bands like the Slickee Boys and White Boy who had records but few places to sell them, Y and T became their outlet. For punk fans weary of mail order or unreliable import distributors, the store became the means to tap into the US/UK punk explosion. From 1977–1979, Groff said, "about seven new punk singles and three new punk albums would arrive in a typical week. We'd have people come in and buy them all every week."

Yesterday and Today gave jobs to more than a few punks, beginning with Kim Kane and Howard Wuelfing. It also evolved into a meeting place where local punk recordings could get a first listen. "People would walk into Yesterday and Today with tapes or test pressings all the time," recalled Kane. "Skip would just put them on the stereo and play them in the store." Groff soon founded Limp Records, a natural outgrowth of the homemade tapes streaming through Y and T. The name was an homage to Stiff Records, home of one Groff's favorites, Elvis Costello.

Although Groff was interested in many of the bands he met through his store, he focused first on the Slickee Boys, who now included ex-Look bassist Wuelfing. "The first time I saw them, the Slickees were so incredibly entertaining that I asked them that night to be the first group on Limp," Groff said.

Before going into the studio with Groff, Kim Kane fulfilled a dream by visiting London in October 1977 to experience the punk explosion firsthand. Upon landing, Kane "just picked up a paper and saw that X-Ray Spex were playing that night at the Marquee." Even though he was a bit worried—"because I had long hair and a goatee and the whole punk thing was 'kill the hippies'"—Kane headed straight to the show.

The night was staggering. Chuckling at the memory, Kane recounted that "I mostly stayed in the back because I was kind of afraid of the dancing. Poly Styrene was great, just screaming, going off. Everyone was pogoing, singing along, and spitting."

At the end of the set, Kane watched in awe as punks exited the club and walked down Wardour Street, singing an a cappella version of "Oh Bondage Up Yours." Kane: "One side would sing 'Oh bondage . . .' and the other side would answer 'Up yours!' Right in the middle of London, out in the street . . . it just blew my mind." Kane spent the next two weeks seeing most of the best English punk bands, visiting the Stiff Records offices and the Rough Trade store, and meeting Mark P., the creator of *Sniffin' Glue*.

After an ebullient Kane returned from London, the Slickee Boys went into Zientara's basement studio and recorded what would be the *Mersey, Mersey Me* 45, Limp Records' first release. Kane had been unhappy with the engineering of their other records. Indeed, he had been so dissatisfied by the sound of *Separated Vegetables*—an album the band had recorded in mid-1977—that he only allowed 100 copies of the LP to be made.

Working with Zientara was different, however. Although his equipment was extremely crude, Zientara proved to be good-natured and helpful, not forcing bands into an existing sound but helping them to find their own. With this flexible yet knowledgeable attitude—and his studio's budget rates—the engineer would become an invaluable resource for fledgling DC punk bands. Zientara's Inner Ear Studio was "the Sun Studios of DC punk—that's just how important it was," said Kane.

The four-song EP's centerpiece was its explosive opening cut, "Put a Bullet Thru the Jukebox." The lyrics were written by New Jersey rock critic Jim Testa, a longtime friend of Wuelfing, in response to a *Village Voice* article that argued that rock fans' oft-expressed hatred for disco music was homophobic and racist. Testa sat down and wrote an anti-disco screed, expressing his belief that "there were a lot of legitimate, artistic reasons to hate disco, reasons that didn't have anything to do with not liking black or gay people."

In a way, the spirit Kane had experienced at the X-Ray Spex show lives on in the song. Besides being a vitriolic attack on the disco craze, it was a punk call to arms, with Martha Hull screaming, "Put a bullet thru the jukebox/Blast it/Blow it/With a nuke!" But if the song—with its talk about "taking a stand on the A.M. band"—hinted at a fight for the allegiance of the broader youth culture, DC punk was not for kids. Most of the people involved in the scene at this point were in their mid-twenties.

However, WGTB was reaching disconnected kids just beginning to discover punk. Kane realized that those people represented DC punk's future. In an 1978 interview with *Argus*, a student publication at the University of Maryland, he argued, "We need to get those kids interested, playing guitars, talking music. That's how a scene snowballs."

Even as Kane was speaking, one crucial knot of kids was finding itself—and punk—at a high school in upper Northwest DC.

positive mental attitude

Success THROUGH A POSITIVE MENTAL ATTITUDE

Now! Proof that dynamic thinking can "awaken a sleeping giant" within you and help you make your dreams come true!

"Whatever the mind can conceive and believe, it can achieve—with PMA."
—Napoleon Hill, *Success Through a Positive Mental Attitude*

Above left: COVER OF *SUCCESS THROUGH A POSITIVE MENTAL ATTITUDE* (by Napoleon Hill)
Above right: COVER OF "THIRTY SECONDS OVER DC," 1978 (by Kim Kane)

positive mental attitude

It was the fall of 1977, and dust was clearing from an explosion in Fort Reno Park. A dozen kids stood across the street in front of Woodrow Wilson High School, watching the last bits of debris fall to earth. One of them was a 15-year-old named Ian MacKaye, who wore a backwards baseball hat to keep his nearly shoulder-length hair out of his face when he skateboarded.

MacKaye had arrived during lunch hour to see the homemade bomb explode. Moments before, bombmaker Jeff Nelson had lit the fuse on a pipe bomb buried in the park and then run across the street. Now Nelson—reputedly a somewhat crazed stoner kid—was chatting excitedly with his friends, flushed with adrenalin. MacKaye took note of Nelson, and walked back into the red brick school.

A self-described "skinny pyromaniacal State Department brat," Nelson had spent much of his life overseas. Perhaps as a result, he had learned to amuse himself, developing many hobbies, including a fascination with the history of warfare. Since arriving in DC, he had become an enthusiastic do-it-yourself bomb manufacturer.

Nelson later dismissed his bomb-building phase as "just another way of getting attention." It worked. In early 1978, not long after Nelson's noontime bomb show, he found himself in the same tenth-grade German class as MacKaye. They quickly became close friends.

MacKaye was already part of a skateboard posse that included fellow Wilson students like Mark Sullivan and Bert Queiroz, MacKaye's younger brother Alec, and neighborhood kid Henry Garfield. They were all what Garfield later called "action kids," bored by their lives in middle-class white DC, always up to something to fill the time.

Garfield was the tough kid, the product of an abusive home. In grade school, he was diagnosed as "hyperactive" and put on Ritalin. A disciplinarian's nightmare, Garfield had been in and out of different schools for years before being sent to Bullis, a strict, all-boys school in nearby Potomac,

Maryland. "It was the whole military school trip—uniforms, buzz cut, all of that," Garfield recalled bitterly. "I was told to 'shut up and sit down' for seven years basically."

At the time, skateboarding was a radical recreation. It appealed mostly to the high-energy kids like Garfield, MacKaye, and others who used their boards to blow off steam. "We were going crazy," said Garfield years later, "skating all night till 4 a.m. just to get up at 9 a.m. to do it more!"

"Skating was such an intense exertion, kind of on-the-edge, at least at the time. Extreme music just seemed to go with it," Queiroz remembered. The skater crew was into what Garfield described as "energy music. Anything with volume and force to it. Anything with that big boom thing happening—Aerosmith, Nugent, Queen."

With the exception of Garfield, this group's social world largely centered around Wilson High. Though it was in an affluent neighborhood, Wilson served a wide area, reaching not only into white and black middle-class sections but also rough inner-city ghettos. Of the roughly 1500 students at Wilson, 60 percent were black, 20 percent were white, with the remainder mostly Asian-American or Latino.

If Wilson's racial composition was not unlike that of most DC public schools, in many ways the school was more like the area's private prep schools. In contrast to the majority of the city's struggling high schools, Wilson sent 80 percent of its kids to college, including every Ivy League university. According to an admissions officer at one elite college, Wilson had a "stellar reputation among universities for producing kids who are smart and self-motivated."

The skate posse was one reaction to the achievement-oriented environment. Another rebellious group of kids centered around the Wilson Players Drama Club, the high school theater group, of which MacKaye was also a member. The old ROTC rifle range in the school basement was the favorite haunt of the Players and other Wilson rebels. Between classes, students would sneak downstairs to hang out, smoke pot, drink beer, kiss, and write on the walls.

MacKaye's individuality and intelligence impressed many of his peers. Garfield recalled that "even when we were really little, Ian was the first person in our age group—in our little gang of shithead kids—who really had ideas of his own and dared to disagree. Like we would all be doing dumb shit, you know, and Ian would just stand there and say, 'Look, that's bullshit!' We'd give him a hard time, but we all saw that the guy had principles. He had his own way of doing things at a very early age."

Perhaps the most striking early example of this was MacKaye's rejection of drugs. Though MacKaye was one of the rifle range crowd, he never joined in the smoking or drinking. "I liked the rebellion," MacKaye recalled, "but I always thought that our thing could be stronger without the drugs."

Several factors informed his view, including a family history of alcoholism. Also, in 1975 the family went to California for a year when MacKaye's father received a fellowship at Stanford. During the year the family was gone, MacKaye's friends back home had begun experimenting with drugs. "Since I was gone, I missed the transition," MacKaye explained, "and this gave me a unique perspective. I could see how dramatically they had changed as a result of the drugs. I didn't like what I saw."

This distaste was underscored when the skater crew started to go to the Capital Centre, then the Washington area's basketball, hockey, and hard-rock arena. The concerts were intensely exciting for them, but some aspects seemed ugly and stupid. As Garfield remembered, "We'd go to the Cap Centre and some guy looped out on quaaludes would come falling down the stairs. We'd go, 'God, this makes us want to skate and rip-roar through life, not fall all over ourselves.'"

The sight of their peers disarmed by dope hardened the anti-drug stance of some in the small group. "We'd go 'Fuck it, we're straight' to set us off from the dopes, to set us off from the boring, dead alkie trip and the take-ludes-and-fall-asleep-in-the-parking-lot-at-White-Flint-Mall thing," Garfield said. "The stoners had their cool, we had ours. With our skates and our music, we didn't need drugs."

Outspokenly anti-drug Detroit rocker Ted Nugent became a hero to the skaters. Disdaining artificial stimulation, Nugent made some of the most crazed straight-ahead rock of the time. It was everything that the skaters sought—loud, aggressive, drug-free mayhem.

For MacKaye, Nugent may have had another appeal: His roots reached back to the '60s. MacKaye was something of a late-'60s nut, old enough to remember being brought to antiwar rallies by his parents, fascinated by that period's counterculture. Nugent had shared the stage with the likes of the MC5 and the Stooges. Unlike those bands or such other MacKaye heroes as Janis Joplin and Jimi Hendrix, however, Nugent was still here.

MacKaye's love for the '60s counterculture was also part of the foundation for his anti-drug stance. Given that the drug culture was a major legacy of the '60s, this might seem odd. But drugs had killed Jimi and Janis, as well as many others. For MacKaye, it was clear that drugs themselves, far from being the lifeblood of '60s rebellion, were actually in part responsible for its destruction.

MacKaye's anti-drug feelings were well-established by the time his circle of friends began to cautiously explore the new music called punk. MacKaye bought his first punk record—White Boy's "I Could Puke"—from junior high friend Seth Martin, who lived near the White Boy house and had frequently roadied for the band. MacKaye listened to the 45 over and over again, amazed by its sheer audacity. For MacKaye and his rebel friends, the White Boy record was like a gigantic "Anything is Permitted" sign.

The skaters also took inspiration from a couple of older Wilson students, Nathan Strejcek and Danny Ingram. The longtime best friends were bored with the music of the day. "We were big Led Zeppelin and Aerosmith fans but those bands had really gone downhill by the late '70s," said Strejcek. "We were looking for something new." They drifted into the Georgetown scene that had grown up around the regular midnight showings of *The Rocky Horror Picture Show*. Ingram took a part-time job at a Georgetown theater.

One day in early 1978, Ingram recalled, "A guy who I worked with who had lived in London brought in the first Damned record, the first X-Ray Spex, the first Stranglers and Wire LPs. He just gave me the records and said, 'Trust me—you'll like these.'" Around the same time, Strejcek got the Sex Pistols' *Never Mind the Bollocks*.

Strejcek and Ingram never looked back. As the former remembered, "The Sex Pistols and those other bands seemed to offer something no other bands had at the time. I thought, 'If this is punk, then I should be one.'" After befriending White Boy, the duo began to hang out in the Kowalski crowd. WGTB became their lifeline to the new music. "We used to sneak out of our house at night and go visit Xyra [Harper] when she did her radio show," Ingram said.

The friends' transformation was soon reflected externally. "Nathan had really, really long hair," Jeff Nelson recalled. "One day he showed up at school with short, spiky, pink hair. It blew everybody's mind. Nathan and Danny were the first punks at Wilson."

As Strejcek and Ingram adopted English punk dress and attitudes, the younger Wilson kids took note from a distance. For them and many other teens in the DC metro area, WGTB—especially

Harper's show—became their connection to what was going on. Eventually they also began to venture out to Yesterday and Today in search of punk records.

xxx

By mid-1978, WGTB had never been more widely heard or influential. But it had also become even more troubling to Georgetown University's administrators. The University's efforts to "tame" the station had plainly failed, and tension was once again building between the station and the administration. Communications between the staff and the station's university-appointed general manager, Robert Uttenweiler, had almost entirely broken down.

At the same time, there was a bitter split at another of the local punk scene's incipient institutions, the Atlantis. Over the first half of 1978, the marriage of convenience between the club and its patrons was unraveling. Owner Paul Parsons was unhappy over the low alcohol sales at even well-attended shows, since this is where clubs usually made most of their profit. As a result, he began to refuse to allow minors into the club.

The Atlantis also stopped booking bands like White Boy, the Rudements, and Ebenezer and the Bludgeons, all of whom attracted a younger, non-drinking crowd. Parsons's authoritarian personality and questionable business practices added to the tension. As Kim Kane recalled, "Unfortunately, Parsons and his assistant Kevin DuPlain were totally obnoxious and crazy. They didn't like to pay bands. And if they didn't like a band, they would literally take bands off the stage in the middle of their set."

In addition, Parsons started to harass his critics, including Mike Heath and Rob Kennedy, who reported in *Vintage Violence* a disagreement between Parsons and the Cramps after the latter's chaotic set at the Atlantis in April 1978. "Parsons freaked out because the Cramps played such wild, uninhibited, crazy rock'n'roll," said Heath. "He was scared for his furniture. To us, it was a little hard to figure—he had a punk rock club, and the Cramps were a real punk rock band. What did Parsons expect? Anyway, he ended up screwing them out of some money. Rob—who was friends with the Cramps—came to me and said, 'We have to write about this!' So we did." On his next visit to the club, Heath was kicked out. Kennedy had an even more dramatic encounter. "The next time Rob came in," Heath recalled, "Parsons literally put handcuffs on him and called the police."

By mid-1978, the various grievances had led to a widely supported boycott of the Atlantis. DC punks found themselves in the ironic position of discouraging business at the only area club for punk or new wave. Still, the boycott was effective. As the *Unicorn Times* reported in August 1978, fewer than 200 of 1100 available tickets were sold for a Dead Boys concert sponsored by the Atlantis at the Ontario Theater.

With no club to replace the Atlantis, most bands were back playing the traditional rock bar circuit and occasional gigs at galleries and art spaces. Limp Records helped out by sponsoring some "beer blasts" at rented American Legion halls. There were meetings about opening a club to compete with the Atlantis, but no one seemed to have the necessary capital.

Keith Campbell—whose short-lived post-Controls band, Nice Guise, had just broken up—expressed the frustration of that moment: "You had to either go back and become a scab at the Atlantis or become a radical and just play private parties with drunken kids crawling up your feet. We said, 'DC really eats.'" This inspired the name of the DCeats, the new band Campbell formed with ex-Overkiller Harrison Sohmer, Vic Quick, and Martha Hull, who had suddenly exited the Slickee Boys.

Hull's exit was the second blow to the Slickees in a few weeks. Howard Wuelfing had just left to form the Nurses with guitarist Marc Halpern and keyboardist Shelly Dietrick. Stripped of its two voices, the band faced an uncertain future.

The Atlantis boycott increased the gap between the Urban Verbs, who were seen as the slickest and best-connected of the city's new wave bands, and some former friends and peers. Although recollections within the band differ—Roddy Frantz recalled supporting the boycott, Robert Goldstein remembered disdaining it—the Urban Verbs were seen by many as refusing to close ranks against the Atlantis.

In retrospect, the Verbs had far more to lose from the boycott than most local bands. Since the Atlantis had opened, the Verbs had become one of the most popular bands in the scene. Goldstein had discovered the place and understood more than most the financial realities Parsons faced. Furthermore, the band had no problems with Parsons, and the Atlantic Building remained their practice space.

Besides, Goldstein didn't intend to be a member of a strictly local band for long. "From the beginning, I thought that the Urban Verbs could go beyond the local community and be a widely recognized band," he said. "I simply wasn't interested in getting bogged down in petty political spats like the boycott."

The rift heralded the beginning of two distinctive scenes: the roots-rock crew associated with the Razz and the Slickees and an art-punk contingent headed by the Verbs.

The tension was temporarily disarmed by the Atlantis management's capitulation to most of the punk community's demands. With or without the Verbs, the boycott was sufficient to convince Parsons and DuPlain to make more significant efforts to keep the bands happy. "It was really cool," remembered Kim Kane, "Parsons invited us down and surrendered to our demands. The boycott was a political thing that really worked." The Atlantis scene, however, would never recapture its previous momentum.

xxx

The commercial success of the Cars and Blondie led some local musicians to consider the possibility of major-label deals, especially after Warner Brothers signed jokey local funk-rockers Root Boy Slim and the Sex-Change Band in 1978. But the first local punk album (aside from the barely released *Separated Vegetables*) was Limp Records' *30 Seconds Over DC: Here Comes the New Wave!* Compiled by Skip Groff and WGTB DJ David Howcroft, the LP showcased 16 local acts. The album's title (drawn from *30 Seconds Over Tokyo*, a movie about the US bombing of that city during World War II that had also inspired a Pere Ubu song) and cover art (a Kim Kane drawing of an aerial assault on the Washington Monument) suggested that the record was a declaration of cultural war.

The album's liner notes denounced disco, metal, and local clubs, while extolling WGTB and the possibility of building a local scene that bands wouldn't desert for the music-industry capitals, New York and LA. One of the songs, the Penetrators' "The Break," made the same point more succinctly: "How much can we take?/This shit has got to break/Our future is at stake/So be different for your own sake!"

Some cuts more than lived up to that challenge. The sidelined Slickee Boys and the Rudements each provided live tracks, the spunky "Attitude" and edgy "Imagination," respectively. The Nurses' "I Can Explain" is a raw, aching pop treasure, while White Boy contributed the driving, splenetic "I Hate."

The album's most striking track, however, was Half Japanese's "I Want Something New." The band was Jad and David Fair, two brothers who had very different physiques but wore similar geeky glasses. Arriving unexpectedly from the Maryland hamlet of Uniontown, Half Japanese was impassioned and original.

The Fair brothers shared the free spirit of White Boy, but replaced its gross-out aesthetic with gawky teen drama and pure rock idealism. Inspired by the Stooges, Patti Smith, and Jonathan Richman, the pair took an untuned guitar and a drum set and created sheets of white noise. Over the cacophony, Jad screamed lines like "No more Beatlemania/Once is enough!/We will not buy your records, no/Once is enough!/Don't let them sell you old-fashioned mania/Once is enough!" After about 100 seconds of chaos, they stopped and called it a song.

Amazingly enough, it worked. Compared to the burning spirit of "I Want Something New," much of the rest of *30 Seconds Over DC* seemed pedestrian. Such songs as Da Moronics' "Mr. President" (chunky stop-and-start guitars churning out a good-humored message of support for then-embattled President Carter), Mock Turtle's "Thank You for Sending Me an Eno" (a tribute to both Talking Heads and Brian Eno) or the Raisinets' "Stay Limp" (a laid-back answer to Devo's anthem to Stiff Records, "Be Stiff") can summon a smile, but they are hardly essential.

Still, it's hard not to admire the spirit and diversity of the collection. Cuts like Mark Hoback's brittle, punky blues "No Fun," Tina Peel's boppy pop "Knocking Down Guardrails," Young Turds' "Murder One" (whose morbid lyrics were obscured by inspired sax/guitar interplay), Billy Synth's Moogy anti-love song "Everytime You Give Me a Call," D'Chumps' jerky blasphemy "Jet Lag Drag," or Judie's Fixation's fuzzy rampage "Martyr Me" showed how far the scene had come since Overkill's tumultuous Keg debut barely more than two years before.

XXX

The punk scene documented on *30 Seconds Over DC* began in neighborhoods and campuses on the city's predominantly white west side, also the locale of Wilson High School and its fledgling punks. In 1978, however, punk crossed the Anacostia River into the city's eastern-most precincts, which were overwhelmingly black. It was carried there by two black teenagers, Sid McCray and Darryl Jenifer.

McCray was from a military family that had moved to Southeast DC in the midst of the riots that followed Martin Luther King Jr.'s assassination in 1968. A DC native, Jenifer came from a splintered home, and had moved frequently from one family member to another. In the early '70s, he arrived across the street from McCray and the two became inseparable.

One of their shared interests was music. They were unusual because, in addition to the popular black sounds of the day, they were also into what Jenifer called "doomsday music": Black Sabbath, Kiss, Budgie, and Led Zeppelin. By the late '70s, however, heavy metal no longer seemed potent to them. "It just didn't give you any energy anymore," recalled McCray.

Then one day in late 1977, McCray saw a TV news report about British punk. Intrigued, the next day he bought the Sex Pistols' and Damned's first albums. The impact of this raw new music was immediate, dramatic, and galvanizing—if initially destructive. "I came back home and played them," he said. "I went into a violent rage and tore my room up!" Vaguely aware that there was a local scene, McCray began searching for it, eventually discovering the Atlantis.

"I always liked the rebellion part of punk," McCray explained. "I was feeling angry realizing that the establishment was killing all our leaders—Malcolm X, MLK, the Panthers. All the other music then was just 'party music,' y'know, the old cliché, 'sex, drugs, rock'n'roll.' I guess I felt that it was time to think about things, to question authority. Basically, punk music was telling me, 'Don't accept these things as the truth unless you check them out.' It was time to get rebellious, to keep up on what was going on."

McCray began to share his new passion with Jenifer, playing him the Pistols and Damned as well as newer finds like Eater and the hyper-fast Dickies. Jenifer liked a lot of it, but was more interested in joining a jazz-fusion band forming in another neighborhood around Paul and Earl Hudson and their friend Gary Miller.

Paul was the older of the two Hudsons and the mastermind of the planned group. Like McCray, the brothers were from a military family and had lived all over the world. When their father retired from the Air Force in the early '70s, the Hudson family settled in a Maryland suburb just across the line from Southeast DC.

Paul Hudson was an outstanding athlete and a creative thinker, but his free-spirited approach brought him into frequent conflict with his father's more conventional outlook. Feeling pressure after graduating from high school in 1975, he half-heartedly went into pre-med only to flunk out. "I would go and sit in the front row, right in front of the teachers, and challenge them all day long!" Hudson recalled. "Eventually I got bored with school and really bored with life in general. It was quite clear that I wasn't going to be able to be a doctor. That's what my mother and father wanted me to do. I had to make some big decisions soon."

Hudson had one great love in his life: music. The first years of his life were spent in Liverpool. Perhaps partly as a result, Hudson's parents used to call their sons down from their rooms to sing along to Beatles songs. "Ever since those days I knew I had to play music some kind of way," Hudson remembered. "But I never really took it too seriously. I would write songs and never show them to anybody."

After dropping out of school, Hudson worked as a security guard at a hospital parking lot in Southeast DC. He dallied with hard drugs, including heroin, and got a woman pregnant. By the time his son was born in 1977, Hudson's future seemed bleak.

"One day I was sitting at home, laying on the couch in the living room, and my father came in, saw me, and started saying, 'What are you doing with your life?' He just went on and on," Hudson recalled. "I said, 'Dad, I'm trying to get involved with music.' He got really angry and said, 'Man, why don't you do something, go read a book or something!'"

Angry, Hudson stalked to his father's bookshelf. "I picked up the first book I saw, sat back down, and started reading it." The book turned out to be *Think and Grow Rich* by Napoleon Hill, a classic forerunner of the self-help genre. Supposedly inspired by a private conversation with industrial magnate Andrew Carnegie, Hill originally wrote and published the book during the Great Depression.

Hudson found himself captivated by Hill's ideas, which were a strange mix of positive thinking slogans, pleas to read the Bible, and proto–new age spiritualist appeals to supernatural powers of the mind. The central concept was PMA—Positive Mental Attitude. According to Hill, this idea—

discussed in *Think and Grow Rich* but only named in a second volume, *Success Through a Positive Mental Attitude*—was the "master key of success" that helped people such as Thomas Edison, Helen Keller, Abraham Lincoln, Henry Ford, and Mohandas Gandhi to achieve their goals.

"Definiteness of purpose" was essential in Hill's philosophy. A person had to know what he wanted in order to focus his entire being on its attainment. This intense concentration required regular use of prayer and a quasi-hypnotic process called "auto-suggestion," as well as other mystical rituals. Hill emphasized that "objectives were achieved because the seeker placed all their energy behind one definite purpose." He also taught that more than one seeker could form a "Master Mind Alliance," which united "the coordination of knowledge and effort in a spirit of harmony between two or more people for the attainment of a definite purpose."

Hudson began to apply PMA principles to his musical ambitions. While not uninterested in the financial aspect, he found special appeal in Hill's call to a great mission, a "Magnificent Obsession" for one's life. "*Think and Grow Rich* had such an effect on my life," Hudson said. "I saw it as a support in helping define directions, to get my music started. Mind over matter, you can do it. So, at the age of 18, I said, 'I'm going to start myself a band!'"

Hudson took his idea for a band based on Hill's theories to his neighborhood friend, Gary Miller, who played bass. Miller switched to guitar and began to teach bass to Hudson, whose younger brother Earl sat in on drums. Other friends, including Jenifer, drifted in and out of the group.

This band was to be called Mindpower, a name drawn straight from Hill's books. "We wanted a name that would represent what we thought the youths needed, what we and our friends needed," Hudson said. Although some friends laughed at Hudson's interest in PMA, Miller, Jenifer, and Earl Hudson also began to study Hill's work.

Hudson was the band's ideological guide, but Miller quickly assumed the musical lead. The jazz-fusion unit band Return to Forever, whose members were Scientologists, was a major influence. Still, Miller said that "we weren't really playing fusion, though I guess you could call it that because it was a mixture of whatever came up."

One of Hill's maxims was "Do it now!," so after practicing for only a few weeks, Mindpower played its first show in the basement of the Hudson family home. Hudson distributed fliers to high school kids and neighborhood friends, drawing a large crowd. Musically, however, the show was a disaster. The set began shakily, then got shakier when Jenifer was too stricken with stage fright to play, forcing the band to improvise. The audience began to boo and throw things. "We bombed, we bombed, we bombed," recalled Hudson, an account ruefully confirmed by the others.

The entire band was chastened by this misadventure, but the show was an especially big blow to Hudson. With the pressures of fatherhood and a dead-end job looming over him, his next move seemed crucial. Hudson returned to Hill's writings, and a new series of messages seemed to emerge: "If one plan fails, try another. Turn defeat into success. Always be ready to try something new."

"I remember sitting with Gary and Darryl saying that we gotta do something original, we gotta think of some sound here that's so fresh and innovative that no one else can copy it," said Hudson. What this sound might be, however, was unclear. Then Jenifer took Mindpower to meet Sid McCray.

Though McCray and Jenifer were close friends, the other band members didn't know McCray well, and had no idea that he had been transformed by punk. They were taken aback by the new McCray, who wore a leather jacket and chains, his chopped hair festooned with peroxide streaks. When he played them his new favorite records by the likes of the Sex Pistols, the Damned, the Clash, and Dead Boys, their astonishment grew. While he had grown up with the Beatles and Stones and still liked rock, Hudson was the most shocked.

"We didn't know anything about any of these bands," Hudson remembered years later. "I'd be sitting down criticizing it and Darryl, who was the rock man, into Black Sabbath and all that stuff, said, 'Hey man, what up? You don't understand.' And he'd break it all down for me."

As Jenifer doggedly defended this outlandish new music, something slipped into place in Hudson's mind. Smiling broadly, he turned to the rest of the band and asked: "Why don't we play some punk rock, y'all?"

*"I've got that supertouch/Chances are I've got too much
I've come to let you see/That you also can be free."*
—Bad Brains, "Supertouch"

HR AND DR. KNOW OF BAD BRAINS AT HARD ART GALLERY, SEPTEMBER 15, 1979 *(by Lucian Perkins)*

supertouch

It was a large, noisy, unconventionally dressed crowd that filed into Georgetown University's Hall of Nations for a concert featuring the Cramps, Urban Verbs, and D'Chumps. The mood suggested both a funeral and a possible riot.

In a way, these contradictory emotions made sense. Three days earlier, on January 31, 1979, WGTB had been yanked off the air by Georgetown University president Timothy Healy. Its transmitter had been sold for one dollar and its frequency transferred to the University of the District of Columbia. The evening, then, was a paradoxical event: a benefit concert for a radio station that no longer existed.

The crisis had been building since at least May 1978, when Father Healy announced that the station was "a financial liability" and would close. Initially, few believed that would really happen. "The radio station had a history of being taken off the air for short periods of time because it did not support the University per se," Xyra Harper recalled. "Whenever we got too radical, they took us off the air for a while."

Neither a petition signed by 20,000 listeners nor resolutions of support for WGTB by the Student and Faculty Senates swayed Healy. This time, the station was not to be merely silenced for a time but actually sold, making any revival impossible.

The exact reasons for WGTB's demise remain unclear. Although the station had nettled the administration for a decade, Healy would not admit to any consideration other than cost. Since a FM radio frequency was of immense potential value, and Georgetown essentially gave its license away, this explanation seems implausible.

The programming of punk and art-rock was probably not a crucial issue. For a station at a Jesuit university, WGTB's gay and lesbian programming and abortion-counseling public service announcements were more controversial. The station's worst offense, however, was something more banal: its unwillingness to air Georgetown basketball games on Saturday nights. "I know it sounds like a really horrible reason to lose a station, but that's what happened," said Harper.

If the end of WGTB was a relief to the university's administrators, it was a severe reversal for the punk community. "When WGTB shut down, it was a tremendous blow," said Mike Heath. "I cried. A lot of people cried."

Some of the grief and rage was expressed in a sizable and spirited demonstration held on the steps of Georgetown's administration building on the afternoon of February 3rd. The emotions were still palpable later that day as the Hall of Nations filled with punk partisans. The loss of WGTB was the end of an era. But that night DC punk's past was to meet its future.

The concert was open to all ages and had been heavily promoted over the air during WGTB's final weeks. As a result, many teens for whom WGTB had been a window to a world of cultural possibilities were in the crowd, many attending a punk concert for the first time.

This included most of the Wilson High skater crowd, who all still wore the long hair typical of male high schoolers of the late '70s. Also there was 13-year-old Guy Picciotto, who attended the private Georgetown Day School. "WGTB was the only station playing remotely alternative music, the first place I ever heard bands like the Adverts," he said. "To see it smashed was a really big deal to me."

His sentiments were shared by David Byers, a young black teen from an all-male Catholic school, Archbishop Carroll, who was also there that night. "The first time that I heard anything good was on WGTB. It hurt to lose it," he said. This was the first punk show for Byers and the friend who accompanied him, Georgetown Day School student Chris Haskett.

While these teens blended anonymously into the crowd, another group of newcomers was harder to overlook. Several wild-looking black punks stood next to the doorway handing out fliers. Their imposing appearance was matched by the bold hyperbole on the handouts: "World's fastest," "devastating," "Are You Ready? We Are!" were among the phrases publicizing the basement show by their new band, Bad Brains.

Bad Brains was Mindpower turned punk, with a new look and sound. Paul Hudson, Gary Miller, and Darryl Jenifer had even taken on new names: "HR Brain," "Dr. Know," and "Darryl Cyanide," respectively. Only sometime vocalist Sid McCray (who was soon to leave) and Earl Hudson didn't assume new identities.

Another book had now joined the works of Napoleon Hill in guiding the band—*1988: The New Wave Punk Rock Explosion*, an anthology of Caroline Coon's *Melody Maker* articles on the Sex Pistols, Clash, Damned, and Slits. Bad Brains had adopted the punk style wholeheartedly upon reading *1988*. Thanks largely to its inspiration, Bad Brains "designed many of our own clothes, our friends helped out with the sewing," recalled HR. "That was the thing that was so great about punk when we first discovered it. You made your music, you made your clothes, you created your whole thing."

Fashion was hardly at the heart of their vision, however. "We dug the militancy happening in punk rock," said Jenifer. "It said, 'If you have something to say, say it.' A lot of the things we saw our people falling for made us mad at the kind of illusions society was trying to create."

This became a recurrent theme in Bad Brains lyrics. One of their new songs, "Don't Need it," rejected advertising ploys: "We don't need Ivory Liquid/Don't need no Afro-Sheen/Don't need the latest fashions/Don't want my hair to smell clean . . . You think I'm going crazy?/It just might be you."

The band's mutation had been sudden, but it was sincere. "If someone were to say to me, it sounds like you were just trying to get a gimmick, I'd have to say they're wrong," said HR in retrospect. "We weren't looking for a gimmick. What we were searching for was what all true musicians do, which is to create. This is the difference between a sellout and what's real. It's a thin line. You have those who do the music because someone tells them to do it—to be popular—and then you have those who do the music because it's what they love, it's what they need to do. When we heard punk rock, we said, 'That's where the energy is!'"

Mindpower took its new name from a song on the fourth Ramones album, *Road to Ruin*. Although Jenifer didn't much like the record, the song title stuck in his head. HR remembers "talking with Darryl about a new name for the band, saying it's got be something dealing with the mind and it's got to be 'bad'—meaning 'great,' in the street sense of the word—and he said 'Bad Brains!' and I said 'yeah!' Only later did he tell me about the Ramones song." With its emphasis on the power of the mind to transform reality, the band's use of the title reversed the meaning of the original song.

The renovated band moved into a rented house in Forestville, a Maryland suburb. There they practiced fervently, preparing to reemerge. Since it was bound to be a big show, the WGTB benefit was a chance for them to get the word out.

Bad Brains caught the eye of many in the crowd. "HR had short dreads, sticking straight up, with the side of his head shaved," recalled Ian MacKaye. "He wore a Johnny Rotten jacket with shit hanging off it. Darryl had his hair peroxided on one side, Earl had a shaved head, and Gary used to wear a surgical gown with blood all down the front and wore a mask and stuff. When they used to walk through Georgetown, they were the scariest motherfuckers you ever saw."

On the Hall of Nations stage were the fledgling Bad Brains' antithesis: the cool, arty Urban Verbs. Thanks largely to a demo produced by glam/ambient cult hero Brian Eno, the Verbs would soon sign to Warner Brothers. Tight and energetic but also moody and atmospheric, the Verbs were a strong live act; one of the gig's organizers, Bob Boilen, described them as "a stunning realization of beat poetry and rock'n'roll." Tonight, however, they were overshadowed by the Cramps, who played two sets, one before and one after the Verbs.

A New York punkabilly band that played Washington frequently, the Cramps already had a strong DC following. Singer Lux Interior opened with an apparent slap at the Verbs' more mannered style: "Some people wondered if this was a concert or a dance. Well, the concert part just ended!" The audience came alive as the singer contorted himself, climbed on amps, and invaded the crowd, living out the B-movie nightmares of the band's songs onstage. People stood on tables, hoping to get a better view, and the tables began collapsing one by one.

The teenagers in the audience, used to the anonymity of shows at the Capital Centre, were riveted. "People were breaking windows and throwing chairs around," marveled Guy Picciotto. "You had no idea at all what Lux might do next. He seemed just totally insane, and the whole scene was like absolute bedlam. Even though I was scared shitless, I was thinking to myself, 'This is the greatest thing that I've ever seen!'"

The Cramps seemed to have tapped into the crowd's rage over the destruction of WGTB. "There was a real anger against Georgetown for what they had done to the station," Picciotto said. "There was an air of total desperation that people were losing their only countercultural outlet. Sure, some people were totally messing around, but there was also a definite sense of protest."

By evening's end, the hall was a shambles. Insurance bought by Boilen and co-organizer David

Howcroft covered the $775 in damages, enabling the night's profits to finance other events. The show could not save WGTB; for some spectators, however, everything had changed.

"I was covered with afterbirth," laughed Picciotto. "Being 13 and having never experienced music outside of giant rock arenas with bands like Kiss and Aerosmith, then to suddenly be here, with the band five feet away, playing so intensely, with people reacting in such a visceral way—to be exposed to that level of interaction just blew my mind wide open."

"At the time I thought Ted Nugent was really wild, so the Cramps show totally changed my life," MacKaye recalled. "It was just unbelievable. It was the greatest shit I'd ever seen. It was everything I thought rock'n'roll should be. I was like, 'This is it, I'm a punk rock motherfucker.'"

David Byers, who soon would help form the Enzymes with Chris Haskett, agreed. "From then on, it was, 'All systems go!'"

By the time they went to see the Clash's first DC show a few weeks later, MacKaye and Nelson had cut off their long hair. "The Hall of Nations show was the first show that made us want to be in a band," said Nelson. He and MacKaye allied with Mark Sullivan and fellow Wilson student Geordie Grindle, a singer and guitarist with cover-band experience. MacKaye had never played bass and Nelson had never played the drums, but they set out to learn by doing. They combined their favorite junk food, Twinkies, with the verb "to slink," to form the band's name, the Slinkees.

The band began with covers like "Louie Louie," "At the Hop," and "No Fun," then added songs that mocked hippie rock (the un-Grateful "Deadhead" and the anti-Skynyrd "Dead Bird") or celebrated a typical teenage diet ("I Drink Milk"). In the new-age-baiting "Conservative Rock," Sullivan proclaimed that "We don't sit in circles/We don't meditate/We don't eat health food/'Cuz Cokes and Twinkies are great." MacKaye would later call these anthems "my first protest songs."

x x x

Just as the Slinkees began to practice, the Atlantis closed. In an interview with the *Washington Post*, Paul Parsons blamed all the club's problems on its patrons: "Every weekend the punks would rearrange the building directory, rip the wiring and toilets out of the rest rooms, and roam through the upper floors of the building like droogs." The newspaper offered no rebuttal from fans or musicians, who might have noted that Parsons had violated fire codes and liquor laws, lied to bands about facilities and wages, banned writers who questioned his policies and had one of those writers put in handcuffs, ended up in court with several of the bands who played there, and become the object of a long—and largely successful—boycott.

Bad Brains had been angling for an Atlantis show, even writing a song called "Jamming at the Atlantis." The band was promised a booking, only to see the club close its doors. Undeterred, the musicians continued to set up shows in the basement of their house, impressing many longtime scenesters. One early supporter was Kim Kane, who said the shows had "the atmosphere of an old rhythm and blues house party. People were sprawled everywhere, holes in the wall, lots of DC's early punks crammed into the basement, listening to these speed demons playing furiously. Their energy was incredible."

In addition to its breakneck, chaotic performances—HR gave up playing second guitar since it invariably got broken as he leaped about—the band had a unique style. "We were searching for an original sound, bringing in all our influences, the jazz, the rock, the funk," said Dr. Know. Such early songs as "Redbone in the City," a knockoff of "God Save the Queen," showed the debt to British punk, but other material meshed jazz chops with punk fireworks, promising something all the band's own.

The lyrics were filled with references to Positive Mental Attitude. A concept popularized by a rich old white entrepreneur was being molded to punk rock by young black men inspired by English kids they had never met. To Bad Brains, however, it all made sense.

One of the more challenging elements of this equation was race. By becoming punks, Bad Brains had entered a largely white world. The band members were often harassed in the black community, where "punk" was an anti-gay slur, but some of their initial experiences in the white rock scene were scarcely more encouraging. While distributing fliers at a heavy metal show at the Keg, McCray says, they were harassed and called "nigger" by some in the crowd. At Bad Brains' first club show, opening for the revamped Slickee Boys in a Baltimore suburb, the band was greeted by racial epithets and threats.

Howard Wuelfing, who attended the show, calls the hecklers "just little boys making a loud noise." But Jenifer bitterly recalled the racist reaction they faced that evening, noting that "some people just couldn't handle black folks playing rock music."

Bad Brains' skills were quickly recognized. In March 1979, just weeks after the band's basement debut, Skip Groff approached Kim Kane about producing a Bad Brains session he had arranged at Don Zientara's home studio. Groff admitted that he enlisted Kane because the group intimidated him. "I thought Bad Brains were an extremely strong group but, quite frankly, I was a bit scared of them."

The day of the session, Kane recalled, "the Bad Brains were way late, leaving only one hour to record and mix seven songs. Half the time was spent miking Darryl's homemade fuzzbox. Because of that, Gary had to overdub all of his leads in a row while the tape was rolling." Miller got it right on the first take. An awed Kane said that "their passion and speed were amazing that day."

Bad Brains were featured in the second issue of a new fanzine, *The Infiltrator*, started by ex-WGTB staffer Mary Levy with the help of fellow former DJs Xyra Harper and Chris Thompson (formerly drummer of the Look and, later, Tiny Desk Unit). Around the same time, Howard Wuelfing began his own 'zine, *Descenes*. "I wanted it to be like the original *New York Rocker*," he said, "where the people in the scene who saw each other's band would write about each other," building a healthy intra-scene dialogue.

The arrival of the *Infiltrator* and *Descenes* was a hopeful step for the embattled DC punk community. So was the return of the Slickee Boys, who regrouped with new singer Mark Noone, an engaging frontman. The band began to gig frequently, introducing new material like "Gotta Tell Me Why," a catchy single written by Noone. With the success of acts like the Cars and the Knack, the Slickees' new power-pop sound had commercial potential. Although one photo showed the band wearing garish wide ties—an obvious dig at the new wave of skinny-tie power-poppers—"Gotta Tell Me Why" was the band's most professional and mainstream release yet.

The Razz bassist Ted Niceley coproduced "Gotta Tell Me Why," and his own band was also moving toward a slicker sound. The quintet became one of the city's top club draws because of its punky blues-rock attack and singer Michael Reidy's abrasive stage presence, but the three singles the Razz released in 1978-79 showed a trend toward power-pop.

This was in large part because Tommy Keene had replaced original guitarist Abaad Behram. Keene was the first prolific tunesmith in the band, which was still playing mostly covers, but the songs he wrote didn't appeal to Reidy. "Tommy would bring me these songs with the most banal lyrics imaginable and I would just tell him, 'Tommy, I can't sing these words.' He didn't like that very much," said Reidy, cackling. "He didn't like it when I put my lyrics to his tunes either! You know, 'I hate you, I hate me, I hate the world.' He'd just go off on me, yelling, 'Reidy, I can't believe you've done this, you've ruined my beautiful songs!'"

The change did make the band more marketable, and several local writers predicted that the Razz would become a major-label act. With the growing viability of "new wave" music, many DC bands began to think about such possibilities.

If judged by sheer tunefulness, DC's leading power-pop band would have been the Nurses, who by mid-1979 had become the trio of Howard Wuelfing, Marc Halpern, and new drummer Harry Raab. Despite the band's assured song-craft, however, its sound was too spare and its attitude too anarchic for mainstream appeal. Wuelfing later described the Nurses as "pop with a nihilist streak a yard wide."

Wuelfing produced the first single by Tru Fax and the Insaniacs, a band that featured former Shirker Libby Hatch. This quartet's punky pop was eminently melodic, and some compared the band's appeal to Blondie's. Although frontwoman Diana Quinn was an engaging vocalist, she wasn't a sleek, iconic blonde, and no major labels came calling.

Not all the local bands that surfaced in this period had power-pop potential. A sibling duo that had begun recording at its exurban Maryland home in 1974, Half Japanese created a skill-free din shaped by stark sincerity and sheer passion. As David Fair sang in "I Don't Wanna Have Mono (No More)": "I don't want to be tired in bed/I don't want to be bored by TV/I don't want to be bored like some punk rockers/I want to live wild in the Half Japanese band/I want to play loud and be in love with a girlfriend . . . get a big stack of Marshall amps/Just blow them up!"

The Fair brothers' brash innocence was genuine and appealing. Their records—released on their own 50,000,000,000,000,000,000,000,000,000,000 Watts label and distributed almost entirely through mail order—began to attract a significant cult following. When D'Chumps split at the end of the year, that band's drummer and sax player, Ricky and John Dreyfuss, joined Half Japanese, as did their friend, guitarist Mark Jickling. The expanded lineup enabled the Fairs to translate their home-studio bashings into live performances. When Half Japanese signed with an eccentric UK independent label, Armageddon, the Fairs decided with typical bravado to make their first album, *1/2 Gentlemen/Not Beasts*, a three-record set.

Under the growing influence of Jake Whipp, White Boy had also been developing a more commercial sound. The band's third single was deemed too mainstream by none other than its lead singer. "For me, the record is too readily compared to other stuff that's out," Mr. Ott said in an interview at the time. "From Jake Whipp's point of view, I guess it's more 'musically competent,' but not being a musician myself, I don't really give fuck if something is 'musically competent.'" Re-affirming the original White Boy ethos of "bizarre subject matter done a bizarre way," Mr. Ott admitted that the new approach "wasn't working for me."

He decided to quit, and White Boy played a farewell gig at a suburban Virginia club, Louie's Rock City, that had initially been hostile to the new rock. (In 1977, the venue had fired LA power-poppers the Nerves for being too punk.) "I've already accomplished what I wanted to do," he told another interviewer. "I've thought about it and I can't be bought. If somebody came to me and offered me money—you know, really a lot of money—to do this, I wouldn't do it."

X X X

Louie's Rock City was one of many local clubs that was beginning to accept punk—but only occasionally and usually on slow nights. Another was the Bayou, a venerable Georgetown hard-rock bar that in the late '70s became a showcase venue for national acts. To the growing punk contingent, the Bayou was notable not only for the big-name punk bands it hosted—Stiff Little Fingers, the Undertones, and 999 among them—but for its hostile bouncers and adamant refusal to hold all-ages shows.

Some underage punk fans became experts at fake IDs and back door and window entry. Many of them nursed a deep hatred for the Bayou, yet it was there that the city's teenage punks would first hear Bad Brains, opening for the Damned on June 24, 1979.

Almost no one in the sold-out crowd came to see Bad Brains. Yet for many, the unknown band stole the show. Years later, Kim Kane still spoke with awe: "It was one of those stupendous shows, an absolute benchmark. I loved the Damned, but the Bad Brains blew them into outer space. There just was no comparison."

For the teens who knew the band only from its fliers, the show was a revelation. Henry Garfield and the Wilson crowd were there, using fake IDs. "Bad Brains blew the Damned with all their makeup and shit right off the stage," Garfield said.

The members of the Damned themselves were impressed. Kane remembered watching drummer Rat Scabies during the Bad Brains' set: "Scabies just stood in the middle of the floor and watched every song, just flabbergasted." As the Damned were leaving, Scabies offered to help Bad Brains get shows in the UK.

Given the band's tenuous finances, this seemed unlikely. Still, playing outside Washington was appealing to HR, especially after Bad Brains got in a hassle with the Bayou and were banned from the club, further reducing their potential venues.

In the suburbs, opportunities were even more limited. In August, the Prince George's County liquor board banned punk from the Varsity Grill, a club near the University of Maryland campus where the Razz, Slickee Boys, Ramones, and Bad Brains had played recently. "This type of music draws undesirables," explained the county's chief liquor inspector, Jerry Kromash. "The citizens of the area were afraid to cross the street to go to their cars."

Ironically, the only act identified by name in the ban was Root Boy Slim and the Sex Change Band, no local punk's idea of a punk group. When the action went unchallenged, the board extended the ban to the University of Maryland and other College Park establishments. Another band, the Original Fetish, was prevented from playing at the university because of its "suggestive" name. When the Varsity Grill attempted a show despite the ban, the county required the bands to sign a paper stating that they were not "punk rock." The headlining Destroy All Monsters (featuring ex-members of the Stooges and MC5) and supporting acts, the Nurses and the explosive, power-chord–driven Penetrators, all refused, and the show was cancelled.

Downtown, the DC scene sought refuge at noncommercial venues after the Atlantis closed. The Urban Verbs staged several shows at the Corcoran Gallery of Art, and punk bands began to play at District Creative Space, better known as dc space. This bar and art space had opened in late 1977 at 7th and E Streets NW, three blocks from the Atlantis. Initially, it hosted mostly jazz, poetry, and performance art, but it soon became a center of the overlapping downtown art and punk scenes.

Bad Brains played dc space's second-floor performance area, but were banned for a practical rather than a moral or aesthetic reason: The crowd danced so vigorously that the floor of the early-

19th-century building—where American Red Cross founder Clara Barton set up her Civil War–era office—nearly collapsed. The band did find one regular venue, however: an Adams-Morgan art co-op run by remnants of the Yippie movement.

Madams Organ had been founded in the early '70s by a group of dissident students from the Corcoran School of Art. By the latter half of the decade, the neighborhood was gentrifying and most of the original Madams Organ members had gone. Initially, the co-op simply agreed to host a benefit concert for the Yippie pro-marijuana-legalization rally held every July 4th on the Mall. Since the Yippies had become interested in punk, such DC bands as the Nurses, Root Boy Slim, and Bad Brains were asked to play.

Transfixed by the energy of Bad Brains, Madams Organ stalwarts Tommy Ashton and Russell Braen began to organize regular concerts at the space. With few opportunities to gig elsewhere, bands were eager to play. Within a month, Madams Organ was hosting two shows a week, and the music was rapidly overwhelming the co-op's other missions.

Musicians were not thrilled with the facility. "Madams Organ was creepy, smelly, and badly run," said Wuelfing. "Everyone was always pissed off at how bad the sound was." Kane had similar recollections: "It had the absolutely worst house PA ever: two mics and one tattered speaker—that was it! No monitors, no nothing."

The technical shortcomings were balanced by other, more agreeable lacks: no age limits and, essentially, no rules. Teenage punks soon became Madams Organ regulars. The co-op was "a place I could hang out with people who weren't concerned with their Trans Am, 8-track players, Boston, the Redskins game, or Dad's credit card," said Garfield. "I was insulated in this all-boy environment all day; this was a chance to do something halfway social. The other kids would be together at Wilson all day, but for me it was a big thing to see people who were different, who were friendly, where everybody looked wild and you could jump around and do anything. At Bullis, I couldn't do anything without getting a judgment trip."

Even a detractor like Wuelfing admitted that "Madams Organ gave a lot of bands a reason to form in the first place, just because it was a place to play. There weren't many of those at the time." For Bad Brains, who quickly became more or less the Madams Organ house band, it was a haven.

The band's energy and skill converted some of the co-op's older artists, who were skeptical of punk. As for the young fans who'd been amazed by Bad Brains at the Bayou, they found them over-whelming in this more intimate context.

"To us, Bad Brains meant everything," said Garfield. "I have never seen anything like 1979-1980 Bad Brains, before or since. You thought they were going to detonate right before your eyes. And there we were, with 35 other lucky people, watching the greatest band in the world for two dollars. HR was three feet away from me singing. It was scary and incredible. I remember thinking to myself, 'I hope this guy doesn't jump on me.' A few seconds later I was on my back. HR had me pinned to the floor and was screaming in my face. It was one of the biggest moments in my life."

It was becoming clear that Bad Brains were something special. They seemed to have what one of their songs called the 'supertouch'—the power to inspire with their energy, their very presence.

x x x

One of the bands inspired by Bad Brains made its debut with a farewell show: Singer Mark Sullivan was headed to college, so the Slinkees arranged a gig in a friend's garage with another young band, the Zones. Ian MacKaye's younger brother Alec remembered the Zones as "a really fun high school rock band who didn't do traditional covers." The quartet played what was arguably the first DC punk version of the Monkees' "Stepping Stone," a song that was later to become a scene standard.

There were complications: The show had to be moved at the last minute, and the Zones' home-made flashpots didn't work as planned. "The Zones had these coffee cans filled with gunpowder that were supposed to go off in this dramatic flash of light," said Alec MacKaye. "But instead they just produced these huge clouds of smoke that filled the garage totally up and chased a bunch of people out into the rain!"

The show, witnessed mostly by local teenagers but also by steadfast local punk booster Kim Kane, convinced the remaining Slinkees to continue. Nelson, Grindle, and MacKaye decided to keep many of the Slinkees' songs but take a new name and singer. They enlisted one of Wilson's punk pioneers, Nathan Strejcek, who MacKaye had only recently met while working at the Georgetown Theater.

"To us, it was a big deal because we saw Nathan as kind of one of the original punks and we were just starting out," said MacKaye. "For all we knew, he might just laugh at us." To the band's surprise, Nathan Strejcek agreed to become the new band's singer. "I had never sung before," he recalled, "but that was how punk was back then—you just found something you wanted to do and just got up and did it."

With the addition of Strejcek, the Slinkees became the Teen Idles. Their first show was in Strejcek's basement in December 1979. Also performing were the Zones and another new band, the Untouchables, which consisted of 13-year-old Alec MacKaye on vocals and three other Wilson punks, Bert Queiroz, Eddie Janney, and Rich Moore on bass, guitar, and drums, respectively.

x x x

Prince George's County's ban on punk was overturned by a judge barely a month after it was instituted, but Bad Brains' attempts at outreach continued to be difficult. When it found a place to play, however, the band usually made converts.

After reading in the Yippie newspaper *Overthrow* that the Clash had played free gigs in the poorer sections of London, Bad Brains decided to do the same in DC, working with a fledgling Yippie-affiliated Rock Against Racism chapter. Ignoring the doubts of the band's informal adviser and quasi-manager, British punk veteran Nick English, HR audaciously arranged a show at Valley Green, a bleak public housing project in the city's Southeast quadrant.

HR called on a Madams Organ cohort, the hard-rocking—and all-white—punk quartet Trenchmouth to open the show. Led by the considerable stage presence of Iggy-esque lead singer Charlie Danbury, and the razor-sharp guitar work of Scott Wingo, the band was able to win over some in the crowd, which consisted mostly of kids and a few skeptical adults. Still, most seemed to view the band as a curiosity, laughing at their contortions, trying to touch their spiky hair; one even poured a can of beer over the good-natured lead singer.

As Bad Brains set up in the courtyard, more kids and older people came out of their homes to investigate. The band opened with some of the loping reggae it had just begun experimenting with. Skeptical residents came to their windows, puzzled by the spectacle; a few stood a good distance from the stage. Then the band tore into its faster material, and little kids started coming closer, followed by the older folks. By the end of the set, a fairly massive crowd circled the tiny stage area.

English was amazed at Bad Brains' ability to win over even this clearly non-punk audience: "At first, people were shocked, but HR has this very upbeat and outgoing quality. He is a natural leader, and knew how to make contact with people and put them at ease. People were absolutely riveted to the spot by Bad Brains."

A free gig in Lincoln Park near the US Capitol was less successful. "The police were circling around on horses," Jenifer remembered. "HR was saying some stuff like 'Why can't we chill out and have our gig without people surrounding and oppressing us?' Finally a policeman just came and turned off all the shit and said, 'Get out of here! There ain't no show now!' That kind of ended it all. It was apparent that they just didn't want us happening in DC."

The song "Banned in DC" was written shortly after this showdown, expressing righteous anger at the clubs that had closed their doors on the quartet: "We, we got ourselves/Gonna sing it/Gonna love it/Gonna work it out to any length/Don't worry about what the people say/We got ourselves/We gonna make it anyway." The song even contained a reference to the band's plans to go to Britain: "Banned in DC/With a thousand other places to go/We gonna swim across the Atlantic/That's the only place we can go."

English advised the band not to make the trip without work permits. He warned that black punks could not hope to be simply waved through by British customs officials. HR listened, but kept on planning. After one final DC show at another stop-gap venue, the Hard Art Gallery, the quartet headed for New York City, to be followed by London.

Bad Brains gigged at clubs like CBGB's and Pier One in order to get the money for plane tickets. With help from friendly New York bands like the Dots, the Stimulators, and the Mad, as well as a growing group of supporters, they departed for Britain.

The band's refusal to surrender had gotten them through many tough situations, but this time it was not enough. When Bad Brains reached Gatwick Airport, they were picked out by customs, detained, and interrogated—just as English had warned. Rat Scabies came to the airport with his father to vouch for them, but to no avail. After being forced to sit on the floor in a detention facility for hours, they were deported. To make matters worse, in the confusion all their equipment mysteriously disappeared.

Back in New York City, Bad Brains were penniless, without instruments or a place to stay. Desperate, HR called Neil Cooper, the owner of the '80s Club, at 3:00 a.m. to try to get an impromptu show to make some money for food. Cooper had never seen Bad Brains play, but he was aware of the buzz. He agreed to let them open a show the following night with the Stimulators, who allowed Bad Brains to use their equipment. Like many others, Cooper was captivated when he saw Bad Brains for the first time, and became a regular at their shows.

Thanks to other gigs using borrowed equipment, Bad Brains were able to survive and even—with the help of Jimi Quidd of the Dots—record two songs for what would be their first single. The potential A-side was "Pay to Cum," a one-minute burst of defiant PMA lyrics built on a ferocious buzzsaw riff. Hyperfast but played with absolute precision, the song sped beyond the punk style of the band's models.

Yet the band lacked both a record contract and the money to press its own single. The tracks went unreleased while the destitute band languished in New York for a few more weeks. On Christmas day, Bad Brains found themselves in a Salvation Army soup line. "New York kicked our ass," Dr. Know said. Three months after they had left DC, Bad Brains returned.

The quartet was soon playing at Madams Organ again. Still optimistic, HR told the *Unicorn Times*, "Some people think new wave is dying but I think it's just getting started." In Washington, this turned out to be true—and in large part because of Bad Brains' example.

Clockwise from top left: 1. WGTB POSTER WITH JIM MORRISON OF THE DOORS *(courtesy of* Infiltrator *'zine)*, 2. XYRA HARPER *(by Lucian Perkins)*, 3. SKIP GROFF, RAZZ BASSIST TED NICELEY, AND DON ZIENTARA AT INNER EAR *(by Kim Kane)*, 4. BARNEY JONES AND RANDY AUSTIN OF OVERKILL *(by Kim Kane)*

Clockwise from top left: 1. MR. OTT AND JAKE WHIPP OF WHITE BOY *(by Peter Muise)*, 2. LINDA FRANCE, RODDY FRANTZ, AND ROBERT GOLDSTEIN OF URBAN VERBS *(by Peter Muise)*, 3. STEVE LORBER *(courtesy of Mark Jenkins)*, 4. KIM KANE OF SLICKEE BOYS *(by Skip Groff)*, 5. MICHAEL REIDY OF THE RAZZ *(by Skip Groff)*

Clockwise from top left: 1. HENRY GARFIELD, ALEC MACKAYE, AND MARK SULLIVAN ON MADAMS ORGAN STEPS, LATE 1979 *(by Kim Kane)*, 2. SLINKEES IN BASEMENT PRACTICE SPACE *(by Theodore or Andy Nelson)*, 3. JEFF NELSON AND RICH MOORE IN VERBS SHIRTS, FALL 1978 *(by Theodore Nelson from collection of Jeff Nelson)*; About this photo, Jeff Nelson wrote, "L to R: Richard Moore and Jeff Nelson in October 1978, before going to Urban Verbs/Ebenezer and the Bludgeons (from Baltimore) Halloween show at the Corcoran Gallery of Art, Washington, DC. This was our first attempt at dressing 'new wave.' I silk-screened both styles of Verbs shirts to sell at this show, my first band shirts ever. Logo on left is band's logo, logo on right is my well-intentioned but completely clueless improvement. I sold shirts to audience members as well as members of the Urban Verbs, only to discover later that I had used water-based inks which ran when washed. Rich is wearing a Dungeons and Dragons black cape, with skateboarding kneepads over his pants. I take the cake, though, with white painter's pants with kung-fu shoes and WW2 spats, a woman's purple ermine evening jacket with wide fur cuffs and collar, and finally my grandfather's WW2 Civil Defense helmet with a purple plume attached to it., 4. AUDIENCE—INCLUDING KATIE

Clockwise from top left: 1. BRYAN GREGORY, LUX INTERIOR, NICK KNOX, AND POISON IVY OF THE CRAMPS, LIVE AT HALL OF NATIONS, FEBRUARY 3, 1979 *(by Peter Muise)* 2. HR AT DC SPACE *(by Gregory R. Stal...)* 3. DR. KNOW OF BAD BRAINS AT THE BAYOU, JUNE 24, 1979 *(by Kim Kane)* 4. HR AND AUDIENCE AT

Clockwise from top left: 1. JAD FAIR (*50,000,000,000,000,000,000,000,000,000,000,000 Watts Records promotional photograph*), 2. CARTOON ATTACKING PAUL PARSONS AND KEVIN DUPLAIN OF THE ATLANTIS (*courtesy of Infiltrator 'zine*), 3. CHRIS HASKETT AND DAVID BYERS OF THE ENZYMES, MADAMS ORGAN (*by Peter Muise*), 4. DIANA QUINN AND LIBBY HATCH OF TRU FAX AT MADAMS ORGAN (*by Mark Jenkins*)

get up and go

*"You keep talking about talent
Talent? What do you know?
Instead of studying theory
We're gonna get up and go . . ."*
—Teen Idles, "Get Up and Go"

IAN MACKAYE, NATHAN STREJCEK, JEFF NELSON (PARTIALLY OBSCURED), AND GEORDIE GRINDLE OF TEEN IDLES AT CHANCERY, OCTOBER 31, 1980 *(by Jay Rabinowitz)*

get up and go

It seemed like another typical roots-rock night at the Psychedelly. The main attraction, '50s-style rocker Billy Hancock, would be on later. But now an extremely young-looking band was setting up onstage, having great difficulty with its equipment. Finally, the lead singer—a thin figure dressed in pink pajamas and a black leather jacket—strode up to the mic and gravely mumbled:

> *You broke my heart*
> *'cause I couldn't dance*
> *You didn't even want me around*
> *But now I'm back to let you know*
> *I can really shake it down*
> *Do you love me?*

Then punk hell broke loose. Guitar, bass, and drums began clamoring at deafening levels in three different keys and in three shifting tempos. The vocalist gave up all pretense of singing and began screaming hoarsely and spinning around the stage like a top. By the time the Contours' 1962 hit had been bludgeoned to death, the audience had split into two camps. The outnumbered group's fans rushed forward to the foot of the stage. The rest of the audience pulled back in dumb horror.

The Teen Idles had arrived, reveling in their ability to simultaneously inspire and shock in the best punk tradition. The chaos described above was captured by *Unicorn Times* writer Monica Regan, who was present at the band's first—and only—Psychedelly show in April 1980.

"The Teen Idles are a band of teenagers too young to be drafted, too musically amateurish to care about making bucks, and perhaps too exuberant and energetic for a DC rock scene dominated by pros," she wrote. "That night at the Psychedelly, the Teen Idles—fueled only by quarts of grape and orange soda they knocked back before the show—ripped furiously through their set. Later, in a scene repeated more than once in its brief career, the band was kindly invited never to play the club again."

This was routine for the Teen Idles, who enjoyed unnerving boring old rockers and club own-ers. "It's kind of nice being feared," said drummer Jeff Nelson at the time. "Of course, it does cut down on places to play."

The Psychedelly show was the Idles' eleventh, and already the band had been disinvited from further performances by three different clubs. Of the remaining shows, two had been in basements or garages and the rest at Madams Organ, the band's early roost.

The Idles were not overly concerned with "professional musicianship," but they were serious about what they were doing. They practiced diligently, trying to write new material and master their instruments. Together with Slinkee holdovers like "Trans Am," "I Drink Milk," and "Deadhead," the Teen Idles had several new songs, including "Fiorucci Nightmare," "Pipebomb," and their anthem, "Teen Idles."

The latter song expressed the fledgling quartet's concerns: "Life has been the same for a long time/Go to school and witness the crimes/Go home and see it on the evening news/We got nothing to do . . .We're as idle as teens can get/ Hanging out in record shops/Go to a concert the boredom stops/Went to the Bayou they said 'no'/You're not 18 you can't see the show."

The song described the band members as "Fucking bored to tears/A waste of twenty years," but they weren't going to waste another second. "We didn't get into bands because we were bored. We did it because we had to. If we didn't, we would have exploded," said Henry Garfield, the band's roadie, number-one booster, and—according to Ian MacKaye—the "fifth Teen Idle."

"We just had so much energy, we were about to jump out of our skins," MacKaye said. "Sometimes when we got onstage, we just played as fast as we could, almost like we were afraid that someone would come and try to throw us off!"

The Idles had started at about the same tempo as the Slinkees, but soon accelerated to hyper-drive. This was largely due to the influence of Bad Brains, who had been invited to use the Teen Idles' equipment and practice space—the Strejcek family's basement—after they returned from New York destitute.

To appease Nathan Strejcek's parents, the two bands practiced on the same evenings. Generally, the Teen Idles would play first, followed by Bad Brains. "Here we are making this racket and complaining how shitty our equipment is, and then they would pick up our very same shit and play this amazing music," MacKaye recalled. "It was like another world."

"Bad Brains influenced us incredibly with their speed and frenzied delivery," Nelson said. "We went from sounding like the Sex Pistols to playing every song as fast and hard as we could."

Grateful for the aid, Bad Brains had arranged for the Teen Idles to open for them at their first shows back at Madams Organ in late January. The Idles' music was ragged in comparison with Bad Brains, but fueled by determination and infectious energy. Their attitude quickly won them allies, particularly among the younger punk crowd. Not all the scene's veterans were enthusiastic, however.

Mary Levy was in the largely unfriendly audience at the Teen Idles' first Madams Organ gig, and wrote about it in *Descenes*: "The teeny-punks held their hard-won places by the stage, drinking soda and laughing, showing off the spike-haired crew's delight in being packed together. It makes their number seem greater and keeps out the sad truth that 'punk' modes of dress and behavior have been 'out' in London or New York for about two years. Theirs is the safety in the pack. They remind me of the die-hard heavy metal fans who dolled themselves up to crowd the now-leveled Keg every Saturday night till last summer. Where do they hang out now? Some of them are die-hard punkers."

"Teeny-punk" was one common term for the Teen Idles and their crowd. They were also called Georgetown punks, after the upscale neighborhood where they hung out (and where many of them had after-school jobs). The teenage punks found both terms condescending.

For some of the older fans, the Teen Idles were too young to be taken seriously—"too young to rock," as one of their later songs would put it. Indeed, Alec MacKaye was barely even a teenager. "That's just the way it is in America, they treat you like shit because you're young," his brother Ian would say later.

In a scene that was increasingly professional, with some bands courting mainstream success, the Teen Idles' rawness was so anomalous as to be laughable to some listeners. Such criticism, however, only hardened the commitment of the Wilson punks. They soon embraced the name "Georgetown punks," turning it from a dismissal to a rallying cry. "'Georgetown punks' became something for us to yell, something to get in people's faces," Garfield recalled.

Not all of the older crowd shared Levy's dismissive attitude. "Initially their thing was maybe too

British, and so until they got their own identity, there was bound to be some criticism," said Kim Kane. "Still, to call them 'teeny-punks' was not treating it seriously and they were trying to be serious. They had the enthusiasm, they were creating something new, doing their own thing. I liked it."

Some older punks found the teenagers "cute," a word that rankled. "They were so cute, you just wanted to pat them on the head," said Xyra Harper. Howard Wuelfing remembered meeting these "goofy high-energy kids who were telling me that they had a band called the Teen Idles while I was at work at Yesterday and Today and thinking 'Oh, that's nice, how cute.'" (Harper later invited the young punks to join her in doing the 'zine *Capital Crisis*, however, and Wuelfing's Nurses became one of several established bands that gave the Idles opening slots at their gigs.)

The Teen Idles' alienation from the older punks did not include Bad Brains. If anything, the two bands became tighter. As Bad Brains' influence deepened, Positive Mental Attitude became part of the Georgetown punk credo. "PMA meant not letting shit get you down and believing in yourself," said Garfield. "The Bad Brains didn't talk that much about it, but they did it by example. They played like their lives depended on it. They made you feel you could do whatever you wanted to do. I couldn't sleep after seeing them. I couldn't even see straight."

PMA took on an even more personal meaning for Garfield when HR befriended him, encouraging him to be more than just the Teen Idles' roadie. "He was talking to me one night and he said, 'You'll be a singer,'" Garfield said. "I said, 'No way—who me? You're joking, I could never do that!'" HR would drag Henry onstage to sing with him; later Garfield would remember these days as "when my life began."

At first, the Idles were followed mostly by their school friends, but gradually they began to draw new fans, forming the core of a group that would support—and, in some cases, play—punk for years to come. It was a diverse group ranging from the brassy, outgoing Toni Young and her precocious friend Vivien Greene, to Jay Garfinckle and Bill MacKenzie, an inseparable pair of boozy troublemakers, to the good-natured Tom Berard and the incorrigible partier Edd Jacobs.

Sharon Cheslow was another of this slowly swelling group. She had left behind her "high school hell" in Bethesda for college, only to find herself once again painfully out of step with her peers. In October 1979 she wrote, "I hate it here at the University of Maryland. If I thought life in Bethesda was unreal, this is insanity. There are no punks here . . ."

A break in her isolation came when she started working at Yesterday and Today a couple of months later and met the MacKaye brothers and Garfield. Cheslow: "In those days, to meet other punks was something special, there were so few of us, you really had something in common then." By the conversation's end, Garfield had invited her to a Bad Brains show the next day where she met the whole Wilson crew. Soon afterward, she encountered another teenage female punk, Anne Bonafede, who became her best friend.

As these kids found each other, they found something worth living for; DC's teen-punk scene became what fervent fan Tom Berard later described as a "misfits club." For some, it began to resemble the family they never had.

Many of them felt like Cheslow. "I spent my whole life waiting for the punk scene," she said. "These bands were kids my own age, so relevant to my life. There were so many doors opening, so much happening, I felt so free. I think that's what punk represented, freedom. All of us, we were really fucked up, in different ways, we had just terrible lives. Just about everybody had fucked up family lives or the incredible sense that you didn't fit in anywhere. Here we did."

The Teen Idles, together with Bad Brains, were the glue that initially bound these teen misfits together amidst skepticism from many quarters. The Idles pushed their attitude in the faces of non-supporters with the song "Get Up and Go": "You keep talking about talent/Talent? What do you know?/Instead of studying theory/We're going to get up and go!" An early flier said it all, listing the members' ages—"Ian 17 Geordie 16 Jeff 17 Nathan 18"—and promising "young fun new clean rock . . . no drugs."

x x x

While the Idles' trumpeted their disdain for drug and alcohol use, one of their inspirations was far from clean. "I was fiending for drugs," HR later admitted in an interview. "I had been shooting up heroin since I was 16. It was a very private life, as heroin use tends to be, but I started getting into drugs too heavy."

HR realized that his new friends disapproved. "It was a reality among everyone that my drug use was wrong," he said. "Henry, Ian, Jeff, David Byers—they all could see what was going on. I wouldn't lie to them and they'd say, 'Don't do that.'"

The singer had written "How Low Can a Punk Get?" about friend with a drug problem. Now his own life was threatening to answer the question. At the time, Bad Brains weren't exponents of moderation. Years later, HR described that period as "days and days of listening to the Damned, the Sex Pistols, staying up all night tripping on acid and acting very indecent and rebellious to any kind of authority of the godly functions of human nature."

HR fell seriously ill with pneumonia. "Everything was falling and crumbling," he recalled. "I knew I was killing myself. I began to see the whole decadent waste of my own body, my own mind, my own soul. I knew what I was doing to myself."

He remembers lying fever-stricken in the attic of Madams Organ, where he found a copy of Gideon's New Testament lying on the floor. In his desperate state, the book seemed to offer a way out. "I picked up that Bible and I started praying, asking Jesus for help. I said, 'OK, that's it, no more drugs and no more bullshit.'"

That night, the fever broke. As HR slowly recovered, he happened to meet a West Indian Rastafarian, Julian Cambridge, at Madams Organ. As they became friends, a chance experience from two years before suddenly had new significance.

In June 1978, HR had gone with the rest of the fledgling Mindpower to see Stanley Clarke and Chick Corea, formerly the heart and soul of their jazz-fusion heroes Return to Forever. Also on the bill was Bob Marley and the Wailers. HR was fascinated by the unusual but compelling music, the dignified yet rebellious image, and above all Marley's shamanic energy and presence.

Marley was a dreadlocked follower of Rastafari, a radical sect that sought justice for Africans and their descendants and promoted a "natural" lifestyle free of chemical poisons. For HR, the Rasta faith provided a spiritual basis for kicking heroin.

Between theological discussions, Julian played immense amounts of reggae for HR. Aside from Marley and the dub Nick English played, HR had never before seriously listened to reggae. He was captured by these lilting, spiritual sounds. "I had never heard a music so incredible, so beautiful," he said. Marley would become HR's major influence over the next few years; he stopped eating meat and began to let his hair dread up.

Marley himself had already begun the process of blending punk and reggae with "Punky Reggae

Party," which identified punks and Rastas as the "rejected of society." And Marley's "Rastaman Vibration"—a "positive vibration," according to the lyrics—suggested a bridge to Positive Mental Attitude. HR clambered eagerly across that span, taking to his new orientation with his usual all-or-nothing fervor.

This zeal could be jarring, spinning into unexpected directions. One day, HR found a bearded man in Lafayette Park across from the White House, decided he was Jesus Christ and brought him back to Madams Organ.

"HR would be big into the Revolutionary Communist Party one week, then into something entirely different the next," said friend Russell Braen. "When he came in with the guy he said was Jesus, we all just thought, 'Here he goes again!'"

This time would prove to be different. HR soon lost interest in his bearded friend, but Rastafari would ultimately overshadow his passions for Napoleon Hill and punk.

x x x

Although there was still plenty of overlap, the DC scene seemed to be separating into three camps. In addition to the bands that took their inspiration from British punk, there were new wave/power-pop groups like the Slickee Boys, Tru Fax and the Insaniacs, and the Insect Surfers, who called their playful, upbeat sound "techno surf." Most prominent, though, were the artier bands inspired by the Urban Verbs, notably Tiny Desk Unit.

Started by synth player Bob Boilen, the quintet had the same instrumental lineup as the Verbs but a funkier foundation. The other members were guitarist Michael Barron, bassist Terry Baker, drummer Chris Thompson, and singer Susan Mumford. Her vocals, which ranged from low, full-throated tones to unearthly shrieks, were arty but rooted in punk attitude. "Someone asked me to sing—not that I can sing but because they wanted my presence," she said. "You're not cut off from this music because you can't sing."

In May, the space that had been the Atlantis reopened as the 9:30 Club, a project of the building's new owner, John Bowers, and managed by his wife Dody Bowers. Former WGTB program director John Paige, who had already promoted concerts featuring such bands as Devo and Pere Ubu, booked the out-of-town acts, providing the first reliable DC venue for touring punk/new wave groups. Joy Division was supposed to inaugurate the club, but the band's tour was cancelled when singer Ian Curtis committed suicide. Instead 9:30 debuted with New York fake-jazz combo the Lounge Lizards, supported by Tiny Desk Unit. The art-punk bill was typical of the club's original musical emphasis.

The Urban Verbs were not conspicuous in Washington at the time, having just released their Warner Brothers debut, which British producer Mike Thorne had given a surprisingly sedate sound. By now, the band was too popular for local clubs; to mark the release of *Urban Verbs*, the quintet played the massive great hall of the Pension Building, a downtown landmark only occasionally used for concerts. Outside DC and New York, however, the band was nearly unknown and found little support.

They'd been slagged as elitist and pretentious in local punk-oriented fanzines, but the Verbs had generally gotten excellent press in Washington. They were unprepared for the mocking review their album received in *Rolling Stone*, written by Washington native Tom Carson. Upon reading the piece, Roddy Frantz put his hand through a glass door in anger; he required multiple stitches.

"*Rolling Stone* was the most important rock magazine in the world," Goldstein said. "Of course, their opinion didn't alienate our existing fans—they already knew they liked us—but it did seem to affect the support we got from Warner Brothers significantly. In retrospect, I think Warner more or less wrote us off." The band was contractually guaranteed another album, but after the release of *Early Damage*, Warner Brothers quickly cut the Verbs loose. Ironically, the little-publicized second album had a more aggressive sound than *Urban Verbs* and would probably have appealed more to the band's detractors—had they ever heard it.

x x x

While teen punk was gaining cohesion, Madams Organ was unraveling. An anarchic punk bastion was not everyone's idea of an ideal use for a structure on Adams Morgan's main street, and the co-op was behind in its rent. Perhaps seeking to dislodge an undesirable set of tenants, the building's landlord raised the rent to $350 a month.

That would have been only $35 a month each for the four-story building's residents, but few of them wanted to pay. "By then, Madams Organ was a de facto Yippie commune, not an artists' co-op," said co-op member John Hagerhorst, who was not a punk fan. "The place was chaotic, dirty, uncared for, and just trashed. Everybody there was just interested in punk music, not in Madams Organ."

"We thought the rent increase was outrageous and we wouldn't pay it," recalled Braen, one of the few tenants who could produce rent money. "We thought we'd just find a better house." When Braen and others searched unsuccessfully for another such space, however, they realized that $350 a month was a deal they couldn't match.

In February 1980, HR organized a meeting of bands to try to create a new cooperative punk club. The participants made plans for a series of concerts at Madams Organ to raise money for the new club. The idea of a co-op performance space was exciting to the Georgetown punk contingent. Sick of bars with age limits and club owners who didn't appreciate their energy, Teen Idles and Untouchables both needed places to play.

The final Madams Organ shows were held April 4th and 5th as part of the series of benefits for the new music co-op. Bad Brains headlined, with the Untouchables and an explosive new band called the Enemy. This band—soon to be renamed Black Market Baby—had been painstakingly assembled by singer Boyd Farrell, who had pirated bassist Paul Cleary, drummer Tommy Carr, and guitarist Keith Campbell from their respective bands, Trenchmouth, Penetrators, and DCeats.

The band members quickly earned reputations as hard-drinking hell-raisers, but their songs were classic punk, with the big chords, anthemic melodies, and the youth-positive spirit of Sham 69. Black Market Baby quickly became the Georgetown punks' most-beloved DC band except for Bad Brains. "I liked those kids, and they seemed to like us," Farrell said. "I was always conscious to have that message there, talking about suicide and troubled youth, all of that. I was mostly talking about myself, but I guess they could relate."

The benefits were successful, and the proceeds were entrusted to the event's main organizer, HR. A potential space only a few blocks away on 14th Street was found. The idea of a punk-run club—first floated during the dark days of the Atlantis boycott—seemed within reach. All that was necessary was to put down a deposit and the first month's rent.

The funds raised by the Madams Organ benefits should have been sufficient. But when HR was approached about the money, he didn't have it anymore. He explained vaguely that he had lent it to a friend, but the loan was never repaid. It soon became clear that the money was gone—and, with it, the dream of the new punk co-op.

The mystery would never be solved, but whatever had happened, it was an incredible blow. Rather than blame HR, the Georgetown punks suspected that the money had gone to one of the Yippies who had perhaps blown it on drugs for another of the never-ending parties. Hagerhorst has another theory: "HR was someone who would give you the shirt off his back. At the time, money was just like water to HR. He probably just gave it away."

HR's erratic behavior both scuttled the music co-op and imperiled his band's own chances. When Madams Organ was evicted shortly after the final benefit shows, Bad Brains were once again without instruments, money, and a regular practice space. The band's unlikely savior came wearing a beard and a three-piece suit: Mo Sussman, a successful restaurateur whose Joe and Mo's catered to affluent downtown attorneys and businessmen.

The connection was made through a Joe and Mo's waiter, Pierre DeVeux. With Paul Bishow and Pam Kray, he was part of an Adams Morgan experimental-film collective called I Am Eye. DeVeux asked Sussman to help finance a new movie, and also asked him to play the part of a record mogul.

DeVeux showed Sussman some of I Am Eye's earlier works, which the restaurateur deemed "utter garbage." Yet something in the films did catch his attention: Bad Brains. DeVeux, Bishow, and Kray had been part of the Madams Organ scene and had filmed Bad Brains both there and at Max's Kansas City in New York. Riveted by Bad Brains' charisma, Sussman convinced DeVeux to set up a meeting.

When HR came to the restaurant, Sussman was sold. "HR just walked in and you could immediately feel this incredible presence," he recalled. He proposed to manage and finance Bad Brains, an offer that the band, facing an uncertain future, quickly accepted.

Sussman was straightforward about his goal: "I wanted them to be the new Beatles and I would be their Brian Epstein. I really believed they could do it." Sussman outfitted the band with top-of-the-line equipment and arranged for the musicians to use a friend's Virginia farm—about an hour outside the city—as a practice space.

Sussman arranged a show at the 9:30 Club, where skeptics of Bad Brains' new manager weren't too surprised to see the band come onstage wearing the suits he had suggested. Other gigs quickly followed, both in Washington and New York. The "Pay to Cum" 45 was finally released—on Bad Brains Records, with "PMA" in large letters on the back cover.

x x x

With the closing of Madams Organ, the Georgetown punks had little reason to leave the neighborhood that provided their nickname. A few clubs there provided occasional venues for shows, but mostly Georgetown was a hangout. Ian MacKaye and Bert Queiroz worked at the Georgetown Theater, Henry Garfield and Eddie Janney at Häagen-Dazs just down the street, and others nearby.

Georgetown was not uncontested territory. At the time, DC had a lower drinking age than nearby Virginia, so the area's bars were packed with suburban kids as well as Marines from nearby bases and Georgetown University jocks—a veritable rogues gallery of punk archenemies.

The same clothing and hairstyles that had earned them scorn from older punks now marked them for harassment and even sudden, unprovoked assault. Garfield remembered the five-block "terror walk" from Häagen-Dazs to Key Bridge. Although this was the shortest way to his apartment across the river in Arlington, it also took him past teeming bars with inebriated and often aggressive patrons spilling into the street.

"Fights were totally common, with punks just getting attacked for how we looked," he said. "Not a day would go by without some incident of harassment." Although Garfield often took side streets to avoid confrontations, he also started wearing a chain around his waist for protection. "I was ready to fucking kill," he recalls grimly.

The clashes only seemed to deepen the sense of group identity and commitment to the punk lifestyle. "At that time, just being a punk meant you were a magnet for getting shit," MacKaye later noted. "You saw how people acted. You kind of understood what it was like to be a black in America, to be just judged by the way you looked. It just made us more determined to do what we wanted, to look just the way we wanted."

Simple necessity led the Georgetown punks to develop a system of mutual defense. Since many worked or hung out within a three-block radius of Wisconsin Avenue and M Street, the neighborhood's central intersection, potential support was rarely far away. If trouble erupted, the word would go out and in minutes a dozen punks would arrive to help their friends. "We backed each other up all the time," Georgetown punk Donald Keesing recounted.

The Teen Idles and the Untouchables would play anywhere they could. Often they would not be invited back, because of the chaotic performance, the slow alcohol sales, or simply because the club considered them entirely unmusical. Still, the bands managed to play at least every couple weeks. "The idea was to go into some place, no matter how goofy or obnoxious it might be, and just make it ours for that night," MacKaye recalled.

One such place was Scandals, a Georgetown new wave disco loosely modeled after New York clubs like Hurrah's. Georgetown Day School student Mike Hampton was there in June when the Idles, the Zones, and the Untouchables played. "The Untouchables just seemed absolutely out of control," he said. "Bert in particular seemed really scary to me. At the end of their set, they just threw their instruments over their heads and walked out! I remember Bert's bass just crashing off a big glass mirror at the back of Scandals and him not even flinching."

Though Hampton was too intimidated to introduce himself that day, he went back to his school and began to work with fellow fledgling punks Lyle Preslar, Wendel Blow, and Simon Jacobsen. Their new band, the Extorts, aspired to the same abandon and chaotic energy Hampton had seen in the Untouchables.

Also at the show was John Schroeder, who came from suburban Rockville, Maryland to see the Teen Idles. He was starting a band, the Stab, with guitarist Pete Murray and bassist John Berger, who became the Stab's bassist after just a few minutes of conversation. Schroeder played drums, although after practicing for months, "I still couldn't pick up on a solid beat." Schroeder told Ian MacKaye about his band and gave him his address. MacKaye put the information in his address book, abbreviating Schroeder's name as "John/Stab." The name stuck.

x x x

While Bad Brains turned toward reggae, the Teen Idles also began to lose interest in British punk, which seemed to have lost its purpose and energy. The band started playing "Fleeting Fury," which expressed their disappointment with the UK scene.

The teen punks began to look west, especially to a pioneering punk label, Dangerhouse, that released an incendiary series of singles including the Dils' "Class War," Weirdos' "Neutron Bomb," X's "Los Angeles," and the Avengers' "We Are the One," documenting the best of early California punk. Even jokey Dangerhouse one-offs like the Deadbeats' "Kill the Hippies" or the Randoms' "Let's Get Rid of New York" struck a special chord with the Idles and their compatriots.

Soon afterward, they also became aware of such bands as Black Flag, the Circle Jerks, and the Dead Kennedys. Like the Idles, these groups played loud-fast-short-angry songs and were often greeted with scorn by the older scene. The next logical step was to check out what was happening on the West Coast in person. After MacKaye and Nelson's graduation from Wilson High, the Teen Idles embarked on a tour of California with Garfield and Mark Sullivan—back from Colgate University for the summer—as "road crew." They booked shows in LA and San Francisco and took a Greyhound bus to California, packing guitars and drumsticks but no other equipment.

What they discovered in sprawling LA was far removed from the close-knit DC scene. At the Hong Kong Cafe, the Idles found themselves playing on a mismatched bill with Vox Pop and the Mentors, while bands they loved played another show across town. They made $15 for a gig they had come 3000 miles to play.

The band had two other missions while in LA: to go to Disneyland and to find Darby Crash, who had just dissolved the Germs. But Crash was in Britain and the Idles were turned away at Disney's kingdom. The group was accosted at the bus station by security guards. When Nelson suggested that the security guards kiss his ass, he was roughed up and temporarily taken into custody.

Things went little better in San Francisco. At the Mabuhay Gardens, the Idles were moved from a show with the Dead Kennedys, the Circle Jerks, and Flipper to one the following night with some forgettable new wave bands. They played to a small, apathetic crowd and made $11.

Still, events at the Mabuhay Gardens made a big impression on the Idles. The club had recently introduced an all-ages policy, which entailed marking a big black "X" on the hands of underage kids so their non-drinking status would be obvious to the bartenders. To the Georgetown punks, this idea made so much sense that they were determined to push the issue with DC club owners.

The Dead Kennedys/Circle Jerks/Flipper show also introduced the DC punks to a new and volatile crowd of suburban fans. One particular group of punks from Huntington Beach, an affluent LA suburb, had taken the vertically oriented "pogo" dance of earlier punk and turned it into a bruising, horizontal one that they proudly called the "Huntington Beach strut." More succinctly, others called the new dance "the slam."

While the pogo had often meant some physical contact with others on the dance floor, now that contact seemed to have became the point. This bruising new dance resembled an unreferreed football game played out to punk music. Such a dance was bound to dismay less macho elements in the crowd—which was just what the Huntington Beach kids wanted. "We went out to show everyone at the Circle Jerks show what LA is all about," said one Huntington Beacher. "The geeks, the people with new wave ties . . . When we see someone at a gig that we don't like, we fuck them up." Dead Kennedys singer Jello Biafra later recalled that night as "one of the most violent shows" he ever saw.

The Georgetown punks had never seen anything like the mayhem unleashed by the Huntington Beach crew on the unsuspecting San Franciscans. "This was the gig where it all went down," said Garfield. "San Francisco punks were older and smarter—kind of like in DC—but the Circle Jerks had brought their entourage of Huntington Beach boneheads. Scary, scary people."

While the DC kids were intimidated by the Huntington Beachers' violence, they were astounded by the power wielded by this relatively small gang of punks. They were also impressed with the Huntington Beach uniform—boots with spurs and bandanas—and their raw energy and stage-diving. When the Teen Idles returned to DC, they brought all of it back with them.

This became apparent at a Bad Brains show at the Bayou in September, which was being filmed by a local news-magazine show. The way the Huntington Beach kids had dealt with bouncers inspired the Georgetown punks to protect one of their own by attacking a bouncer. More security came and the face-off turned into a general melee.

It was an intoxicating feeling. "Just imagine all your life you've been hounded by rednecks, jocks, cops," said Garfield. "All of a sudden you're charging one with a chair. Eighteen years of rage just comes out on some stranger."

x x x

Thanks to the Rasta influence, Bad Brains "began to see me as an 'evil capitalist,' a 'Babylonian,'" Sussman remembered. "HR was always talking about 'the music must be free, music is for the people'. I told him it can't be free all the time or the band doesn't have any money. At that time he didn't seem to realize that."

Against Sussman's wishes, Bad Brains returned to play another free show at the Valley Green projects that spring, this time with the awestruck Teen Idles and Untouchables as opening acts. "This wasn't like the Yippie RAR [Rock Against Racism] gigs, which were really 'Rock for Pot' shows, this was the real deal," according to Ian MacKaye. Although the young white bands met with some non-comprehension, the day was a powerful, even formative one—and probably marked the pinnacle of Bad Brains' influence on the teen punks.

While the gig did little to ease tensions with Sussman, Bad Brains nonetheless spent much of the summer at the farm he had arranged for them to use. Without Sussman's full knowledge, the farm became an incubator that helped complete the group's transformation. With the assistance of some older dreads, they turned the place into a Rasta commune: music, "ital" vegetarian food, lots of pot smoking, and "reasoning" sessions where theological points were exhaustively discussed.

The band did not reach immediate unanimity on the issue of Rastafari. Veteran local punk Edd Jacobs remembered drinking with Darryl Jenifer on the streets of Georgetown while he made fun of HR's latest obsession. Soon, however, even Jenifer began to decrease his drinking and drugging in accordance with Rasta edicts. "Rasta was a way of life we chose to recognize," he said later. "I was raised Catholic but that was a white man's religion and that's not my heritage."

By this time, Bad Brains' Rasta conversion was becoming apparent to those outside the band. The Georgetown punks were taken aback by the transformation. Garfield: "Instead of HR saying, 'Hey, what's happening man!?' he's like 'Yes, Ian, righteous, Henry' and we're like 'Hunh?' We couldn't understand it. It was like Ian and I had gone to Philadelphia for two months and came back with English accents."

Despite accepting Rastafari, both Jenifer and Dr. Know resisted transforming Bad Brains into a reggae group. "It was a dream for me to play reggae," said HR, "but Darryl and Gary always insisted,

'We're a rock'n'roll band and that's what we're going to play.'" Integrating dub into the band's already potent mix interested Jenifer and Miller, but to abandon melting-pot punk for standard roots reggae would be to turn back at the edge of a breakthrough.

Jenifer and Dr. Know's insistence on sticking with the band's original vision was validated when "Don't Bother Me," recorded at Don Zientara's studio in March 1979, surfaced on *Best of Limp (The Rest of Limp)* in the summer of 1980. On a compilation album that seemed less diverse and contemporary than *30 Seconds Over DC*—in part because it reprised such older material as the Slickee Boys' "Gotta Tell Me Why" and the Shirkers' 1978 single, "Drunk and Disorderly"—"Don't Bother Me" was a leap into the future.

In rural Virginia, however, Bad Brains looked less like musical pioneers than possible subversives. Under the apparent assumption that black people with dreadlocks equaled guns and drugs, the local police had placed the farm under surveillance and were preparing a raid. "They had all these ideas that we had a bunch of guns and some big dope operation," Jenifer laughed. "All we had was one of these BB guns, a kid's toy. The day of the raid, I was using it to shoot at rats—out toward the same clump of trees, it turned out, that the cops were waiting!

"Out of nowhere, they broke the doors down, all these heavily armed cops pouring in from everywhere! They put a gun to my head and started screaming at me to tell them where the guns were, where the dope was. They didn't believe me, they just kept pushing it, threatening to kick my ass if I didn't give it up."

The police busted Jenifer, Dr. Know, and some friends—HR and Earl Hudson were on an errand—but there were no guns. Aside from one pot plant in the living room window, there also were no drugs. When Sussman made it clear that he was going to fight the charges and make an issue of the police's excessive force, the charges were settled out of court.

Although the raid's consequences were small, the experience seems to have further hardened the appeal of the apocalyptic Rasta worldview. The antiestablishment message of songs like "The Regulator" or "Big Takeover" grew more militant. Earlier that year, HR had said that their music "knocks the rich people who have forgotten how to feel." Class oppression, racial injustice, and impending confrontation began to replace Positive Mental Attitude in the band's lyrics.

For HR, every new event seemed to add to the certainty of his new worldview—especially the imminent election of Ronald Wilson Reagan. Rastas whispered that Reagan might be the Beast prophesied in the Book of Revelation, the six letters in each word of his name indicating the mark of the Beast, 666. A deadly spirit was in the air, reflected in such new Bad Brains songs as "Riot Squad," "I Against I," "Destroy Babylon," and "We Will Not."

x x x

A week and a half after playing at the Mabuhay Gardens, the Teen Idles opened for the Cramps and Slickee Boys at the Ontario Theater in Adams Morgan, just a few blocks from the shuttered Madams Organ. The largest show the band had ever played, it exposed them to a whole new spectrum of suburban kids.

Some were like suburban Maryland teen Kenny Inouye—son of Hawaiian Senator Daniel Inouye—who was drawn by the Cramps but left talking about the Teen Idles. "I came to see the better-known bands," he said, "but the one that really captured my imagination was this really energetic, young-looking opening band. From then on, I started trying to see them whenever they played, which brought me into the DC punk scene for real."

Another link was made when Extorts made their debut at the opening of Blitz, a Georgetown punk store, playing with the Teen Idles and Untouchables. Although the Wilson and Georgetown Day School kids had often gone to the same shows, this was the first time they really got to know each other. "I had been scared of Untouchables for the longest time," remembered Hampton, "so to go up and finally talk to them was great."

Other than the streets of Georgetown, the teen punks' main hangout had become Yesterday and Today. "Skip Groff was our Big Daddy," said Garfield. "We'd be in there all the time, scouring the bins, asking questions. Skip was a great source of information." Skip recalled that "they were nice kids and good customers, full of energy, really interested in the music. Some of them—especially Ian—you could really tell had something going."

Not long after returning from California, the Teen Idles were hanging out at the store when one of them mused, "Wouldn't it be wild if we made our own record?" The whole group burst out laughing. "It was so far out, so insane, so impossible, that we'd joke about it," said Garfield.

In the corner of the store, Groff straightened up from his work. "Sure you can do it," he said. "I'll help you."

He introduced the band to Don Zientara and his home studio. Zientara was "a really great guy," Garfield said. "You'd go into the studio and other guys would say, 'Get them the fuck out of here!' to a band like the Teen Idles. But Don would go, 'That's good. Here's how we can make it better.' He'd help you, not make you feel like talentless junk."

The record was funded by a year's worth of gig money the band stored in a cigar box, and was to be released by the Idles' own label, Dischord, inspired in equal parts by Limp and Dangerhouse. As the 45 neared completion and the band approached its first birthday, however, the Idles were coming undone.

In large part, the tension centered on a split between Nelson and Grindle. The latter had a new girlfriend, a born-again Christian who disapproved of the band. Grindle began to question what he was doing, bringing him into conflict with Nelson, a vociferous atheist. Hostilities erupted onstage, at least once leading to physical combat between the two. Grindle decided to quit the band.

MacKaye was hurt by Grindle's change of heart. Once the guitarist made the decision to leave the band, however, MacKaye pushed for its breakup. This was mainly because Teen Idles had been a group of friends. Without Grindle it wouldn't be the same unit anymore.

But there was another, less openly stated reason for MacKaye's plan. Strejcek and Grindle had written songs for Teen Idles, but almost all of the new songs were coming from MacKaye, who was increasingly dissatisfied with how Strejcek sang his words. MacKaye decided that he would form a new band with Nelson but without Strejcek so he could sing his own songs.

MacKaye recruited Extorts singer Lyle Preslar, known as a more accomplished guitarist than vocalist. Preslar brought a fellow Georgetown Day School student, the young but musically gifted Brian Baker. There soon was unanimity about Baker within the new unit. "Brian was this snotty little fucker," said MacKaye, "and a great bass player."

Preslar's exit left the Extorts without a singer, which became an opportunity for Garfield. The new SOA—for "State of Alert"—started practicing in October. MacKaye and Nelson were also eager to begin their new project. Even before the Teen Idles split, the duo's new band was practicing semi-covertly. One of the first songs they learned was a tune called "Straight Edge," which MacKaye had written as an Idle but never brought to the band.

The Teen Idles' raucous Halloween show at the Chancery, a club near Union Station, was supposed to be their last performance. But shortly before the gig, the Idles were offered an attractive opportunity: a chance to play the 9:30 Club, where Dody Bowers had agreed to try identifying underage patrons by putting a large X on their hands.

The X quickly evolved into a badge of honor, a signifier of the emerging new scene. "It was a really powerful thing," said Garfield. "Imagine 35 kids with the X on them!" Later the X would become an internationally recognized symbol of a phenomenon known as "straight edge." Ironically, in DC the X was more a symbol of youth solidarity than of an anti-drug philosophy, although for many the two went together.

The 9:30 gig paired the Idles with SVT, a new wave band featuring former Jefferson Airplane bassist (and Washington native) Jack Casady. This meant that the Idles' final show would draw the older audience they increasingly despised. "We showed up in force," remembered Garfield. "It was a half-SVT, half–Teen Idles crowd. We were going to show them, we wanted to go kick ass—'Yeah we're teeny-punks, Georgetown punks, we're too young to rock.'"

The Teen Idles charged through their set, finally coming to "Minor Disturbance (Too Young To Rock)." As the band prepared to start the song, a loud chant went up in the room: "Georgetown punks, Georgetown punks, Georgetown punks." The chants faded and the band tore into the song. When they reached the final power-chord-backed chorus of "We're too young to rock/We're too young to rock," the whole teen-punk faction of the crowd screamed along. The live version of the song recorded that night, complete with chanting, would provide the title and closing track for the forthcoming Teen Idles record.

Soon after the Idles' last show, MacKaye and Nelson resumed practicing with Preslar and Baker. The new band would be called Minor Threat. Later, Nelson explained that "minor" referred to the "ongoing problem of underage kids not being able to get into bars to see shows," and that the "threat" was ironic, since the teen punks had never been taken seriously.

While the Georgetown punks began create a self-contained scene, Howard Wuelfing made plans to bring together the larger punk community. He organized a two-day festival at dc space, which he described as "a forcibly mixed bag of subcultural styles intended as a convocation of the committed fringe." It was called "The Unheard Music Festival" and would be recorded for a live album.

MacKaye and Danny Ingram, who was now drumming for the Untouchables, arranged for SOA, Minor Threat, and the Untouchables to play. MacKaye had called "John/Stab" to see if his band wanted to play, but found out they didn't exist anymore. Schroeder assured him that he now had a new and better band, one in which he had traded drums for vocals.

Years later he recalled, "I thought, 'Why don't I sing? If Johnny Rotten can do it, so can I!'" Adding one more "b" to his accidental name, he became John Stabb. He was joined by drummer Mark Alberstadt, bassist Brian Gay, and guitarist John Barry, a student at DC's academically prestigious St. Anselm's Abbey School. "We thought he was so great because he was so fast," said Schroeder. "When we asked him his secret, he told us, 'I just take old Rolling Stones chords and speed them up!'" The band took its name, GI, from the Black Market Baby song, "World at War."

Alberstadt couldn't make the gig, and the GI's had rarely rehearsed, but a chance to play with other teen-punk bands couldn't be passed up. Schroeder immediately said yes. The Unheard Music Festival would host the first club performances of Minor Threat, SOA, and GI.

Wuelfing and Marc Halpern also booked their own Nurses, Martha Hull's new group the Steady Jobs, Charlie Trenchmouth's hard-rocking new Abbreviated Ceiling, and perverse progressives like Gross Suckling and Blitz Bunnies.

On the night of the festival, Stabb recalled, "our drummer didn't know any of our songs. We were going onstage trying to teach him drum beats!" The result was hilarious. If that version of GI had ever played together in the same room before, it was not proved by its performance. At one point, Stabb sang one song while the band played another—with no one realizing the error until the song was over.

Stabb jumped up and down, spitting out incoherent, incomprehensible vocals, shaking with stage fright but determined to somehow get through their short set. The evening hardly represented an auspicious debut for the GI's, but there was triumph in the fact that they had gotten up and done it.

SOA's sound was tougher and more musically accomplished. The clear visual focus of the band was a lean, bald-headed Henry Garfield. With an imposing physical presence, Garfield showed what he'd learned watching HR at Madams Organ. He spent almost as much time in the crowd as onstage. His monotone singing style—like SOA's songs—was rudimentary, but his raw anger was cathartic. Hampton showed aggressive flair on guitar, complemented by Blow's bass and Jacobsen's simple but solid drumming.

With the demise of the Teen Idles, the youthful Untouchables were the scene's most seasoned band. "Alec was in top form, sliding on the stage, rolling around on the floor, under people's feet, constantly diving onto the crowd," recalled Kim Kane. "Once he hit the floor and got the wind knocked out of him, but just kept going crazy anyway!" During the set-closing Sham 69 anthem, "If the Kids Are United," MacKaye went out into the crowd again, which closed in around him, pogo-ing and singing along with great fervor.

It was Minor Threat, however, that set the festival standard. The band played concise, melodic songs at Bad Brains hyper-velocity. While Ian MacKaye lacked the sheer physicality of Garfield, his presence was nonetheless arresting. No longer shackled by his bass duties, MacKaye's engaging, self-mocking theatrics were unleashed to considerable effect. If MacKaye appeared jovial, his vocals were clear, impassioned, and convincing.

"A quantum leap had taken place," said Wuelfing. "Minor Threat had songs and played them well. I was blown away to see that they could play with such speed and not have the structure of the song melt down underneath. The difference between Teen Idles and Minor Threat was Bad Brains. They set the example of how to play extremely fast but with extreme precision. Teen Idles may have tried to pull that off, but they never really could. From day one, however, Minor Threat could—and did."

Another observer thrilled by Minor Threat was a precocious teen transplant from Washington State, Calvin Johnson, a punk fan for several years. In his hometown of Olympia, Washington, he had worked at KAOS-FM, the Evergreen State College radio station.

Johnson had recently moved to Bethesda, a Washington suburb, with his family. Eager to work at WGTB, whose exploits were known at KAOS, Johnson searched for the station only to discover it had been closed. He had returned to Evergreen to attend college in the fall, but was back in town for Christmas vacation in time to attend the festival.

Although ambivalent about the music of the Georgetown punk bands other than Minor Threat, Johnson recognized their crucial accomplishment: They had built their own scene deep within hostile territory. Still, he wrote at the time, "trying to dance to one of the bands can be like hand-to-hand combat. Some people are just using the music as an excuse to wear leather and hit people."

Johnson faulted the teen punks for walking out on the Steady Jobs, a conventional roots-rock band. The musicians were, he noted, "just a couple of Joes and one Jane getting onstage to play music they believe in. Isn't that what the Georgetown punks like to think of themselves as?" He warned the teen punks "to open their minds if they don't want to end up like the musical conservatives they go to school with."

"Another problem is their attitude toward women," Johnson also argued. "Only one band had a female member and when a girl is dancing, she gets special abuse." He was "really impressed by the code-of-honor behavior," but he "wished that some of their female friends would get involved in the music side of the deal."

This observation echoed the misgivings of some of the older musicians who had encouraged the teen-punk bands. Once at Madams Organ, while the Untouchables played, Tru Fax bassist Libby Hatch had surveyed the high school girls in the audience, asking why none of them was in a band. She didn't get any interesting answers.

Despite such concerns, the event was a turning point. "The Unheard Music Festival was when you really started to

REGENERATION GAP
by Mark Jenkins

According to some of the founders of Washington's teen-punk scene, they were abused and ostracized by their elders. But that's not quite how those of us who were "older"—early to mid-20s, mostly—remember it. Bands like the Teen Idles and the Untouchables weren't universally accepted, but they were encouraged by some over-21 punks (and non-punks). Skip Groff, Don Zientara, Kim Kane, Howard Wuelfing, and others helped these bands get gigs and make their first records. I included them in my coverage of the scene for the *Washington Tribune* and other publications.

The Slickee Boys, the Nurses, Tru Fax and the Insaniacs, and other bands regularly offered opening gigs to bands like the Teen Idles and Tony Perkins and the Psychotics, a band that grew out of the Enzymes. (The Psychotics played punk-funk, not hardcore, but they were roughly the same age as the Idles, and included guitarist David Byers, who was later to play with HR.) These gigs were often frustrating for the headliners, however, because few of the teen bands' fans would stay for the older groups' sets. "They weren't very interested in anyone outside their clique," remembered Insaniacs singer-guitarist Diana Quinn.

Howard Wuelfing, however, noted that "all my anecdotes would be about how gracious the DC hardcore ("harDCcore") kids were all along. Fuck, Ian produced the first sessions by Underheaven," the band Wuelfing formed (with Don Zientara and Half Japanese's Mark Jickling) after the Nurses. But he did add see that this new thing was starting to take off, that it might be able to exist on its own," said scenester Tom Berard.

The festival had a bitter epilogue, however. The live album that was to be financed by the evenings' profits never materialized. Many of the teen punks speculated that the money had instead subsidized Halpern's heroin habit.

Told a decade later about the rumors, Wuelfing didn't disagree. "They thought the money went into Marc's arm? Yeah, I'd have to say that's about right. I didn't get any of the money and I didn't know about it at the time, but when I did ask Marc about it, he just said, 'Those bands are shitty. Why should we put them out?' I guess I was naïve. I didn't know how bad Marc's problems were. He told me it was under control, that he only did heroin once in a while."

Halpern's own explanation will never be known. The following May, the guitarist was found in a heap on the sidewalk outside dc space. After three days in a coma, Halpern died of complications resulting from a heroin overdose. He was 28.

When the album didn't happen, the Georgetown punks were stung, but it hardly mattered. They had definitively split from the older scene.

"When we first got into the punk scene, we were just stupid kids from the viewpoint of the 19-to-25-year-old punk," MacKaye later recalled. "We were just stupid little 'teenypunkers' to them, especially because of the fact that we weren't all druggies. They started calling us all this shit and I said, 'Man, you think

that "they never returned the favor of putting us on bills with them—outside of Lyle [Preslar] and Brian [Baker] having Underheaven open for their post Minor Threat band at the 9:30 Club."

When harDCore went its own way in 1981-82, it was partly because the principal venues of 1979-80 had vanished, and partly because some of the bands that used to offer them opening gigs had split. Neither harDCore nor teenagers were welcome at some clubs, and the 9:30 Club seldom booked local bands except as opening acts. There was no way groups like the Insaniacs could get gigs for the Teen Idles or the Psychotics when all they could get for themselves were opening slots.

It was in this period that harDCore first developed a reputation for elitism. The scene seemed a private party to which people who hadn't attended Wilson High School or Georgetown Day School weren't invited. I faithfully bought all the Dischord releases, and as editor of the *Tribune*, edited and published one of the first non-fanzine features on harDCore. Yet I was rarely in the know about upcoming shows.

For those who had been punk fans since first hearing Patti Smith, the Ramones, and Television, harDCore's separatism didn't make musical or ideological sense. The music's diversity was its strength, and punk wasn't a question of how you dressed or how fast you played. Still, I was stunned when I first saw Minor Threat. I didn't approve of harDCore's self-imposed quarantine, yet it had yielded something far more powerful than the Teen Idles or the Untouchables foretold.

you're punk—well, we're *hardcore* punks!' That's when the whole hardcore thing started. Before long, we started getting our own identity and were separating ourselves from the older bands. Our whole thing was to bust out in our own way."

putting DC on the map

"You set the standards of society
But we don't want to live that way
So we're gonna change 'em
We're the Youth Brigade
The Youth Brigade is growing
Another punk everyday
We hope you'll be the next one
Join the Youth Brigade!"
—Youth Brigade, "Youth Brigade," 1981

EARLY DISCHORD T-SHIRT DESIGN WITH IAN MACKAYE OF MINOR THREAT AT WILSON CENTER, 1981
(design by Jeff Nelson, photo by Susie Josephson)

putting DC on the map

On January 20, 1981, Ronald Reagan became the 40th President of the United States, ushering in the most conservative administration since the 1930s. Reagan's policies would soon inspire dramatic political responses from many in the punk underground. At the time of the former actor's inauguration, however, Minor Threat was not thinking about the future.

"Hey! What I want to know is," demanded Ian MacKaye, "when is '77 coming back?"

With that taunt hanging in the air, Lyle Preslar hit the chords of "Minor Threat" and the band's anthem rang out, rousing the small group of teenage punks at the front of dc space's stage. In what was only Minor Threat's third public performance, its confidence and power were impressive.

MacKaye's crack was directed at a pair of reviews of the Unheard Music Festival that had suggested the Georgetown punks were hopelessly nostalgic for 1977. Former *Unicorn Times* editor Richard Harrington, now writing for the *Washington Post*, had dismissed the Georgetown punk bands as "caught in a vapid time warp that transported them to 1975 punk London" and claimed that "of the six bands last night, none showed an ounce of originality, style, or substance." *Unicorn Times* writer Charles McCardell also identified the bands as class-of-'77 wannabes, and suggested that "their perfunctory playing and overt posing implied that they wished not to be taken seriously."

Of course the teen-punk bands wanted to be taken seriously, but they were increasingly interested only in the reaction of their peers. They felt that older rock fans and critics had missed the point entirely, and were far more guilty than they of pining for the music's past. Four years away from the seemingly distant 1977, these kids had something new and they knew it.

Minor Threat was opening that night for the Slickee Boys, who were loved by many Georgetown punks. Next to the younger scene, however, the band now seemed antiquated. "We'll try not to be long," MacKaye jeered. "We know you're all eager to see the Slickee Boys!"

With the Slickees banner hanging behind them, Minor Threat tore through the rest of its set. MacKaye dedicated "I Don't Wanna Hear It" to Marc Halpern, in honor of the missing funds from the Unheard Music Festival. The set was indeed completed quickly, and the younger band made way for the Slickees. It was the last time the two groups would share the same stage.

The next night at 9:30 Club, Minor Threat shared the bill with SOA, Black Market Baby, and another, officially unscheduled act. The Untouchables were about to disband and wanted to play a farewell show, but club co-owner Dody Bowers had said no. Midway through Minor Threat's set, MacKaye mourned the end of the Untouchables and told the crowd to "watch for their last show soon." It wasn't a long wait. As the final chords of "Stepping Stone" faded, the Untouchables emerged from the crowd, grabbed Minor Threat's instruments and launched into "If the Kids Are United."

Furious, Bowers pushed her way through the crowd toward the soundboard. Halfway into the song, Eddie Janney's guitar went out, but the crowd's singalong propelled the tune to its last verse. The guitar came back just in time to bring the song to its closing chorus.

As the club owner confronted the conspirators, SOA took the stage. "Minor Threat has just been banned from the 9:30 Club," Henry Garfield proclaimed. "Guess who the fuck is next!" The band smashed into "Gonna Have to Fight," a call for the Georgetown punks to battle to protect each other and their growing scene.

By now, the Georgetown punks had a reputation as brawlers. The day after Reagan's inauguration, the teenagers were the subject of a *Washington Post* story that described "a small but flourishing, youth-oriented, music-centered subculture that has gravitated to the streets of Georgetown. Too young to get into many of the clubs, they just hang out at places like Station Break, a Georgetown arcade, or the Häagen-Dazs ice cream shop." The pictures showed the "atypical, apolitical, and seemingly amoral" punks walking down M Street, proudly wearing their chains, boots, and leather jackets.

The article, the first where the teen punks defined themselves as "hardcore," explained that "punks dress to maim if not quite kill," a characterization supported by a Garfield remark: "We have a strict policy—if a bouncer at a nightclub lays a hand on one of us, it's ten on one till his ears bleed."

"We don't say 'fuck the world,' we say 'fuck the people around us'—you know, the people who put us down for the way we act, for the way we dress," MacKaye told the *Post*. Despite Reagan's arrival a mere dozen blocks from Georgetown, teen-punk politics didn't tend to look beyond their own neighborhood.

Not all the teenage punks ignored the new administration. John Stabb wrote "Hey Ronnie" for the GIs; Danny Ingram, just beginning to work with Nathan Strejcek in a new band called Youth Brigade, penned a broadside called "Moral Majority." Reagan's early actions also helped confirm Bad Brains' increasingly apocalyptic outlook. To HR, "It was like a vision. It just dawned on me that things were going to get bad—really bad—for America."

Still, Garfield recalled, "Early DC punk was not political. It comes from what I'm into: soul. Guitars with politics bore me. I relate to music on the level of sex and death—sweat, blood, cum, sleepless nights, insecurity."

At the time, MacKaye echoed this inward-looking ethic: "If you want to keep an eye on what's going on, that's cool, but you are not as capable of changing politics as you are capable of changing yourself. If you're able to change yourself, that's for the better. When you get that out of the way, then maybe other things will shape up."

Even if most of the teenage punks were not politically engaged, they seemed revolutionary to their high school peers. "Anytime a group of kids get together outside adult authority, it's political," said Guy Picciotto. "When you became a punk, you knew it was a big deal. You were going to lose old friends. It was a radical step."

X X X

One thing did open the DC teen-punk scene to a wider world: the release of the Teen Idles' single. ("The first of many posthumous releases!" laughed Jeff Nelson in retrospect.) The records dribbled out, and the feedback rushed in. Michigan fanzine *Touch and Go* called it "this year's best single." An obscure San Francisco punk radio show called *Maximum RockNRoll* made "Get Up and Go" its number one pick for several weeks in a row, after one of its DJs, Tim Yohannon, happened upon the 45 in a used record bin. Clearly, there were others out there who shared the DC punks' vision.

Initially, Dischord partners MacKaye, Nelson, and Strejcek had thought of the label as a one-off project. But with all the new bands that had formed, they decided to keep the label going as long as there was local music they wanted to put out. "Our goal was not to make a lot of money," Nelson said, "but to help as many of our friends' bands as we could."

Money, however, was immediately an issue. Before any new records could be released, the $600 invested in the Teen Idles' single had to be recouped. Minor Threat was the obvious follow-up release, but MacKaye and Nelson didn't have the cash to do it. Eager to get an SOA record out, Garfield raised the money himself. Thus SOA's *No Policy* EP became the second Dischord release.

"No" was the band's operative word. "SOA songs were anti-everything I didn't like," said Garfield. "I hated my job, hated cops, hated girls . . . It was all about no fun, fear, oppression. My message was 'Kill The World.'"

Stabb's new fanzine, *Critical List*, was among the first to hail SOA: "They're what it's all about—a bunch of kids making a lotta loud fast noise!" Of course, Stabb also wrote that SOA and his other favorite bands—including Black Market Baby, Minor Threat, Youth Brigade, the Untouchables, and his own GI—"prove that you don't have to have lots of fucken talent to be good, ya just hafta play fast!!"

Of the EP's songs, "Gate Crashers" attacked the older punk scene, "Lost in Space" derided Garfield's drug-addled peers, and "Blackout" detailed the singer's psychic struggle: "War going on inside my head/I can't get to sleep/I'd rather be dead." Many of the songs—"Gang Fight," "Warzone," "Gonna Have to Fight," "Riot"—reflected Garfield's enthusiasm for hand-to-hand combat.

Garfield tended to explode when faced by physical conflict, going to unpredictable extremes. "I was in lots of fights," remembered MacKaye. "I'd just try to teach the guy a lesson, no permanent damage, just a bruise or two. I'd be stopping, I'd look over my shoulder, and Henry would be dragging his guy down the stairs and kicking him! I'd have to go and try to stop him."

The teen punks' zest for rough dancing, fast music, and street skirmishes was a way to set themselves apart from the older crowd, which they saw as tame, arty, pretentious, and drug-addled. Watching the Huntington Beach kids in action, Garfield and his friends had realized how much power a gang could wield. Gang-like solidarity was also a practical reaction to the continuing problem of attacks in Georgetown.

"I am fascinated by gangs," MacKaye later told the *Washington Post*. "I don't like going out and beating people's asses but I like the idea that if I have trouble, I have a lot of friends that are going to help me out. 'Stand Up' was like the first song that [Minor Threat] wrote. At the time, there was a lot of violence at shows. To me, it was a great thing to see all these people get out there and be able to put back the bouncers, put back whoever was hurting somebody else. It's good to see that you have friends like that.

"It's a fine line," he admitted. "I like to bruise the ego, nothing more. But sometimes you get taken overboard. I might get in an altercation with someone and just want to cool the guy down basically. My friends might destroy him—which is certainly not what I had in mind."

The teen-punk scene's reputation began to draw outsiders who wanted only trouble. "Like any new society, it started off idealistic," Garfield recalled. "The scene was so small everyone knew each other. By late summer of 1980, violence started as new people came in from the suburbs. We'd get Marines, bikers, rednecks, tough guys, thick-necked young wise-asses. We'd fight outsiders. We didn't care if it was fair, this guy was fucking with our little piece of the world, so we'd stomp the shit out of him. That was our attitude. We didn't go out to start any fights, we just wanted to do our thing like we had the year before."

When the Georgetown punks took their gang ethos and underdog attitude to New York, conflict was inevitable. The first clash came at a Black Flag show at Manhattan's Peppermint Lounge, which MacKaye recounted in Glen Friedman's photozine, *My Rules*: "The club was packed. We sat content that we were finally going to see them. They were so important to us, almost living legends, they represented that total release, that personal rebellion that we felt so strongly. We had driven 250 miles to a town we loathed, waited in line to all hours of the night. We were laughed at, ridiculed for our social etiquette. We were definitely un-cool. How could we, coming from DC, have any idea what it was like to be Punk?

"It must have been 2 a.m. when they finally came on. All 14 of us gathered in front of the stage. There were eyes looking down on us and sideways comments all around. We were a little scared but hell-bent on doing what we set out to do. The tensions ran high but we ran higher, the atmosphere was hard but we were harder. And when it was over, we had the last laugh. The city was still there but we had beaten it and it would remember. And it did."

To fanzine editor and musician Jack Rabid, "DC ruined the Black Flag show. They brought slamdancing to New York. I hated them. You're just standing there to watch the band and suddenly you're getting rammed into." He thought the DC kids "were jerks. I didn't like their shaved head thing. It was just too macho."

The members of Black Flag, however, were impressed, especially after a 9:30 Club show with Minor Threat and Youth Brigade a few days after the Peppermint Lounge gig. Ending its brief embargo on hardcore, the club had allowed the music's return, but had prepared for the date by hiring extra bouncers to stand in front of the stage. To the teen punks, this was another provocation.

"That made the night so fun for us," MacKaye remembered. "Those motherfuckers were leaving with blood pouring. To me, that was justified aggression because it's our stage, that's the way it is."

"There is an old guard, there's about 10 of us or more, this is in our blood," he said at the time. "I'm fucking 20 next month and it's not fucking 'fun-time' for me anymore, it's much more serious for me and I'll not have them fuck with my band, my music, my friends. This is what I do, I don't go to school, I got a fucking record label, I got a band. It's my life and I won't have people fuck with my life." Impressed by such vehemence, Black Flag began extolling the DC scene in interviews.

The next California band to make the DC connection was Dead Kennedys. When they reached New York in April, the show began with MacKaye shaving heads onstage. This led *Village Voice* rock critic Robert Christgau to label the DC punks "muscleheads." In the same paper, Lester Bangs referred to the Georgetowners as "a phalanx of big ugly skinhead goons imported from Washington, DC, apparently the same guys Black Flag brought up for their show to hurl themselves on the crowd with brutal but monotonous regularity in suddenly institutionalized slamdancing."

Dead Kennedys frontman Jello Biafra, however, sided with Washington over New York. "New York is the most overrated cultural center in the world except for Paris," he said. "In DC you've got a bunch of young original bands. Here it's leftovers from the New York Dolls. When I heard about how all of the DC people we had met had showed up for Black Flag and wreaked havoc, I thought, 'Yeah, cool!'"

The Georgetown punks' most conspicuous New York outing came late in the year, when LA hardcore quartet Fear played *Saturday Night Live's* Halloween show. John Belushi had championed the band, but doubted that its appearance would have the impact of a punk club performance without a slamdancing crowd. So he called MacKaye to recruit some DC punks to supply the requisite mayhem. Roughly 30 Washingtonians showed up, creating enough havoc that the cameras cut away in the midst of Fear's performance. "Saturday Night Riot," a *New York Post* headline blared the next day.

As Dead Kennedys prepared to perform in DC, Biafra was surprised to receive a petition urging the band to play the all-ages 9:30 Club rather than the Bayou. The petition was organized by Sean Finnegan, who was just beginning to assemble a band called Void in the "new town" of Columbia, Maryland, midway between Washington and Baltimore. "I knew there was a different kind of scene going on," Biafra said, "to get a petition signed by real people rather than some guy on the phone who you could visualize chomping on a cigar saying, 'Why don't you play my club?'"

Despite his concern that the band might be a "total art-student disaster" live, Biafra arranged for the decidedly non-hardcore Half Japanese to open the show. He was enthralled that night by the group's new big-band lineup. Later, he would claim that "Half Japanese is the best art band in the world because they come from the gut and don't plot out what they're doing on graph paper. They just attack people with what they're doing."

The Dead Kennedys' set was a paroxysm of slamdancing and stage-diving during which Biafra repeatedly plunged into the crowd but never stopped singing. Energized by the crowd's abandon, he laughed and exclaimed, "Now all you've gotta do is take this kind of attitude and storm the White House and the Capitol Building!"

"We haven't had anything near this extreme so far," Biafra said after the show. "Instead of a few people standing around guzzling beer, here you've got everybody out on the dance floor, sweating, screaming, and mixing it up. DC is the only place around with a good hardcore punk scene like the West Coast's."

x x x

As the DC hardcore scene expanded, it grew a bit more distant from a crucial inspiration, Bad Brains. The group was faulted for both its commercialism—embodied by the man Howard Wuelfing called "money bags manager Mo Sussman"—and its new Rasta spirituality, which caused HR to prefer reggae to punk. As HR attributed his band's new musical direction to "the power of Jah," Stabb dismissed the group in *Critical List* as lost to religion.

Sussman paid for sessions at Omega Studios, a sophisticated 24-track recording studio in suburban Maryland. The band recorded a demo that included polished versions of five songs, including "I Luv I Jah," a roots reggae track, and two bracing punk outbursts, "I Against I" and "At the Movies." But the band's idealism often trumped the pragmatism of Sussman, who was trying to make Bad Brains more commercial without compromising their musical vision.

Sussman prepared to shop the tape to major labels, but the band was retreating from its former career goals. While Sussman tried to find a place for Bad Brains in the commercial mainstream, HR continued to look for a non-profit venue for the band to play. Through a friend, he found the Wilson Center, a place that would prove even more important to DC hardcore than Madams Organ. The center's basement space was simple, spacious, and virtually indestructible, with a large sturdy stage—perfect for hardcore punk shows.

The Wilson Center was located at the confluence of three neighborhoods, Adams Morgan, Mount Pleasant, and Columbia Heights, all of which were home to an increasing number of refugees fleeing war-torn Central America. The center housed an employment center, a free clinic, and other social service facilities; to raise funds, the basement was rented for everything from Latin American dances to a Yippie-sponsored anti-Reagan "Counter-Inaugural Ball."

The venue's first punk performance was an overview of the burgeoning hardcore scene, including such established bands as Bad Brains, Minor Threat, Black Market Baby, GI, and SOA, as well as more than a half dozen newer or lesser known ones: Red C, Law and Order, Broken Cross, Mod Subs, Prophecy, Scream, and Void. The latter two were the most prominent early hardcore bands to hail from the suburbs.

While HR was clearly eager to accomodate as many bands from the rapidly burgeoning scene as possible, 13 bands on any bill—even with 20-minute sets—was a bit much. At least one person's attention waned before the night was over; Susie Josephson photographed Alec MacKaye asleep on the steps of the Wilson Center. The photo became the cover of the first Minor Threat EP.

A less distracted member of the audience was Malcolm Riviera. It was the first DC show for the Raleigh, North Carolina resident, who had seen Bad Brains in his hometown and had driven five hours to investigate the DC punk explosion. Already a Bad Brains devotee, Riviera was elated by Minor Threat.

"I wasn't into it so much for the message," he remembered, "but I liked the fast, angry, alienated music. It was what I had been looking for. Minor Threat was better than the Sex Pistols. They were more angry, fast, loud, and tight and they were right there in front of my face. It was something all our own, watching the greatest bands in the world perform in front of you—what a rush, what an inspiration!" He made the decision then and there to move to DC. In 1982-83, Riviera would sponsor a series of Wilson Center shows that would help make the basement space the home of DC hardcore.

Another new site for shows was Woodlawn High School, an alternative public school in nearby Arlington. The first gig featured two local bands, mod-revival quartet Count 4 and teen-punk band the Necros (not to be confused with the better-known Ohio group). In May, the school hosted Canadian agit-punk group DOA, which was accompanied by Jello Biafra, and four local bands: Minor Threat, SOA, Youth Brigade, and Scream.

The reaction to the latter demonstrated the hardcore crowd's clannishness; when Scream began to play, most of the audience walked out. Although Scream was strongly influenced by Bad Brains and lived only a few miles from Georgetown—in the Virginia suburb of Bailey's Crossroads, once the winter home of the Barnum & Bailey circus—it appeared to a puzzled Biafra that the quartet was not in with the in-crowd.

Aside from being suburban, the band's only offenses were not dressing punk and occasionally playing covers. "They called us 'jocks who were trying to play punk,'" singer Pete Stahl remembered. Scream—which featured Pete's brother Franz on guitar, bassist Skeeter Thompson, and drummer Kent Stax—would later be accepted as one of the scene's most powerful bands, but their initial sense of being outsiders was never forgotten.

x x x

Sussman's relationship with Bad Brains was increasingly strained. The crisis broke at a show in Chapel Hill, North Carolina that was scheduled for simulcast on radio and cable TV. Sussman flew down for the event, only to find the band without a singer as the 9 p.m. airtime approached. "It was 8 p.m., no HR. 8:30, no HR. 8:45, still no sign of HR," he remembered. "Finally, at 8:59 p.m., HR comes in, disheveled, whacked out on marijuana or whatever, incoherent." The band was ultimately able to play, but the TV crew, already dismantling its gear when the vocalist arrived, packed up and left.

"After the show, I sat down with HR to find out the reason he was late and incoherent," said Sussman. "He had driven from Chapel Hill to DC"—a six-hour trip one way—"to help someone move furniture with the van and then had driven back again. I said, 'HR, you were going to be on television!' He said, 'Fuck you, my friend needed the van.'"

By then, Sussman estimated, he had spent more than $40,000 on the band. "I said, 'That's it, I can't take anymore. You guys aren't going to get anywhere. I quit.'"

"It wasn't the rest of the band," he noted. "It was HR. As he metamorphosed into a full-fledged Rasta, he just wouldn't listen to reason."

Bad Brains still had ambitions, and without access to Sussman's checkbook, DC didn't seem the place to fulfill them. The band returned to New York, where a teenage friend they knew from the Mad, David Hahn (later known as Dave Id), became its informal manager. Jerry Williams, who ran the Lower East Side performance space and four-track recording studio 171-A, was the band's soundman. Williams and the group were soon living, practicing, and recording at 171-A.

Once in New York, HR joined the Twelve Tribes of Israel, the Rasta sect which had included Bob Marley. HR's obsession with Marley grew when he discovered that he and Marley were born in the same month, February, making them both members of the tribe of Joseph. Later describing himself as "engulfed" by his new faith community, HR began calling himself "Joseph I." The depth of commitment showed in his latest lyrics, which were full-throated exhortations for the destruction of Babylon and a cleansing revolution that would be led by what he described as "a new breed of youths who are going to be unconquerable"—kids like those in the Bad Brains' growing audience.

While such views surely seemed a bit much for the average concert-goer, if ever there was a band who could live up to such rhetoric, it was Bad Brains during this period. HR exhibited absolute, riveting conviction in live performance, backed by a band whose speed, precision, and power was staggering. A New York area teenager named Lou who first saw the band around this time recalled thinking that "Bad Brains were these untouchable Rasta gods who were going to lead some revolution." Later he would help form a band of his own called Sick of it All.

Alerted to Bad Brains' burgeoning reputation, their old heroes, the Clash, offered them a slot on a series of shows they were doing at Bonds, a Manhattan dance club. The idea was to showcase diverse opening acts, including Grandmaster Flash and the Furious Five, Funkapolitan, Bush Tetras, and the Slits, as well as Bad Brains. The shows soon went awry: Police shut down the club on the first night for overcrowding and some Clash fans heckled the supporting acts, especially Grandmaster Flash. Bad Brains went over well, but the band was disappointed by both the audience and the headliner.

"The Clash were something back in 1977, but now they've been sucked into the system, the record company bit, this world of drugs," said Darryl Jenifer at the time. "They've got to have their collars starched up real straight. That's real false. We don't have no gimmick, I ain't no gimmick, man. You see the Clash onstage and they're all high on some kind of speed. If I want some energy, I just drink some orange juice and go out and rock harder than all of them."

Neil Cooper, who had recently started the cassette-only label ROIR (Reach Out International Records), approached Bad Brains about releasing some of the work they were doing at 171-A. He wanted them to sign a contract, but they were wary.

"They would just be hanging out in my office, sitting on the floor, smoking some weed, and we would talk about it," Cooper recalled. "Finally I had a contract drawn up. I watched as they tore it up. I got another and they tore that up. I got a third one which they tore up as well. They were very suspicious of record companies, of contracts being meaningless, feeling that things should be done on a matter of trust. They didn't understand the commercial aspects of a record company or the need for a contract to protect both themselves and the record company."

The stalemate could have lasted indefinitely if Bad Brains had not learned that in the late '60s Cooper had been employed by the government of Ethiopia, establishing a national mint, working directly with the Rasta God-on-earth himself, Haile Selassie. At first, HR and company didn't believe it, but Cooper showed them letters as well as medallions he had with the likeness of Selassie on them. "Bad Brains just flipped," Cooper said. "They said, 'We want to be on your label!' One of the stipulations of the contract was that I give them each one of the coins to hang around their neck. I think they were more excited about the medallions than being on ROIR." Cooper set to work on *Bad Brains,* the tape that would be the band's first national release.

Centered on Lower East Side venues like 171-A and A7, a New York City hardcore scene began to grow. New bands like Beastie Boys, Reagan Youth, Cro-Mags, Kraut, Heart Attack, the Mob, and the Nihilistics joined existing ones like the Mad, the Stimulators, False Prophets, and Even Worse (which included Jack Rabid). As in Washington, Bad Brains were the catalyst for a punk eruption.

x x x

Henry Garfield was feeling desperate when he went to New York in June for a show at Studio 57 with Bad Brains, Black Flag, and LA's UXA. "Looking at 20 with just a high school education didn't look good," he said. "I knew I could be doing this—working at Häagen-Dazs, living in an apartment smelling of insecticide and dirty socks—for the rest of my life. Everything was closing in on me."

Garfield jumped up and sang "12XU" with HR and danced and sang along with abandon to Black Flag. He followed the latter band to A7, where it played an impromptu show long past midnight. By the time Black Flag hit the stage, Garfield needed to get back to Georgetown to open the Häagen-Dazs shop. Several songs into the band's set, he requested "Clocked In" to send him on his way. On an impulse, he jumped onstage and sang with the band. Then he drove back to DC, arriving just in time to go to work.

Days later, Garfield got a call from Black Flag vocalist Dez Cadena. He'd decided to play second guitar and the group wanted Garfield to try out as singer. "This band was as big as Elvis in my mind," Garfield said. "What else could I do? So I just went and did it. I'd never have a chance like that again in my life." When practices in New York went well, Garfield was officially asked to join.

Garfield returned home and began making preparations to leave for good. Before he left, SOA still had one more gig: with Black Flag at a club in the working-class Philadelphia neighborhood of Kensington. The Georgetown punks went with the same attitude as they had taken to New York. "We really didn't come up to beat up Philly punks, but I guess we came up to fight for something," Garfield allowed. "It was sorta to show people what was going on in DC."

They had chosen the wrong place for the demonstration. When the dancing got rough during Black Flag's set, one of the locals took offense and a fight ensued. After the immediate mass response of the DC crew, the locals ran from the club, chased by the DC kids. Fighting indoors on a dance floor controlled by the DC crew was one thing; fighting outside on the local turf was another matter entirely. Suddenly the visiting punks faced not just a few local kids but a whole neighborhood.

Stabb was inside when a comrade came back with blood streaming down his face. "Police had lined up blocking the street and just watched it all," he recalled. "More fights erupted and out of the woodwork came the local gang—Kensington Boys with baseball bats!" One of the DC contingent, Jamie Biddle, was struck in the head with a bat. "We were standing about 10 feet away and couldn't do anything," said Stabb. "We were frozen with shock. We grabbed Jamie and took off to the nearest emergency center. By the time we got there, we were covered with blood. Jamie ended up with 22 stitches." Fortunately, no one was killed or permanently injured in the confrontation.

The sight of police watching the mayhem without intervening inspired Stabb to write "No Rights," a song that would appear on the GI's first EP, *Legless Bull*, Dischord's fourth release.

In retrospect, Garfield would feel that the Philadelphia battle had a message: He had gotten out just in time. Defecting from Washington, he decided to leave something behind: the name of the father he hated. Henry Garfield became Henry Rollins, taking his new surname from a college T-shirt worn by MacKaye's older sister, Susannah.

The musicians who recorded for Black Flag's label, SST, became the renamed singer's new extended family. "Our practices were our world. We hung out with the Minutemen, Saccharine Trust—crazy people wired out on music, just like us. Black Flag was a big gang, music was what was happening."

Rollins was less sanguine about what was then America's largest hardcore punk scene. "The LA punk community was jaded people into it for the wrong reasons," he said. "It was not my pure energy trip, drugs were all around, kids on quaaludes, 15-year-old girls, high school dropouts shooting smack, fucking anyone who came along."

Shortly after returning to LA with its new vocalist, Black Flag recorded its first album, *Damaged*. The record was a hardcore landmark, but it didn't make a fan of MCA boss Al Bergamo, whose company was supposed to distribute it. After listening to the album, Bergamo cancelled MCA's distribution deal with Unicorn, SST's sub-distributor. Black Flag was left with 20,000 copies of its already completed LP, all bearing the MCA logo. The band covered the MCA logo on each album with stickers bearing Bergamo's verdict: "As a parent, I found it to be an anti-parent record."

The incident was just the beginning of Black Flag's distribution problems, but for Rollins the important thing was that the album was out and the group could return to the road. As the fierce, even intimidating presence fronting hardcore's hardest touring band, he had found a reason to live.

x x x

Bad Brains' relocation and Garfield/Rollins's farewell left large holes in DC's hardcore scene. The older punk scene was also sputtering, with the demise of the Nurses (who split upon Halpern's death), the Razz (because of strife between Michael Reidy and Tommy Keene), and the Urban Verbs, who didn't last long after Warner Brothers dropped them. The Slickee Boys soldiered on, joined by such promising new bands as the Velvet Monkeys (whose leader, Don Fleming, would ultimately make his name as a producer) and REM (soon to become Egoslavia to avoid conflict with a band from Athens, Georgia). But increasingly Washington was known for hardcore, which some locals were now spelling harDCore. And the focus of harDCore was Minor Threat.

Minor Threat's music caught up with its nationwide buzz with the release of Dischord #3, Minor Threat's first single. Like the Teen Idles and SOA EPs, it had been recorded with Skip Groff at Don Zientara's basement studio, Inner Ear. On the label was the motto, "Putting DC on the Map," a joke that nonetheless revealed the band's self-confidence.

The music's velocity made an immediate impression, but the eight songs also had cogent lyrics, catchy melodies, impassioned vocals, and tight, precise performances. It was a veritable blueprint for "thrash," a sound that would launch thousands of imitations.

The songs raged, but not blindly or inarticulately. Each one was simple yet well-spoken, taken straight from actual experience. "I Don't Wanna Hear it" and "Screaming at a Wall" were inspired by Halpern and the disdain of the press and the older punks. "Bottled Violence" was an anti-alcohol and -violence rant rooted in the misadventures of Black Market Baby's Paul Cleary. "Seeing Red," the only song written by Nelson, was about being judged simply on appearances.

At the time, no one could have guessed that "Straight Edge" would be the most influential of the EP's tracks. For MacKaye it was—and would remain—simply a song, not a philosophy or move-ment, but for others it would take on a broad and lasting significance.

The band made plans for a national tour with Youth Brigade, and played a show at the 9:30 Club with GI (now being called Government Issue) to raise money for the excursion. In the audience was Cynthia Connolly, a recent transplant from LA who would soon begin writing DC scene reports for LA-based *Flipside* under the name Morticia.

Also there were Tesco Vee and Dave Stimson, publishers of *Touch and Go*, which was known for its taste for the tasteless. Vee, who put his critical outlook into practice with the taboo-tweaking Meatmen, had been a fan of DC hardcore punk from afar, and experiencing the music live completed his conversion. He and Stimson began to not only tout the scene in their fanzine but also to make plans to move to DC.

A harDCore mythology was beginning to develop, with phrases like "straight edge" intriguing and in some cases inspiring kids in punk scenes across the country. The scene's most visible symbol was the X on the hand, which was included somewhere in the packaging of each Dischord release. Once a practical solution to the problem of underage shows, it was now becoming an identifying mark for a growing teenage tribe. Some punks, including Woodlawn student Amy Pickering, wore it in school.

x x x

Pickering was one of harDCore's most devoted fans, but she and other young women began to feel excluded—by force. At hardcore shows, slamdancing and stage-diving were separating the boys from the girls.

In the *Washington Post*, Richard Harrington depicted slamdancing in prose that, if somewhat breathless, had the ring of unwelcome truth: "The pit is ferocious and frightening: Young men's bodies slam into each other, arms and elbows out, fists flailing, like razor-edged Mexican jumping beans popping madly on the dance floor. This ritual of resistance is fueled by dancers who are young, white teenage boys given to shaved heads more extreme than a Marine cut, sometimes in a 'Taxi Driver' mohawk. DC's punks are given to torn shirts and jeans, black leather jackets littered with names of bands and ideology. Their dancing feet are enveloped by combat boots, the heels that wound. Years ago Iggy Stooge used to damage himself in performance, throwing himself on broken glass or into the audience. Now the audience completes the cycle."

"It's not about hurting anybody," the article quoted Henry not-yet-Rollins. "It's just letting go, just going off. A lot of kids live in good places, their parents are rich. That doesn't keep you from being mad or feeling angry or outraged or alienated."

By mid-1981, the punks' "letting go" had effectively barred women from both the dance floor and the stage. The dozen bands who played the first massive Wilson Center show included only one woman: Toni Young, bassist of Red C. This was particularly striking since so many of the earlier local punk bands, including the Urban Verbs, the Slickee Boys, the Nurses, Tru Fax and the Insaniacs, Tiny Desk Unit, DCeats, and the Shirkers had female members.

Early scene-maker Sharon Cheslow recalls dancing to Teen Idles and Bad Brains at Madams Organ. "I was right up at the front of the stage. It wasn't called slamdancing then, but it was very physical. I could withstand it. So for me to say it was rough by 1981, you know it's rough. I started looking at the scene and asking myself, 'Am I really with a group of friends?' A lot of the girls felt the way I did and started dropping out."

In 1979-80, there were nearly as many women as men in the audience for hardcore shows, but by late 1981 new female converts like Pickering, Connolly, or Janelle Simmons were rare. "At the time I was blind to it," said the latter, "but looking back now, women didn't really have a place."

"I wasn't into slamdancing," recalled Anne Bonafede, another longtime punk fan. "It was too male oriented. Around Minor Threat and SOA I started feeling really alienated from the scene. I used to love to go out to shows and dance but by then you couldn't really because you might get hurt seriously."

The women who did continue attending hardcore shows had to do so on the terms set by their male peers. "We were trying to be boys," said Pickering.

Cheslow and Bonafede formed Chalk Circle, the first all-female band to emerge from harDCore. "At the time my life was lived through boyfriends or guys that I knew rather than for myself," Bonafede said. "With the beginning of Chalk Circle, that really changed. I could be a drummer if I wanted to be. All my [male] friends had been playing in bands so I knew I could just do it, that was the punk philosophy. It tied very much into my feminist growth as well, just being able to say that I don't have to live through guys, I can do it myself. Chalk Circle helped me deal with all the alienation I was feeling from the hardcore scene at the time."

Like Scream, Chalk Circle initially was not accepted by the scene that had inspired it. After the group played its first show—with REM and Velvet Monkeys rather than any hardcore bands—a *Critical List* review called the show "bimbo nite at dc space" and dismissed Chalk Circle as a "boring all-girl band."

"It was very unusual to have an all-female band," said Bonafede. "That definitely had a lot to do with us not being taken seriously. There were a lot of bad all-male bands at the time and they wouldn't have been trashed as much as Chalk Circle."

Male supremacy wasn't harDCore's only dubious new element. A young band called Iron Cross became the earliest local group to emulate Britain's violent and sometimes racist skinhead scene. Frontman Sab Grey had lived in the UK and returned home inspired to form the first American skinhead band. He was joined by 13-year-old guitarist Mark Haggerty, 14-year-old drummer Dante Ferrando (both from the now-defunct Outsiders), and 15-year-old bassist Wendel Blow (fresh from SOA). Theirs was a slower, English-oriented punk style that rejected speedy DC hardcore.

Interviewed for *Touch and Go*, Grey made some remarks that were more controversial than his boredom with "the fast shit." The singer found himself defending members of Britain's far-right National Front. "Sure they are Nazis to a certain extent," he said. "I'm a Nazi, everyone is." When challenged, Grey added that "blacks are the biggest racists."

The singer's ill-considered words had lasting repercussions for him and his band. Interviewed years later, Grey recalled sadly, "I was just talking out of my ass. I had no real idea that people all over the country would be reading what I said. Who in the scene did at the time? We were just dumb kids."

Although it surely doesn't justify the ignorance of Grey's comments, there is a certain ring of truth to his explanation. Over the course of the last year, something had happened. With only the slightest warning, DC was becoming one of the most closely observed and influential punk scenes in the United States. As Alec MacKaye recalled, "When we started out, we never believed in our wildest dreams that what we were doing in DC would matter to somebody outside the Beltway." Now clearly it did. But while DC as a scene would rise even further, the specter of racism and fascism would follow Iron Cross until its end.

x x x

The Minor Threat/Youth Brigade tour began in August, with 10 dates between Chicago and the final scheduled gigs in San Francisco and Los Angeles. Biafra helped the bands arrange shows, as did Nevada's Seven Seconds and Ohio's Necros.

The two bands packed their equipment in a van, a more professional approach than the Teen Idles had taken on their California jaunt the summer before. But the plan had one flaw: The van belonged to the mother of Youth Brigade guitarist Tom Clinton, who was never informed of the scheme. When she learned that her van was in the Midwest and on its way to the West Coast, she demanded its immediate return.

The musicians had no choice but to return to DC with less than half their planned dates completed, scrapping entirely the important West Coast gigs. For Lyle Preslar, the bungled tour was the final indignity. He had been accepted at Northwestern University and saw little reason to remain with Minor Threat, whose frequent internal squabbles wearied him.

Without Preslar, Minor Threat would not continue. MacKaye and Nelson began to work with former Untouchables guitarist Eddie Janney and John Falls, who was then known primarily for his daredevil stage-dives. The new band was to be called Skewbald (MacKaye's idea) or Grand Union (Nelson's).

"Jeff and I have a policy, we don't keep the bands alive, the members are the bands," MacKaye explained at the time. "It's kind of cool to break up, rebuild, and write a whole new set of songs. It humbles you, you never get too good, and you stay underground. In DC, right at the point when people start hearing about your band or you put out a record, the band breaks up. It keeps it really underground, gives room for a lot of progression."

Before the split, Minor Threat recorded its second EP, *In My Eyes*. The sessions were done at Inner Ear, and Skip Groff helped pay for the recording. The record was a major advance, rivaling the power of the band's former inspiration, Bad Brains.

"Out of Step" was both the EP's most influential and controversial song. "Don't smoke/Don't drink/Don't fuck/At least I can fucking think," proclaimed MacKaye. Jeff Nelson didn't like the lyrics because it seemed that MacKaye was ordering people not to drink, smoke, or fuck. That this was a personal code of conduct rather than a set of instructions was obvious to MacKaye, but not to Nelson.

Interviewed by *Flipside*, Nelson carefully noted that "Ian and I agree on almost everything, but he and I do think differently on some things. If it was his way, the whole scene wouldn't drink or smoke ever. But it's not like that, there's more and more drinking just 'cause the kids that were there are two years older now and they can drink, they're of age. I agree with Ian on all of his [anti-drug] views, it's just what I actually do." Although he didn't publicly advocate either activity, Nelson did sometimes drink and smoke pot.

After a final few Minor Threat gigs, Preslar left for school and Baker joined Government Issue. Red C split as frontman Tomas Squip headed to college, and within two months Youth Brigade also called it quits. When Skewbald didn't develop as hoped, MacKaye headed to Britain as a roadie on Black Flag's first UK tour. (He raised the money for his plane ticket by passing a cup at a DC Black Flag show.) To the American punks' surprise, such British counterparts as the Exploited and Chelsea treated them with disdain.

The opening left by the defunct groups was filled by new teen-punk bands, notably Artificial Peace, Faith, and Deadline. The first of these was a thrash band that included former members of Red C and Assault and Battery: singer Steve Polcari, bassist Rob Moss, drummer Mike Manos, and guitarist Pete Murray. The musicians hailed from Bethesda, an affluent Maryland suburb just a few miles up Wisconsin Avenue from Wilson High School. The Bethesda crew's dancers were known as the "B-Town Thrashers," but one of Artificial Peace's early songs had another name for their town: "Wasteland."

Faith marked Alec MacKaye's return to action after a series of bands which never quite escaped the basement. Initially, Garfield had tried to recruit the younger MacKaye to replace him in SOA, but MacKaye didn't want to sing Garfield's words. Instead, he began working with SOA's guitarist and drummer, Mike Hampton and Ivor Hanson; they were joined by bassist Chris Bald, a Wilson dropout. He and MacKaye quickly found a creative connection, with Bald writing many of the lyrics MacKaye would sing.

Faith debuted in November at Woodlawn, and soon had a reputation for intense, confrontational performances. The quartet always opened its set with the rampaging "It's Time," which was built on a relentless bass line. The song's refrain expressed the adolescent rage characteristic of harDCore—"I know what I want and I take what I need/I'm gonna make this society bleed"—but the band's music also presaged the raw emotion and almost spiritual striving that would distinguish later Dischord bands.

Formed from several basement outfits, Deadline was comprised of singer Ray Hare, guitarist Chris Carron, bassist Terry Scanlon, and drummer Brendan Canty. Almost as important to the band's hijinks were their pals Guy Picciotto, Mike Fellows, and Chris Bald. One chaotic night, the group of friends jokingly named itself "DOD" for "Dance of Death." Although it was just one of many running jokes, DOD stuck. "It was one of those little things that has an esoteric non-meaning that just happens to mean everything," recalled Picciotto.

The DOD crew built a special bond with Faith and Deadline. The Dance of Death, which involved playfully crawling under the legs of humorless slamdancers, was performed at Faith shows. "Every fucking show they all shave their heads, they write DOD on their heads, they're berserk," marveled Ian MacKaye. "The last night Faith played, these kids put their jackets up around their heads and zipped them up tight. They just fucking ran out [onstage], couldn't see anything, fucking ran out smashing. At the UK Subs show, this kid did a back flip off the stage, smashed his fucking head, and knocked himself out. I picked him up and carried him outside. He was back on the floor in like two minutes!"

x x x

HarDCore's reputation grew as Dischord continued to release ferocious, committed music. By the end of the year, the label had issued seven singles (including one by Ohio's Necros that was a joint release with Touch and Go). Next up was a compilation album originally titled *Hardcore* but eventually released as *Flex Your Head*, a rebuttal of Robert Christgau's description of the DC punks as muscleheads. "I'm not too much into the whole 'hardcore' thing now," MacKaye noted at the time. "It becomes a selling point now, you see albums saying 'hardcore' on them and I'm not into that. I consider myself a punk but a punk on my own terms, nobody else's."

The album included songs by many bygone groups, including Teen Idles, Untouchables, Minor Threat, Youth Brigade, SOA, and Red C, but also offered evidence of the scene's continuing vitality with tracks by established bands like GI, Void, and Iron Cross as well as such new ones as Deadline and Artificial Peace. Similar compilations would soon document the hardcore scenes in Boston, San Francisco, Los Angeles, and New York.

If MacKaye and Nelson didn't always agree on Minor Threat's drug policy, they were allies in running Dischord. Nathan Strejcek began to feel that he was being ignored. After Strejcek left 100 copies of *Minor Disturbance* atop a hot motor in a van, thus making the Teen Idles single more of a collectors item than expected, MacKaye and Nelson began to make Dischord decisions on their own.

The gap widened when MacKaye and Nelson found a house to share in the Clarendon area of Arlington. It was ramshackle but cheap and close to a Metrorail station, and right across the street from a 7-Eleven. The house became Dischord headquarters, which put the label's operations even further from Strejcek. He became angry when he learned that Dischord had planned a GI release without consulting him, and angrier when he saw a Dischord ad mentioning a "possible EP by Youth Brigade." Stung that his own band's release was considered only a possibility, Strejcek titled the Youth Brigade record *Possible EP*.

Strejcek began to withdraw, not only from Dischord but from hardcore as well. When Youth Brigade broke up, Strejcek started a new group with his girlfriend, ex-Chalk Circle member Jan Pumphreys. But their planned band didn't appear, and Strejcek rarely returned to the scene. MacKaye and Nelson's world shifted to Dischord House, and hanging out in Georgetown became less important. The tight-knit teen-punk clan was beginning to grow up and apart. Soon the larger hardcore community would too, caught on the horns of its own contradictions.

I against I

"In the quest for the test
To fulfill an achievement
Everybody's only in it for themselves . . .
I don't want to have I go against I
It's the same old story
No factual glory
I against I against I against I"
—Bad Brains, "I Against I"

HR OF BAD BRAINS, NYC, EARLY 1982 *(photo ©Glen E. Friedman, reprinted with permission from the Burning Flags Press book,* Fuck You Heroes*)*

I against I

Ian MacKaye couldn't get the phone conversation out of his head. He had been talking to HR, now on Bad Brains' first US tour, when HR had brought up the subject of Minor Threat. "HR said, 'A lot of people are asking about you guys, you should get back together,'" MacKaye would recall later. "I said forget it. Then he said, 'You don't understand, you came on with this really strong message, a whole philosophy, then you left everyone hanging. You've left a lot unsaid.'"

Like Bad Brains, Minor Threat had been a band with a mission, at least for its lead singer. So he took it seriously when HR—who, for all their disagreements on specifics, had been one of MacKaye's main inspirations—said so strongly that he considered the band's purpose unfulfilled.

MacKaye had regrets of his own about Minor Threat's split. He had not left the band; Lyle Preslar had. And the effectiveness of the group as a vehicle for MacKaye's message was becoming clear as Skewbald spun its wheels. Both HR's remarks and the rave reviews that greeted the posthumous *In My Eyes* EP indicated that Minor Threat had spoken deeply to an audience far beyond Washington. The only course MacKaye could see was to press forward with his sputtering new project, yet he knew that Minor Threat's kind of chemistry would not easily be recaptured.

Preslar had also concluded that the band's breakup was a mistake. The most pragmatic and careerist of the four members, Preslar had left Minor Threat because it didn't appear to be going anywhere. Yet life at Northwestern University seemed just as fruitless. As it became clear that Minor Threat was developing a national audience, Preslar, in his own words, "dropped out of school with the express intent of re-forming Minor Threat."

The first person he approached was Brian Baker, who turned out to be just as dissatisfied with GI as Preslar was with Northwestern. Going from the preeminent harDCore band to a second-string one, Baker would later admit, had delivered an unexpected jolt to his ego.

John Stabb was simply not Baker's idea of a frontman. The singer had taken to wearing increasingly obnoxious clothes—"If it was irritating to the eye, I wore it!" he later bragged, poking fun at punk's increasing fashion-consciousness—and engaging in the antics that had earned him the nickname of "BoBo the Clown." Baker was embarrassed at a February 9:30 Club show with the Necros and the Misfits, when one of the latter asked him how he felt about playing behind Stabb, who that night was wearing a lime-green leisure suit. It was easy for Preslar to convince Baker of the wisdom of re-forming Minor Threat.

Preslar and Baker didn't expect Nelson to resist, but they were dubious about MacKaye. They didn't know he was also open to a reunion, albeit for reasons unlike those of the other members. When gingerly approached, MacKaye readily signed on. The band members would later repeatedly explain that Minor Threat—in Preslar's words—"broke up because I went away to college and we got back together because I came back from college, that's all, simple." But it really wasn't that simple. The motives of the different members were quite distinct, and over time the differences would become increasingly clear and troublesome.

Still, at first the reunion seemed uncomplicated. The band had, after all, been apart only from September 1981 to April 1982. It was merely a case of the musicians realizing an error and picking up where they had left off. The first priority was to get out and play, not just in DC, but across the country.

Baker was still only a high school junior, so he had to make arrangements with his parents and school. That accomplished, he sold his 1966 Mustang so the band could buy a van. They planned two local dates—one with Bad Brains at 9:30, the other a Malcolm Riviera–organized show at Wilson Center with harDCore allies Faith, Void, Artificial Peace, Iron Cross, and Double O—followed by a full US tour.

Minor Threat's decision had a major impact on the DC scene. When Preslar later said, "It wasn't a popular decision with my parents," MacKaye wryly noted that "it wasn't a popular decision with anybody."

Many younger fans were elated by the prospect of a resurrected Minor Threat, but dismayed, cynical mutterings were heard from harDCore veterans. Many apparently shared Chris Bald's judgment that "Minor Threat was a band that made more sense apart than together." It was well known that the musicians had frequently been at odds with each other. Some people who admired MacKaye's integrity nonetheless distrusted Baker and Preslar's motives. Others were simply envious of Minor Threat's stature.

There was nothing about that Wilson Center show that suggested that Minor Threat had lost its commitment to harDCore principles: Admission cost three dollars and there was no age limit and no bouncers. The band even played before Faith and Artificial Peace, hardly the sign of superstar egos. (The reason was that Ian MacKaye still worked at Georgetown Theater; he needed to go back and lock up for the night.)

Given Minor Threat's popularity, it wasn't surprising that many audience members left right after the band's set. Though it was not encouraged by the band, the exodus suggested to such observers as Sharon Cheslow—who wrote about the night in a new fanzine, *If This Goes On*—that Minor Threat had become just another entertainment option rather than part of a community that supported all its bands out of principle.

x x x

By this time, straight edge was no longer solely a DC phenomenon. It had reinforced the outlook of Nevada's Seven Seconds camp, and transformed the growing group of people centered around the Boston band Society System Decontrol, known more simply as SSD. The band's founder, Al Barile, was particularly influenced by the power of Bad Brains and a discussion with Henry Rollins. "He told me how united and tight the DC scene was. I realized Boston didn't have anything like that." Barile stopped drinking and took up the "X" and the all-ages crusade. SSD rapidly became the biggest East Coast hardcore band aside from Bad Brains and Minor Threat.

SSD's agenda, as expressed in the song "Ex Claim," could have been cribbed from an unwritten harDCore handbook: ruling the dance floor, hatred for New York, no barriers between performer and audience, all-ages shows, no drugs, scene unity, and a DIY ethic. Although Dischord remained adamant about releasing the music only of local bands, MacKaye and Nelson helped SSD put out *The Kids Will Have Their Say* on the new Ex Claim label—just as they had helped the Necros launch Touch and Go.

SSD's first visit to DC showed that some of harDCore's character had been lost in the translation. While Washington had its share of tough-guy posturing, the fans that accompanied SSD to Woodlawn High School took their slamdancing much more seriously than their DC counterparts.

The DOD crew was already part of DC folklore, and the Boston kids were apparently expecting to see an army of fierce rumblers. They were taken aback to discover that Picciotto, Fellows, and their friends, for all their abandon, were more nerds than bruisers, with a style that subverted the rituals of slamming. Their creative, more-fun-than-fury dancing starkly contrasted with that of the Boston crowd, who treated slamming as a contact sport combining tackle football and outright assault.

"The first time SSD came down with their boys," Alec MacKaye said, "they wanted to prove to DC that they were rough and tough. Nobody really danced or anything. These guys were all mad. So while the other bands were playing, there were two guys—they had long hair—who were kind of pogoing. So all the Boston guys got out there and did all this thrashing around. And then they hit the guy and the guy kinda hit them back. Then all of a sudden they all turned around and jumped on him—just jumped up and down on him and broke all his ribs. I couldn't believe it, it was the stupidest and sickest thing I ever saw."

Sab Grey, however, endorsed the Bostonians' savage style in his new fanzine, *Skin Flint*: "What's the matter with DC lately? No dancing, no band support, just sideline soap operas and complaining about the 'dancing being too rough' from the snotty brats who came in with punk over the summer. I'm not saying we should all be musclebound goons who fight everyone in sight but if you wish to 'prove your individuality' you must be prepared to fight for it!" As these words suggest, the Boston approach simply took the old DC credo—on display in New York City and Philadelphia the year before—one step further.

Ian MacKaye was also worried about the harDCore scene, but for different reasons. "I've seen Washington grow from the Teen Idles, Untouchables, and Henry—those nine people, that was it, that was our 'hardcore scene,'" he told *Forced Exposure* in March. "I don't believe in 'slamdancing.' I'm sorry, I hate that fucking word. I hate when people start a trend with it."

MacKaye was particularly annoyed that Boston record and comics store Newbury Comics—which he felt had brushed him off when he tried to sell it Teen Idles EPs just a year before—had suddenly jumped on the hardcore bandwagon by putting together its own compilation, *This is Boston, Not LA.*

"When suddenly people start putting out 'hardcore' compilations, realizing that the word 'hardcore' is so financially viable, then it's time to get the fuck away from those people," he said. "Why don't people just do it themselves? That's what Dischord is. Put it out, man, be proud of what you're doing, make it your project. That way, when it's not financially viable, it's still yours."

MacKaye was regularly asked to address the controversial "Out of Step," whose don't-drink-smoke-fuck message had been puckishly characterized as "monk rock." "Sex is a great, great thing," he said. "I am not anti-sex, I am anti-fucking, if you can understand the distinction. All this 'adolescent sexual discovery' crap is twisted. You watch TV shows, everyone's getting laid all the time, no one gets pregnant or VD. [Yet] when kids [have casual sex], they get burned. If people want to sit around and go, 'Oh, he's a fucking monk,' then they've got their own problems."

In one 60-second song, the avowedly anti-religion, anti-authority, antiestablishment punk had challenged the entirety of the hedonist mantra, "sex, drugs, and rock'n'roll." The outraged and often willfully distorted interpretations of the song suggested that people were threatened by MacKaye's critique. To him, that showed the accuracy of his aim.

x x x

Before going out on tour, Bad Brains had released their ROIR cassette. Finally, many of their best songs—most at least two years old—would be available, in raw recordings engineered by Jerry Williams at 171-A that captured the band at its best. Lest anyone miss the drift of the lyrics, the cover graphic showed a lightning bolt erupting from the heavens to shatter the US Capitol dome.

The cassette was—in the words of Dr. Know—"crucial music for crucial times" and would become ROIR's top seller, with almost 150,000 sold in its first 10 years. The cassette expanded the band's reputation nationally and even internationally. A flattering feature in British weekly *Sounds* called Bad Brains "one of the true miracles to have emerged from punk rock."

The article included apocalyptic pronouncements from HR and Darryl Jenifer. Alarmed by Reagan's hostile rhetoric and unprecedented arms build-up, the *Bulletin of Atomic Scientists* had shifted the hands on its Doomsday Clock to just four minutes to midnight, the moment that symbolized nuclear war. To Bad Brains, it was the Armageddon Time that the book of Revelation foretold. "We don't have time for joking, man, these are serious times," said HR. "The world could end at any time. It's a matter of consciousness, making sure that when the time does come you'll be prepared." Added Jenifer: "Our music is a reflection of the times. It's like sticking your hand in a microwave and out comes your hand, all charred."

True to their original PMA credo, however, Bad Brains still had hope to share. "Our music is a way of revealing the revolutionary," Dr. Know told *Sounds*. HR added that "money don't mean a thing to us—that don't make it. Who got the highest number on the charts—that doesn't make it no more. It's going to be rough and it's going to be hard and the one thing we don't have is money, but we've got unity. We're setting an example for the youth. The youths don't want to be part of [Babylon] and we don't want to be part of it. If we have to die fighting, we will."

Such words might seem grandiose, but Bad Brains had inspired hardcore bands all along the East Coast. And the band was hoping to further the cause of national punk unity with a double-LP compilation of bands like DC's Scream, Skewbald, Peer Pressure, and Double O; Chicago's Articles of Faith; and Florida's Crucial Truth.

The musicians took the tapes with them on tour, planning to complete the record in California, where they were also to work on some 171-A tapes intended for the second Bad Brains album. As the musicians hit the road, with Jerry Williams doing sound and a Rasta "I-tal" cook, they were at the height of their powers and certain of the absolute necessity of their mission. Tragically, their behavior on the tour would throw all that into doubt.

X X X

In *Sounds*, Tim Sommer had commended Bad Brains' "very active but unobtrusive religiousness [that] fuels every positive and visible thing that they do." Not every aspect of the band's spirituality, however, was positive.

While HR often spoke of being on the side of the poor and the oppressed—asking, "Who is more revolutionary than Jesus Christ?"—he had little affection for some outcasts. Like many religions based in the Old Testament/Hebrew Scriptures, Rastafarians viewed gay and lesbian sexuality as an "abomination." After moving to New York, old friends recall that HR and Earl Hudson would make remarks like "fire and brimstone, Babylon" when encountering gays on the street in Greenwich Village.

HR was not one to do things halfway. As with Positive Mental Attitude and punk before, he had seized Rasta with mighty fervor. Part of the singer's power was that he truly seemed to lose himself in his expression. This was riveting to behold—"HR is as close to a true shaman as punk has produced," Jello Biafra once said—but his intense drive and absolute belief could lead to fanaticism.

HR began to use the name Ras Hailu Gabriel Joseph I. Apparently convinced that he was a prophet with God-given powers, he tried to exorcise friends who had drug problems. He began to look for 12 wives in emulation of the Biblical King Solomon, and to view people like Jerry Williams—who, although white, had adopted Rasta ways—as his disciples.

HR told one interviewer that "capitalists try to instill fear into people, [but] we don't have to be afraid anymore, we've got Jah to protect us." When the journalist professed not to understand, HR said, "That's why I'm here to help you." Annoyed, the interviewer responded, "I don't think I need help." Replied HR: "That's why I'm here to help you."

That kind of messianic condescension was bound to rankle. HR's beliefs had nurtured his vision of spiritual growth, unity, and revolution, but such anecdotes suggest he was swinging out of balance.

When Bad Brains hit the road in March, there was no sign of the coming explosion. In San Francisco, the band played before more than a thousand people, their biggest headlining show yet.

In 1992, Biafra still spoke of that night with awe: "It was one of the best shows I've ever seen any band play. There was so much positive energy burning off the stage that some of the worst thugs in San Francisco—including Bob Noxious, infamous leader of the Fuck-Ups who sometimes wore a shirt with swastikas on the front and 'Niggers Beware' on the back—were actually dancing with their arm around a black person. They seemed to have the effect of easing a lot of the tension that had been building up in San Francisco. There was a serious racist thug element starting to grow in the scene and some of that really dissipated after the Bad Brains [played]. They had an incredible force to unite so many people."

That wasn't so clear after the show, when Williams took the band to stay with a friend who lived in the Castro, perhaps the world's best-known gay neighborhood. Flushed with Rasta fervor and a sense of triumph after the show, the band was outraged to encounter transvestites, male prostitutes, and men kissing other men in public. The band fled to another apartment in a different area.

The following day, the band was off to LA for its next gig and an interview with the popular punk fanzine *Flipside*. Asked how the band had liked San Francisco, HR announced that the city had "too many faggots. Mostly if they acted sensible it wouldn't be so bad. Most of them act so crazy even out in public, it disturbs me, makes me want to go and shoot one of them." This was a remarkable digression from Bad Brains' message of positivity and revolution. And it was just the beginning.

As Bad Brains toured California, they linked up with MDC (Millions of Dead Cops), a militant band that had recently moved from Texas to San Francisco. Partly because both bands were vegetarian, unusual in punk at the time, they hit it off and planned to tour back to the East Coast together. "They were the greatest band I had ever seen," MDC singer Dave Dictor recalled. "I fell in love."

Bad Brains didn't realize that Dictor was a cross-dresser who sang lyrics like "Cops don't like us fags and punks who don't conform." For MDC, it was obvious that gays and punks were fellow outcasts who should make common cause. Bad Brains, however, now took the Bible as the final authority on homosexuality and virtually everything else.

Ultimately, HR and Dictor had a tense encounter. "MDC came to us and wanted us to read their lyrics," HR remembered. "They kept saying how gays didn't have any say, that everybody was persecuting gays. I-mon sat down with [Dictor] and had a long talk about fornication and that homosexuality was Babylon. He said that I was hypocrite because I say I deal with unity but I don't want to unite with the faggots and it got real serious."

Without resolving the dispute, Bad Brains headed off for Texas, with MDC to follow. In Austin, Bad Brains were set to spend the night at the home of Big Boys' guitarist Tim Kerr. MDC called ahead to warn the gay-friendly Austin punk scene of Bad Brains' views, but the easygoing Kerr didn't worry.

The Bad Brains/Big Boys show went well, and Big Boys singer Randy "Biscuit" Turner even bought some pot for the visiting band. After the show, Biscuit and HR embraced warmly, Kerr recalled, "like two new friends." What happened during the embrace is a matter of dispute. HR has said that Biscuit made a pass at him. Other witnesses suggest that Biscuit made a remark that HR "interpreted" as a pass at him. According to Kerr, Biscuit simply made an innocuous remark indicating that he was gay.

"Immediately HR pulled back and said something like, 'But you're not gay, are you?'," Kerr remembered. When the puzzled Biscuit nodded, HR was shocked. "All I remember is HR spinning around screaming, 'Babylon bloodclot faggot!'" at Biscuit, Kerr said.

Kerr nonetheless let Bad Brains stay the night, heading off to work early the next morning. Several hours later, his wife called, hysterical. She was so upset that Kerr couldn't understand what she was saying, so he raced home. On his front lawn, he found members of MDC and Bad Brains, screaming at each other. After finally silencing the combatants, Kerr ordered MDC to leave. Bad Brains were about to depart anyway. Just before leaving, one of Bad Brains gave Kerr an envelope for Biscuit; Kerr assumed it was the money for the pot purchased the day before.

When Kerr returned home after work, he discovered a few things in his house were not right. A photo collage that happened to include a picture of the Pope—a hated symbol of Babylon to many Rastas—had disappeared. A punk poster that featured a male nude—something of a collector's item, since it had been banned by the city—had been permanently defaced with tape over certain parts of the man's anatomy.

Kerr had no proof that Bad Brains had done these things, but he had reason to suspect them. Then, when Biscuit opened the envelope left for him, he discovered that it contained no money. All that was inside was a pile of ashes and a note that read, "Burn in hell bloodclot faggot!"

As word of the incident spread, Bad Brains' reputation underwent a dramatic revision. MDC wrote "Pay to Come Along," a song that roasted Bad Brains' "Jah fascist doctrine": "People gave you homes and their love/You gave back hate from high above," Dictor sang. "You hide your eyes from the truth/Not to be free, but to be right."

There was disappointment as well as rage in these lyrics. "We'll never know what was lost," sang Dictor, who believed that Bad Brains "could have been the most important band." Biafra admitted his own "heartbreak when the homophobic side came out." For many former fans, Bad Brains' message of love and unity would never be credible again.

In an interview later that year, HR conceded that the band had left without paying for the pot they were given by Biscuit, but claimed they did so because the Big Boys "attacked us. They came at us spiritually. After that happened, I-mon felt that I didn't owe them no explanation for nothing. They were my enemies. They got their money though." (According to Kerr, the money didn't arrive until much later—and only after threats of additional bad publicity.) HR also denied that he had "called anybody faggots." Moments later, however, he termed the Big Boys "faggots" to justify not paying Biscuit.

It is important to note that none of the other band members spoke in public with HR's vehemence—or incoherence—about these issues. Interviewed years later, both Darryl Jenifer and Dr. Know expressed their discomfort with HR's rhetoric and actions.

It wasn't simply Bad Brains against Babylon; there were also divisions within the band. Williams sensed internal problems, although the musicians kept them private. At that time, he guessed that some band members had not agreed with HR's treatment of the Big Boys and MDC. Musical direction was also an issue, with HR again pushing for an all-reggae approach.

At an April show in Raleigh, North Carolina, Bad Brains played 12 minutes of punk and 75 minutes of reggae. "The youth need reggae," HR explained. "They don't have anyone showing them the true way." When asked about doing that through rock, HR responded, "I've done that already."

Days later, HR told *Forced Exposure* that Bad Brains were about to become an all-reggae band called Zion Train. This startled the interviewers, but not as much as it surprised the other band members. "All of us are together in it," HR claimed, but Jenifer and Dr. Know had not agreed. Stymied by the band's internal process, HR had decided to commit the group publicly to his preferred course of action.

"HR wanted Bad Brains to become HR and the Wailers," Jenifer said later. HR had in fact taken the band's proposed new name from a song on *Uprising*, the last studio album Marley recorded before his death the year before.

Something else was testing band solidarity: HR wanted his friend Ras Freba to be Zion Train's vocalist. Dr. Know didn't mind Freba's singing a number or two, but the guitarist didn't think Freba was qualified to be their frontman. As HR began to hang with Freba more and more, he drifted away from the band, neglecting his previous close relationship with Dr. Know.

Freba had been HR's friend for some time, and the singer's interest in reggae was longstanding. Why then did HR—in the midst of the band's first major tour—suddenly need to make such changes? Apparently the incidents in California and Texas had sparked his desire to exit the world of hardcore. "I guess the final decision was made [when] we went out to California and saw all the faggots and went to Texas," HR told *Forced Exposure*. "There the 'in-thing' was being gay and all the hardcore bands were gay. That was the last straw, I couldn't take no more. Somebody got to go out there and show the youth the truth."

The tour still held one more crisis. When Bad Brains arrived at the 9:30 Club for the show with the reunited Minor Threat, Williams called friends in New York to tell them he was about to return. He was horrified to learn that no rent had been paid on 171-A during the two months he'd been gone. The landlord had evicted Williams, and his recording equipment had been saved only because several friends had scrambled to rescue it.

Williams was furious. He had put up money for the tour himself, with the understanding that Bad Brains would pay his rent with the money they received from their shows. "We just didn't have the money, we needed what we had to get to the next gig," said Dr. Know later. Williams had lost both his home and his livelihood.

Williams had been a true believer, not a mere employee. When the band reached NYC, he collected his tapes—including the 171-A material planned for Bad Brains' second album and some of the tapes for the planned compilation—and walked out of their lives. It would be years before he resumed his friendship with the band.

In the course of the tour, Bad Brains had lost their soundman, their next album, their compilation, and much of their moral authority. Next they lost the equipment Mo Sussman had bought for them. While HR watched the show the following night at the Wilson Center, some kids looted Bad Brains' van. A fan leaving the hall sounded the alarm, and Ian MacKaye was one of those who ran out to see the culprits racing off.

The band had not one but two shows the next day, and now it had no equipment. When the musicians arrived late for the May 1st Yippie pro-pot parade in New York, another band had set up on the flatbed truck. The other group refused to let the late-comers commandeer its equipment for the event, so HR threw himself in front of the truck's wheels to prevent it from leaving. Then he jumped onto the vehicle and took over the microphone, denouncing the Yippies as the truck moved down the street.

The band rushed to Boston for its evening gig, again arriving late. They had to beg the opening act to use its equipment. Dr. Know was annoyed as SSD singer Springa kept trying to tell him that somebody important was backstage waiting to meet them. When he mentioned the man's name, it didn't click.

"Springa [was] saying, 'Man, Ric Ocasek is backstage,' and I'm, 'Who, what? I don't want to hear it, man.' I was like asking this other band who was opening if I could use not just his guitar but his pick and Earl was like, 'Yeah, can I use your drumsticks?' After I secured what it was I was supposed to play, I went back. Once I saw him, I finally realized who Springa was talking about."

Ocasek was the singer-songwriter of the Cars, the Boston band that had helped make new wave a top-ten commodity. Based on the ROIR cassette, he had become a huge Bad Brains fan. Learning that they had no equipment, Ocasek re-outfitted them and took them to record at his studio, Synchro-Sound. At the brink of self-destruction, Bad Brains had a new patron.

"It was like Cinderella or something," said Jenifer. "I didn't have a bass to play, so I had to play this other guy's stuff. After the show, Ric just came out and said, 'Do you need amps or whatever?' I was like, wow! We got our [new] manager at the same time too." Longtime scenemaker and activist Tony Countey was reluctant to take the job, but decided he couldn't refuse when Dr. Know "told me that my mission was to save Bad Brains—who I thought were the greatest band in the world—from breaking up."

x x x

As Bad Brains regrouped from its tumultuous tour, Minor Threat was on its way across America. In a sense, the two bands' trajectories had crossed: Bad Brains had peaked and Minor Threat was barreling past its former mentors. While Bad Brains' compilation album remained unfinished, Dischord's *Flex Your Head* sold its entire first pressing of 4000 in a week.

For MacKaye, any celebration was tempered by the fact that many people, including some close friends, were upset or at least ambivalent about Minor Threat's return. "We caught a lot of shit, people said we were selling out, that we'd get too popular, steal the shows, that we were just cashing in," MacKaye said. "They were all really threatened, which was really silly." Hearing the grumbling as lack of faith in him, MacKaye was hurt. At the 9:30 Club gig, he and the rest of the band had decided to defuse the tension with humor.

As the singer was carried onstage, the band tossed coins into the crowd, then launched into a tuneful new song called "Cashing in." MacKaye introduced himself in a show-bizzy voice, "Hi! I'm Ian—I don't think that we've met!" as Preslar screamed at the crowd, "We cashed in! We sold out! We cashed in!"

"It was our big *fuck you* to all the people who gave us shit when we got back together, telling us that we were cashing in on our popularity, that we were doing it for the money," said MacKaye. "That hurt the fuck out of me 'cause loving DC so much I just couldn't believe that it was DC that was doing it to me. The lyrics are as ridiculous as the idea that we were actually doing it for money."

The actual performance could easily have been overshadowed by the controversy and the band's mocking rebuke to its critics. But the chemistry was still there. Howard Wuelfing, now freelancing for the *Washington Post*, raved: "They raged, they soared, they conquered. In fact, the re-formed Minor Threat very nearly surpassed the grotesquely high expectations everybody held for them on this, their first public appearance since last year. The playing was consistently outstanding, a superlative display of disciplined high energy, the band was speedy yet precise, forcible yet expressive." He ended the review by asking, "Are Minor Threat the best punk band in the world? I don't know, I haven't seen them all. Maybe."

Minor Threat hit the road quickly after its two reintroductory DC shows, determined that this tour would be everything that the earlier one was supposed to be. Still, for the musicians to spend long periods in a cramped van was challenging. "We don't necessarily get along that great," MacKaye noted. "We'll practice for about two, three hours at a time and maybe 20-30 minutes will be actual playing, the rest of the time we'll be discussing, arguing, going off on each other."

As the tour wound through smaller cities like Reno, Lansing, Minneapolis, and Austin, they met kindred bands: Seven Seconds, Big Boys, Dicks, Hüsker Dü, Toxic Reasons, Articles of Faith, Crucifucks, and more. In those smaller scenes, the band found what Preslar described as "more [of a] sense of people together and doing something they like doing"—like DC and unlike such more established scenes as San Francisco's.

These bands were supported by a burgeoning array of fanzines, dances, music, and labels. These were the makings of a permanent underground that mavericks like MacKaye began to dream might challenge the monopoly of the hated corporate rock industry. "I think it's great," he said, "what is happening right now, this kind of local or regional music scene, as opposed to the nation-wide music we've been living with all these years."

MacKaye was energized by the big, enthusiastic crowds his band was attracting, but determined not to let prominence alter his personal code. His vision was that Minor Threat could "become a popular band without picking up the usual shit that most of the big bands get into. Where we stay a pure band, where we stay true to what we started out as."

The band came to embody an unofficial but clearly understood ethos: all-ages shows, low door prices, minimal PR, no rock'n'roll bullshit. After playing in front of over 1000 people in LA, MacKaye told *Flipside*, "Out here you hear 'record label' and 'getting signed.' You don't hear that in Washington. Bands just want to play. Out here it's a big market, people form bands with the intention to 'make it.' We formed Teen Idles out of boredom and formed Minor Threat as a vehicle to express what we were thinking about. If we have nothing to say, then I don't want to become 'popular.'"

It was a powerful, even revolutionary creed. Yet although MacKaye said "we," he was the only band member totally committed to it. Over time, the other members would grow tired of living with his sweeping idealistic statements.

Minor Threat also found that it was preceded by DC's tough reputation and the straight edge controversy. While MacKaye enjoyed the local tribal customs, he was not very excited about facing potential physical assault from kids who wanted to prove that their scene "ruled" or resented straight edge.

Onstage at the Tool and Die in San Francisco, MacKaye was jumped by Bob Noxious and a cohort. "Unfortunately, it's even gotten to point of gang warfare in some areas," he said after the brief incident. "Who rules what city and which bands are tougher. I felt people were challenging me because I was from DC, which had this apparently incredible reputation. I am talking basically in the fighting sense, who is tougher than who." To MacKaye, it seemed that there were more important battles.

The straight edge issue was almost always the first question asked in the many interviews Minor Threat did on the tour. "Everywhere we went," MacKaye said, "people wanted to fight me to prove I was wrong" about his opposition to drugs.

While the singer seemed to take some satisfaction from his ability to so threaten people with a simple idea, he and the band also repeatedly tried to emphasize that straight edge was not a monastic canon but a commonsensical idea of personal responsibility. "We don't pull any of this 'if you drink you suck, if you take drugs you suck,'" said Preslar. "It's the idea that if you want something, you're not going to allow yourself to be distracted, to be fucked up with a lot of bullshit."

Straight edge "is not just not taking drugs or not drinking," echoed Baker. "It's an outlook on life. In the sense that you want to be in control of your body and yourself, you want to have a clear view of what's going on. We will never, never tell you what to do."

In San Francisco, the band was interviewed by a new fanzine that would ultimately be nearly as hotly debated as straight edge itself. *Maximum RockNRoll* had evolved from the radio show of the same name. The publication became controversial for its outspokenly left-wing orientation.

The magazine's founders, Tim Yohannon and Jeff Bale, were aging counterculturists who sought to force the implicit politics of punk to the surface, into a more conscious, systematic, and active opposition to Reaganism and American society at large. Their first step had been to release a heavily political hardcore compilation called *Not so Quiet on the Western Front*.

In its way, *MRR* was not far from the revolutionary fervor of Bad Brains or MDC. Unlike in the '60s, however, there was no unifying youth-culture cause like Vietnam and the draft. Even the threat of nuclear war seemed vague and distant compared to bodies of friends coming home in boxes as in the '60s. While impressed by the passion and openness of Yohannon, Bale, and the rest of the *MRR* crew, a skeptical Jeff Nelson said, "They want a movement like in the '60s but it's just not there." Such attitudes, combined with the divisions created by incidents like those on the Bad Brains' tour, made it seem unlikely that hardcore punks would ever expand their fight beyond their narrow subculture.

x x x

For all the controversy about straight edge and the band's internal bickering, MacKaye returned to DC full of excitement over what he had seen. While Bad Brains had been mortally wounded by their tour experience, Minor Threat had upheld its lofty reputation. The musicians made "a relationship with this band more than just 'fan' and 'band,'" wrote Al Flipside. "They themselves are living examples of what they talk about in their songs."

Minor Threat carried Washington's banner as well as its own. "We're really proud that in Washington, DC, which is not an entertainment town, not a music or a club town of any sort, we put together a band and got records out and financed it all," said Preslar. "What you hear about DC is true, very few fights, people being positive. Being in DC has its advantages. Because it isn't an entertainment town, we don't have the exploitation that goes on out here."

"We are proud to be a part of a scene that has a big reputation that is true," agreed MacKaye.

"Washington was giving me a bad feeling so we wanted to tour as soon as possible. Now I can't wait to get back."

Shortly after his return, however, MacKaye read an interview with a new Bethesda band, Hate From Ignorance, in *If This Goes On*. He found the words of guitarist Kevin Mattson: "I think going out and touring the world isn't very sincere. I don't think touring the world makes you a punk band." Bass player Eugene Bogan and singer Clark Chapin dismissed Minor Threat even more directly.

Then MacKaye found Cheslow's review of the Wilson Center show, which extolled Faith but questioned Minor Threat's very legitimacy. After writing that the band seemed "stale" and "bored," she asked, "What about Ian's statements not five months ago that it's good to start a new band with new songs so that you remain underground? Playing old songs just to please an audience and using the name Minor Threat to attract an instant audience seems far away from Ian's original attitudes."

MacKaye was stunned. He felt as betrayed as Cheslow had when her band, Chalk Circle, had been rejected by the harDCore crowd. "It was just a slap in the face," he said later. "I was really hurt by all that crap."

Underlying MacKaye and Cheslow's hurt was an idealism forged in the intimate camaraderie of the once-tiny DC teen-punk scene. As Cheslow noted in an interview with MacKaye for the next issue of *If This Goes On*, the dispute "all came about due to misunderstanding and lack of communication . . . I was so disillusioned, I thought, 'How could Ian be doing this?'"

Cheslow apologized, but the flap showed how harDCore had changed. The scene had once been a tight-knit group of friends—a family even—but now it was much, much larger, and as a result, increasingly fragmented. Communication wasn't as direct, cliques were more hardened, relations were more impersonal. It was an ironic but painful turnabout from two years before. To many new fans who didn't know MacKaye, Nelson, and their circle personally, Minor Threat and Dischord now constituted the punk establishment.

Top to bottom, this page: 1. ALEC MACKAYE'S HANDS, ON DISCHORD #1 *(by Susie Josephson)*, 2. DC SPACE

Clockwise from top left, opposite page: 1. HENRY GARFIELD AND WENDEL BLOW OF SOA, WILSON CENTER, APRIL 4, 1981 *(by Susie Josephson)*, 2. TEEN IDLES AUDIENCE AT HARD ART GALLERY, LATE 1979, INCLUDING ANN APTAKER, EDD JACOBS, PAUL CLEARY, BERT QUEIROZ, MARK SULLIVAN, KARI WINTER *(by Lucian Perkins)*, 3. TEEN IDLES AT PSYCHEDELLY, APRIL 1980 *(by Jem Cohen)*, 4. BETSY SALKIND, DANNY INGRAM, AND NATHAN STREJCEK AT HB WOODLAWN HIGH SCHOOL, FEBRUARY 14, 1981 *(by Lloyd Wolf)*, 5. ALEC MACKAYE, EDDIE JANNEY, AND BERT QUEIROZ OF THE UNTOUCHABLES, MADAMS ORGAN, MARCH 1980 *(by Mark Jenkins)*

XXX

HARDCORE

WILSON CENTER 6/25
15th & Irving St. NW, WASHINGTON DC *Doors Open 7:00 p*

GOVERNMENT ISSUE • From Boston **GANG GREE**
FAITH • **ARTIFICIAL PEACE** • **SCREAM** • **DEADLIN**

SPRING THRASH
WILSON CENTER
18th and Irving street NW
Friday April 30th
doors open at 8:00 pm

MINOR THREAT
FAITH
ARTIFICIAL PEACE
IRON CROSS
VOID
DOUBLE-O

DC
DC
DC
DC
DC
DC
DC
HARDCOR
HARDCOR
DC
DC

Clockwise from top left, opposite page: 1. CROWD OUTSIDE MINOR THREAT/YOUTH BRIGADE/GI 9:30 CLUB SHOW, JULY 16, 1981; BACK: MIKE HAMPTON, BRIAN BAKER, MANOLO LAGDAMEO, IVOR HANSON, BRENDAN CANTY; MIDDLE: TESCO VEE, BARRY HENSLER, COREY RUSK, KEVIN FARRELL, TODD SWALLA; FRONT: TONI YOUNG, CHRIS BRAY, VIVIEN GREENE *(by Lucian Perkins)*, 2. WILSON CENTER XXX FLIER, JUNE 25, 1982 *(by Bob Raiter)*, 3.WILSON CENTER HARDCORE FLIER, APRIL 30, 1982 *(by Bob Raiter)*, 4. CHRIS BALD, IVOR HANSON, ALEC MACKAYE, AND MIKE HAMPTON OF FAITH AT CHANCERY, 1982 *(by Malcom Riviera)*, 5. FRANZ STAHL, KENT STAX, SKEETER THOMPSON, AND PETE STAHL OF SCREAM, 1980 *(by Mimi Baumann)*

Clockwise from top left, this page: 1. HR AND DARRYL JENIFER OF BAD BRAINS ON TOUR *(by Malcolm Riviera)*, 2. MARC ALBERSTADT, TOM LYLE, MITCH

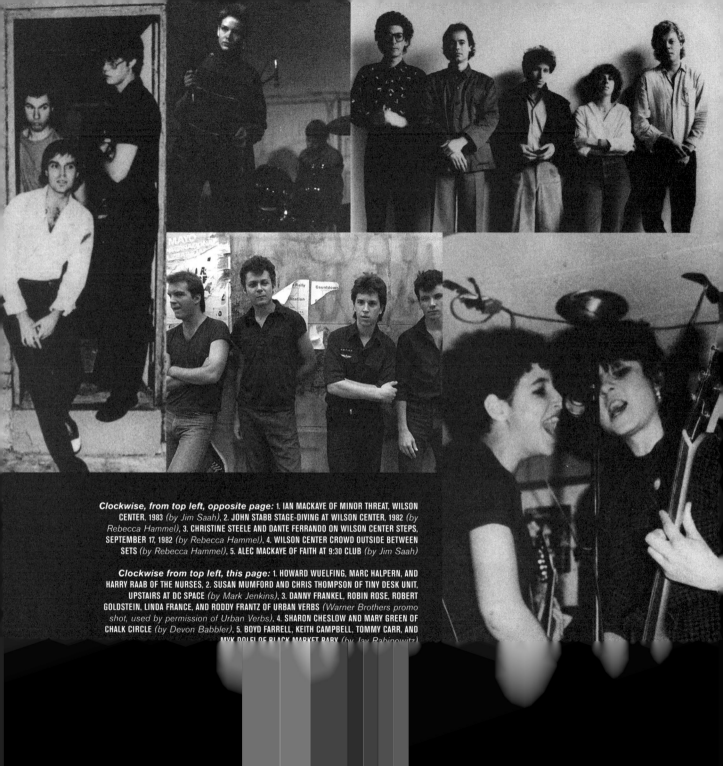

Clockwise, from top left, opposite page: 1. IAN MACKAYE OF MINOR THREAT, WILSON CENTER, 1983 *(by Jim Saah)*, 2. JOHN STABB STAGE-DIVING AT WILSON CENTER, 1982 *(by Rebecca Hammel)*, 3. CHRISTINE STEELE AND DANTE FERRANDO ON WILSON CENTER STEPS, SEPTEMBER 17, 1982 *(by Rebecca Hammel)*, 4. WILSON CENTER CROWD OUTSIDE BETWEEN SETS *(by Rebecca Hammel)*, 5. ALEC MACKAYE OF FAITH AT 9:30 CLUB *(by Jim Saah)*

Clockwise from top left, this page: 1. HOWARD WUELFING, MARC HALPERN, AND HARRY RAAB OF THE NURSES, 2. SUSAN MUMFORD AND CHRIS THOMPSON OF TINY DESK UNIT, UPSTAIRS AT DC SPACE *(by Mark Jenkins)*, 3. DANNY FRANKEL, ROBIN ROSE, ROBERT GOLDSTEIN, LINDA FRANCE, AND RODDY FRANTZ OF URBAN VERBS *(Warner Brothers promo shot, used by permission of Urban Verbs)*, 4. SHARON CHESLOW AND MARY GREEN OF CHALK CIRCLE *(by Devon Babbler)*, 5. BOYD FARRELL, KEITH CAMPBELL, TOMMY CARR, AND MYK DOLEL OF BLACK MARKET BABY *(by Jay Rabinowitz)*

"I thought I left it behind
In another fucking time
Where boys were boys, girls were girls
And faces were hard to find . . .
All the stupid thinking
Stupid people thought
The rules that we lived by
The friends that we bought . . .
I thought I'd outrun it
When I crossed the tracks
I thought I had gotten away
When it tapped me on my back
IT FOLLOWED ME . . ."
—Minor Threat, "It Follows," 1982

it follows

John Stabb was not overjoyed by Minor Threat's reunion. It meant that Government Issue had lost its second guitarist in six months. In addition, the band was sure to be overshadowed by Minor Threat's return.

Still, Stabb was simultaneously relieved by Brian Baker's departure. He felt the young guitarist had been trying to control the band, even offering Stabb money to stop dressing so obnoxiously. The singer worked to get GI back in action as soon as possible. Tom Lyle shifted—reluctantly—back into the guitar slot he had filled in his previous band, while his friend Mitch Parker was recruited to play bass.

Before Baker left, the band had recorded an EP, *Make an Effort*, that included the anthem "Teenager in a Box." The song showed that GI was leaving behind its previous themes and musical style. The new tunes, while still fast, had more structure and melody—the result at least in part of Baker's influence. "The DC scene at first was 'play as fast as you can, make the songs as short as possible,'" said Lyle. "Now we're kind of evolving away from that."

Stabb's model had shifted from Jello Biafra to Henry Rollins. His new songs, he explained, were about "personal politics. I don't write about El Salvador or things like that. More on a gut level in the vein of Black Flag and bands like that. Music is an intense therapy session for me." Yet, he added, "I try to put a real positive mental attitude in and put in humor and intenseness. We're not too punk rock to smile."

It wasn't clear who was going to release *Make an Effort*, since Dischord was busy with other projects. The second pressing of *Flex Your Head* was on the way, and there were also plans for a Faith/Void LP, a split-label (Dischord and Skinflint) Iron Cross EP, and eventually new Minor Threat material. Moreover, when Ian MacKaye and Jeff Nelson were on the road, Dischord's operations ground to a halt.

While Minor Threat continued to tour, the new GI headlined a June 25th show at Wilson Center with Artificial Peace, Scream, Faith, Deadline, and Boston's Gang Green. The show's poster featured the latest emblem of harDCore: the stars-and-bars design of the DC flag—derived from George Washington's family crest—with its three stars replaced by X's.

A new band from the DOD ranks had asked promoter Malcolm Riviera to play, but was told the bill was full. So at the end of Deadline's set, Chris Bald jumped into Brendan Canty's drum seat, Guy Picciotto grabbed the guitar, and Mike Fellows the bass. Riviera, who was filming the show with a new video camera, was briefly puzzled, but then put down the camera and evicted the unbilled group.

When GI took the stage, Stabb was in fine form, racing across the stage, singing with the exaggerated mannerisms that became his trademark. One punk got up with a specially prepared T-shirt: a black cow assembled from Black Flag's logo, with the slogan "beef edge." He led the crowd in a boisterous chant of "beef edge, beef edge, beef edge!"

Such playfulness had been characteristic of harDCore, but was threatened as the scene become larger and less cohesive, diluted in part by new fans who were more interested in slam-pit action than community. In the past, the intensity of slamdancing had been tempered by camaraderie. As the crowds grew, though, it became difficult for the core group to police the activities of troublemakers; harDCore's self-protection mechanisms were being overwhelmed.

In the crowd at the next Wilson Center show were *Washington Tribune* writer Alan Keenan and photographer Rebecca Hammel, reporting on the proceedings for a cover story on the DC scene. The opening of the article—which featured a photo of John Stabb diving into the crowd—confirmed what careful observers already knew: "Washington, a city often scorned as bereft of indigenous culture and identity, has a nationally known music scene. Among cognoscenti, this scene is widely admired for its innovation and spirit and is increasingly emulated. It is recognized as having achieved a trend-setting cultural position rare for a movement based in DC."

Although Keenan noted that "the movement is little known and less understood in the city it champions," ironically, the scene's popularity was now becoming an internal issue. William Dagher, who played guitar for both Law and Order and the Bollocks, spoke for many of the scene's veterans: "I hate the new punks," he said. "The new punks are old jocks trying to be as macho as anything." By 1982, he noted, punk had become "an establishment. It consists of conformists conforming to a nonconformist movement."

In this increasingly divided community, the lightning rods were the most prominent surviving institutions: Minor Threat and Dischord. In the North Carolina fanzine *Southern Lifestyle*, a Norfolk band called Frontline accused Minor Threat of taking Dischord profits that rightfully belonged to other bands to subsidize its touring. Actually, MacKaye and Nelson had borrowed money to underwrite the tour, and Dischord had no profits: It was nearly $5000 in debt.

Lara "Lynch" Connolly, a member of the noisily experimental band Nuclear Crayons, used the same fanzine to announce that she was starting a new DC label, Outside Records. "We're aiming to get local bands that Dischord won't take," she wrote. "The Georgetowners seem to think that their bands are the only ones worth recording."

In fact, Dischord never intended to be the city's only punk label. As their aid to Touch and Go, Skinflint, and Ex Claim showed, they encouraged others to do it themselves, just as Limp had once done for Dischord. "We don't deny other bands because they're arty or poppy or whatever," MacKaye protested. "We say, 'OK, you got your thing, do it for you.' We did it for us—we're a hardcore label."

He also noted that "not one member of Teen Idles or Minor Threat has ever made a cent off the bands. On tour, we use the money to live on and that's it. All the money from our records goes to Dischord."

Another sign of anti-Dischord backlash was "bent edge," a term coined by DC punk old-timer Micro. This anti-movement was headquartered at Flipper House, the home of two recent arrivals to DC, Don Diego and Linda LeSabre. The place was named in honor of the San Francisco band Flipper, which was notorious for its drug use and noisy dirges.

To MacKaye, this development was painful, because "there were always plenty of kids who didn't adhere to all the straight edge rules, but who were totally part of the family," including close friends like Mark Sullivan. As straight edge became a movement, however, there were many who did not approach the idea with such tolerance, thus adding fuel to the "bent edge" fire.

Diego and LeSabre formed the Joy Division–influenced Wurm Baby (later known as Grand Mal) with Malcolm Riviera and Joey Aronstamn and became notorious for drug-sodden parties. Tombstones stolen in midnight raids on graveyards decorated their house. Early Georgetown punk inspiration Black Market Baby, whose members certainly weren't straight edge, became a bent edge favorite.

Wurm Baby was one of a new crop of bands that were bored with the loud-fast-short mode, including Nuclear Crayons and the other groups that would be associated with Outside, Chalk Circle, United Mutation, and Hate From Ignorance. The most outspoken anti-harDCore band was No Trend, which was strongly influenced by Public Image Limited and Flipper. Although the band wrote such scabrous songs as the ironically titled "Teen Love," the key to the No Trend experience was its confrontational stage behavior. In addition to mainstream society, the group targeted harDCore itself: "We used to be into hardcore," Chris No Trend said at the time. "But it evolved in just another teen youth subculture with an even stricter system of social status."

x x x

Of all the bands associated with Dischord, Iron Cross was the most controversial. While on tour, MacKaye and Nelson were asked to explain their connection to the band, and the former did not offer a ringing defense. "They claim not to be racist or Nazis," he told *Maximum RockNRoll*, but "a couple of people in that band are extremely ignorant. They literally beat up gay people for no reason. I think that there are some people with mental problems in that band."

Iron Cross frontman Sab Grey insisted he was not a bigot, but his ill-considered remarks to *Touch and Go* were followed by a racist cartoon in the first issue of his fanzine *Skinflint* and several controversial songs on the Iron Cross EP, *Skinhead Glory*. The title song boasted, "You don't know how it feels/To put the boot in!," while "Psycho Skin" tells the story of a skinhead who kills a gay man and is sentenced to jail.

Written by Wendel Blow, "Psycho Skin" was in fact semi-autobiographical. When MacKaye had referred to attacks on gay men, at least one of those he had been talking about was Blow. It could be argued that the song—with its repeated cry of "this day will be the last"—was actually a gay-basher's tortured self-critique, but the lyrics were ambiguous. Grey ultimately refused to sing the song, and would later say he had never wanted the song on the EP, but it was—and Iron Cross would have to bear the burden of its inclusion.

Homophobia had always been present to some degree in DC punk, as in society at large. Still, it had never been expressed violently—except by threatened outsiders against punks. In fact, there probably was greater tolerance for homosexuality within the punk scene than in most arenas of American culture.

However, as the scene's founders withdrew from Georgetown's streets, they left a certain vacuum of leadership. Wendel Blow was one of those who felt this acutely. While Blow was a troubled teen who had already had run-ins with parents, school, and other authority figures before punk, his involvement in SOA had given his life a tenuous center. When he found out—on the way to Philadelphia—that the Starlite show was to be the band's last, Blow felt shocked and betrayed by Rollins. The singer, who was five years older than Blow, had become something of a role model to him.

The violence that erupted that night, and Blow's perception of Rollins's disdainful reaction, made the split all the more bitter. Blow recalled years later that on that night "our Pied Piper led us into a trap . . . I'll never forget getting hit in the back of the head by a blackjack helping a friend back toward the Starlite, and then hearing that Henry had come out and looked at his friends getting hurt, just shook his head in dislike, and walked back inside . . . Henry turned his back on us like we were some kind of disease."

Blow later acknowledged that "we all were very young and had our own inner battles to fight," insisting that "I don't blame Henry, Black Flag was definitely the hotter ticket." But the bitterness was real, as was his subsequent lack of direction. "After SOA broke up, I was real confused and hurt," Blow said. "The real problem was lack of communication between this supposed family of friends."

Hanging out in Georgetown was becoming a separate subculture of the DC punk scene, and one way to create that alternative "family." One of the new punk subgroups called itself "Rat Patrol," after the TV series about World War II in North Africa. This crew included most of the "DC Skins" Grey had helped form during his now-repudiated skinhead phase, including Blow and Iron Cross bandmate Dante Ferrando. They would hang out and drink, squatting in an abandoned factory near the Potomac River.

For Ferrando, as for the others, the Rat Patrol brought a new sense of power. As Blow recalled, "We used to have to walk in packs just to keep people from messing with us . . . Fighting came with the territory. The whole thing behind Rat Patrol was to incorporate a sense of support to those who might need it." This made immediate sense to Ferrando who, since he was small in stature, had often been the victim of harassment and violent attacks by non-punks. Now he had allies, and could—and did—retaliate.

The next step, however, was worrisome. "We started out fighting just in self-defense," Ferrando recalled a decade later. "Then as time went on, we seemed to realize that we could go on the offensive. Now we had the strength to fuck with people. And so we did." Driven by an intense distaste for homosexuality learned initially from the mainstream world, this violence began, in part, to focus on gay males who frequented nearby Dupont Circle.

Ferrando's misgivings culminated one night when he went with Blow and fellow Rat Patroller JC to P Street Beach, a forested park between Georgetown and Dupont Circle that gay men visited for anonymous trysts. As Ferrando watched, JC and Blow attacked an unsuspecting man with a baseball bat. Later Ferrando—whose father owned and operated the restaurant Food for Thought, a '60s holdover that was now a gay and lesbian stronghold—would say "that is when I knew my days in the Rat Patrol were over."

To horrified older Georgetown punks, such actions suggested the disintegration of the once-precious Georgetown hang. Blow and JC were subsequently arrested for one of their assaults, with Blow getting probation and JC—who was black and already had a police record—doing prison time. (The disparity in sentences led to some bitterness and suspicion of racist favoritism.) Blow later acknowledged that "I've done some pretty ugly things in my life that I'm not proud of," and both he and JC repudiated their past homophobia. But at the time, their arrests did not end some DC punks' enthusiasm for gay-bashing.

Among the Iron Cross fans who had begun to hang out in Georgetown was a stocky young woman named Kendall Hall; like JC, she was black, yet attracted to a crowd that emulated an often racist British movement. While she was first known for her cartooning skill, under the nickname Lefty, she would later become notorious.

x x x

In the fall of 1982, Minor Threat was laying low. In part, this was because the band was adapting to a new lineup. Eager to switch to guitar, Baker recruited an acquaintance, Steve Hansgen, to play bass. Then he had to sell the change to MacKaye, who was always skeptical of shifts that might upset a band's delicate chemistry. "We did it mostly because Brian was unhappy playing bass," MacKaye said later, adding drily that "if we had continued with Brian on bass, we obviously would not have been too happy."

Working a new member into the band took some time, but that wasn't the only reason Minor Threat was seldom performing. Although the band's popularity continued to grow, the chorus of criticism that had greeted the group on its return from its tour had left MacKaye confused and demoralized. "DC is the hardest city for us to play," he would say later. For MacKaye, harDCore had been "us against the world." What to do, then, when harDCore seemed to have become "us and the world against Minor Threat"?

One of the new lineup's first shows was filmed for a documentary, *Another State of Mind*. The film's most exciting moment captured the newly augmented Minor Threat at a Baltimore concert with MDC, Agnostic Front, and the Bollocks. As Minor Threat played, a careless stage-diver broke a microphone. The nervous sound company retaliated by quickly removing all the mics from the stage, leaving the band with only its amps. Undeterred, it launched into "Minor Threat." With MacKaye dancing wildly and screaming without a microphone, the crowd became a punk chorus, singing along with him, word for word.

Something similar happened two weeks later at the University of Maryland ballroom, where Minor Threat played with GI and the Velvet Monkeys. After MacKaye ordered the bouncers to let people come onstage, there was an incredible crush on the two-foot high stage. When the sound company rebelled, the encore turned into a confrontation between the singer and a mic-stand-wielding technician. Once again forsaking microphones for communal mass-howl, MacKaye sang the set-closing "In My Eyes" together with the crowd, all directing their voices at the unrepentant soundman.

It was the spirit of these incidents that MacKaye feared losing. In an effort to boost the scene, he became the Washington correspondent for *Maximum RockNRoll*. In his first report, he noted that "DC has lots of bands, lots of kids, and lots of spirit, but nowhere to play. The only club, 9:30, may do one or two shows a month. They don't feel that they can deal with the amount of people and aggression the shows bring."

Even as he wrote this, MacKaye was working with Dody Bowers to institute hardcore matinees at the 9:30 Club. The Sunday afternoon shows, played while no alcohol was served, soon gave harDCore a regular venue besides the Wilson Center.

On Halloween 1982, Minor Threat returned to the University of Maryland. This time, they played the larger Ritchie Coliseum, opening for Public Image Limited before almost 2000 people. It was an odd but instructive pairing. The new group fronted by former Sex Pistol John Lydon was artistically venturesome but as remote from the audience as any art-rock band. Minor Threat was more focused and potent than PiL—whose original lineup was already unraveling—and more connected to the crowd. PiL was interesting; Minor Threat was triumphant.

Backstage, however, the show seemed less successful. MacKaye was rankled by mutterings that Minor Threat had been paid extravagantly for the gig; in fact, the band had agreed to play solely for the exposure—and some food and Cokes. "When we got there it was shitty [store-brand] soda and the deli-plate had been eaten by the security men," MacKaye recalled. "I put my foot down and made them bring us a case of Coca-Cola and two pizzas!"

xxx

Dischord bands had been splitting and re-forming at their usual pace. When Dischord released *Flex Your Head's* third pressing in late 1982, Nelson noted on the lyric insert that "since the release of *Flex Your Head* in March both Deadline and Artificial Peace have broken up, which leaves Minor Threat, Iron Cross, Government Issue, and Void as the only surviving bands on this record." He added, however, that "lots of new bands have formed and a whole new generation of kids have been coming to shows."

Void lasted long enough to release its first record—a split LP with Faith—before its November farewell gig at Wilson Center. After the show, the band reconsidered and decided to carry on, pleasing fanzines like a new one from Seattle. "*Void* is one of the most intense records I've ever heard," wrote *Sub Pop's* Bruce Pavitt, who was later to help transform the 'zine into an influential label.

Void featured Bubba Dupree's chaotic, Greg Ginn–influenced guitar and singer John Weiffenbach's frenzied performances held together by the rhythm section of Chris Stover and Sean Finnegan. The band offered the customary critique of mainstream hypocrisy—"We all live their lies/No one asks them why," declared "Ask Them Why"—but did it with such conviction and fury that they soon earned a small but devoted posse of followers across the United States.

Among most listeners who knew the bands only from the record they shared, Void overshadowed Faith. But in DC, Faith was assuming a position second only to Minor Threat, largely because of the band's intense performances. Mike Hampton was a hard-edged yet increasingly melodic guitarist, Chris Bald was a vehement live performer, and Alec MacKaye seemed to embody utter conviction. The band's fanatical following included Malcolm Riviera, who booked Faith at virtually every Wilson Center show. A decade later, a friend of Riviera's named Thurston Moore (by then ringleader of New York's Sonic Youth) would still list Faith as one of the five most amazing live bands he ever saw.

Closely allied to Faith was the unruly band of DOD insurrectionists who had briefly seized the stage at the June Wilson Center show, as well as at numerous house shows around the DC area. When Deadline broke up, Canty and Scanlon formed Insurrection with Picciotto and Fellows, drawing their inspiration from the early work of the UK's Discharge. Instead of knocking themselves unconscious with their frenzied dancing—as Picciotto had done more than once, hitting his head on the ceiling—the DOD boys grabbed guitars and went wild. "They jumped around so much," one observer noted, "sometimes they forgot to play!" When the musicians' only attempt at seriously recording their songs didn't satisfy them, they held a ceremony and burned the tapes.

A similarly exuberant spirit animated the tiny but active scene that developed at Bethesda Chevy-Chase High School in nearby Maryland. Teenagers Colin Sears and Geoff Turner and scene veteran Sharon Cheslow established a small cassette label, WGNS, a name that commented on the sad state of alternative radio in post-WGTB DC: It stood for "We Gots No Station." Cassettes were simply the most accessible medium for underground DIY groups, but with their diverse music and clever inserts and drawings, WGNS tapes had a special creativity and flair.

Together with other Bethesda punks like Alec Bourgeois, Charles Bennington, Roger Marbury, and Alex Mahoney, Sears, Turner, and Cheslow would form one-off bands with names like Fungus of Terror, Bozo Brigade, or Gang of Intellectuals. The bands would come into existence, play a party or two, record in Turner's bedroom studio, and then disappear—only to re-emerge as another oddball entity with an equally unlikely name a few weeks later.

The Bethesda crowd was known for smart and playful music, but it was also influenced by such British leftist post-punk groups as Crass, Poison Girls, and Zounds—all generally overlooked by harDCore regulars, who favored the rougher, "street-oriented" style of UK Subs, Blitz, and the Exploited. The result was an explicitly radical political consciousness, exemplified by the fanzine *If This Goes On*, the band Hate From Ignorance, and its guitarist Kevin Mattson.

The original Hate From Ignorance split after just a few gigs, but the band quickly regrouped with a new singer, Monica Richards. Mattson was frustrated by what he saw as the conformist, apolitical nature of harDCore, as well as its often monochromatic music. Songs like "Oliver Was a Good Soldier" attempted to add political content to DC punk while challenging its accepted form. The band never attracted a large audience, but Mattson was to ultimately play an important role in the DC scene as an activist.

Hate From Ignorance was not the period's only explicitly political DC punk band. The once-maligned Scream had devised a powerful mix of rock, reggae, and hardcore, energized by '60s idealism and the passion of singer Pete Stahl. The quartet's debut record, *Still Screaming*, was the first album from a single band in Dischord history. It showed the legacy of Bad Brains, especially in songs like "We're Fed Up," Scream's response to its initial lack of local acceptance: "We're from the basement/From underground/We'll break all barriers with our sound/We're sick and tired of fucking rejection/But we're not down, we got a direction."

Another striking new band, Marginal Man, was founded because members of Artificial Peace, according to guitarist Pete Murray, "had gotten tired of [bassist] Rob Moss and so we broke up the band and quietly but quickly re-formed it without him under a new name." The remaining members—Murray, Steve Polcari, and Mike Manos—recruited new bassist Andre Lee and second guitarist Kenny Inouye who had played drums in the initial version of Hate From Ignorance. The band took its name from a term Inouye had encountered in a college sociology class, while adapting its two-guitar sound from melodic British punks like the Buzzcocks.

Some Marginal Man songs addressed political issues, including the American class system ("Missing Rungs") and Reagan's MX-missile plan ("Pandora's Box"), but in tunes like "Friend" the band discussed more tender feelings than rage or pain. "We're trying to say something that's pertinent and interesting that everyone can relate to do, something where people will say, 'Hey, I've felt that way before,' something other than the '1-2-3-4, I hate Reagan' style that had its day," explained Lee at the time.

As Marginal Man developed, Faith added Eddie Janney as its second guitarist—principally because he didn't have a band. Aside from his short, unrewarding stint with Skewbald, Janney had been out of action since the Untouchables broke up nearly two years before. Now Minor Threat, Marginal Man, and Faith all had two guitarists.

The three bands demonstrated their two-guitar power at a January 1983 9:30 Club gig. It was one of the first hardcore matinees, and so many people came that a second show had to be added. There were lots of younger fans in the audience, and some veterans were unhappy. "Most of the new people were morons," said one longtimer. "I heard at least five people explaining their theories on how to stage-dive and a few more asking their friends why they weren't slamming."

x x x

For MacKaye, the influx of slam-crazy dilettantes inspired songs like "It Follows." The message, he said at the time, was that "here I am punk rock and we're all so fucking happy to be different from this [mainstream] crap and now I turn around and the shit we ran from is right with us." This realization haunted all the songs for the third Minor Threat EP, *Out of Step*.

MacKaye's confusion began to coalesce into lyrics that alternated between defiance and self-examination: "Everybody's right/Everything I've done is wrong, wrong, wrong/You know I tried to keep it short/I know it took too fucking long/Too much has been said/You think it fucked my head?/THINK AGAIN." By the time Minor Threat went into the studio in January 1983, MacKaye had finished the words to "It Follows," "Think Again," "Betray," and "Look Back and Laugh." They were the expression of his anguish and disillusionment with the scene that had nurtured him—his harDCore blues.

While he pondered the future of DC punk, MacKaye also wondered about his relationship with Nelson. Their visions were beginning to diverge, as Nelson argued that Dischord should be more businesslike. "We sell our records too cheaply for there to be a lot of money," Nelson noted at the time, which meant that projects were put hold while Dischord waited for money from distributors to finance the next release. For MacKaye, however, keeping prices as low as possible was crucial to his ethic.

Discussing "Betray," MacKaye joked that "all my songs are about Jeff," only to turn serious the next moment: "My songs usually come out of pure anger. Jeff and I have been together for so long. I don't change much, I'm pretty much the same fucker [I was] and it's hard for me to handle change [in Nelson]. But when I start writing songs about Jeff, by the time I get through my song is about everybody." The changes in Nelson's attitude just personified what MacKaye saw happening in the scene; punks were not only betraying each other, but punk was betraying itself.

In late 1982, the most obvious dispute was not over business practices but about the song "Out of Step." Nelson wanted to re-record it with some sort of spoken or written explanation to clarify any misunderstandings. MacKaye agreed, but he took exception to Nelson's idea of adding an "I" in front of the "don't drink/don't smoke/don't fuck" mantra; he felt that the "I" was already implicit. The argument grew so heated that MacKaye kicked a hole in Nelson's bedroom door, but Nelson ultimately prevailed. The lyrics of the new version had become "I don't smoke/I don't drink/I don't fuck," the "I" clearly enunciated. Moreover, where Preslar's guitar solo had been in the previous version, MacKaye now impatiently intoned a public service announcement that further clarified the song's intent.

Ironically, the struggle between Nelson and MacKaye about precisely what to say raged till the band was actually in the studio working on the song. As Nelson and MacKaye fought over what the spoken part should say, Don Zientara surreptitiously recorded the argument. The rap that ultimately appeared on the EP came from this recording.

The most powerful of *Out of Step's* nine songs was not even credited on the record's label or sleeve. It was the throwaway "Cashing In," written as a joke for Minor Threat's first post-reunion show. Despite its origins, it was a well-crafted song; its energy, tunefulness, and sardonic edge provided an ideal conclusion to a disheartened yet still committed LP. Earlier Minor Threat material had mostly attacked the outside world, but these songs located the enemy within, the "little friend" at the rotting core of the scene that had put DC on the map. MacKaye did not exclude himself from his own critique: "Every song on the record, I consider myself to be on both sides of the coin," he said. "It goes both ways."

x x x

As Minor Threat recorded the songs that expressed MacKaye's frustrations, *Flipside's* reader's poll voted the group "band of the year" and MacKaye the year's best vocalist. The best gig of 1982 was Minor Threat's show with Dead Kennedys at the Barn in LA. Dischord was the best label, and *Flex Your Head* ranked third among the year's albums. All this acclaim was especially striking because *Flipside's* readership was primarily in LA.

Two other bands with DC links made the best-band list: Black Flag was number three and Bad

Brains number five. The full story of the latter's year, however, was reflected in another ranking: number three on the "Asshole of the Year" list, two spots behind Ronald Reagan.

Once a source of inspiration, Bad Brains had become the enemy to many. "They're really talented musicians and their message on the surface is real cool—the idea of Positive Mental Attitude—but they don't live up to it," said Dave MDC in an interview published in the first issue of *Maximum RockNRoll*. A letter published in *Flipside* was harsher: "The Bad Brains are religious fascists," wrote Johnny Rat.

Even the quartet's former friends and admirers began to lampoon HR's Rasta fundamentalism. Minor Threat started playing a reggaefied version of the GI song "Asshole" that poked fun at both John Stabb and Bad Brains. When MDC played at Club 2+2, the successor to the now-defunct A7, the opening act was a joke band called Lucifer's Imperial Heretical Knights of Schism, a reference to Rasta's idea of the gap between Jah's laws and the ways of Babylon. Composed of members of Beastie Boys and Reagan Youth, the group facetiously read from a pamphlet called "What is Rastafari?" over improvised musical backup.

Earl Hudson took the bait. During a break in the set, he stepped to the mic, warned that "we must all be held responsible for our actions," and declared the set finished. After the Knights opened the mic for discussion, members of the Bad Brains contingent pelted them with eggs.

Next up was a band pointedly named Blood Clot, featuring former Bad Brains soundman Jerry Williams on guitar. Introducing an anti-Rasta song called "Fire Burn," Williams announced that "September is Death of Hardcore Month here at 2+2." Needless to say, this only added more fuel to the fire. Heated discussions between the two factions continued inside and outside the club, stopping just short of violence.

It was now open season on Bad Brains. The band was accused not only of homophobia—a charge that at least had the salutary effect of raising the consciousness of gay rights in the hardcore scene—but of anti-white racism, a groundless allegation. The damage to the group's reputation became clear when the band toured again at the end of 1982. In Richmond, Virginia, an audience member repeatedly yelled "bloodclot faggot," until Hudson abandoned his drums to challenge the heckler and then refused to play any more. In San Francisco, site of a triumphant show on the previous tour, Biafra recognized that "there was a real dark cloud over them. You could tell that they felt it."

"It's rough," HR said at tour's end. "We've been together now five years. I thought it'd get easier but it's the opposite. It's harder to do your job because everyone is against you. Everywhere we went we were faced with the rumors ordeal. People are saying we sold out—but they don't know us."

Manager Tony Countey, who had booked the US tour, also managed to keep the band sufficiently focused to finish the Ocasek sessions, which yielded a Bad Brains Records EP, *I and I Survive*. He then negotiated a deal with Jem, an indie label that had begun as an import distributor, to release more Ocasek-produced material as the band's first full-length LP, *Rock for Light*.

Despite the upcoming release of a Bad Brains album, HR continued to publicize the band under the name Zion Train. He ambushed Jenifer and Dr. Know again by telling *Southern Lifestyle* that only contractual obligations had kept Bad Brains playing under that name, and that Zion Train would commence on January 1st.

Pressing ahead amidst the chaos, Countey booked a European tour, where the band played before large crowds in offbeat venues like a chocolate factory, a slaughter house, and a bomb shelter. Already alienated from the American hardcore scene, HR was horrified by the spitting, drunken, and often violent European version of punk.

When the band returned, *Rock for Light* had been released to great acclaim. Ocasek hailed Bad Brains on the Grammy Awards and hired Jenifer to do session work on his new solo album. The band remained controversial within the hardcore scene, but corporate-rock decision-makers were getting curious. According to Countey, Elektra Records proposed a multi-million-dollar deal.

This was a dilemma for a band that publicly disdained the music industry. "They're just middlemen, they don't do nothing so [it's best to] avoid them completely," Jenifer told *New York Rocker*. "They can 'Knack' you, but that's false. What we're saying has to be felt as the truth, not just 'Oh I've heard that song on the radio so much I must like it.'"

"We got something better than money," HR had said in early 1982. "We've been trying our best to keep what we have, which is the right to play what we want to play. [We] set an example for other people—you can be independent and survive. You don't have to sign the contract to make it."

Now, after more than a year of struggle and vilification, some of the band members were not quite so eager to reject a major-label offer. They allowed Countey to arrange a meeting with Elektra A&R man (i.e., talent scout) Tom Zutaut.

HR, however, was not interested. Disillusioned by the punk audience and increasingly drawn to Rasta, he no longer really wanted to be in Bad Brains or play punk music. He certainly did not intend to sign a contract that would obligate him to the band, once again forestalling his dream of Zion Train.

HR again resorted to guerrilla tactics. By this time, Jenifer said, "it was like anything to do with Bad Brains was bad, it was like HR was trying to sabotage Bad Brains." When Zutaut arrived, the bassist recalled incredulously, "HR met him at the door and brought him back to see us. He walked up to me and introduced Zutaut: 'Darryl, this is Satan. Satan, meet Darryl.'"

The introduction undermined both Bad Brains' chances with Elektra and HR's relationship with Jenifer and Dr. Know. The singer then sealed the deal's—and the band's—fate by abruptly returning to DC with Hudson. For the bassist and guitarist, the hasty departure was a betrayal of both their friendship and Bad Brains.

As Bad Brains went down, more dark clouds were gathering on the horizon of Reagan's America. Had the band been in a state to do so, they may well have played a memorial concert with Beastie Boys, Reagan Youth, and others for Patrick Mack, former lead singer of the Stimulators, one of their old allies. A less-than-sympathetic NYC fanzine reported that Mack had died from "some fag disease."

The mysterious new disease had a name: Acquired Immune Deficiency Syndrome, or AIDS. By the time Ronald Reagan cared enough to speak out about the epidemic—four years later, after Rock Hudson's death—nearly 40,000 human beings would be dead or dying from the disease in the US alone.

x x x

With *Out of Step* finished, Minor Threat planned its second full US tour. In late February, shortly before going on the road, the band played another Wilson Center show, this time with Social Suicide, GI, and ENB. ("ENB" stood for "Eric's New Band," the successor to Eric Lagdameo's Bad

Brains–inspired Double O. The new group included Red C compatriot Toni Young on bass and flashy newcomers Pete Moffet and Stuart Casson on drums and guitar respectively. The quartet later became known as Dove.) Spoofing their detractors, Minor Threat went onstage in Vegas-style gold lamé jackets that Amy Pickering and Cynthia Connolly had bought on a whim at a nearby thrift store.

Two weeks later, Minor Threat hit the road. With 31 dates in 49 days, this tour was twice as long as the previous year's. It was tough at first; exhaustion plagued the musicians as they crossed the South doing small shows. The band had played barely more than six gigs in the last eight months and was suddenly playing virtually every night. "At the beginning of the tour it was weird because it almost started to feel like an act," MacKaye said during the tour. "It didn't feel right. But by the time we got to Texas, things were really rolling. I just loved playing so much that the more I sang the songs the more I learned about the songs. [Now] I feel more sincere, I think about it even more than I did in the beginning."

The band members were unhappy with the first copies of *Out of Step*. It had a thin, uneven mix, and a printing blunder had left the back entirely black. Still, the record sold all 3500 copies in a single week, and was garnering rave reviews. MacKaye was pleased by comments like one in DC fanzine *Truly Needy*, which wrote that "Minor Threat are still true to us and themselves."

Having the LP available was important for the singer; he wanted audiences to know the new songs so they could sing along. The communal nature of Minor Threat gigs was vital, with dozens of audience members taking turns on the mic as MacKaye played master of ceremonies. At the first shows in the South, MacKaye recalled, "I had to sing every word of every song!" He was uncomfortable that the record's first pressing was flawed, but "the idea was to get it out before the tour. Thank God we did, because it really helped. The beginning of the tour was a real drag but by the time we got out west, people knew some of our songs."

The band members were losing their patience with the ritualized, self-centered slamdancing and stage-diving they encountered, which made it difficult simply to play the songs. MacKaye still supported the idea of minimizing the distance between band and fan, but even he admitted that slamming and diving seemed to detract from, rather than add to, the communal spirit. The worst night was in LA, with CH3, Aggression, and Suicidal Tendencies in front of 1500 people. When someone got stabbed outside—an incident apparently unrelated to the show—the LAPD closed down the gig in the middle of Minor Threat's set.

The musicians were also unimpressed by most of the groups they encountered while touring. "We saw eighty bands and with a very few exceptions, I never want to see any of them again," said Lyle Preslar. MacKaye was a little gentler, but admitted that "we ran into a lot of 'echoes.'"

One band, however, did affect MacKaye: MDC, which now stood for "Multi-Death Corporations" (instead of "Millions of Dead Cops"). Minor Threat's initial dialogue with MDC had come on the previous tour when the two bands met for the first time and—as Minor Threat roadie Seth Martin recalled—"we opened up the door to our van and a bunch of McDonald's wrappers fell out!" As committed vegetarians and foes of corporate fast-food giants, the members of MDC began a vigorous discussion.

This time, MacKaye ran into Dave Dictor in a bookstore where the latter was perusing a book on Guatemala, site of a CIA-sponsored coup in 1954. MacKaye was impressed. The difference between MDC and most hardcore bands, he said, "is that MDC are knowledgeable about what they're saying, they're not just a bunch of fucking kids getting onstage and shouting 'Fuck Reagan.' These guys check into it. I have great respect for that."

MacKaye had known other vegetarians—HR and Rollins were both veggies at the time—but hearing Dictor explain the connection between meat-eating here and starvation elsewhere had an impact: "I know when we talk with MDC, they definitely leave an impression on me," MacKaye said. "I certainly don't take everything they say 100 percent because I don't allow myself to take anything anyone says 100 percent, but I'll tell you one thing—when I hang out with these guys, I feel guilty about going to McDonald's."

Increasingly, MacKaye would deny being political while expressing interest in many political issues, from American intervention in Nicaragua to animal rights and environmental activism. He also began to understand how his personal message fit with the political one of bands like MDC. As he told *Maximum RockNRoll*, "What it all boils down to is that I choose to speak about one thing and [Dave] about another. When we were in San Francisco, we got into this whole multi-death corporation thing and what is happening [with US policy] in Latin America which I agree is a very fucked up thing. But also four blocks away or downstairs, there are 13-year-old kids shooting speed. While I may be ignoring what's happening in Latin America, it's sort of vice versa for MDC. I like to see it as the two of us kind of being a full novel, filling the whole picture."

MacKaye's politics emphasized issues closest at hand, and one topic very close to any male touring band is sex on the road. Even within the underground scene, there was a substantial amount of groupie action. Unlike Black Flag, however, Minor Threat was what MacKaye described as "anti-scam." To him, this was part of the ethic he had described in "Out of Step." It was enough of a departure from customary rock-band behavior to lead to rumors that the members of Minor Threat were gay.

Not everyone in the band was as strict as MacKaye, but he was a formidable example. "Girls would totally come on to Ian because of 'I don't fuck' and he would turn them down," Brian Baker recalled. "It seemed like a challenge to them." Later, Preslar said that Baker and he "were scared [of girls]. We were very young at the time and Ian's influence had a lot of impact on us."

Perhaps the musicians' greatest challenge, however, was simply keeping themselves on speaking terms. "When you go on tour with Minor Threat you sit in the van of hell," MacKaye said at the time. "We just had the stupidest fucking arguments. We'd argue about the color of the stripes on the road. And Jeff Nelson is Mr. Arguer. Red is blue to him no matter what!"

MacKaye's outspokenness led to resentment, and Baker would sometimes bait him with bratty remarks while the band was being interviewed. Their relationship blew up in Vancouver, where Baker contracted tonsillitis. He didn't want to play, but since the show was a big one and the band had never played Vancouver, MacKaye was adamant about not canceling. Finally, Baker went to a hospital. When he got a medical opinion that supported him, he screamed at MacKaye, "You were wrong, you fucker!" The band cancelled the gig and rode in silence to the next one.

Adding to the tension was the fact that the new bass player, Steve Hansgen, was not working out. Steve was "always on the outside," Preslar later noted. "It was getting to be a four-plus-one situation and conflicts with the one were causing conflicts with the four. I think the pressure was really high on Steve and he just couldn't handle it." In addition, Baker seemed less focused on guitar than he had been initially, making it hard for Preslar, who described himself as "the unofficial 'musical leader,'" to direct the songs.

When the band returned to DC, MacKaye told Baker to fix the problem. Baker broke the news to Hansgen, and returned to bass. Hansgen soon joined former Untouchables Bert Queiroz and Rich Moore in Second Wind. The name promised a revived energy for harDCore, but the band was never able to overcome the perception that it was "Minor Threat Jr."

Hansgen's role wasn't the biggest issue facing Minor Threat on its return. Dischord was growing larger, and people were beginning to buy Dischord records solely due to the label's reputation. To Nelson and MacKaye, this was a big responsibility, and one they could not ignore. Massive backorders had piled up for *Out of Step* while they were gone, leaving recent recruit Amy Pickering to run the office.

(On her first day of work, Pickering tore down a goofy sign Eddie Janney had put on the front door of Dischord House: "No Skirts Allowed." This was just one artifact of a harDCore scene that still seemed all too much like a boys' club. Another example was the DOD slogan, "SAG," which stood for "'Stroy All Girls." A chant of "Girls Are Poop" even rose at one 1982 Wilson Center show—a spectacle bitterly attacked by Lara Lynch in Barbara Anne Rice's fanzine *Truly Needy*. While all of these slurs were surely as facetious as their progenitors later claimed, the underlying attitudes they suggest clearly had an effect. Of the 16 bands who played four separate harDCore blow-outs at the Wilson Center in 1982, not one had a female member. As Alan Keenan noted at the time in his otherwise flattering cover story on harDCore in the *Washington Tribune,* "the scene's extreme masculinity is disturbing . . . [and] offers a stark contrast to other forms of new wave which in the last few years has given women far more and varied roles than any previous form of popular music." Sadly, this male dominance has been reflected in virtually all hardcore scenes.)

The partners devised a special certificate that they sent to everyone who had been waiting for the record, thanking the fans for their patience. Because of those loyal buyers, Nelson and MacKaye faced another big step: making Dischord a tax-paying business.

"We could easily say 'fuck the government,'" said Nelson at the time, "but that's irresponsible to all the bands who have supported us, all the people who have put out records and never got paid—they put all the money back into the label. I'd say it'd be pretty bad money management if we folded. We'll have to pay taxes. Trying to recreate the financial history of Dischord is going to be very hard but it occurred to us that we'd get busted this year and we better do something about it."

Previously, the Minor Threat band members had all worked when not on the road—Preslar as a waiter at a French restaurant, Baker at a lawyer's office, Nelson at a 7-Eleven, and MacKaye at the Georgetown Theater and Häagen-Dazs. Now the latter two found that Dischord had become a full-time job. Dischord didn't pay Nelson and MacKaye salaries, but it did begin to pay their rent. This irked Baker and Preslar; Minor Threat was responsible for the bulk of Dischord's sales, yet they weren't seeing any money.

XXX

The 9:30 Club matinees continued, but with variable attendance. With more shows, each one seemed less special and fewer people came to all, supporting certain bands but not the scene in general. Riviera and other promoters continued to put on shows at Wilson Center. Another fairly stable venue, Space Two Arcade, opened in mid-1983. One of the first shows there was GI with the Circle Jerks.

GI had finally released its *Make an Effort* EP as well as a whole LP of other material called *Boycott Stabb*. The records were released by a new label, Fountain of Youth, but Dischord was willing to lend its logo—"which helped sales," according to GI's Tom Lyle. In documenting the music of the prolific DC scene, Fountain of Youth joined Dischord and Outside, whose compilation, *Mixed Nuts Don't Crack*, included Chalk Circle, Nuclear Crayons, Hate From Ignorance, Media Disease, United Mutation, and Social Suicide.

Another new venue was the Lansburgh Cultural Center, a former department store in downtown Washington that was owned by the city government and subsequently redeveloped as an apartment building. When Dead Kennedys, Scream, Void, and No Trend played there, more than 1000 people turned out despite what was then a high ticket price: eight dollars.

Observing was Charles M. Young, who was researching a *Playboy* article on hardcore. He watched as DC fire inspector T.R. Gardner tried to shut down the show during Void's set, accusing promoter Steve Blush of not having the right permits. Blush went onstage to tell the crowd that the concert was over; the crowd began to boo angrily and then spontaneously sat down on the floor and started chanting, demanding a show or a refund. The fire marshal refused to back down, instead calling the police. As the crowd began to sing songs like "I've Been Working on the Railroad" and "God Bless America," the Dead Kennedys' Jello Biafra was asked to try to convince the audience to end its sit-down strike.

Outside, there was a line of police cars and some arrest vans and ambulances; inside, MacKaye warned Biafra not to jeopardize punk-police relations, which weren't nearly so adversarial in Washington as in California. Biafra later recounted being "caught between a rock and a hard place, DC cops on one side and Ian on the other, saying, 'Don't you dare cause a riot in my town, don't you dare fuck up my town!'"

Returning to the stage, Biafra encouraged the fans to continue their nonviolent sit-down, while entertaining them with a cappella versions of Dead Kennedys' songs—including "Let's Lynch the Landlord," which to some in the crowd became "Let's Lynch the Fire Marshal"—as negotiations continued.

"The DC punks seem to instinctively know to sit on the floor and save the threat of violence for a last resort," Young wrote in *Playboy*. "They are, nonetheless, very close to the last resort. The faces of the dozen or so cops [inside the hall] change from horrified fascination with the female punk aesthetic to barely concealed fear that their precinct is about to be trashed. Gardner locks himself in a side room. 'This is a test,' Biafra tells the crowd between blasts of feedback from a bass amp the band had managed to get working. 'We can't lose our tempers or they'll make it impossible for us at other shows.'"

The building manager announced that a compromise was possible. Young detailed: "The crowd cheers and Biafra takes the mic back to lead them in another rousing a capella until negotiations are complete. 'If you've come to fight, get out of here,' 1000 punks sing as one. 'You ain't no better than the bouncers/We ain't trying to be police/When you ape the cops, it ain't anarchy/Nazi punks/Nazi punks/Nazi punks—fuck off!'" Ultimately, the Dead Kennedys were allowed to play for 40 minutes. Disaster had been averted by flexible, united action, a testament to the power punks could wield if they agreed on an objective.

The possibility of directing such moments into a genuine political force led to a national "Rock Against Reagan" tour that brought Dead Kennedys back to town a month later. With them were MDC, the Dicks, Crucifucks, and DRI. This adaptation of Britain's "Rock Against Racism" campaign was conceived by New York City's Yippie chapter. Not being fans of the Yippies, some of the original Georgetown punks stayed away. However, many younger fans came; one was a junior high school student from suburban Virginia named Dave Grohl.

Grohl's first punk connection was a cousin who lived in Illinois. "She had hundreds of singles by bands on their own labels and I just couldn't believe it, that there was this amazing underground network," Grohl remembered. "I fell in love with it." After accompanying his cousin to a couple of Chicago shows, Grohl started writing songs. "I had a guitar and I had learned my basic three chords," he said, but "after hearing punk rock I suddenly realized, you don't have to be Eddie Van Halen to be in a band. You can pick up a guitar and learn three chords and write a song."

Back in DC, Grohl searched for the local scene, which brought him to his first DC show, the Rock Against Reagan gig. "I went pretty much for the reason that the Dead Kennedys were playing and at the time they were one of my favorite bands. I remember Biafra staring up at the Washington Monument and calling it the 'Great Eternal Klansman with the two blinking red eyes.' There were police helicopters all over the place and buses filled up with riot police. As a 13-year-old kid, that was like my own little revolution."

The power of Washington punk solidarity expressed itself differently when the Damned came to town with Anti-Nowhere League, and Minor Threat was offered the opening slot. After the PiL show, the band members had some misgivings about performing with another popular British punk band, but the chance to play with the Damned—long one of their favorite bands—was irresistible.

In his *Washington Post* review, Howard Wuelfing wrote that "it'll probably be a while before the Damned show their faces in DC again. On their first visit, they were upstaged by the Bad Brains. Last night at the Ontario Theater, they were decisively outmatched by Minor Threat." The real contest, however, was on the dance floor.

The crowd, as usual, had been all over the stage during Minor Threat's set, and the barely controlled communal chaos had unsettled the Damned. The British musicians insisted that bouncers be onstage to protect them during their set. At first, the security crew simply pushed people off the stage. But then, Jeff Nelson said, "they started trying to drag kids back to teach them a lesson. A more militant faction of the punk rockers decided to take things into their own hands." Among the militants was Ian MacKaye.

The kids managed to pull one of the security guys into the crowd, which precipitated a sudden invasion by all the bouncers. "Some bottles got thrown and then a [bouncer] pulled out a lead pipe and was swinging it at us," said MacKaye. Ultimately, a larger confrontation was averted and the bouncers did not return to the stage.

"It was just total chaos and the Damned and [the promoter] chose to ignore it for the longest time," Preslar recalled. "I think basically the whole thing could have been averted if the Damned had been concerned enough to say, 'Hey, we don't want anyone onstage,'" said MacKaye. "People here love the Damned, fanatically love them. To have the Damned not acknowledge the audience at all was obnoxious."

MacKaye found something else about the show offensive: a ticket price of $13, including the Ticketron fee. In fact, the planned charge had been 50 cents higher, and MacKaye had negotiated a decrease. The only way he could do so, however, was by reducing his own band's pay from $1000 to $500. MacKaye considered the gesture important, but Nelson called it "silly" and the rest of the band agreed. Preslar was especially outraged. The extra money could have paid to repair old equipment or bought new stuff. The incident left Preslar convinced that he needed more say in Minor Threat's business affairs.

The Damned show also highlighted Preslar, Baker, and Nelson's growing irritation with fans swarming the stage. They became visibly angry at several points, and Baker later complained to *Truly Needy* that "it doesn't really register with their mind that they are preventing the music." Even MacKaye allowed that "I don't mind having tons of people onstage really, but to me there's no more stupid waste of time than when some guy runs up and skanks into Lyle's tuning and we have to spend the next five minutes tuning again."

Despite concerns that the scene was being overrun by heedless youngsters, Minor Threat continued to insist on playing only all-ages shows. In New York, one promoter lied to them, and the band arrived and was horrified to discover the show was for ages 18 and over. They refused to play unless it was all-ages, and the promoter yielded. "I'm not so proud about the fact that we have huge shows and we're getting bigger and bigger," said MacKaye at the time. "I'm so fucking proud that we've had an impact on people. The other good thing is being able to swing our weight around with clubs" on issues like all-ages shows.

x x x

Once back in Washington, HR returned to setting up shows at the Wilson Center, usually with a mix of local and New York bands. One of the first of these gigs featured a new band called Madhouse that included original Georgetown punk Danny Ingram on drums and singer Monica Richards, who had left Hate From Ignorance. Rejecting "loud, fast rules," Madhouse played a moodier style derived largely from British goth-punk.

In an interview with the *Washington City Paper*, Richards called the local punk scene "a big joke now. Fashion models spike their hair. Five years ago I was dressing like this and my parents were saying I looked like a prostitute. Friends at school, who are now dressing the same, were calling me a dyke."

Fashion was one conspicuous sign of disaffection among the scene's founders. Clothing had played a crucial role in defining the group against the outside world—first UK-style garb, then the LA boots and bandannas, shaved heads, and kilts and boots for girls. "It looked great for a while, then everybody said, 'Fuck it, it's too much of a hassle,'" MacKaye explained. "I had to lace up boots and for me to tie a bandanna around my foot was a pain in the ass because I could never get them off!" The reasons for abandoning the look weren't simply practical, however: "All of a sudden there were stupid motherfuckers fighting for stupid reasons and we didn't want to be associated with them."

Punk couture had also turned conformist and commercial. In Georgetown, boutiques like Commander Salamander were selling punk fashion to kids who couldn't or wouldn't create their own style. John Stabb loved to taunt the new punks by dressing as a hippie, while MacKaye turned to a functional style based on a small wardrobe of secondhand-store clothes. This potentially defied consumer society more so than early punk fashions.

It also made punk a lot less shocking or even recognizable to outsiders. Now only MacKaye's shaved head served as a visual cue of his punk status. The ability to blend into mainstream society began to suit other older punks like Nelson—but for a different reason. Once one of the most outrageous dressers in the teen-punk scene, Nelson had begun to view this previous orientation as an immature attempt to gain attention. Nelson had not deserted his values, but for him punk now seemed merely a phase that he was willing, even eager, to leave behind.

This difference was probably the true source of the growing split between Nelson and MacKaye. For MacKaye and an apparently dwindling number of other true believers, punk was about independent thought and not about easily definable styles of dress, music, or dance. This stance, however, was being lost. As older punks began to drop the clothes, they seemed to be losing the commitment—while the younger ones picked up only the apparel, not the ideas.

A new Faith song, "Slow Down," captured the community's ebbing spirit: "Inspiration's thin these days/With everyone going their separate ways/All of sudden it's hard to find the song/And still you act as if nothing's wrong." The band itself was also flagging. Under pressure from his parents, drummer Ivor Hanson had decided to attend Vassar, and Mike Hampton and Chris Bald were not getting along. Hampton had begun to play with former SOA drummer Simon Jacobsen, experimenting with a more tuneful style—an interest that irritated Bald.

The band that, for many, had come to represent the soul of harDCore played its final show in August 1983. Witnesses to the Space Two Arcade performance said it was a shattering celebration and a funeral all in one. "I had never seen a band so intense, so into it," said Cheslow. "It was like, 'OK, we're going to give it all we got, band and audience, because it was the last time it was going to happen.'"

After the show, MacKaye wrote the words to a new song: "Goodbye to you my friend/What you had to offer will not be seen around here again." He entitled it "Last Song." Though Minor Threat later practiced the song's music, the singer didn't share the words with the band. He felt alone, even within his own band.

Again a crisp four-piece, Minor Threat played a triumphant gig (despite their simmering internal disputes) at the 9:30 Club that was filmed for a never-finished documentary. (The footage, taped by Mitch Parker and friends, later became the Minor Threat live video released by Dischord.) Then the band did a short tour of the Northeast, including a stop in their old nemesis city, New York.

In the audience at New York's Gildersleeves was John Loder, who ran Southern Studios, a home recording studio in England that had worked closely with Crass. Dischord was interested in having Southern distribute *Out of Step* in Europe. Loder thought Minor Threat was "quite rock'n'roll," Nelson remembered, but he was interested in working with Dischord. It was to prove a crucial connection.

Also present was Tom Carson, a once and future Washingtonian who had savaged the Urban Verbs' debut in *Rolling Stone*. The Minor Threat show was the "most galvanic and inspiring hardcore set I've seen," he wrote in the *Village Voice*. Carson was one of the first writers to portray MacKaye in clearly spiritual terms: "Because its reason for being isn't taste or even sensibility but first and foremost no-way-out spiritual need, it's less music as religion than religion as music. Ian MacKaye respects hardcore liturgy because he believes in its necessity. Like his West Coast counterpart, Jello Biafra, he's not just the frontman for his band but the organizer and main spokesperson for a whole community and he's committed to his flock above all."

Back in DC, Minor Threat's rehearsals became debates over the band's direction. Preslar and Baker were taken by the sound of U2's *War* album, and to MacKaye their new compositions showed that influence. He wasn't sure how to sing to the new music, and was uncomfortable that Minor Threat might align with an already distinct and more mainstream sound.

The other band members didn't see it that way. While they acknowledged the influences MacKaye sensed, they felt that the new elements were assimilated in a way that retained the band's sound and spirit. They wanted Minor Threat to continue to grow musically, but they also hoped the band could be their livelihood—a not unreasonable idea, given its popularity. They didn't object to making the music more accessible.

The result was stalemate. MacKaye was uncomfortable with the band's new direction, and for him that feeling was enough. All he had was his instinct, and to ignore it would be false. He began to skip practices.

With this conflict unresolved, Minor Threat played what would be its last show: September 23, 1983 at the Lansburgh Center. Also on the bill were Austin punk-funkers the Big Boys and Trouble Funk, a group that played the distinctive DC big-band funk style called Go-Go that Minor Threat greatly admired. The show was an effort at encouraging links between harDCore and Go-Go, much like the punk and reggae alliance in Britain's Rock Against Racism.

The show went well, although the hopes of a racially mixed audience were unfulfilled; most of the 1200 fans were white. The crowd danced amiably to the Big Boys and Trouble Funk, but surged as Minor Threat mounted the stage. It was a "freak show," said John Stabb, as fans slammed, dove, and stormed the stage. Preslar found himself constantly being knocked out of tune by stage-divers. Furious, he resolved that the band would have a riser in the future. At such large shows, the joyous blurring of boundaries between audience and performer that had formed the heart of the initial harDCore experience no longer seemed possible.

The whole band recognized that Minor Threat was on the edge of breaking out and could leave harDCore behind. In a way, Baker, Preslar, and Nelson already had. "We have all the natural aspirations to be a big band, but we're already feeling what it's like to be in a big band and it's pretty weird," Nelson told *Musician*, a glossy national mainstream magazine. The challenge was clear, and lines within the band were drawn. After the Lansburgh show, MacKaye made his choice: He stopped going to practices at all.

Infuriated by the singer's unexplained absences, Preslar and Baker quit. Nelson tried to get the band back together, managing to arrange a band meeting. The parlay quickly soured when Preslar and Baker presented MacKaye with a list of demands. They included more say in business matters and a riser for the band. Predictably, MacKaye resisted. "If Minor Threat had had a marriage counselor, we could have worked it out," Nelson said years later. Instead, the band agreed to divorce.

Nelson did win one concession: that the musicians would come together one last time to record their final completed song, "Salad Days," which had debuted at the Lansburgh show. A strong believer in documenting the punk scene, MacKaye agreed, as long as the song would not be released. In December, Baker, Preslar, and Nelson went to Inner Ear to record the instrumental tracks for "Salad Days," an unfinished song called "Stumped," and a cover of the Standells' "Good Guys Don't Wear White."

The words to "Salad Days" were a sharp, painful autopsy of harDCore: "Wishing for the day/When I first wore this suit/Baby has grown ugly/It's no longer cute . . . Do you remember when?/Yeah so do I/We called those the salad days/We called those the good old days/What a fucking lie/I call it a lie." On the last word, the music stopped dead.

Yet MacKaye had hope for a re-born punk community. "The DC hardcore scene is very disorganized, confused, and unfortunate at the moment," he said at the time. "I think you basically have a group of people who are so half-assed that they'll be gone in a year anyway." He recalled a Bob Marley line that HR had once quoted to him: "When the smoke clears, only the true rebels will stand."

Those were words to live by—and obviously MacKaye intended to. Still, the final words of "Cashing In" lingered, questioning MacKaye's cherished DC scene: "There's no place like home/There's no place like home/So where am I?"

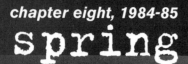

"Caught in time so far away
From where our hearts really wanted to be
Reaching out to find a way
To get back to where we've been
And if summer left you dry
With nothing left to try
This time . . ."
—Rites of Spring, "Spring"

spring

Minor Threat had split, tensions were rising at Dischord House, the label was several thousand dollars in debt, and Ian MacKaye—as he recalled a few years later—"was so depressed that I seriously was suicidal." As for DC punk, the usually upbeat MacKaye foresaw a sort of living death: "I think hardcore or punk or whatever it is could last for many years. But it's like the soul could die while the body lives on."

One person who noticed MacKaye's mood was Skip Groff. He asked MacKaye to work part time at Yesterday and Today, hoping the job would shake some of the unmoored musician's gloom. "I started to work there," MacKaye said, "just to give myself something to do because I really was not happy."

MacKaye wasn't the only original Georgetown punk who suffered a crisis of faith. Many of the old crew were now in college, returning to a more typical course for children of white-collar parents, although some of them chose schools in the DC area to stay connected to the punk community. After Faith broke up, Chris Bald remembered, "I felt kind of stuck because this was going to be my life and all of sudden there wasn't any Faith. Friends were going off to college, and I thought, why are they doing this? Everyone still wanted to make the right career moves—but I thought we were all saying 'screw the career world.' I got really disillusioned."

Bald went to work at the *National Journal*, a small but influential inside-government publication. He learned more about national politics while his personal politics unraveled. "I've never been the king of self-control," he said. "I started drinking again, got into the boring 9-to-5 routine [where] the only time you have are weekends. What do you do with friends on weekends? You drank." His slide was mirrored by more than a few of his old allies.

MacKaye and Bald's despair had nothing to do with a decline in DC punk's audience. The scene was still growing, and such stalwarts as Government Issue, Scream, and Marginal Man remained active. GI released *Joyride* on Fountain of Youth; the album added some metal to the band's personal lyrics and pop-punk music. With Mike Fellows's melodic bass underpinning John Stabb's vulnerable lyrics, one track—"Understand"—was a classic of the form.

Marginal Man had released its first album on Dischord, but its second was on Gasatanka, a subsidiary of Enigma, a large independent California label. "At the time, it looked like Dischord might go under," Pete Murray explained. Scream began to negotiate with Rough Trade to issue an album recorded at two separate sessions in 1984; when it finally appeared in mid-1985, the record was a Rough Trade/Dischord co-release.

These three bands were more popular than ever, but no new groups had risen from the ranks of the old Georgetown punks. The sense that harDCore was a special community was ebbing away. "We sat around and watched it all fall apart," MacKaye said later.

For years, Georgetown punks had gained perverse satisfaction from upending people's prejudices. "We'd fuck with the merchants in Georgetown so royally," MacKaye remembered. "We had our heads shaved, right? We were punk-rock motherfuckers but we'd be totally polite and not steal anything. It fucked with them so badly."

Now Georgetown was a different scene. Kids hung out aimlessly, getting drunk or high, smashing bottles, shoplifting, starting fights, committing acts of vandalism, begging spare change for cigarettes or beer. One of the first signs of the transformation had been when Bryant DuBay, a Rat Patrol member, drunkenly smashed the plate-glass window at Clyde's, a Georgetown restaurant. DuBay escaped capture, but MacKaye was chagrined: "The police stopped by while I was working at the Georgetown Theater. We knew each other and they didn't hassle us, but they asked me, 'What's up with your friends?' What could I say? It was a stupid thing to do."

Even shows were becoming less appealing to harDCore veterans; gigs seemed overrun with kids they didn't know, doing things they didn't like. When GI played, the stage was constantly commandeered by younger punks with less interest in the music than in being seen. "The folks who had been into Minor Threat at the end just switched over to us," said John Stabb. "We got the freak show."

Outright antagonism developed between the Dischord crowd and the kids who now congregated in Georgetown and nearby Dupont Circle to drink, talk, and sometimes fight. The Dupont kids were dismissed as "drunk punks" by many in the Dischord crew, while many of the newer punks viewed Dischord as elitist, cliquey, and self-righteous. Once harDCore had been a family. Now, Wendel Blow wryly noted, "it became a dysfunctional family."

The malaise was felt elsewhere as well. In early '84, the cover of *Maximum RockNRoll* asked a simple but unavoidable question: "Does Punk Suck?" In New York, an increasingly macho and reactionary scene formed around bands like Agnostic Front and Cro-Mags. In Boston, SSD added a second guitar player and turned toward heavy metal. Kenny Inouye remembered playing with them and being astounded. "I figured it would be a joke, but it wasn't. They were serious about it [but] it wasn't even good heavy metal."

Black Flag was prolific, releasing six albums and EPs in under two years, while *Family Man* marked Henry Rollins's recorded debut as a spoken-word performer. The band toured doggedly, often playing smaller towns that had never hosted a punk show before. In April 1984, the group played its first DC gig since Kira Roessler replaced Chuck Dukowski on bass; the venue was Pierce Hall in All Souls Unitarian Church, a promising new space just two blocks from Wilson Center. The performance was strong, but marred by fighting and the destruction of the bathrooms. An All Souls employee "showed me the destruction and said, 'This is your last show here,'" Rollins recalled. Indeed, it was the last punk show there for years to come.

Rollins was not used to this kind of behavior in his hometown. "In the beginning there were so few of us," he said years later. "I felt responsible, we all did. It meant a lot to you, you wanted [the space] to be there next week.

"Today's music [scene] is not responsible, people aren't saying the real thing," he continued. "It was do or die then. Now it's a casual attitude—casual youth casually shitting where they live because there's always some kind of Mom to clean up for them. In those days there was no 'Mom'— we did it. There were always bad eggs in punk but now the ratio of jerks has gone up to where there are 40 jerks at a show breaking bathrooms. And All Souls had this beautiful marble bathroom—it took some breaking! Crowds today just take it for granted."

Rollins knew that kind of irresponsibility was a betrayal of DC punk's original promise. Yet at the time he, like John Stabb, generally didn't comment on the audience's behavior during shows lest he be seen as a "preacher."

x x x

There was one harDCore pioneer who had no such compunction. HR was organizing not one but two bands: the long-promised all-reggae Zion Train and another group more in the Rasta-punk mold of Bad Brains. HR asked Dr. Know to join Zion Train, an offer declined in favor of working with Darryl Jenifer on a new project. The second band, "HR," came together more quickly.

The singer recruited guitarist David Byers, formerly of the Enzymes and Tony Perkins and the Psychotics, a playful punk-funk band. The gig was a dream come true for Byers, a longtime Bad Brains aficionado, as well as a boon for HR. Byers was a hard-edged yet jazzy guitarist who joined Earl Hudson in crafting a potent musical framework for HR's return. HR, Byers, and Hudson worked with a shifting lineup of musicians who could move easily from thrash into many other styles. HR described the new band as "not as much hardcore, more reggae, jazz, more variety. The basic set is rock'n'roll but we mix it up a little more" than Bad Brains.

HR's lyrics were as militant as ever. The singer had taken to wearing military fatigues and writing songs like "Let's Have a Revolution" and "Free Our Mind." "I have always been committed to the struggle of the poor man, the unfortunate, the slaves, the prisoners, the exploited, and against the innocent bloodshed of victims and the overall demeaning of civilization today," HR told *Metrozine*, a new publication. "I will be forever against hypocrites, murderers, thieves, and oppressors of the people. Until Babylon falls, we will not rejoice."

HR was supporting himself by selling marijuana, a righteous occupation for a Rasta, but one that brought him directly into conflict with Babylon. A distribution ring operated from the row-house that HR and other dreads and punks occupied during 1984. The house was on the corner of 17th and U Streets NW, directly across the street from the 3rd District Police Headquarters.

HR would often spend his days on nearby Columbia Road, selling pot and talking with other dreads and passersby. Then came the day in mid-May, shortly before the band was to make its debut; the venue was a new one HR had discovered, the Newton Theater, a former moviehouse near Catholic University in Northeast Washington. As the singer prepared to sell some herb to a customer outside the Ontario Theater on Columbia Road, police swooped in. HR was handcuffed and taken in.

HR was released on bail in time to play the gig, where he still proved to be a riveting performer. The show, which the singer dedicated to "all the hungry, poor, rebellious youths in Washington, DC," was a Bad Brains–style unity production, bringing together Philadelphia's McRad, New York's Antidote, and Underground Soldier, a pop-punk band from the DC suburbs with a strong female vocalist, Helen Danicki. HR's debut was followed with a mini-tour of the East Coast and a recording session at Cue Studios in the Virginia suburbs.

Then, however, the singer had to serve two months at DC's prison in Lorton, Virginia as a result of his arrest. "It was a test," HR would later say. "I give thanks to Jah that I was able to grow in there still. You can even find unity there, there's unity even in the depths of Hell." But there were soon signs that his incarceration had not made HR any more stable.

Because of the jail sentence, it would be nearly six months between HR's first DC show and its second, at the 9:30 Club in mid-November. The bill was an odd pairing with DC's most popular "new" band of the moment, the Meatmen. The latter had existed in some form since 1981, but only in the past year had frontman Tesco Vee turned the concept into a real band. He had recorded an EP, *Dutch Hercules*, featuring the usual sophomoric joke-punk songs but a new cast of musicians, including Lyle Preslar, Brian Baker, and Ian MacKaye, as well as Bert Queiroz, Rich Moore, and Mike Brown—all uncredited on the record.

Technically, the EP was a solo release credited to Tesco Vee and the MeatKrew, but it was a short hop from the record to the return of the Meatmen. With the end of Minor Threat, Preslar and Baker could make a serious commitment. The resurrected band played its first show at a 1983 benefit for *Touch and Go* magazine.

Meatmen shows were massive productions with props and costumes. Perhaps it was this reputation for outrageous spectacle that drew more than 600 people to the Wilson Center—the largest show there yet—in January 1984 to see the Meatmen's second DC performance. Tesco rode onstage on a moped wearing tight gold lamé pants to begin a show quite unlike the usual harDCore concert.

The Meatmen were irreverent, energetic, and occasionally clever, but much of Vee's humor was best suited for a junior-high locker room. The band was hardly an artistic progression for Preslar and Baker. They had briefly joined Glenn Danzig's new band, Samhain, an experience Preslar wryly described as a "date with Satan." Then the guitarists began playing with the Meatmen while developing a new band that continued the more melodic direction they had planned for Minor Threat.

With Deadline alumnus Ray Hare as the vocalist, the 400 was a pop-punk band in the mold of U2 and the Alarm.

In retrospect, he and Preslar viewed the project as a mistake, but "at the time we thought we were going to be pop stars," Baker laughingly recalled. When the 400 debuted at the University of Maryland with Government Issue, the group demonstrated much musical skill but little soul. In the fanzine *WDC Period*, Dave McDuff called the band "very tight but also very uninspiring." Preslar and Baker soon accepted this assessment, and the 400 folded after a few shows.

Preslar and Baker weren't the only DC musicians struggling to find a direction. Void was falling apart onstage. The band had increasingly shifted toward heavy metal, and its shows seemed to be public practice sessions. The apparently unrehearsed group struggled erratically through its new material, mirroring the chaos in the audience. In late 1984, the Wilson Center hosted a series of shambolic shows marred by fights and vandalism. Thirteen-year-old *Metrozine* editor Scott Crawford went to see HR and Void only to leave in disgust before the latter played: "There were too many fucking fights. Is it really worth it?"

HarDCore seemed increasingly to be merely providing a soundtrack for mayhem, with crowds breaking windows, smashing bottles, and fighting in the street. Understandably, few venues wanted to host punk shows anymore. The 9:30 matinees had ended, replaced by the occasional gig, mostly with out-of-town headliners. Pierce Hall was gone almost before it opened, and Space Two Arcade closed. The usual problems soon shut down HR's discovery, the Newton Theater.

Gordon Ornelas's *WDC Period* became one of the most prominent voices lamenting harDCore's auto-destruction. "Gordon Gordon" (as he called himself in print) had recently moved to Washington from the Midwest, starting *WDC Period* mostly as a humor mag. Unfamiliar with the local scene, he committed an ironic blunder when, looking for filler for issue #4, he reproduced a Dischord ad clipped from *Flipside*. Knowing only that Dischord was an important local label, he put the ad next to a "DC Drug Report," a half-serious listing of local prices for illegal drugs.

MacKaye was not amused by this act of generosity, and told the startled Gordon as much. "Until John Stabb pulled me aside and explained the whole straight edge thing, I had never heard of any kind of youth philosophy that didn't encourage drug use, let alone discourage it," Gordon explained. While Gordon was scarcely a puritan, over time *WDC Period* became a voice for responsibility and sanity in the punk scene.

HarDCore's founders didn't know what to do about the deterioration. Ten years later, MacKaye recalled standing next to HR at one chaotic show, complaining about the ugliness: "I was like, 'Man, how did this happen?' HR just blew me out of the water. He turned to me and said, 'You want to know who did this? You did.'" MacKaye was startled, but he knew that there was some truth to HR's judgment.

Despite its violent moments, the Dischord crowd had provided a sort of moral center for DC punk. Now they seemed directionless. No one was able to get a band together. MacKaye had an ambitious idea for a group called Grand Union that would have a large, changing cast of members. Others were skeptical, preferring to stay with more traditional musical lineups.

Yet no such bands appeared. In the first half of 1984, meetings were even called to jump-start the process. Nothing resulted, and the community disintegrated. With Dischord in crisis both financially and creatively, Amy Pickering later noted, "we had to get our shit together before we could help anyone else."

DC punk was going in new and sometimes disturbing directions. In 1984, anyone who looked at band posters in Washington knew of 9353. The quartet's skillfully crafted, multi-colored fliers were pasted throughout the city. The confrontational images were mostly done by singer Bruce Merkle, who had already unsettled more than a few commuters with his sidewalk spray-paint stencils of such phrases as "Penis Cancer."

9353 was the most powerful of the bands from the artier side of post-harDCore. With a voice that "could shift from a deep drawl to Ethel Merman warblings in a flash," as *Trouser Press* marveled, Merkle delivered caustic rants over spare pop-art-punk generated by ex–Double O guitarist Jason Carmer, bassist Vance Bockis, and drummer Dan Joseph. With its distinctive music, live charisma, and vigorous PR work, 9353 soon became one of the city's most popular punk bands.

By late '84, 9353 was also known as a "heroin band," with at least two of its members in an enduring liaison with the drug. Partly as a result, the group gained a reputation for volatility. "9353 broke up after every show," one observer later noted. By August, the band announced the first of what would be many "final" performances. 9353 was not the only DC punk band to include heroin users, but its popularity and the relative openness of its narcotic tastes suggested a change in attitudes within the no-longer-teen-punk scene.

"It's sad, all those little kids who were on skateboards a year or two ago are on heroin now,"

Black Market Baby's Boyd Farrell told *Flipside* in late 1984. "It's like DC lost its innocence. [HarDCore] has been deteriorating ever since the end of Minor Threat. It's lost the sincerity, the energy, and just become cynical."

The same could have been said of Farrell's band. He and Keith Campbell, once the group's creative heart, had largely stopped writing songs. The Sham 69–style idealism that was once BMB's trademark was eclipsed by its reputation as a hard-drinking, fist-fighting kind of band. "Black Market Baby could play a redneck bar one night and a hardcore show the next and find acceptance both places," Wendel Blow said. In part, this was because BMB was a good band. But it also reflected the appeal of songs like "Strike First," "Killing Time," and "Gunpoint Affection"—a non-judgmental first-person account of a rape—that accommodated traditional male aggression and excess.

It took three years, but BMB managed to record and release its first LP. *Senseless Offerings* (on Fountain of Youth) featured sharp, strong, well-played songs. Yet the band was unable to rouse itself to tour, languishing in inertia that Farrell later attributed largely to drug and alcohol use.

In late 1984, Myk Dolfi left BMB. He briefly played in the final lineup of Iron Cross and then formed a new band, Lethal Intent, with Blow and Doug Caldwell, a recent arrival from LA. Thanks to Caldwell's influence, the band added glam-metal to its punk. BMB boosted Lethal Intent, helping it get shows.

The two bands often shared a stage with the Obsessed, a group from the Maryland suburbs. Initially, Vance Bockis had been the Obsessed's singer, and the band had mixed songs like the Sex Pistols' "Problems" with its own material. After Bockis's departure, the covers were excised from the set and the vocal chores fell to guitarist-songwriter Scott "Wino" Weinrich.

Wino had a strong, clear voice and a rugged guitar style that bridged metal and punk; the Obsessed's poorly recorded first single showed debts to both Black Sabbath and harDCore. By the time the single appeared in 1983, however, the band had created an original sound that combined some of the heavy rock elements of the MC5, Sabbath, and Stooges with punk power and speed.

Black Market Baby, the Obsessed, and Lethal Intent drew most of their support from the Dupont Circle/Georgetown drunk-punk scenes. This crowd gravitated to Smash, a new punk record store/clothes boutique in Georgetown. While the store necessarily catered to "punk as a commodity," just like Commander Salamander, it had a more friendly, less commercial atmosphere. Doug Caldwell worked there, and it became a place for the new crop of Georgetown punks to hang out.

Few of these kids had a vision of punk as something revolutionary. They were trying to survive, searching for a tribe, for family, for fun. Blow later recalled that he saw hard drugs spread "like wildfire" during this period, including within in his own band and its audience.

x x x

A ROUGH LANDING IN DC
by Mark Andersen

My first direct exposure to DC punk was via graffiti that read, "Nazi Punks rule! Oi Oi Oi!," complete with a crudely drawn swastika. This rude introduction came in early September 1984, two weeks after I had moved to the DC area to attend Johns Hopkins School of Advanced International Studies on Embassy Row.

My own punk journey had taken me from lost rural misfit to radical activism and academic excellence at Montana State University and, ultimately, to the master's program at SAIS. It is fair to say that punk–by helping me find purpose and identity–had saved my life in a literal sense.

While DC punk was far from the main reason for my relocation, the glowing reports of Bad Brains, Minor Threat, Henry Rollins, straight edge, and PMA that had reached me in Montana had not prepared me for the sight of Nazi-punk graffiti, much less the violence, drug abuse, conformity, and ignorance that seemed rampant at the time. When I bought Minor Threat's "Salad Days"–which the ever-persuasive Jeff Nelson had managed to get permission to release that fall–I heard the word that seemed all-too-appropriate: ugly.

These initial encounters with DC punk were wrenching. In Montana, to be punk was almost unheard of, and required a deep commitment. Pretty much only idealists or lunatics gravitated to punk there; it is fair to say that I was something of both. While my life was now on a promising career track, I was struggling with deep questions about my increasingly conventional and compromised direction.

Since my apartment was near Dupont Circle, I soon became aware of the crew who hung out there, including skinheads like Victor Potocki and Steve Squint. Eventually we became acquainted, sometimes even discussing music and politics. Although we rarely agreed, respect for one another as people resulted, a fact that saved me at least twice from being beaten up, thanks to interventions by Victor and Steve. Years later, another of the skinheads–Eamon "Eddie" Clifford, who eventually became a police officer–apologetically explained that, at the time, "we were squatting in abandoned buildings, drinking a lot, and everything was getting really sick."

Violence was also spreading, most conspicuously because of a new skinhead gang dominated by a punk called Lefty. As a black woman, Lefty didn't seem a likely neo-Nazi. Yet she enjoyed wearing swastikas and sieg-heiling cars that passed by, apparently for shock value.

If the Nazi stance was a bit of a joke, Lefty's politics were extremely conservative, especially for someone associated with the punk scene. She was outspokenly pro-Reagan and anti-leftist. Her charisma, however, attracted a group of loyal young skinhead followers. This was not the only violent group within the scene, but it was the most tight-knit and thus the most dangerous. Her gang was generally the most powerful force at shows, doing pretty much what it wanted.

Among the targets for this group and some of its "drunk-punk" allies were gay men around Dupont Circle. From late-night ambushes of gays, the skins soon turned to attacking those within the punk scene. By the end of 1984, Lefty and her crew had embarked on a reign of terror. Shows, once the sacred ground that punks protected against assault, became sites of regular punk-on-punk violence and intimidation.

In Philadelphia, Lefty and two others brutally beat a fellow skinhead. According to Lefty, it was because "he had ripped me off on an acid deal." Others, however, said it was because he was Jewish.

This story quickly became common knowledge, but few openly challenged Lefty and her followers. Ironically, among the first to do so were Wendel Blow and Sab Grey—who some of Lefty's followers claimed as inspiration. A decade later, Blow recalled going out with Lefty and her crew in her pickup truck: "Lefty saw some folks hanging in an alley and decided to jump them. I told her to let me out 'cause I wanted nothing to do with this shit."

Grey was also disgusted, especially since many members of this new gang claimed to be Iron Cross fans. It might seem strange that the author of "Fight 'em All" and "Skinhead Glory" would be angered by skinhead violence. For Grey, however, there were crucial differences between the past and present violence. "Fight 'em All," Grey argued, "was written about a specific time and place. All the old crew used to fight a lot at gigs, [but] there used to be a reason to fight. We were protecting the scene, we weren't stupid bully boys who ran around and beat up people for no reason."

Still, at least some of this new violence grew out of the earlier punks' brawling. Lefty claimed to have first become aware of violence's power at a Wilson Center show where the Georgetown punk "scene police" were at work. Later she defended herself to Ian MacKaye by saying, "I'm only doing what you taught me to do."

Some old-timers began to reevaluate their previous conduct. Mark Sullivan, who admitted to having started more than a few unnecessary fights, pondered whether "our violence was more 'holy' than theirs simply because it was *our* violence."

To Grey, however, there was a difference. "We had 'DC Skins,' which wasn't a gang, it was just a bunch of friends who happened to be skinheads. Then all of a sudden it went sour. Some people who had shaved heads were beating up people [so] we decided to bag it. We grew our hair out and went back to being punks, which is what we were in the first place," he said. Now "if there's nobody else to fight, they beat each other up. I don't see the point of beating somebody up because you don't like his looks or where he sticks his dick or whatever."

Grey called the new kids fascists, not skinheads. "In the 1930s, it was [Hitler's] Brownshirts. It's the same mentality, they're just dressed up differently. I saw one kid who had 'Iron Cross' on his arm and there was a swastika in the middle and I said, 'Take that off!'"

If Grey seemed defensive, perhaps it was because Iron Cross had never lived down its early image. That reputation—combined with the loss of Dante Ferrando and Mark Haggerty to Gray Matter, a band they formed with Geoff Turner and Steve Niles—would soon end the group. Its last (and best) EP, *Hated and Proud*, contained the song "Wolf Pack," an attack on Lefty and her crew.

At one of the last Iron Cross shows, opening for Suicidal Tendencies at 9:30, Grey directly confronted Lefty and her pals from the stage. He was frustrated that few were willing to denounce Lefty's gang, apparently hoping that it would simply fade away. It didn't, and instead many older punks like Grey left the scene.

Another disenchanted Georgetown punk was Madhouse drummer Danny Ingram. While some dismissed his band for its musical resemblance to Siouxsie and the Banshees, Madhouse was a welcome change from generic macho-punk. Such Madhouse songs as "So Sad" and "Advice" expressed a feminist viewpoint rarely heard in the largely male scene, and several Madhouse songs attacked the new punks. "We hate ourselves for making you," declared "Repulsion."

In an interview with *Truly Needy*, Ingram denounced the younger punks as "just sheep looking for someone to herd them around." His despair may have been heightened by his heroin addiction, a problem he flaunted in the interview by naming "12th and W"—an open-air drug market—as the best place in DC to visit.

x x x

At the Neighborhood Planning Council office near Wilson High School, Amy Pickering had plenty of time to think about the scene's plight. She was one of many teens provided make-work positions by the summer jobs initiative of DC's mayor, Marion Barry. The idea was to give productive work to every young person seeking summer employment, yet few serious jobs were available. The NPC office where Pickering worked did sponsor the annual free summer concert series in Fort Reno Park, an important venue on the harDCore circuit, but seemed to accomplish little else.

While Pickering continued to work at Dischord, at NPC she got paid to "sit in the back room, make goofy [Xerox] copies, and hang out." Laughing, she recalled later that she "was supposed to be teaching some kind of video course—I had never used a video camera in my life!" In fact, Pickering wasn't even qualified for the jobs program, since she didn't live in the city; she applied by using her friend Molly Burnham's address.

Increasingly aware of harDCore's lack of direction, Pickering felt ashamed when uprisings in South Africa began in the fall of 1984. A new wave of anti-apartheid activism had begun—and some of its leaders were people her own age. "It was really nice to hang around and goof off at NPC," Pickering said. "But then there were the South Africa protests and I thought, 'Man, here we are just being lunkheads.'"

Another punk looking for purpose was Tomas Squip. After being kicked out of school in Georgia—"for getting naked," he reported unrepentantly—he had moved back to DC and into Dischord House. Squip rejected both adult cynicism and the fatalism of many of his punk peers. "My mother was always saying, 'When are you going to grow out of this punk thing and get a real job?'" Squip said in 1985. "Sure enough, 75 percent of the people I knew were out getting regular jobs. Or going to big colleges. I had complete faith in these motherfuckers. When the Georgetown punk scene was at its height, I thought this was the revolution because these people wouldn't let go. But they all disappeared, they all went away and even the people at the very core sold out."

Part clown, part mystic, and part radical activist, Squip could be a challenging presence at Dischord House, particularly for Nelson. But Squip influenced all his housemates, especially MacKaye. Together with Sullivan and MacKaye, Squip created the Marvelous Sit-Coms, an acoustic joke band that seemed to reinvigorate MacKaye.

At the same time, Dischord hatched a plan to resolve several problems simultaneously by releasing an LP comprising four of the label's most sought-after out-of-print singles: Teen Idles, SOA, GI, and Youth Brigade. The LP would make this music available again, and—together with the earlier 12" of Minor Threat's first two singles—pull Dischord out of the red. The record would also undercut the over-priced collector's market for the original 45s. When Dischord started, the label had pressed one or two thousand copies of records, never expecting to sell even that many. But now the popularity of Minor Threat and Rollins, and DC punk's still-growing international reputation, was driving a strong demand for early Dischord releases.

Working at Yesterday and Today, MacKaye could see how high prices were going. He could do nothing about people who spent tens, even hundreds, of dollars for DIY items that were intended, at least in some vague way, as refutations of consumer society. But he could ensure that those who wanted only to hear music from Dischord could do so without paying absurd prices.

It was at Yesterday and Today that MacKaye had a breakthrough. "One day I was sitting there getting all bummed out," he recalled, "and Skip went 'What's the problem?' I said, 'Man, life is bull-shit.' I was so fucking down. He goes, 'Give me a break. How old are you?' I said, 'I'm 21.' He goes, 'You're 21 and you've fucking touched so many people in your life. I'm 30 and you know I'll never even meet that many people in my life, I'll never know that many names.' Those were really saving words for me, it really made me feel a lot better."

At Dischord House, Squip began to badger MacKaye about one of his pet issues: vegetarianism. It was not the first time MacKaye had discussed this subject. He parried the playful yet persistent digs, but he also took Squip's ideas seriously and appreciated the challenge.

The signs were small, but something was shifting. Nelson remained outside this resurgence, while the bonds between MacKaye, Squip, and Sullivan grew stronger. All three were aiming to form new bands, but the first to succeed was their other housemate, Eddie Janney.

As a member of Faith, Janney had been on the fringes of DOD and Insurrection. The group's spirit of abandon fascinated him. "I think he was impressed by the fact that we just went for it," said Guy Picciotto. "When we played, we just pushed it hard, we went over the top." However, Insurrection never really jelled musically, which became clear when the band recorded a demo with MacKaye at Inner Ear. The demo "was really bad, and we never finished it," Picciotto recalled. "The songs weren't great. We were unhappy with how limited it was. I had started to write lyrics, which I had never really done before. Everybody was getting into new things, high school was coming to an end, and people were trying to figure out what to do. So, toward the end, the band just broke apart."

After Insurrection split in mid-'83, Fellows joined GI, but he, Picciotto, and Canty continued to play together. In December, as one cycle of DC punk ended with the recording of "Salad Days," another was beginning. One day Picciotto and Canty were jamming in the former's basement when Janney called. They invited him over, and soon began writing songs together.

It was immediately clear that this band was not just a harDCore rerun. Nor was it going to be just for fun. "The whole original idea of Insurrection [was] to play very fast and jump around like madmen and have a great time. We were writing songs and having fun but it didn't seem really serious," said Picciotto. "So I thought if I ever started a band again, I had to do it full-on serious."

While the new unit emulated the verve of Faith and Minor Threat, musically it was a progression beyond Insurrection or the thrash of many DC bands. Canty—who was the drummer but wrote several of the early songs on guitar, his first instrument—remembers being inspired at the time by the Buzzcocks and MC5. Whatever their inspirations, the new songs added emotional and musical nuance to harDCore's bristling intensity.

As the music began to jell, the band faced another challenge: Who would sing? Although he was writing the lyrics, Picciotto had never sung before. Neither had anyone else in the band. Ray Hare came from school in New York to sing at a couple practices, but it didn't really work out. "Already me, Eddie, Brendan, and Mike were achieving this kind of solidity and we decided that we were just going to try to do it as the four of us," remembered Picciotto. "That was when I decided that I wanted to sing."

The new band was nearly ready to play live when Fellows announced he was moving to LA. It was a crushing surprise, but there was no question that the band would end with the bassist's departure. More than even most other DC punk bands, the group drew its power from the members' friendships and near-telepathic connection. Before Fellows left, however, the group decided to record its finished material, a total of six songs.

As he had done with scores of others before, MacKaye went to Inner Ear with the new band. He had liked Insurrection and had always enjoyed the creativity and energy of the DOD boys. In addition, Janney was his housemate and a longtime comrade. Still, the Insurrection sessions had not gone very well, so MacKaye didn't expect much.

Yet what he heard electrified him. The songs were potent, wiry outbursts, startlingly realized for a band that had never played live. Another revelation came when Picciotto opened his mouth to sing. "I was just blown away," MacKaye recalled later. "The songs were great and Guy's vocals were amazing. Right then I knew that this was something special."

The demo made the power of the new group apparent, but what should have been a clarion call seemed more like a eulogy. Shortly after the session, Fellows left for California. The others finished the demo without him, inserting humorous effects and sonic scraps, finally sending the finished product to him in California. "Mike Fellows is dead" was the echoed goodbye on the tape—part jokey Beatles reference, part requiem for the unfulfilled band.

The remaining musicians didn't know what to do without Fellows. "So the three of us just kept practicing without him, just for something to do," said Picciotto, "kind of burning the torch for it." Then, one day months later, Picciotto was working at NPC and Fellows "just walked in." He had returned, unannounced, to rejoin the band. The reconstituted quartet took on the name Rites of Spring. "Within a week, we did our first show," Picciotto recalled.

That July gig also marked the return of punk to Food for Thought, the Dupont Circle hippie hangout and health food restaurant owned by Dante Ferrando's father. A new band, Gray Matter, that contained the core of the old Outsiders—Ferrando, Haggerty, Turner—and new addition Steve Niles on bass, headlined the bill.

Gray Matter was clearly descended from the goofy, energetic WGNS bands, and was a dramatic shift away from Iron Cross' macho. Such songs as "Crisis and Compromise" and the bittersweet "Give Me a Clue" matched a pop sensibility with crashing punk chords, while grappling with the confusion faced by idealistic kids leaving their high school years behind. Perhaps their best tune was "Retrospect," an anti-nostalgia anthem whose spirit exemplified the hoped for DC punk resurgence.

Gray Matter was very good, but from its first show Rites of Spring was a difficult act to follow. The band took its name from the Stravinsky piece that outraged its audience upon its premiere in 1913, but it also had another meaning. "All the bands that I cared about—Minor Threat, Faith, Insurrection—had broken up and nothing else was going on," Picciotto said. "When we formed, we hoped it would come together again. 'Spring' was cool because of the rebirth idea."

The quartet quickly became notorious for punishing its equipment, playing so hard that instruments detuned or simply broke, while leaving astonished audiences in their wake. Among the band's early converts were Lois Maffeo and Calvin Johnson, who were visiting the latter's parents in Maryland. They attended Rites of Spring's second show, at Hard Art Gallery, where they persevered though the opening band, industrial noisemongers Peach of Immortality. Johnson had begun Beat

Happening and K Records in Olympia, Washington, both embodiments of his taste for easygoing pop-punk played with childlike simplicity, but he was impressed by Rites of Spring's turbulent sound.

The show was so energetic that the band was left with little usable equipment. "I broke my guitar about three songs into the set," Picciotto later noted, "and Eddie destroyed his at the end. Here we are, we've played two shows and we'd broken so much stuff that it was hard for us to play anywhere." Eventually they patched up enough stuff to go on, but they remained so short on gear that some bit of equipment was borrowed for nearly every show they ever played.

The band not only survived these technical difficulties, but seemed to thrive on them. "The cool thing was that it never was really very secure," Picciotto later said. "We never had a full line of equipment, we never had amps, we were always rushing around trying to get everything together. All the essential things that really hold a band together weren't really there, but we made it work anyway."

Not surprisingly, Rites of Spring shows tended to be infrequent. "The shows were always 'events' for us," Picciotto said. "Back then, a bad show was really crippling. Every show had to be momentous. We put everything into them. We treated them almost like religious occasions." This was manifested in the beautiful set lists the band designed; almost as much an art object as a practical item, the list would hang at the back of the stage for all to see.

"The reaction we got was incredible," Picciotto remembered. "At least with the words I wrote, my main goal was to be honest and real about everything. And when we played, it wasn't anything we worked out; it just clicked. It always seemed to me the way that music should be played was the way that we were playing it."

"They really were the nucleus around which the community began to regroup," said Sharon Cheslow, who had recently been left bandless with the demise of Bloody Mannequin Orchestra. "You started to see some of the old faces again." Rebirth was a central theme, as the band's name and early songs like "End on End" and "Spring" reflect. The latter tune was about "a positive thing coming out of a negative situation," Picciotto noted, a reference clearly relevant to the situation in the DC punk world.

Rites of Spring was meant as a reinterpretation of hardcore. "It wasn't spikes and bloody meat and skulls with hammers in the head and the violent bloody macho thing," the singer said. "It was more open-ended, which I thought was good, because everyone got into the band. It wasn't just people posturing in front of the stage." The now-clichéd slamdancing was not expected or particularly welcomed.

Unlike most hardcore lyricists, Picciotto wrote about love, but in multi-leveled ways that allowed and even encouraged wider interpretation. The band's performances expressed this broader emotional scope. In the place of unfocused anger, they had a soulful passion that suggested that any given song could be about the end of a relationship—or the beginning of a new world.

Such songs were anguished, but not self-pitying. "I am serious and I deal with realistic things [but the music is] not despairing," the lyricist said. "It's a constant friction between what you see and what you want to achieve, the things you know are right. That rub is what creates the pain and the emotion. Then there's the hope that maybe you can overcome it. It's the same personally and politically. To me, it's all one issue."

Picciotto distinguished Rites of Spring from bands he thought didn't "really have any real purpose in being there. I mean everything I sing and we mean everything we play. I've had my share of kidding around, I'm not kidding around anymore. This is the biggest thing in my life. You've got to try to stir people and try to get into them and have them get into you, which is what I hope our shows are about. I would say that the way we play is a protest."

x x x

This challenge to "punk-as-usual" expanded when another new band, Beefeater, joined Rites of Spring and Gray Matter at a Food for Thought show in September 1984. Squip had allied with bassist Dug Birdzell, from the defunct Underground Soldier; drummer Bruce Atchely Taylor, formerly of Hate From Ignorance and Subtle Oppression; and metal-funk-punk guitarist Fred Smith, a DC government worker by day and an Obsessed fan by night. In its own way, Beefeater was as significant as Rites of Spring. It introduced a craggy punk-funk hybrid to the scene's expanding musical mix, as well as explicit radical politics. Although bands like Bad Brains, Scream, and Hate From Ignorance had written political songs, Beefeater bridged the gap between the personal politics of bands like Minor Threat and larger issues.

The pro-vegetarian anthem "Beefeater" is a good example: It was, Squip explained, "a dialogue between the subject and its conscience, then myself and the subject." Similarly, "Satyagraha" invoked the spirits of Gandhi and Martin Luther King Jr. for what could be a song about violence at punk shows—or the danger of international war. Some of Beefeater's subtleties were lost in their live performances, in part because Squip, Birdzell, and Smith were extremely energetic presences. Still, the band's power was undeniable, and Squip, though an inexperienced frontman, was not shy about speaking his mind from stage.

Food for Thought was a congenial place for DC punk's rebirth. By necessity, most of the shows were held with little publicity on early Sunday afternoons—before the restaurant would ordinarily open—in a space cleared by moving tables and chairs aside. They were far smaller than the hardcore hall shows, but, while often filled with intense audience participation, lacked the mindless, violent rituals too common at the other venues. As a result, some viewed the gigs as elitist "cool shows for the in-crowd"—but the gigs did attract fewer troublemakers, creating a free zone for the new punk to germinate.

THE BIRTH OF POSITIVE FORCE DC
by Mark Andersen

Although I lived three blocks from Food for Thought at the time, these lightly publicized shows passed below my radar. Meanwhile, my disillusion with punk was being augmented by other ugly American realities on display before my small-town eyes.

Mere blocks from the Capitol and White House, wretched pockets of violence, poverty, and despair festered. In what the re-elected Ronald Reagan dubbed "Morning for America," some Americans had learned to step over other Americans, the multiplying street people who were the consequence of Reaganomics. When a homeless World War II vet named Jesse Carpenter froze to death across the street from the White House shortly before Reagan's multi-million-dollar inaugural, some activists protested, most visibly the inspirational "Christian-anarchist" Community for Creative Nonviolence. Beyond that, few seemed outraged–including punks–as far as I could see.

For me, if punk was to remain relevant, it needed to step past rhetoric to organized action. I was not alone in this sentiment. Although few were willing to take matters as far as the Subhumans' Gerry Hannah had done–imprisoned as one of the "Vancouver Five" for his involvement in a series of political bombings in Canada–such actions bespoke a growing sense that now was the time to turn from word to deed.

Even before Reagan settled in for his second term, there was a process underway on the West Coast that was pushing hardcore punk–or what remained of it–toward more explicit and active radical politics. According to an analysis by Jeff Goldthorpe in *Socialist Review* in 1993, "by 1983, squatter activism, critiques by popular bands and fanzines of punk's impulsive self-destruction"–including straight edge, of course– "and other activist initiatives (like the Rock Against Reagan Tour) had set the stage for a punk style of protest, if not a full blown politics."

A key step in the development of this "punk style of protest" was the linkage in the Bay Area between punks and the Livermore Action Group that organized events like the nonviolent blockades of Livermore Labs, perhaps the most important nuclear weapons development facility in America. A small but growing (and very visible) faction in the LAG coalition were what would be called "peace punks," many of whom had been inspired by the anarchist UK punk band Crass and the confrontational "Stop the City" punk-connected demonstrations in the financial district of London in 1982 and 1983.

According to Goldthorpe, this punk protest style "took on a definite form" during LAG's "Hall of Shame Tour" in San Francisco's financial district. "Unlike most affinity groups, who were sitting in the entrances of target institutions and waiting to get arrested by prior negotiation with police, punk affinity

The importance of this space was illustrated by the contrast between Beefeater's Food for Thought show and its not-so-friendly second show with the Meatmen and Void at the Wilson Center in October. Squip wore storm-trooper boots, a leather jacket and hat, a sword-shaped swizzle stick as an earring, and 10 differently colored combs he had found in the street taped to his head. There's no record of how the audience responded to this wry comment on punk fashion's dead end. Possibly they were too busy scuffling to notice, for once again the evening was marred by violence.

groups held screaming 'die-ins' in the middle of the street, moving on before the police could catch up with them. The sober decison to 'get arrested' was replaced by the anxious and exhilirating game of avoiding arrest while continuing to disrupt normalcy, and inventing theater in the city streets."

Soon punks were to apply these tactics on their own, most notably at the Democratic and Republican Conventions in the summer of 1984 under the name "the War Chest Tour." The basic approach, as Goldthorpe noted, was "to invade corporate space (usually just the lobby) creating a playground of protest, raucously denouncing, leafletting, dying-in, and generally disrupting business as usual." While Goldthorpe believed that "the War Chest Tour had been consistently outmanuevered and marginalized by the authorities," he also saw that these actions nonetheless helped to create a "loose new community" that was labeled as "punk rock protesters." Inspired by the tour, punks in and around the Nevada band Seven Seconds created an affinity group called Positive Force.

This development sent out ripples across the nation. One of those energized by the actions was Kevin Mattson, who Sharon Cheslow later called "DC's first peace-punk." Kevin had long felt marginalized by harDCore's general insistence on "personal politics." As time passed, his attacks on the narrowness of DC punk had grown increasingly savage. After the demise of Hate From Ignorance and its successor, Subtle Oppression, Kevin had more or less forsaken music for ever-more serious activism, helping to organize a "Student Union to Promote Awareness" (SUPA) at Bethesda Chevy-Chase High School, and working with the Student Action Corps for Animals and the Washington Peace Center.

Since its birth in the early '60s, the Peace Center—which was lodged in a Quaker house of worship—had become the major hub for peace and justice work in the DC area. Indeed, during the Vietnam War, it had the dubious honor of having its offices burglarized and its phones tapped by the FBI. When the "punk politics" that had originated in the UK and SF came to DC, mostly via Kevin, the Peace Center would play a support role similar to that of LAG in California.

After the Convention actions, a national coalition called "No Business As Usual" was formed to focus this new style of protest on preventing nuclear war. Although NBAU was influenced by the Revolutionary Communist Party—never too popular in DC punk circles—Kevin quickly became involved. As he later wrote, "It is time to step out of the boundaries of 'protest and dissent as usual.' Our actions must become much more effective and disruptive . . . The normal day-to-day routines of people have to be creatively disrupted. People have to be challenged and made to deal with the situation . . . The normal processes of government have to be shut down." The Peace Center agreed to provide space for Kevin to help organize the DC portion of a nationwide NBAU day of protest on April 29, 1985.

The new bands led the Dischord crowd to reevaluate harDCore. Perhaps it was true that the scene as a whole was beyond reclamation, but there was another approach: to create a "scene within a scene." In effect, this was what the Georgetown punks had initially done by inventing their community out of the original DC scene.

As the Georgetown punks stirred, new teenage bands emerged. Mark Sullivan's younger brother Bobby, his friend Chris Thomson, and neophytes Scott McCloud and Alexis Fleisig formed a band called Lünchmeat. In suburban Virginia, high school freshman Dave Grohl was switching from guitar to drums to join a group with Chris Page, Bryant Mason, and Dave Smith. Originally called Freak Baby, the quartet became Mission Impossible. "Lünchmeat and Mission Impossible were totally inspiring to see, high school kids playing again," said MacKaye. "Their whole scene was similar to how ours was in early Minor Threat and Teen Idles."

Not surprisingly, MacKaye was one of those pushing for a revival from behind the scenes. Every Rites of Spring and Beefeater show made MacKaye yearn to be back in a band. Equally inspired was Chris Bald, who was in the front at the first Rites of Spring show and many after that. "ROS was the most incredible band ever to come out of this city," he said years later. "They came as close as any band ever has to putting words on the feelings I felt for this whole movement." Bald began to work with MacKaye and Nelson as they tried to assemble the right band to follow Minor Threat.

MacKaye was also working to expand Dischord's horizons. In early 1985, he went to the UK to make a business arrangement with John Loder and Southern Studios. After the

In a spotlight on a Dead Kennedys concert set to happen in DC the same day, *City Paper* writer (and old-wave DC punk) Michael Marriote noted that "last July's Democratic National Convention proved the potential of a burgeoning punk politics: four days of roving, creative demonstrations condemning both political parties culminated in a number of arrests and an end to the notion of American punks as apathetic, inconsequential counterparts to their British brethren . . . This year the movement goes national. April 29 has been declared No Business As Usual Day. Exact details of the day's demonstrations are unclear but the objective is to create an ongoing movement to prevent World War III—no matter what it takes."

The details of the demo were "unclear" for a good reason: most were made up on the spot to make it difficult for the police to stymie the plans. Although there were at most 100 demonstrators, nearly as many police showed up. The protest lurched through the federal district, one moment staging a "die-in" in the street or next to a crowded sidewalk café as Kevin or one of the other organizers gave speeches with bullhorns explaining the action. Just as suddenly as we had fallen, we would leap up and run down the street, the cops in hot pursuit, only to dodge into the lobby of a government building. After "dying" yet again, the group would charge out the door before the startled guards could react.

Tense, exhilarating scenes like these were repeated in more than two dozen cities and college campuses across the USA that day. The protest went on for several hours with a slowly dwindling number of protesters and police, ending up at the *Washington Post*, where the only arrest of the day took place when one of the protesters rushed too far into the building and got nabbed. At the time, Kevin wrote that the day "was an extreme success in that it disrupted the normal processes of Washington, DC and made people see that (other) people are angry at the threat of nuclear war and are beginning to ACT."

While few objective observers would have echoed Kevin's enthusiastic assessment, the day was significant. Unlike the movement of the late 1960s, we were up against a newly re-elected, popular president without a galvanizing issue like the draft. In this context, NBAU was a good beginning, even if its rhetoric seemed dangerously out of touch with its actual strength. If NBAU had hardly succeeded in stopping "business as usual," for many of its young participants, it was nonetheless a powerful first step into action.

Kevin became a big inspiration to me, as did Chris Bald, who I met through my new friend Danny success of *Out of Step*, Loder was willing to use Southern's money to help underwrite more Dischord projects. With this funding to float the label between projects, it could release more records and keep the older ones in print.

While in Britain, MacKaye met the anarcho-punk band Crass. Surrounded by new friends and abundant vegetarian food, another personal puzzle was solved. "My final thing was that out of all animals, humans are the only ones that can make the choice" to kill or not to kill, MacKaye realized. "Since we can make the choice, we should use it. I suddenly realized that the only reason that I rejected the vegetarian thing was out of convenience, because everywhere you go they serve meat, because everybody else was eating it."

MacKaye emphasized that this was his own decision. "It was the same thing as alcohol, I realized. [Vegetarianism] is such a logical step for straight edge, it's such a logical step for my thing. As much as Tomas influenced me, he did not make me a vegetarian. I made myself a vegetarian. [Personal decisions] are the only ones that make a difference."

Ingram. Chris shared his excitement about Rites of Spring and plans for what was beginning to be called "Revolution Summer." Already I had begun to turn my angst toward the creation of a punk activist group, a way to give back some of the energy punk had brought to me years before. During a pilgrimage to SF punk mecca, the Mabuhay Gardens, shortly before my move to DC, I had learned of *Another State of Mind*, a film about the 1982 Better Youth Organization tour that featured DC and Minor Threat prominently. Since the film had never been shown in DC, I decided to arrange a benefit premiere that would also help to launch the new activist group.

The final element of my plan fell into place when I picked up the March issue of *MRR* and read about the Positive Force affinity groups that had sprung up in Reno and then spread to Las Vegas. According to PFLV member Michelle Cernuto, "Positive Force is meant to be a network of affinity groups in places like Las Vegas, San Francisco, Los Angeles, etc . . ." The next step seemed obvious: Why not have a Positive Force DC?

At about the same time, Kevin also read the *MRR* article and arrived at much the same conclusion. Although we had slightly different concepts of what the group would be about—I focusing on its work within the punk community, Kevin on building a DC-area youth-activist group that expanded on his work with SUPA, SACA, and NBAU—it seemed to make sense to work together.

Another State of Mind proved an effective fundraiser and outreach tool, bringing out a broad spectrum of DC punks and raising $800 for CCNV and the Coalition for a New Foreign and Military Policy. The following Saturday—June 15, 1985—Positive Force DC held its first public meeting. Given that American punk was a largely white, middle-class movement, the original PFDC was a diverse group. Neo-hippie high school activists mixed uneasily with mohawked Crass-punks, RCP members, older anarchists, bright-eyed young posi-punks with no ideology but a desire to learn and to do—and me, a farmboy grad student beaming amidst the chaos.

Although the Yippies and RCP had skulked on the edges of DC punk since the late '70s, Positive Force was the first organized political group from within the DC punk scene, and one of the first anywhere. Soon we would have powerful new allies, for the energy within the resurgent Dischord scene was also building toward eruption.

X X X

As 1985 dawned, DC punk shows were crowded and frequently dangerous. On New Year's Eve, a planned Lansburgh concert with Black Market Baby, Scream, Reagan Youth, Malefice, and Sacrilege was shifted at the last moment to Georgetown's Key Theater—without the theater owner's knowledge. The disorganized event became a frenzy of violence. Rumors that a fan had died proved untrue, but a concertgoer was stabbed, and more than one left bloody and bruised.

Less than a week later, the Wilson Center hosted its largest punk show ever, with nearly 1000 fans. No problems were apparent when the opening act, Madhouse, took the stage. Although Madhouse's music was by design slower and more nuanced than most hardcore punk, and thus only marginally "skankable," slamdancing began almost immediately. Midway through the set, Monica Richards made an innocent joke about skinhead girls.

Suddenly, the front of the stage was swarming with skinheads taunting Richards, who had once sported a shaved head herself. "I really made a mistake because this was the new generation of skinheads," she said later. "They were throwing lit cigarettes at me and saying things like 'take off your shirt.'" As the abuse continued, Richards motioned for the band to play "Cut," a chilling song based on personal experience. "I said, 'This song is about rape—which I've been through!' These stupid boys, who had just discovered their penises, all said 'Fuck you!'"

Richards threw herself into the song, spitting venom straight at the skinheads: "I see your face in every man/I feel your hate in every man/I smell your breath/I feel your body/I feel your hate/Hate . . . hate . . . hate. . ." It was a gripping moment, entirely wasted on the front row. The kids continued heckling, unchallenged by anyone in the crowd. When the set ended, Ingram leaped from behind the drum set to confront the skinheads, who just slinked away. Later, Richards and Ingram would recall this show as their definitive break from harDCore.

There was a parade of stage-divers as Marginal Man and Corrosion of Conformity continued the show. Between sets, the venue was brazenly vandalized, including a small partition systematically destroyed while onlookers chatted obliviously or even cheered on the destruction. When the headlining Circle Jerks came on, singer Keith Morris requested that fans stay off the stage, for a very good reason: He was still recovering from a broken back. Although most people honored Morris's request, the slamdancing grew even more fevered. When the band began its anthem, "Live Fast, Die Young," Morris pulled up his shirt to reveal the back brace underneath. It wasn't clear if he intended the gesture as warning or glorification, but the crowd cheered. After this chaotic show, the Wilson Center was closed to punk.

A new venue, Sanctuary Theater, opened—and just as quickly closed when the first two shows (one with GI, MIA, and Phlegm, the other with GBH and Lethal Intent) were accompanied by violence. "There were some real radical punk rockers throwing bottles at cars and throwing a rat at a taxi," *Metrozine* reported tartly. "There were plenty of great fights to see. As for the bands, hell if I know."

x x x

At the Neighborhood Planning Council office, the term "Revolution Summer" popped out. Initially, it was just a joke about an imaginary uprising against an unpopular NPC supervisor, but something about the term clicked with Pickering. Since her work at NPC was not very strenuous—"I was bored out of my mind!" she laughed—Pickering began making a series of missives, assembled from cutout letters like ransom notes. "NPC paid for everything, they had the Xerox machine, they had the stamps, they had envelopes. We had a lot of energy at this point and we thought maybe we could inspire other people." The notes were a variation on a general theme: "Be on your toes. This is . . . REVOLUTION SUMMER." She began to send them out in unmarked envelopes to the old Georgetown punk core group.

Pickering later called the anonymous notes "corny and cheesy," yet they roused some of the people who received them. "I think it kind of reinspired the group ethic, the family ethic that people were thinking of you even if you weren't hanging out, they were thinking of you, they knew you wanted this," Molly Burnham reflected later.

"Amy was the 'mother of the revolution,'" said Squip later. "The original punk philosophy was 'fight bullshit' and 'do something real.' The punk scene was doing neither of those things. Revolution Summer was about getting back into fighting bullshit again."

Increasingly politicized by his work at the *National Journal*, Chris Bald was interested in the daily demonstrations organized by TransAfrica outside the South African Embassy. One night he had a strange dream: Beefeater was playing its song "Apartheid No" on a flatbed truck on Massachusetts Avenue, the DC street with a stretch known as "Embassy Row." Bald told Squip about the dream. After deciding that such an exploit was unlikely in the waking world, they struck on a different idea. Why not just take drums and a bunch of punks to the Embassy to make as loud a racket as possible?

For all the good that TransAfrica was doing, the protests were becoming routine. Kept two blocks from the Embassy by a regulation banning protests within 200 yards of a diplomatic building, the protesters marched in all-too-orderly pickets, getting arrested as if on cue. "We thought we'd inject a little spontaneity into it," Picciotto said. As Pickering's anonymous letters heralding "Revolution Summer" began to arrive, plans were laid for what would be the first punk percussion protest.

X X X

Although HR had to cancel a planned national tour when his parole officer refused to let him leave the area, he was beginning to send his music to the world through his new label, Olive Tree. The first release contained the seven songs he'd recorded at Cue Studio just before entering prison, but the label was also developing other bands. It became the nucleus for a mini-scene that included Go-Go punk band Outrage and the metal-punk groups Scythian, Revelation, and Press Mob, which was fronted by an astonishing, dreadlocked female singer, Spyche.

As *It's About Luv* was being readied for release, HR returned to Cue to record some new songs. One of these, "Keep Out of Reach," was his most fully realized song since the end of Bad Brains. This hybrid of reggae, rock, and jazz counseled would-be rebels to escape the system: "Keep out of reach/Don't compromise," HR warned as one guitar played a morse-code riff over a second's swelling chords. "Only Jah Jah know/What's in the future." The potent new style hinted at the new band's potential and showed that HR was moving beyond Bad Brains.

Although HR's muse seemed intact, the singer was living in a hazy, ganja-steeped world; ominous conversations about guns and revolution mixed with band rehearsals, Bible meetings, and street scuffling. HR was the same energetic, eccentric, fundamentally kind person he had always been, but he could also explode in violent rages, sometimes aimed at the women he was involved with. Once he savagely attacked a woman during an argument in front of a room of witnesses, apparently because she took off a ring that he had given her and threw it across the room. This was not the only such incident.

His behavior was largely kept hidden, but became public when Jimi Riley, a former 17th and U housemate, interviewed the singer for *WDC Period* in May, 1985. Riley had been an HR follower since the Bad Brains days, and was now the art director for Olive Tree; he had designed the HR band logo and a series of HR concert posters. His own band, Revelation, was produced by Byers and included another HR follower, Kenny Dread, on guitar.

Riley was a member of Olive Tree's inner circle, but he was struggling with an internal crisis, sparked by his realization that he was gay. Despite the hostility he anticipated from some of his acquaintances, he decided to come out. The revelation had strained his relationship with HR—as had HR's erratic behavior during the period they both lived in the U Street house.

Nonetheless, Riley began the questioning as a friend and believer. If he had hoped the interview would bring understanding, however, he was disappointed. From the start, the exchange was strained, full of long pauses and odd answers. HR dismissed the soon-to-be released *It's About Luv* as a "piece of shit." When asked a generic question about upcoming gigs, HR replied, "If a gig comes up, it comes, if it doesn't, it doesn't. I'm going to concentrate on saving my soul and forget about everything else."

Riley began broaching the more sensitive issues by noting that some people said that HR felt that a woman's place was "barefoot in the kitchen making babies." The singer replied that "every woman belongs to Jah and they are soldiers. They must take their place on the battlefield alongside the man, so that doesn't involve the kitchen."

The interviewer then asked directly if HR and members of his band had "exerted physical violence toward your women." Riley had in fact seen some of these incidents, and HR didn't even try to dodge the question. "When a woman is disobedient to her man and is consistent in the disobedience," the singer replied, "it is the man's responsibility to administer justice to protect her from herself."

Asked about his anti-gay rhetoric, HR responded that "faggots can't have babies!" Riley noted that the Bible says "Judge not lest ye be judged"—a verse used by HR's hero Bob Marley in an early song—but HR responded that the "Bible also says 'blessed are those who execute his judgement.'"

Confounded by HR's unrepentant manner, Riley retreated from this line of questioning. HR insisted that he still intended "never ever to be disloyal to the underprivileged or God," but after this interview songs like "It's About Luv" or "Let's Have a Revolution" could never ring entirely true.

x x x

MacKaye had finally formed a new group, but with one conspicuous absence. After four bands and a half-decade playing together, MacKaye and Nelson were no longer a musical unit. Initially, they collaborated, writing several songs together. Then MacKaye made an offhand remark. "I said that I was hoping not to have fights over money with him in this band, like we had in Minor Threat," MacKaye recalled. "I told him I hoped to do a lot of free shows. Jeff told me he would have no trouble doing free shows when we started out, but that when we got more popular, he thought we should get paid what we were worth. I said, 'Does that mean that you wouldn't want to do free shows if we got popular?' He said, 'Yes, I think we should get paid what we're worth.' I said, 'Jeff, I don't think I can be in a band with you.'"

After adjusting to this development, MacKaye's new bandmates turned out to be Bald, Mike Hampton, and Ivor Hanson, who had returned from Vassar. In other words, the new band—which Bald named Embrace—was the original Faith with Ian MacKaye instead of Alec MacKaye on vocals.

After a year and a half without a band, MacKaye was ready to play. There was also bad news, however: DuBay, one of the most troubled members of Rat Patrol, had died of a heroin overdose. His death shook many, including his old comrade, Wendel Blow, who later said, "I had no idea how much pain Bryant was in during that last year . . . After he died, I kept wondering, where were we?"

This question hit MacKaye with perhaps even greater force. In many ways, DuBay had been a fuck-up, but he had been part of the DC punk family. Where had his family been when he needed help? MacKaye felt that he had turned away, too self-righteous and confused to extend a helping hand.

The death inspired a new song, "Past": "I suppose I'm naïve/But I find it hard to believe/That a person could make life so cheap," the song begins. But then the judgment suddenly turns on the singer himself: "I am guilty/I failed you/As a person who should have cared/I shut my mouth/Because I was scared/I hid my feelings/When they should have been bared." Perhaps the most naked song MacKaye had ever written, it would help set the tone for Embrace.

In February, Rites of Spring recorded again at Inner Ear with MacKaye and Zientara, a session Canty later remembered as "the best four days of my life." Except for the vocals, the music was all recorded live, with strobe lights blinking and the musicians wrestling each other. "It was mayhem! It was very much like playing a show," Picciotto said. "I don't know how the song 'Persistent Vision' came out—we were jumping all over the place."

With its new funding, Dischord planned to release the Rites of Spring album followed by a Beefeater LP recorded shortly after the Rites session. Meanwhile, Gray Matter was about to issue its first album, *Food for Thought*, on a label started by Rich Moore and Bert Queiroz—R&B Records.

The last show of spring came in early June at the Chevy Chase Community Center, in a neighborhood not far from Wilson High School. Mark Sullivan's new band, King Face, was set to open for Rites of Spring, but fell apart just before the gig. It was replaced by Lünchmeat, which was followed by Beefeater. Then Rites of Spring took the stage, with Mike Fellows playfully introducing the opening song as "in the key of jelly." The band played its first four songs back-to-back, then paused to tune.

"It's going to be Revolution Summer, so get ready!" Canty proclaimed. "Let's get the male-bonding in the back and the dancing up front!" said Picciotto, who then announced the next Rites of Spring and Beefeater shows and the first major punk percussion protest at the South African Embassy. The chatter died, Picciotto said one word—"Spring!"—and the band was off. As the musicians tore through the song, Picciotto's voice rose to an unearthly shriek: "If summer left you dry/With nothing left to try/This time . . ."

After sprinting through another four songs, Picciotto leaned forward on the mic stand and hung there, panting, and launched into an impassioned rant: "It's time to get things happening! We've been waiting around and waiting around and waiting some more till the whole thing goes down. Letting people steal stuff right from under your nose." He hesitated, struggling for the right words. "And they're wearing the clothes you wore last year and you don't even feel like you should be around"—he straightened up, his eyes flashing—"but you gotta be around, you gotta stay around! We're coming back! This song is called 'Persistent Vision,' and I've still got it, and everyone in this fucking room better get it!" Then the initial chords screamed out and the band was off, racing through the song with fire and utter conviction.

With only a shouted "This is it, it's all yours!" to mark the transition, the band went from

"Persistent Vision" straight into "End on End." This had been the band's very first song and, like "Spring," carried a message of renewal. As drums, guitar, and voice strained at their limits, the audience picked up the "Ooo-ooo-oooh" background vocals. The music dropped back and Picciotto's voice overwhelmed the near-silence: "It's just the beginning/It's not the end/It's not the end/Take it back/Take it back, it's yours!"

The most astonishing part of the evening, however, was still to come. "End on End" shuddered to a halt and the band began to leave the stage. As if in response to the challenge the singer had flung moments before, the crowd took over, continuing the background vocals, refusing to let the song end.

An unprompted and unexpected a capella chorus rose from the audience. As it grew louder and louder, the musicians lingered offstage, unsure what to do. Then, as the crowd continued singing the song, they came back. First the drums rose, then the bass, then the guitars, till the band and audience were back into a full-throttle reprise of the song. Picciotto's cries of "It's end on end/We won't let it end" chased the song to its final, frenzied crash of drums and feedback.

Spring was over. It was time for the Revolution Summer.

TRANSPARENT MOMENTS
by Mark Andersen

This Rites of Spring show was my first experience with the band, and, in a way, I've never really recovered from that night. A more longtime DC punk who was present that night, Rich S., called the show "mind-blowing," writing in *WDC Period* that "ROS had such a powerful presence I found myself yelling along without knowing the words . . . I read where, in a review of "Salad Days," Gordon said he often felt he were 'waiting for the moment.' This show was the moment. The feeling in the hall was incredible, it was no different than the way it was in '81 or '82 . . . change was in the air."

Rereading his words, as well as my own feeble attempts at communication, they seem so lifeless, so stiff, so empty. That is tragic, for the moment was as full as life can be. Never before had I seen or heard anything quite like it. Although the band was the catalyst, the evening went far beyond them, was far more than a mere "concert." Words can barely scratch the surface; indeed, they may only somehow cheapen or limit it all.

All I can really say is that I experienced something in that room that today seems barely short of a miracle. A new community was being invented out of the rotting body of the old. The evening didn't erase DC punk's violence, drugs, or stupidity, much less homelessness, starvation, or injustice, but it changed me—and it was just the beginning. For the second time in my life, punk was about to radically rearrange my world. Once again, everything else would be measured by that sense of immense possibility. The next day I was on a plane to Central America, where my personal revolution would continue.

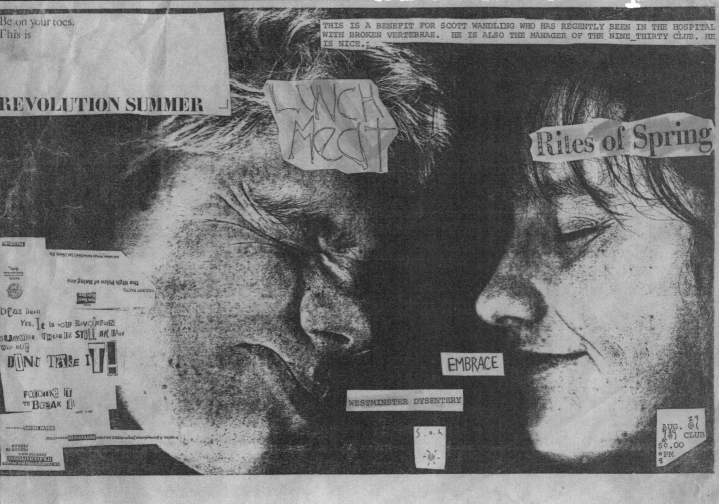

Be on your toes.
This is

THIS IS A BENEFIT FOR SCOTT WANDLING WHO HAS RECENTLY BEEN IN THE HOSPITAL WITH BROKEN VERTEBRAE. HE IS ALSO THE MANAGER OF THE NINE_THIRTY CLUB. HE IS NICE.

REVOLUTION SUMMER

LUNCH MEAT

Rites of Spring

EMBRACE

WESTMINSTER DYSENTERY

S.O.H.

AUG. 29 @ ((#) CLUB $¢.00 *PM

"Drink deep/It's just a taste/And it might not come this way again/I believe in moments Transparent moments/Moments in space/Where you've got to stake your faith . . ."
—Rites of Spring, "Drink Deep"

FLIER FOR RITES OF SPRING/LÜNCHMEAT/EMBRACE/WESTMINSTER DYSENTARY 9:30 CLUB SHOW, AUGUST 29, 1985
(with Chris Thomson and Amy Pickering, courtesy of the NPC copy machine)

drink deep

By June 1985, protesters were a common sight outside the South African embassy. But on the first day of summer, something unusual was clearly underway. Drivers craned their necks as they passed several dozen punks pounding on drums, trash cans, buckets, or anything else that made some noise when struck. The din even puzzled the regular demonstrators at the embassy, whose invitation to the punk group to join them across the street was politely declined.

The event was the punk percussion protest announced at the Rites of Spring show the week before. Members of that band as well as Beefeater and Gray Matter had brought their drums to the rally, a punk variation on the pots-and-pans protests of Latin American human rights groups. After about ninety minutes, the clamor rose to a climax. Then, just as suddenly as the protesters had arrived, they were gone, leaving only a few shattered drumsticks in their wake and a promise to soon return.

A few hours later, Rites of Spring was onstage, opening for the Jet Black Berries at the 9:30 Club. After the multiple equipment casualties of the previous week, the musicians were using three borrowed amps. Tom Berard, a longtime DC punk who was now a club employee, introduced the band: "Spring is over—now it's time to begin the Revolution Summer . . ."

With that, Mike Fellows hit the bass snaps that heralded "Drink Deep," and the band crashed into the song, their movements broken into an eerie stop-action by the blink of a strobe light. Guy Picciotto's vocals cut through the tumult: "Drink deep/It's just a taste/And it might not come this way again . . ."

After the song spiraled to its heart-stopping conclusion, Picciotto thanked those who had attended the protest. "When the guy introduced us as 'Punk Percussion,' I said, 'Damn right it's punk!' because it's creative outrage and not just a bunch of people hanging out in Georgetown, begging for fucking change!"

The remark announced the musicians' intention to battle for the meaning of punk. In an interview, Fellows had declined to call Rites a punk band, lest it be associated with "people who just want to be drunk and don't do anything creative." Picciotto, however, declined to surrender the word, explaining that "I know what Mike means, those people are totally alien to me, but it's too hard for me to say, 'No, we're not a punk band.' Who represents the ideal of punk more? Them or us? I think we do."

As usual, the band's onstage frenzy led to the need for on-the-spot repairs. During one pause, the crowd revived that afternoon's "Apartheid No, Freedom Yes" call. Picking up the chant, Picciotto leaped onto an amp to reveal that the set list had been written on the back of an anti-apartheid poster. "It's not really that far away," Picciotto noted of South Africa. "The same kind of thinking that is going on down there is going on here."

More equipment breakdowns followed, until Picciotto ruefully joked that "everything onstage has broken." Yet the quartet managed to keep its momentum, reaching a crescendo with "End on End." Picciotto grabbed his guitar by the strings, systematically popping them; he battered the guitar with his hands, bouncing it off the floor. After raising squeals of protest from the instrument, he tossed it aside and climbed onto an amp. As the band returned to the song's whirling clamor, Picciotto let himself fall limply, almost as if in slow motion, face first onto the stage. Rising unhurt from his fall, he grabbed the mic and threw himself into the song's finale.

As had happened the week before, the audience continued the song after the band left the stage. The musicians returned, obviously moved. With Picciotto's guitar thoroughly trashed, they launched into a ragged one-guitar rendition of "All There Is," Picciotto imploring the crowd to sing along. The song came to its climax with the singer on the edge of the stage, staring straight into the crowd and improvising: "It doesn't have to end/No end/I said, no end!"

Beefeater's show the following night was equally vigorous. The band, which—at HR's request—had recorded an Olive Tree EP to follow its imminent Dischord LP, opened with "Laurel Grove." Tomas Squip had written this poignant song, taking its name from a beautiful but desolate graveyard outside Savannah, Georgia, for former Red C comrade Toni Young. Long a harDCore stalwart, Young had retreated from the scene—and, apparently, life in general—after leaving Dove. "We seen truth as deep as bones/And love for all we know," Squip sang. "Now you sit at home with some makeup and a telephone/Don't even know you've never been so alone."

After playing several more jagged, propulsive songs, including "Reaganomix," "Apartheid No," and "In America," Squip dedicated the show to Amy Pickering "for setting a season into motion," and lauded the punk percussion protest and Revolution Summer ideas. When some barflies in the back of the room heckled him, Squip turned the next song, the anti-Reagan "Wars in Space," into a potent, improvised attack on his detractors. Such direct confrontation of the audience by a Dischord band had not been seen since the early days of Minor Threat.

Only a few people were consciously constructing Revolution Summer, but others began to share the spirit. Positive Force sponsored a free festival in Dupont Circle—combined with an NBAU-style protest—on the anniversary of the bombing of Hiroshima, followed three days later by a similarly chaotic but creative "Zombie Walk" on the anniversary of Nagasaki's bombing. As it grew, the group developed tentative bonds with the Dischord crowd. Beefeater, which played several Positive Force events—and had done a NBAU fundraiser shortly before PF coalesced—was one of the principal links.

A smaller "positive punk" scene was also developing in Burke, one of the bland, cookie-cutter Virginia suburbs. This group centered on teenagers Brian Gathy, Sean Lesher, Frank Charron, and Sohrab Habibion, who were involved with the fanzine *Yet Another Unslanted Opinion* and a new band sardonically named Kids for Cash. Through Gathy, the Burke kids established ties with both Positive Force and Dischord, and *Yet Another Unslanted Opinion* became an important forum for the reinvigorated scene.

Not all the older punks were receptive. Even Squip noted that Positive Force's "peace punks" didn't "seem to share our sense of humor," while some veterans thought that the young "posi-punks" were overly influenced by harDCore past, as well as a bit too perky. (For example, one rising new band from New York City's Connecticut suburbs, Youth of Today, took its "physically strong, morally straight" chant from a Boy Scout oath.) Still, the Burke kids were logical allies, especially for the younger Revolution Summer bands like Lünchmeat and Mission Impossible.

This alliance was cemented when the Burke punks, inspired by the Chevy Chase gigs, set up a show at their local community center. This July gig "was where we and Mission Impossible really got together for the first time," said Lünchmeat's Chris Thomson.

The two bands played a more accessible style of punk to younger kids who didn't necessarily view the Dischord elders as peers. If the bands were less politically pointed than their predecessors, their shows did recreate the egalitarian spirit of the early harDCore gigs. At one Burke show, the only thing physically dividing the band and the audience was a line of athletic tape on the floor, with one side labeled "stage."

xxx

Embrace's first performance was at Food for Thought in late July, with Gray Matter and Rites of Spring. Since previous gigs had interfered with the restaurant's operations, this was a morning show. Despite the hour, the restaurant was crowded when Embrace took the stage at 11 a.m. Nearly two years since Minor Threat's farewell, many younger fans knew the musicians' former bands only by records and reputation. Descriptions of Embrace as "Ian's new band" or "Ian singing with the Faith" were circulating widely, and many were eager to see harDCore history in action.

This band, however, did not play circa-'83 harDCore. MacKaye welcomed the crowd, and the musicians began "Past." Mike Hampton uncurled a guitar figure, underpinned by Ivor Hanson's building drums, and seconds later MacKaye and Chris Bald leaped in. While the quartet was not tight by Minor Threat standards, its music was impassioned and distinctive.

No one had anticipated this moment more than MacKaye himself. After watching for so long from the sidelines, he was eager to redeem his lost time. He sang so hard that the action seemed to involve his whole frame, which was trimmed considerably from the soda-plumped chubbiness of his late Minor Threat days.

"Past" was a mid-tempo song by harDCore standards, but it demonstrated that intensity did not require speed. The band shifted to an even slower pace with the next song, "Spoke," while maintaining the emotional pitch. MacKaye slid from a hoarse scream to a gentle chant and back again: "No compromise/No co-opt/No giving out, giving up, or giving in," followed by a simple repeated "spoke." Words that he said years before, MacKaye seemed to mean, still stood.

The emotional tenor of MacKaye's singing and lyrics was well-matched to Bald's lyrical bass and Hampton's guitar. The latter was the center of the band's sound, with the melodic style begun in the Faith now approaching fruition. Hampton was no longer the aggressive-if-baby-faced kid he had been in the early days of Extorts, SOA, or even the Faith. He had become an introspective craftsman, focused intensely on his playing; his style was strongly influenced by Empire, a Generation X offshoot that, while little-known even in Britain, had attracted a following in Washington. Bald was his old self, barely contained by the small stage—much less the beat—after his agonizingly long absence from live performance.

"This is Revolution Summer," MacKaye announced. "This next song goes out to Rites of Spring, Gray Matter, Beefeater, Lünchmeat, Mission Impossible . . . and Amy too. It's about Revolution Summer; it's called 'Dance of Days.'" With a drum roll, the song charged and MacKaye leaped forward, his eyes blazing: "We all struggle/For our dreams to be realized/They end up/Objects of our own despise/Why?"

What the song confronted was nothing less than the collapse of harDCore and the singer's own subsequent despair and inertia. Written largely by Bald, "Dance of Days" was a shimmering steamroller. Its title was a play on words: the "Dance of Death" that had represented so much to a teenage Bald and his DOD comrades now faced the "Dance of Days," the inevitable passage of time and with it the encroachment of the adult world and the loss of purpose and direction. The song, however, was a commitment to renewed struggle.

As strong as "Dance of Days" was, the set had not yet hit its emotional peak. As the band tuned, MacKaye addressed the crowd: "If anybody out here came to listen to what I was thinking about being straight or anti-alcohol or whatever, well, listen to this song. I think drugs are shit. So, this song is called 'No More Pain.'" The singer's voice was clipped by Bald, who hit the ominous first notes, making way for its opening challenge: "No more lying down/You've got to speak and move . . ."

The rest of the band crashed in, and MacKaye's voice rose to a shriek: "No more righteousness/Everything is far too wrong/No more selfish tears/You have not paid for them." The song was an account of the scene's ills and an attempted exorcism, attacking first the young media-punks— "No more dressing up/Please leave your costumes home"—and then the elitist older crowd—"No more looking down/You might bump your head."

Abruptly, the band hit a dead stop. Then MacKaye returned to the verse, his voice anguished: "No more alcohol/It's a Kool Aid substitute/No more heroin/Death is not glamorous." The tension built as MacKaye's litany continued: "No more number one/It's time to quit that game/No more attitude/Give it back to the TV set/No more tough guy stance/I hear your mommy call." His choked voice screeched the song's denouement: "No more suicide/It kills everyone/No more petty love/No more petty hate/No more pettiness/No more pain."

As if overwhelmed by the pent-up ugliness of two years, a hunched-over MacKaye screamed, "No more pain/No more pain/No more pain" over and over. Then he sprang up and unleashed a riveting diatribe: "No more bullshit! No more fucking punk rock dicks! No more fucking alcohol shit! No more common American teenager shit! No more sitting home watching TV all day! No more 'get drunk and party all fucking night' bullshit! *No more fucking pain!*" A voice from the crowd drunkenly mocked him. MacKaye stopped, glared straight at the loudmouth, and added heatedly, "And if you don't like it, then fuck you too!"

MacKaye's return to the stage could hardly have been more dramatic. If the actual performance was a bit ragged—with frequent bum notes and unintended gaps—its intensity and nakedness was a revelation, even in a town that had already experienced Rites of Spring.

Gray Matter followed with an impressive set. The band had powerful new songs like "Take it Back" and "Chutes and Ladders," clearly influenced by Rites of Spring. (Soon after, however, the band was sidelined when Mark Haggerty moved to New Zealand. After one last show on Food for Thought's roof, Gray Matter went on indefinite hiatus.)

The Rites of Spring set that ended the show was the band's first since the 9:30 Club gig more than a month before. The band played a powerful set to an overwhelmingly appreciative crowd, yet the musicians were beginning to be troubled by aspects of their success. Their shows' most potent moments had been the most spontaneous ones, but these were solidifying into ritual. The musicians were concerned that the audience singalong of "End on End" would become what Picciotto called "a rote thing." To prevent this, the band went from "End on End" straight into "Spring," preempting a replay of the past two shows' coda. Rites of Spring would never again conclude a concert with "End on End."

By now, the group faced intense expectations. Although the musicians generally handled these with grace, they recognized the increasing possibility of disappointment. "In a way, Revolution Summer was ominous because it couldn't last," said Natalie Avery, a close friend of the band.

xxx

Not all the challenges to the revived Dischord scene were so abstract; there was also the threat of violence as troublemakers infiltrated the "scene within the scene." "This was a real period of pacifism," Molly Burnham recalled. "If someone was dancing too roughly at a show, everyone would get around the person and totally chill them out." This approach had no appeal to the brawlers who Gordon Gordon dubbed "Rambo-punks."

Only some of these combatants were skinheads, but the most visible and consistently violent at the time were the skins associated with Lefty. This curiously chauvinistic crew once precipitated a biker/punk confrontation by knocking over an entire line of motorcycles, apparently because they were not American-made. At the 1985 Rock Against Reagan concert, skinheads attacked a person who was playing "disrespectfully" with an American flag, sending him to the hospital with a broken jaw and other injuries.

Some of the worst brutality came when Margo Buckley, who had begun managing Lethal Intent and Black Market Baby, helped promote a show at the Lansburgh Center. A self-described "suburban housewife" who was fairly new to the scene, Buckley simply wanted to help bands. Not having been warned about Lefty's skins, she agreed to hire them for security.

The show was "a nightmare," Buckley recalled years later. "I raced from one part of the club to another with the horrified representatives of the Lansburgh. As soon as we'd stop one of them from beating someone, another fight would break out." It was the only show she did with the skins as security—and it was the last punk show at the Lansburgh.

Asked about such incidents years later, Lefty complained that she was blamed for things she never did—and then proceeded to justify many of the actions. Kids who used to hang out around Dupont Circle told stories of having "a hit" put out on them by Lefty. One claimed that "she would just tell the others to get someone—even other punks in the Circle. I thought it was crazy. After all, we were all involved in the same thing, weren't we?" One acquaintance from that period noted that "there was a side of Lefty that was very nice—and another side that was psychotic."

xxx

Darryl Jenifer and Dr. Know were frustrated. The former had begun to earn a reputation as a session musician, but the band the two had developed with guitarist Billy Banks, Cro-Mags drummer Mackie, and singer Michael Enkrumah (son of reggae cult hero Ras Michael) had not meshed. Their solution was an unlikely reunion with HR and Earl Hudson, grudgingly recognizing both the four's lasting bonds and their limited success while apart.

The bassist and guitarist were now married with children, and had fled the drugs and violence of the Lower East Side for Woodstock, a quiet upstate New York community with longstanding musical connections. They needed to make a living, and—despite anger over Bad Brains' dissolution—had remained in chilly but regular contact with the Hudson brothers. It was not entirely unconvincing when Jenifer explained the four's decision to reunite by saying, "We missed each other so we all just came back around again."

Not everyone was persuaded; some punks considered the reunion a crass commercial move. Yet HR—a.k.a., Joseph—had previously walked away just when significant cash was offered. "Joseph doesn't do anything just for money," David Byers said.

Much had changed during the quartet's two-year absence, most of it favorable to its reunion. Bad Brains were still remembered as one of the greatest punk bands of all time, while few outside of DC recalled HR's 1982 miscues or knew of his more recent travails. The band returned, as razor-sharp and energized as before, with two July shows at New York City's Rock Hotel. It followed these gigs with several shows in the Northeast, playing to capacity crowds.

Despite the far more enthusiastic reaction than his new band had received, HR was cautious. The singer emphasized that he would continue with his other projects. He agreed to do a new record and a full tour with Bad Brains, but made no longterm commitment.

One challenge was writing new material that would justify the regrouping as more than nostalgia. By the time Bad Brains played their first hometown gig in August with Dove, Beefeater, and Scream at WUST Radio Hall, they had begun to play new songs, some adapted from work Jenifer and Dr. Know had done with Mackie and Banks. This material charted a course between hardcore and reggae, forging a sound that was slower than the band's blistering rastacore and much heavier than its reggae. The songs were sinuous, assured, and more accessible than much of the quartet's earlier work. They were as powerful as early Bad Brains hardcore but less frenetic, a progression rather than a repudiation.

x x x

Several days after the Bad Brains show, Rites of Spring returned to the stage on a bill with Embrace and Lünchmeat. A poster for the show included one of Pickering's ransom notes: "Dear dear: Yes, it is now Revolution Summer. There still is an easy way out. DON'T TAKE IT! Forsake it to break it. Don't give up 365 days a year."

That directive was hard to follow. The night was to be Lünchmeat's last show, since several of the members had decided to go to college. (Indeed, two of them flew back from Colorado—without their parents' knowledge—to play the gig.) "I didn't even think about it, I just did what everyone else was doing," said Lünchmeat singer Bobby Sullivan. "Before I knew it, I had made a commitment to go to college and now it's too late. I guess I'm doing it for my parents."

Mission Impossible also

NEW PALS AND PUNK PERCUSSION PROTEST
by Mark Andersen

The Rites of Spring 9:30 gig was one of my first shows since returning from a two-month trip to war-torn, impoverished Central America. Having left in highly charged spirits, I returned sobered by my experience yet even more determined to do something.

As I threw myself back into work with Positive Force, three people began to become key comrades. The first was Tomas Squip, who I called up to offer my help in publicizing the next punk percussion protest, planned for the week after the Rites of Spring show. My visit to Dischord House to make copies of a flier led to our first serious conversation. Our shared interest in activism and spirituality would draw us into ongoing collaboration.

Tomas's flier—to which I added info on South Africa and PF—became the catalyst for my next connection. As Rites of Spring left the stage, I hurried to the long hallway leading out of the club to F Street, to hand out fliers to the exiting crowd. Among the dozens filing out of the room was a striking, red-haired young woman, drenched in sweat. Moments after taking a flier, she was back, chatting animatedly, eager to get involved with Positive Force. Her name was Jenny Toomey.

Jenny was a fanatical ROS follower. Later she joked, "I was a heart-broken 16-year-old and that summer I lived from Rites of Spring show to Rites of Spring show!" By chance, she had witnessed BMO defy her high school authorities by playing their anthem "Cool As Shit" at a talent show. Impressed by the subversive humor, creativity, and wit of the WGNS scene, Jenny became interested in the larger DC punk world. Energetic and gifted, she swiftly became a central member of Positive Force and a close friend.

She and I collaborated on what would be the first punk show either of us had organized: a benefit at dc space to raise money to pay for PF's free Alternatives Festival, to be held outdoors in Dupont Circle. Beefeater and Embrace played the show; as a result, I found myself working for the first time with Ian MacKaye. Our relationship was a bit rocky at the beginning, in part because of his suspicion of Revolutionary Communist Party influence in Positive Force. Our first in-depth talk consisted mostly of Ian listing his concerns about a flier I had made for the dc space show. Chastened by his largely accurate critique, I quickly canned the old flier and made a new one, an action which apparently impressed Ian—and the seeds for many a future conspiracy were sown.

succumbed to higher education. Before disbanding, however, the two bands made a combined farewell single for their own label, Sammich, begun by their teenage co-conspirators, Amanda MacKaye and Eli Janney, with some help from Dischord and Skip Groff.

These bonds were strengthened by the shared catharsis of the punk percussion protests. While both of the previous protests had between 40 and 50 people, this one was larger and even more spirited than the first two had been. At least 75 punks gathered with two complete drumsets and numerous other noise-makers, creating a massive roar of punk percussion. As Tomas leaped up and down, drumming and vaguely orchestrating the rhythmic chaos, car after car passed, offering support by blowing their horns. Used to more mannerly and choreographed demonstrations, the police were nonplussed by the scene.

Cynthia Connolly remembered that "everyone came after school and work. The drumbeats went through Rock Creek Park. You could hear the thumping for miles. It was so great." As Molly Burnham said to me later, "The punk percussion protests were completely unifying and amazing. It was finally what punk was always meant to do . . ." She paused, laughed, and continued, "It was what everybody really loved, which was making a really big scene but totally having a purpose . . . and everybody who was involved totally believed in what was going on." (Not everyone has quite as idealistic a recollection as Molly. For example, Mike Fellows later described the protests in these terms: "I went and it was cool but it wasn't that big of a deal. I mean, I was against apartheid, but mostly I went because other people did . . . it was fun.")

After the protest, I was convinced of the necessity to work more closely with the Dischord group, but my PF compatriot Kevin Mattson was skeptical. He was not in favor of bringing Positive Force any closer to the punk scene than it already was. Moreover, while he had respect for some Dischord-related individuals, he dismissed Revolution Summer as "just another in-crowd thing by that clique."

It was true that the Dischord people seemed distinctly less likely to be seen at our protests than vice versa. While Kevin's explanation may have had some merit, no doubt this was partly due to lasting suspicions of outsiders like the RCP and Yippies trying to use the scene for their own ends.

In the end, I think Mark Jenkins—who observed these events with more than a modicum of journalistic distance from his perch at the *Post* and *City Paper*—got it right when he noted that "Revolution Summer really was a striking thing . . . when the harDCore scene started to collapse with bands like Minor Threat breaking up, I figured that was it, that those people would return to a more typical life path for their age and class group like most 'youth rebels' do . . . But instead of giving up and moving on, they made a new beginning. It really was a unique and impressive occurence."

Mission Impossible had transcended the posi-punk clichés of peers like Uniform Choice with lyrically nuanced songs such as "Helpless" and "I Can Only Try" (released on the WGNS/Metrozine compilation 45, "Alive and Kicking"), which were driven by Bryant Mason's jazzy guitar and Dave Grohl's frenetic but assured drumming. Such Lünchmeat songs as "Under the Glare" and "Lookin' Around" showed a keen sense of melody and song structure.

Both bands hoped to keep going somehow, but school was a major obstacle. The split EP was covered with slogans like "Revolution Summer is for always," but the musicians' college plans suggested that Revolution Summer might not long outlast the summer itself.

Embrace followed Lünch meat's last performance with a riveting set, its second show ever. Bald and MacKaye had made lyric sheets that were distributed to the audience at the door. "It was really important to us at the time that people know what we were singing about," MacKaye noted.

In the audience were two *Flipside* staffers. The magazine was soon to report that, while Embrace was "a band to be reckoned with," the headlining Rites of Spring was overwhelming: "They burst onstage with the power of the early Jam. The band and audience were in some weird communication to the point you expected an explosion."

The Flipsiders decided to interview the band. Impressed by the spirit of Dischord House, they also did a separate interview with MacKaye, Squip, and Mark Sullivan. If this period produced any manifestos beyond the songs themselves, it was these interviews.

"Revolution Summer is a revival," said Squip. "It [builds on] the energy and commitment that was in the original punk movement. The original punk philosophy was—for us—first of all, 'fight bullshit' and second of all, 'do something real.' And [by 1983] the punk scene was doing neither of those. Most people were submitting to exactly the same bullshit that everybody else was submitting to: the alcohol thing, smoking, being the tough guy, or being a lawyer—exactly the bullshit that punk was supposed to defy. [Revolution Summer] is putting the protest back in punk."

Denouncing "drunk punks" and "fag-bashing," MacKaye noted that "we could just go on with our lives and reject our past, or we can get up and fight against it and speak out again. We sang out against people in the beginning and we'll sing out again. I think the gist of all of this is that you have a group of people in their 20s now who want to continue to do socially relevant things. We're not giving up on the punk thing."

Squip was careful to say that "Revolution Summer is so self-understood and ethereal that there are no doctrines or rules or members. It's a spiritual thing." Still, in addition to criticizing "punk as usual," MacKaye endorsed vegetarianism: "It's such a logical step for straight edge."

A related concept was what Mark Sullivan called the "economic vote." As Sullivan put it, "I do vote, (but) in the end I don't think that my vote counts for very much . . . what I think is more important in our society is the way that we spend our money. People should vote with their money. And my big vote is against mechanized death." While this idea was implicit in straight edge and other aspects of punk, the economic vote made explicit what MacKaye argued elsewhere: "I consider my life a protest."

Given DC punk's reputation for "personal politics," the Flipsiders were surprised to learn of the ongoing series of punk anti-apartheid demonstrations. "Whether it's 'political' or not, I don't know," MacKaye responded. "It's an emotional issue just like the civil rights thing was. It still pisses me off when I see Kent State pictures" of the Vietnam War protesters killed by the Ohio State National Guard.

The Revolutionaries had also come to recognize a special significance in the apartheid issue. "We live in a black town run by whites," noted MacKaye. "South Africa junior," added Squip. Then as now, Washington had no voting representation in Congress; it was scarcely more than the American equivalent of a South African "homeland," a colony without genuine self-determination.

After the Rites of Spring, Gray Matter, and Beefeater albums were released, *Flipside* published the interview as part of a package on the DC scene. Also included was an interview with Scream and a Squip-designed Dischord ad that featured a photo of severed cows' heads at a slaughterhouse with the plea, "Help us." The issue helped re-establish the DC scene as a vibrant, cutting-edge community in the eyes of the larger punk world.

Underlying the redefinition of punk was what Squip called "the heartfelt thing. This is a movement where the whole emotional aspect is brought in, which I don't think punk ever had." Much to the confusion of some angry kids, this meant breaching the boundaries between punks and hippies. Punk could—in fact, *must*—express not just hate or anger but also love or any other real emotion.

Revolution Summer's ideas also spoke to the moment, as many 20-something punks considered adulthood. "If the enemies are parents and teachers," Molly Burnham noted years later, "what do you do when you're not in high school anymore and you've moved out of your parents' house? The obvious course—return to the mainstream—was not acceptable, so you rebel against each other— that's when the fractionalizing comes—and then you start rebelling against something even bigger, the political conditions."

"I'm waiting for an explosion where people just let themselves go," said Squip at the time, "where the whole concept of going to concerts for entertainment is going to be obsolete. People will go there to revolutionize what they're doing."

Perhaps the most articulate expression of this feeling was a new Rites of Spring song, "Hidden Wheel," in which Picciotto revealed his amazed disbelief of past ignorance: "It never seemed that close to me/No, it never seemed all that real to me/Now it feels so real to me/Now it feels so much to see." The music pulls back as the singer contemplates a whole new world somehow revealed to him: "Is this the first time I've seen the color of this room/Is this the first time?" A bitter query—"Is this the first time I've seen the size of these walls?"—rolls into the song's blistering conclusion: "Now I'm the angry son/Everything I've learned was wrong/I'm the burning door/Once I'm opened I can't be closed/I found a hidden wheel and it rolls to reveal/That I'm the angry son/I'm the angry son."

xxx

While skeptical of both its political and musical direction, Brian Baker was nonetheless sufficiently inspired by Revolution Summer to leave the Meatmen and abandon a embryonic pop project with Lyle Preslar and Jeff Nelson. The guitarist began what Preslar derisively called his "punk band." His cohorts were Colin Sears and Roger Marbury, who had played in such WGNS joke bands as Bozo Brigade and the high-spirited but decidedly un-hardcore BMO.

Singer Shawn Brown, whom Sears had met at Montgomery College, had no previous band experience, but he fit Baker's call for "an energetic shouter." The group took the name Dag Nasty from a German children's game, and adopted a flame-haired logo inspired, Sears reported, by a "bad '30s movie I saw where the guy's hair caught on fire at the end because of all the pain and anger that had built up inside of him."

Dag Nasty took an ambiguous position on the edge of the Revolution Summer crowd. While the band was motivated by the scene's energy, its music revived an earlier sound, and thus was often compared to Minor Threat. "I can think of worse comparisons," said Baker. "I'd like to avoid the stigma, but it's really hard. We're playing fast music because we like fast music. It is coincidental that Minor Threat played fast music as well. Part of it also comes from me writing songs and Shawn, who is still learning about being a singer. He's very conscious of trying to avoid being attached to Ian's style, but just because of the way the songs are structured and the speed of the song, it's hard not to."

Lyrical parallels were also apparent in songs like "Under Your Influence," which denounced drinking and fighting. Dag Nasty "was trying to avoid the militant straight edge bandwagon," Baker explained. "I don't think it's coincidental that none of us drink or do drugs [but] I don't think it could feasibly be the focus of our band."

Far from an intimate Food for Thought gig, Dag Nasty's first DC show was with Government Issue and DOA at WUST. The band made a powerful debut, but that was overshadowed by fights and aggressive stage-diving. DOA confronted the Rambo-punks, with guitarist Dave Gregg suggesting that fans "could ease up a bit and give your sisters some space to dance as well." Singer Joey Shithead announced an upcoming Positive Force–sponsored anti-apartheid demonstration, drawing taunts, sieg heils, and anti-communist epithets. He didn't back down, however, and the band finished its set without further major disruptions.

A week later, Revolution Summer mainstays Embrace, Rites of Spring, and Beefeater were confronted by violent punks—including Lefty and her crew—at Baltimore's Clubhouse. That this was not the typical Revolution Summer crowd became clear when Embrace started to play. Almost immediately, scattered slamming began.

Jon Kirschten—Chris Bald's younger brother, who had started coming to shows in the last year—confronted some slamming skinheads in exasperation. "I was nearly in tears," he remembered. "I just took a lyric sheet and pushed it at the guys, saying, 'Here, please read this.'" Instead, one of them gave Kirschten a hard shove, the usual prelude to a fight.

From the stage, Bald could see what was happening. He stopped playing and leaped off the stage to protect his brother. As Embrace ground to a halt, the skins and a group of Embrace supporters found themselves in an angry face-off. A massive free-for-all could easily have erupted—but didn't, largely due to MacKaye's calming influence.

Now a more or less committed pacifist—having seen the effects of his own earlier punk violence—MacKaye did not want to descend to that level again. Picciotto remembered being "so angry that I wanted to kill them, but Ian was like, 'No, let's try to cool it out, talk to them.'" Successful in their peace-making, Embrace returned to the stage, finished the few songs left in its set, and then went outside for a heated but nonviolent discussion.

Beefeater was next, with Squip making a plea for people to "not be so macho." The slamming continued, so the singer tried a novel approach to upstaging the brawlers: He undressed. Once entirely naked, he moved directly toward the pit. This so startled the skankers that they fled, and the band finished its set without further incident.

Before Rites played, Picciotto requested that no one thrash during its performance, and the band performed an intense set with no violence. If the night bordered on triumph for the Dischord crowd, it was not the final resolution of the friction between the divergent punk factions.

A few new bands that had nothing to do with Rambo-punk defined themselves in opposition to the Dischord crowd. The most noteworthy of this ilk, the defiantly raw Pussy Galore, encouraged divisiveness as a means of attracting attention, writing songs like "Fuck Ian MacKaye," "You Look Like a Jew," and "Die Bitch." These taunts and tantrums didn't draw much of a reaction, and the band soon moved to New York. When they later unveiled a song entitled "Revolution Summer," it was not a tribute to the DC scene.

Meanwhile, harDCore stalwarts Marginal Man, Scream, and GI all continued to tour, record, and release new albums. GI was now on a California label, Mystic, which John Stabb wryly described as the "K-tel of hardcore." All three groups remained popular, but were too busy with their ongoing work to participate in any reinvention of the DC scene.

In its way, Revolution Summer was probably the death knell for hopes of "scene unity" in DC. While some of the Dischord crowd denounced such bands as Lethal Intent and their fans, old-timers like Danny Ingram and Nathan Strejcek dismissed the idea of a punk revival as "rubbish" and "nostalgia bullshit" respectively.

Asked if Embrace would play with such bands as GI and Black Market Baby, MacKaye said yes, but added that "we try not to play big shows like the WUST shows right now. It's hard to get your message across to 700 people who just want to get down and rock out. I like to play small shows where at least you have a fighting chance of influencing a few people. It's nothing against [the better-known bands]. They've been around longer and are in sort of a different thing and we're just trying to establish ourselves as a band. Once we do that, we can play with them."

Stabb apparently resented this position. By late 1985, he was lampooning Revolution Summer from stage, heralding instead what he called "Degradation Winter." Ironically, guitarist Tom Lyle would later note the musical influence of Revolution Summer on GI's subsequent self-titled album, which used backwards guitars and electric sitar.

"I'd love to play with bands like ROS," Stabb later admitted, "but a lot of those bands don't want to play for our audience. I can accept that we have reached the level of Minor Threat in their days when things got out of hand." He added that "I wouldn't want to be associated with the kind of shows we play. The only reason we do them is because these are the only shows we can find." He didn't note, however, that venues like the 9:30 Club largely stopped booking GI for a time in part because Stabb made no effort to control the band's often destructive fans.

xxx

Embrace confronted the issue of violence with a new song, "Said Gun," it debuted at dc space in October. "You're looking for a reason to hate so you can fuck somebody up/You'd hate yourself if you got the chance/I guess you already do/You fuck yourself up every night," MacKaye jibed. The song's punchline: "If you have to fight/Then fight the violence that rules your life."

MacKaye's outspokenness made him the lightning rod for the skinheads. The battle was joined again at Embrace's next show at Chevy Chase Community Center, with Rites of Spring and Bells Of (a new Rites-influenced band whose bassist was skinhead Bleu Kopperl). Bells Of played without incident, but Embrace was greeted with abuse. Between songs, MacKaye asked one of his critics, "Are you angry at me?" and stuck the mic into the crowd for a reply. The eventual response was only, "Yeah, I am!"

"And why are you so angry, sir?" MacKaye queried the skinhead, who could muster only a flustered, "Because, man . . ." before shoving the mic and stalking away. "Well, that sure makes sense to me," mocked the singer to widespread applause. The humiliated skins began calling the band "dicks," to which MacKaye responded, "So I'm a dick? Oh and he's a dick too? And him also?," pointing at various members of the band. "OK, we're Dick, Dick, Dick, and the Embrace Boys—and I'm Dick. Hi!"

Sullenly, the skins began to leave; a skinhead girl shouted, "We'll see you after the show, asshole!" MacKaye's shoulders drooped in feigned terror and then the band was into "Spoke," with

MacKaye pointedly addressing the line "I couldn't care less" to the spot where the skins had been. The band finished its set without interruption, ending with another new tune, "Money Song," a scorching statement of MacKaye's anti-greed ethic.

The skinheads did not return, but slamming resumed when Rites of Spring began its set. The band opened by throwing flowers into the crowd—hardly the exhortation to a football match—but when it roared into "Spring," the flailing grew. "There are people here who don't know what this song is about or what this band is about," said an obviously distraught Picciotto, an outburst that quelled the rough elements in the crowd.

While Picciotto confronted the slam ethic, Fellows began to question the increasingly ritualized audience reaction. He doubted the sincerity of the fans who were moved to tears by Rites of Spring performances. "Maybe it was real to begin with," he said, "but to cry every time? Come on."

As the band worked on new material, Fellows wanted to make dramatic changes to upset audience expectations. While the other musicians shared his desire to keep the band fresh and challenging, they didn't share his confrontational approach.

Rites of Spring's next two shows were both benefits for local alternative radio stations: the University of Maryland's WMUC and a new version of WGTB with a signal that was restricted to the Georgetown University campus. The latter benefit—held in December at the Hall of Nations where the Cramps and Urban Verbs had played seven years before—was a climactic show. The three central Revolution Summer bands, Rites of Spring, Embrace, and Beefeater, played their first concert together in DC, with Dag Nasty opening.

Dag Nasty had grown immensely since its first performance at WUST four months before, increasingly forsaking Minor Threat–style harDCore for catchier pop-rock. Brown seemed slightly uncomfortable with the newer material, but his gruff performance of the anti-nostalgic "Never Go Back" was heartbreakingly convincing.

Once again, the skinheads came out to dog Embrace, only this time instead of entering they waited just outside the door. For MacKaye, it was a special evening, playing on the stage where the Cramps had sparked his punk odyssey. He told the audience as much, then introduced the opening "Money Song."

Embrace had become considerably tighter, though it was still short of Minor Threat's cohesion. After ripping through "Past" and "Building," MacKaye paused to note that "everybody thinks that punks are a bunch of stupid asses, let's not prove them right tonight. If you've got a bad fucking problem, some bad vibes, then check it at the door." Looking in the direction of the skinheads skulking outside the front door, MacKaye continued: "This song is called 'Said Gun' and it's for everybody who has trouble with their lives being destroyed by violence."

When the show's organizers began closing the doors to block the skins' view, MacKaye asked to keep them open. The band played another new tune, "Do Not Consider Yourself Free," its most explicitly political song yet. As the song reached its climax—"And you can stay cool behind your window/And choose the things you want to see/But as long as others are held captive/Do not consider yourself free"—MacKaye did a mock sieg heil. The music paused and then lunged forward, and MacKaye wrenched the word "Free!" out of his throat as he turned the salute into a thumb's down aimed straight to the back of the hall. The message apparently was received and understood, for despite all their posturing, the skins left without any violent disruption.

The evening's most jarring note came from an entirely different source. Although Rites would ordinarily have closed the show, it was scheduled to play third in order to accommodate Fellows's job at the Georgetown Theater. The theater was mere blocks away, but when the time came, there was no sign of the bassist. This was a real problem, since the hall had a midnight curfew. When Fellows finally arrived, the vibe was tense. The band played as hard as usual, but the usual onstage banter all but disappeared. Twice, Fellows got in visible spats with Brendan Canty.

Nearly half of the songs in the abbreviated set were not on the album, including "All Through a Life," "In Silence/Words Away," "Hidden Wheel," and "Patience." These songs were slower, more mannered, and less incendiary than the best of their earlier work. Audience reaction also seemed a little muted.

What had made the band so affecting was its unity, its common fire—which tonight was missing. It could have just been an off gig, but it wasn't. When the final chords of "Drink Deep" faded, a certain moment passed. No one knew it then, but Rites of Spring had just played its last show.

As the band left the stage, with Canty and Fellows verbally sparring in the hallway, Beefeater rushed to set up. The band had begun playing a new song that encapsulated Squip's message and, in a way, the ethic of Revolution Summer: "Live the Life" was actually an old song, written in the

1930s by Thomas Dorsey, the "Father of Gospel Music." Squip heard it once on the radio, and searched for years for a recording. When he finally found a version by Dorsey's collaborator Mahalia Jackson, the band reworked the hymn into a reggae-metal anthem. Its message was simple yet profound: Talk is cheap. If punk was to mean anything at all, punks needed to get past rhetoric and live the life they sang about in their songs.

The use of a gospel song in this new context made some punks nervous, but it suited Squip, an unabashed spiritual seeker. It also reflected the intensity of the commitment of many in the new DC punk scene, and the importance of this community in their lives.

Bassist Dug Birdzell gave a heartfelt intro to "Song for Lucky": "This song is about honesty in the form of jazz saxophonist Lucky Thompson. Honesty is a very important thing, especially here"—motioning to the crowd—"as opposed to pulling bullshit trips, power trips. This is the opportunity to get rid of bullshit, to stand up to it, to put it aside. Sexism, racism, whatever you want to call it, as it exists here—and it does exist, I see it—you can stand up to it, that's why we're here."

At the song's end, the hall's staff shut off the power even though they knew

DEAD KENNEDYS VS. SKINHEADS
by Mark Andersen

That there was no violence at the December 1985 Hall of Nations show was a relief, given the chaos of a recent Dead Kennedys/Government Issue WUST show, where the skin crew showed up with US flags and a bad attitude. As many indulged in the mainstream punk rituals of slamdancing and stage-diving—with at least one person visiting the emergency room of nearby Howard University hospital with a head cracked open by a diver's boot—the skinhead group used the cover afforded by the massive crowd to pursue its agenda of mayhem.

After a flurry of fights broke out during GI's set, WUST's security intervened, accidentally attacking one of the DK's road crew who was attempting to stop the skinheads' mischief. After calm was restored, a group of skins were summarily kicked out, including some who claimed to have played no part in the battle. Enraged, they waited outside outside to attack the DKs.

The DKs started to play amidst heckling and a sporadic beer can barrage from the remaining Rambo-punks in the crowd. Biafra repeatedly paused to challenge his shadowy opponents. Finally, when a full beer can missed the band but hit a bystander, Biafra himself leaped into the crowd and collared the cowardly assailant.

After this, the DKs were able to play the remainder of their set without further interruption. Biafra ended the show with "Stars and Stripes of Corruption" and a pointed reminder that the punk crowd had the power to defeat the ugliness by standing up against it.

The night's drama had not ended, however. Outside, a group of people—including Ian and myself—talked with the skins, trying to get them to not take the confrontation any further. I listened incredulously as one skin told me, "I am not a Nazi—I am a fascist!" The distinction—apparently meant to clarify that the skins didn't support Hitler, lest they appear somehow not patriotic—was hardly reassuring.

Finally, the skins retreated, although apparently with the intent of following the DKs to their motel for a surprise attack. The situation was finally defused when, by chance, cops pulled the skins over for a routine traffic violation as they sought to tail the DKs' van.

Beefeater had only one number left. Angered, guitarist Fred Smith led a group of punks in an impromptu rendition of "Fred's Song" on the sidewalk just outside the hall. It had been the biggest Revolution Summer gig yet, with perhaps 400 people in attendance.

xxx

Further evidence of the growing strain within Rites of Spring came when the band entered Inner Ear to record its new songs. It was a difficult session, and the result had a distinctly less spontaneous sound. The songs were strong, with words that clearly showed that Picciotto had succeeded in "not writing the album over again," but they did not always benefit from the musical restraint.

As the musicians tried to write more new songs that broke the previous mold, it became clear to the others that Fellows was no longer fully committed. Not long after the Inner Ear sessions, he confirmed it: He didn't want to continue with the group.

"This band is such a unit that it would be impossible to continue with someone else," said Eddie Janney at the time. Picciotto echoed this: "There are tons of bands who aren't close as human beings but they can make great music, because those people can play together. But for us, it was much more than playing, it was totally interacting together." Picciotto, Janney, and Canty continued together, hoping to eventually perform as a threesome.

One of those shaken by the news of the band's split was MacKaye. Rites of Spring had been an inspiration to him at one of the darkest periods of his life. MacKaye returned to the final Minor Threat song he had written, "Last Song," which had been composed for the Faith when that band split. Now the lyrics—which appeared to refer to both Rites of Spring and Embrace, but actually had been written long before—were set to new music and dedicated to the passing of Rites of Spring.

xxx

As 1986 began and DC punk struggled to build on Revolution Summer, Henry Rollins announced, "I'm extremely jaded. There's nothing you can do at a show that hasn't been done, not a whole lot of bands doing anything new." During breaks from the Black Flag touring grind, he moved from sporadic spoken-word gigs to a growing focus on writing, inspired by Henry Miller's *Black Spring*. The man who in SOA had screamed, "I'm not a book/You can't read me," began writing and publishing his own books with help from his friend Joe Cole, who ran a small company called Illiterati Press.

Rollins saw himself as a man with a mission. If it was a solitary one, it was nonetheless lived in public. And while his life took him far from his old hometown allies, their ethics were still connected. In November 1985, while on tour in Amsterdam, Rollins wrote:

> America is a place that destroys the minds of its young people at an early age. By the time they are of any age to think for themselves, it's much too late. That's why Journey and Bruce Springsteen fill stadiums. Kids look to others to make them feel good about themselves. Those who rebel usually go to the shop next door to buy their new clothes. They are compensated for their choices. Their avenues of rebellion have been provided for them by the same people that will apply the chains in a few years. How many of these upstarts will end up cops? More than you think. The hands are invisible, the hands are subtle, the unseen hands mold and push ceaselessly until the human clay molds and sets without question.

> Change has to come from the inside. No bullets have to fly. Thirst. Hunger. The soul must be set aflame. Self expression must be realized. Do you remember that line from that old Earth Wind and Fire album, "You're a shining star/No matter who you are"? It's so true . . . Just because they built a desk for you that does not mean you have to sit behind it . . . Wouldn't it be great if they built a jail and nobody came?

Jails were made to be filled, however, and before these lines would be published, the man who was Rollins's original inspiration would be behind bars again. Although he was preparing for more work with Bad Brains, HR had returned to Washington late in 1985 to rehearse with his other project, the HR Band. Returning from practice one night in February 1986, HR, Kenny Dread, and Earl Hudson were pulled over by police. Pot was found in the car.

After the trial, HR returned to the prison in Lorton, Virginia with a four-month sentence. This time Hudson accompanied him to the prison, where their father was a guard.

Bad Brains were able to record most of their new album before HR and Hudson went to Lorton, but one song was left without a vocal track. Producer Ron St. Germain decided to record the vocals over the phone from prison. The lyrics to "Sacred Love" were written by HR for a faithful friend during his incarceration, and they gained an extra poignancy in the process.

Given his mainstream-pop resumé, St. Germain had seemed a strange choice as producer. But his production gave Bad Brains a broader, livelier sound that complemented its new songs. The result was an album that sounded artistically uncompromised, but also seemed commercially viable.

St. Germain had insisted that the band make a rock record, downplaying reggae. In effect, the producer had resolved—at least temporarily—the musical dispute that had helped tear the band apart in 1982-83. A skeptical HR was mollified by assurances of the tactical wisdom of this step and that subsequent records would have much more reggae.

In their own way, Bad Brains had made the same move as the Revolution Summer bands. Rather than continuing to compete in the louder-faster drag race, the band eased up on the throttle and integrated influences more deeply, crafting a new style that was both a musical progression and more accessible. Despite the challenge of having half the band in jail, it appeared that Bad Brains were ready to make a leap forward.

In Washington, a few protested HR and Hudson's imprisonment. Most DC punks, however, no longer considered Bad Brains part of the scene. Even though HR celebrated the underground in the new "House of Suffering," the band was headed above ground, toward the realm of such commercially promising groups as REM, Hüsker Dü, and the Replacements who were (or soon would be) signed to major labels.

It was this looming development that MacKaye warned about in an agonized new song, "End of a Year (Words Are Not Enough)." He still wanted to create a genuine alternative, one that could provide vital music while making the corporate music business irrelevant. "There will be no victory/No progress made/If we do not stand apart from the enemy," the song warned.

If Embrace's music had the potential to reach a larger audience than Minor Threat, the initial reaction to the band was far less fervent than if MacKaye had simply reprised his former band's approach. That did not bother him. "I think people should always be attempting within themselves to do something that is new and challenging," he said.

"Within my own little community of people there's a lot of reestablishing going on, but we feel like we're moving forward pretty well, we feel like we're doing something," MacKaye said. Yet his new songs hinted at a darker side of the story, suggesting his fear that the scene's new purposefulness might last no longer than Rites of Spring, Mission Impossible, and Lünchmeat.

MacKaye may have sensed Embrace's coming breakdown. He was well aware of the friction within the band, especially between Bald and Hampton. The singer was caught between them, appreciating Bald's commitment and spirit, but also empathizing with Hampton's discomfort with the bassist's explosive nature.

While MacKaye continued to be unsatisfied by the band's tightness, several successful gigs in the first two months of 1986 suggested that Embrace was starting to establish itself. "Once the [demo] got around and people got to know the songs, we definitely got a much better reaction," he noted at the time. "People are knowing what I'm singing about and wanting to sing along and that's great." In addition, since the Hall of Nations show, the band had encountered no further crowd problems.

After recording its new songs at Inner Ear in February, Embrace played another 9:30 gig in March. It was perhaps the band's most assured and relaxed show yet. One hard-to-please observer, Jeff Nelson, felt the band was finally hitting its stride.

For all its intensity, Embrace onstage was not a grim entity. Tonight was no exception, with even Hanson repeatedly wandering out from behind his drums to crack jokes. The element of humor was nearly as significant to DC punk as its idealism, but was often missed by outside observers. In part, this was because the playfulness wasn't always captured by the bands' recordings.

At this gig, MacKaye rejected a new label. *Thrasher*, a slick skater magazine, had dubbed the city's new punk sound "emo-core." Although the singer called this "the stupidest fucking thing I've ever heard of," the name would stick. Driven in part by this tag, a new stereotype would replace the old image of DC punks as drug-free macho baldies: tortured ascetic/romantics crying at the drop of a hat.

MacKaye pointedly added a message to the fallen Rites of Spring—part consolation, part challenge—onto the end of the night's version of "Last Song": "Come, let me sing for you/You sang for me/Come let me play for you/You played for me/Hey, Guy, does a movement die with a band?/No, it just loses some of its soul/It just loses some of its soul."

Near the end of the set, after an explosive rendition of "End of a Year," frustration came to the surface. As the music faded, MacKaye continued, his voice husky with feeling. On his knees, slightly out of breath, he spit out, "Words are never enough. We can talk all we want, we can plan all we want, we can project, talk and talk and talk. But we can't fucking do anything until we do it."

In contrast to the lightheartedness of so much of the earlier banter, MacKaye's words seemed to have a special urgency and the crowd grew quiet. "We should try a lot harder to do it. Everybody here has so much fucking potential. We should do something about it." He shook his head, rose from the floor, and began pacing back and forth. Over the opening guitar/bass interplay of "Building," MacKaye informed the audience that this would be the last song of the night and that there would be no encore. He threw himself into the song, a wrenching portrait of failure; as it hit a climax, MacKaye crashed to the stage.

With MacKaye face down on the floor, Bald—frustrated by tensions within the band and filled with the spirit of raw abandon that overtook him in live performance—took his bass and began to methodically smash it into the column in front of the stage. Pieces of the rapidly fragmenting bass flew erratically off into the crowd; one caught Bert Queiroz in the head and knocked him out cold.

Hearing the noise, MacKaye looked up. Annoyed at what he saw as a senseless act, he rose to stop the bassist, kicking him in the ass and pushing him offstage. This moment would be the final snapshot of Embrace.

XXX

The resistance the Rambo-punks had faced from the Revolution Summer crowd had pushed them away from those shows, but they continued to wreak havoc at other gigs. After an incident at an April dc space gig left a person hospitalized, members of Positive Force proposed making a flier denouncing the culprits by name. The group as a whole endorsed the idea, but some wanted to see the actual document before it was distributed.

Without informing the group, several Positive Force members made such a flier to distribute at an upcoming event opposing Reagan's not-so-secret war on Nicaragua. The handout was not attributed to Positive Force, but copies were placed on the ticket table at the entrance to the show, so it was widely taken to be a Positive Force publication.

Below a large handwritten headline of "Warning!," the flier announced that "certain violent skinheads have been terrorizing our scene. During the last year these cowards, who had once been a small presence in our scene, began to grow in numbers and visibility and are now messing with more and more people's lives." This was followed by three examples of their actions and a list of the nine main skinhead thugs, beginning with Lefty. The circular gave advice on how to resist, ending with a plea to "stand up to the skinheads before they step on you!"

Given what was going on at the time, the flier may have been necessary. Still, it would have seemed more credible if its supposedly definitive list of the most visible suspects hadn't been adjusted at the last minute. Two names were crossed out, apparently because someone decided that they weren't so thuggish after all. (The names could still be read through the ink, however.) The message was further undermined by the fact that the flier's creators didn't

CHAOS WITHIN POSITIVE FORCE
by Mark Andersen

Although it may seem a bit funny at this late date, I was nearly thrown out of Positive Force DC in early 1986.

While many PF members seemed to enjoy the prolonged "cat and mouse" games with the police, I did not. Although my initial experiences with the roving, spontaneous protests were energizing, after my trip to Central America, these actions seemed shambolic and self-indulgent.

In addition, our weekly meetings tended to go on for hours, with no agenda or decision-making process. Often we would discuss an event or action at length and then drift into another topic, only to realize after the meeting was over that we had made no decision. The next Saturday, the process would begin all over again. While the aim, in principle, was to keep things spontaneous and leaderless, in practice it often seemed to degenerate into simple chaos, dominated by the few who felt at ease speaking.

The limitations of this sort of "structureless" group had first been outlined in "The Tyranny of Structurelessness," an influential essay published in 1970 by feminist writer Jo Freeman. Although PF supposedly disavowed ideology beyond "the idea of young people working together to make a better world," de facto, the motivating ethos of early PF was a version of anarchism. While anarchism does not necessarily oppose organization itself, many in early PF seemed to dismiss all structure as inherently bad.

reveal their identities. If even the authors wouldn't directly "stand up to the skins," why should anybody else?

"When I saw it, my first reaction was to want to go out and shoot someone," recalled Lefty of the flier. There were no incidents at the show, but rumors spread that skinheads were going to attack a Positive Force meeting.

At the next PF meeting, some members brought baseball bats to the Peace Center. A heated exchange ensued about bringing weapons into a Quaker meeting house. Finally, the bats were left outside in the hedge, accessible but technically outside the meeting house. The arrangement was not tested, since the skins didn't show up.

Although some skinheads later reported that reprisals had been planned, the expected violent confrontation never came. Lefty and her crew had blinked, signaling the end of their grip on the scene. Apparently, the resistance of the Dischord group and Positive Force had undermined the skins' confidence.

There were other factors as well. Incidents attributed to the group had now come to the attention of the police, which were investigating, and some skins had followed the example of Harley Flanagan of New York's Cro-Mags, who had joined the Hare Krishnas. DC skins began to frequent the Krishna temple near Dupont Circle—at first, no doubt, simply for the free food. Krishna doctrines didn't ease the skins' homophobia—indeed, it gave them a supposedly spiritual basis for their hatred—but it did seem to

Freeman saw that such groups had undeniable strengths, especially in providing a forum for discussion. The problems appeared, according to her, when "groups exhausted the virtues of consciousness-raising and decided they wanted to do something more specific . . . At this point they usually floundered because most groups were unwilling to change their structure when they changed their task . . . People would try to use the structureless group for purposes which they were unsuitable out of a blind belief that no other means could possibly be anything but oppressive."

I tended to agree with Freeman's position. I was goal-directed, and impatient with what I saw as the group's simplistic politics and go-nowhere meetings. In turn, many viewed me as domineering and interpreted my emphasis on the complexity of issues as proof that I was a "liberal"–a characterization that I considered an insult.

Unfortunately, I was not fully sensitive to the dynamics of the group and pushed my views far too hard. For PF members like Jenny Toomey, the lack of structure was seen as positive; they enjoyed the free flow of ideas, and found the long meetings enlightening and energizing. In its way, PF was a laboratory for them to learn on their own terms, in their own way. After one meeting, I was confronted by a half dozen PF members and a choice: accept the majority opinion on how the meetings would run or leave the group. Chastened, I tried to work with the group in a less prominent but hopefully more positive role.

The issue did not go away, however, as is suggested by the skinhead flier fiasco.

interrupt their cycle of self-abuse and violence. Some skins also began to challenge Lefty's authority.

The bands popular with the more drug-and-drink–oriented punks were also faltering. Lethal Intent ended with Doug Caldwell's suicide in early 1986, the Obsessed had split when Scott Weinrich left to join LA's St. Vitus, and newer bands like Purevil and the Unclassified were also fading away. While Black Market Baby soldiered on and such new hard-punk bands as Factory arose, this scene was being submerged into the larger rock and metal crowds.

xxx

After Dag Nasty completed an EP for Dischord, vocalist Shawn Brown was ejected from the band and replaced with Dave Smalley, formerly of Boston straight edge band DYS. Rather than release an outdated EP, the revamped band returned to the studio and re-recorded the seven songs plus five more to make a full LP.

Ostensibly, Brown was banished for missing practice. Rumors soon circulated, however, that he was actually replaced because Smalley's voice was better suited to the poppier direction Baker had now chosen. Later, the guitarist admitted as much.

In other words, the realignment was a blatant career move. In corporate rock, personnel decisions are just business, but DC punk opposed such calculations. The local distaste for the change was heightened when, after playing only a few shows, Smalley also split, to be replaced by Peter Cortner (also known as "Pete Moss") from the young Maryland hardcore band Pro-Tem. Dag Nasty's popularity continued to grow, but its image was permanently tarnished.

King Face was struggling to find a new drummer and bassist. Gray Matter, which had tried to continue with Jon Kirschten replacing Mark Haggerty on guitar, quit when the new lineup didn't seem to jell. Soon, virtually all the Revolution Summer bands would be history.

Embrace had collapsed on the eve of its first serious out-of-town shows. While MacKaye and Nelson were in England on Dischord business—and recording what would be the Egg Hunt single at Southern Studios—the group was supposed to practice for the tour. "I kept calling Mike, but the practices never happened," Bald later recalled. MacKaye returned to an unpracticed band, and a heated dialogue ensued. As the musicians discussed what to do about the shows, Hampton said "I quit" and walked out. After nine shows in as many months, Embrace was suddenly, unexpectedly, over.

Given the longstanding conflict between Hampton and Bald, the bassist years later called Embrace "the band that should never have been." At the time, however, he felt betrayed by what he saw as Hampton's lack of commitment. Furious, he moved to San Francisco within days after the breakup. There he tried to deal with his frustration by working for *Maximum RockNRoll* and trying to get a new band together.

MacKaye was no less devastated. He too left for the West Coast, to visit Cynthia Connolly, who was also working for *Maximum RockNRoll*, and to consider his next step. Hanson returned to school, and Hampton quickly began playing with Picciotto, Canty, and Janney in a band called One Last Wish, feeding Bald's suspicion that this was why the guitarist had left Embrace.

The loss of Embrace left Beefeater as the only intact part of the Revolution Summer triumvirate—and pressure was building in that band too. It had lost its second drummer, Mark Shellhaus; replacement Kenny Craun was a skilled player who adapted well to Beefeater's style, but ideologically he was more in tune with Ronnie Van Zant than Mahatma Gandhi.

The Olive Tree EP recorded with Shellhaus was released, and in early 1986 the band recorded enough material for an entire album at Inner Ear with MacKaye. The band played so many benefits and protests that it seemed almost literally the "Positive Force band."

Not all the musicians, however, shared Squip's emphasis on politics. "Tomas is 'message first,' Dug is debating the question, and Kenny and I are definitely 'music first,'" Smith told the *Washington Post*. Although sufficiently politicized to have a MLK tattoo on his shoulder, Smith ate meat, drank alcohol, and did not abhor slamming. Craun was even less supportive of Squip's ideas. He scandalized the band by getting into several fistfights, including one with the members of UK Subs that started over a beer and ended with him hospitalized. These tensions came to a head when the band toured in the summer of 1986. By the tour's end, Beefeater had also decided to quit.

Not surprisingly, the band's final show was a Positive Force–organized benefit and protest. The issue was animal rights, and the other bands were One Last Wish and Philadelphia's Follow Fashion

Monkeys. Beefeater played one of its most pumped-up sets ever, dedicated by Squip to "all the girls in this town who want to make music," adding, "I hope you do."

Near the end of the show, the singer gave one last talk encouraging people to take straight edge into vegetarianism and beyond. "Don't worry, you're not going to have to listen to any more 'preaching' after this because we're breaking up," he quipped. Greeted with a chorus of boos, Squip quickly added: "I'm only kidding. I'll be back with another group and I'll start preaching all over again."

The band then tore into "Out of the Woods." With his bass decorated by a rose picked up from the stage, Birdzell played like man possessed. As the song skidded to its close, Squip hurried off and Birdzell repeatedly threw his bass into the air, finally taking it by the neck and smashing it. After it splintered, Birdzell lost himself in a feverish dance, whirling amid flurries of feedback from Smith's guitar. Finally, Birdzell collapsed onstage and the din slowly faded.

It was an appropriately intense end to a powerful musical, political, and even spiritual force. What had started so promisingly seemed now to be fading. When asked years later about Revolution Summer, Bald replied, "What was it? It was something that never happened." Even Squip, who was responsible for so much of the period's vision, was flippant in retrospect: "Well, it was when I stopped smoking, I can tell you that much."

MacKaye offered a more earnest comment on Revolution Summer in a song he recorded with help from Nelson. "We All Fall Down" was released on a 45 under the name Egg Hunt (because

POSITIVE FORCE ON THE ROCKS
by Mark Andersen

It wasn't merely the bands who had fallen upon evil times. By late 1986, Positive Force was also headed for the rocks, hounded by a series of internal splits.

The first came when PF broke with the national NBAU coalition, which many felt had shriveled into an RCP front group. Anarchist vs. communist tensions grew; most PF members who were sympathetic to socialist politics felt unwelcome and left the group.

This was not the only problem, however, as a flier largely authored by Kevin Mattson in May 1986 suggested: "Positive Force is one year old, and some of us feel that the group has strayed from its original goals and ideals. We think it is time to decide upon a direction, to break out of the stagnant rut we've fallen into. It's time to redefine the group . . .'

The flier identified three major problems within the group: "#1, Personal commitment and personal initiative have fallen by the wayside . . . projects are simply not being completed because few are willing to participate; #2, Positive Force is increasingly plagued with a sense of cliqueishness . . . not only newcomers but even people who have been coming since the beginning feel alienated largely because they do not identify with the hardcore-oriented discussion that dominates; #3, Sociability has overwhelmingly replaced action and pertinent discussion . . . without a sense of accomplishment (or, rather, without actual accomplishment) the meetings are vacuous and boring, not to mention pointless."

it was recorded during Easter) in fall 1986, while the Embrace sessions languished without plans for release. MacKaye's vinyl debut as a guitarist and his final collaboration with Nelson, the song was originally written for Embrace, whose other members rejected it. ("They thought it sounded like Led Zeppelin," MacKaye said.)

"We All Fall Down" began with an impatient bass figure, rising wisps of feedback and drums, and a bitter question: "Why do we act like we just learned how to walk/When we've been walking all this time?" Challenging both the punks who turned to the mainstream and those who had tried and failed to create an alternative, the song blasted: "In search of the quiet life/We all fall down/In search of the righteous life/We all fall down."

"Revolution Summer was a climax, the end of something," Amy Pickering said in 1987. The innocence and isolation of the original harDCore scene was gone, a development that was both threatening and promising.

To me, much of this seemed the predictable outcome of the group's "structurelessness." Kevin, however, tended to blame the ennui on the fact that most of the newer PF members were political neophytes coming from the punk scene. This critique begged the question of why efforts to engage other youth had failed and conveniently ignored the massive gap between aims and means that had been present from the very beginning with NBAU. If raising a ruckus and yelling at people made emotional sense, it hardly seemed likely to create the kind of broad-based movement that could actually "stop World War III." Quite simply, the lofty aims embraced by at least some in PF were so far mismatched with the group's actual strength, skills, or approach as to be almost laughable.

At the same time, to simply dismiss the group was a bit unfair. Although early PF did not achieve everything some had hoped for, this did not mean that the group achieved nothing. PF had helped to inject political consciousness into DC punk, built a social group that gave support to alienated young people, helped protect them from violent attack, and had nurtured political skills and education that they could use in other contexts.

However, the over-the-top idealism of many involved made the group ripe for swift disillusion, disintegration, and collapse. Kevin himself would leave the group in June 1986, spewing negativity. Others soon followed, including, ultimately, Jenny Toomey. While some kept the group going, PF was hemorrhaging members and falling apart. As 1987 loomed, the group seemed destined for extinction.

"It feels like everything you've done is destroyed, but it's just not true," said Picciotto of Rites of Spring's breakup. "The shows existed, people came and saw the shows, I played the shows, the record came out—it's just changed my whole life. Whatever I do from now on will be a continuation of that. The name will be different, but the whole feeling I had in Rites of Spring will always be there."

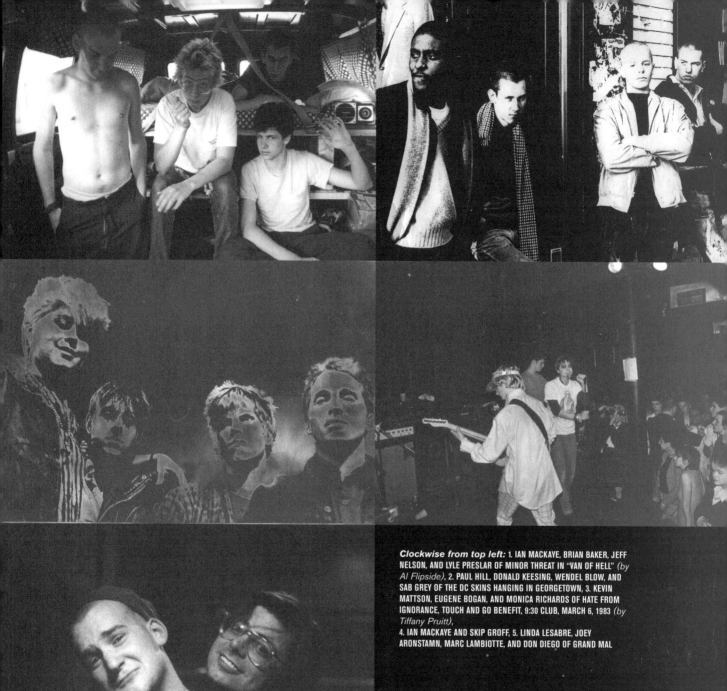

Clockwise from top left: 1. IAN MACKAYE, BRIAN BAKER, JEFF NELSON, AND LYLE PRESLAR OF MINOR THREAT IN "VAN OF HELL" *(by Al Flipside)*, 2. PAUL HILL, DONALD KEESING, WENDEL BLOW, AND SAB GREY OF THE DC SKINS HANGING IN GEORGETOWN, 3. KEVIN MATTSON, EUGENE BOGAN, AND MONICA RICHARDS OF HATE FROM IGNORANCE, TOUCH AND GO BENEFIT, 9:30 CLUB, MARCH 6, 1983 *(by Tiffany Pruitt)*, 4. IAN MACKAYE AND SKIP GROFF, 5. LINDA LESABRE, JOEY ARONSTAMN, MARC LAMBIOTTE, AND DON DIEGO OF GRAND MAL

Clockwise from top left: 1. BOBBY SULLIVAN AND SCOTT MCCLOUD OF LÜNCHMEAT AT LAKE BRADDOCK COMMUNITY CENTER, JULY 25, 1985 *(by Amanda MacKaye)*, 2. CHRIS BALD, IAN MACKAYE, AND MIKE HAMPTON OF EMBRACE, FOOD FOR THOUGHT, JULY 28, 1985 *(by Leslie Clague)*, 3. TOMAS SQUIP, FRED SMITH, AND DUG BIRDZELL OF BEEFEATER, 9:30 CLUB, 4. MOLLY BURNHAM, AMY PICKERING, NATALIE AVERY, AND TED NICELEY AT YESTERDAY AND TODAY *(by Skip Groff)*

9353

DC SPACE · HALLOWEEN · 10 O'CLOCK · FIVE DOLLARS

Clockwise from top left: 1. 9353 FLIER (by Bruce Merkle), 2. DOUG CALDWELL OF LETHAL INTENT (by Valerie Rousette), 3. LARA LYNCH OF NUCLEAR CRAYONS, 9:30 CLUB, MAY 22, 1983 (by Jim Saah), 4. BRUCE MERKLE, JASON CARMER, VANCE BOCKIS, AND DAN JOSEPH OF 9353 (by Fatimah Balbad)

Clockwise from top left: 1. PUNK PERCUSSION PROTEST FLIER *(by Tomas Squip)*, 2. PUNK PERCUSSION PROTEST AT SOUTH AFRICAN EMBASSY, JUNE 21, 1985 *(by Bert Queiroz)*, 3. STEVE NILES, GEOFF TURNER, DANTE FERRANDO, AND MARK HAGGERTY OF GRAY MATTER ON ROOF OF FOOD FOR THOUGHT AFTER LAST SHOW, AUGUST 4, 1985 *(by Bert Queiroz)*, 4. NO BUSINESS AS USUAL DIE-IN, 5. NBAU POSTER, APRIL 29, 1985

Clockwise from top left: 1. DAVE GROHL OF MISSION IMPOSSIBLE, LAKE BRADDOCK COMMUNITY CENTER, JULY 25, 1985 *(by Amanda MacKaye)*, 2. BRYANT MASON (LOWER LEFT COR-NER) AND CHRIS PAGE (WITH MIC) OF MISSION IMPOSSIBLE WITH AUDIENCE DURING FLOOR PILE-UP AT LAKE BRADDOCK COMMUNITY CENTER, JULY 25, 1985 *(by Amanda MacKaye)*, 3. PETE MURRAY, ANDRE LEE, KENNY INOUYE, AND STEVE POLCARI OF MARGINAL MAN, 9:30 CLUB, JANUARY 2, 1983 *(by Tiffany Pruitt)*, 4. THE OBSESSED

Clockwise from top left: 1. MONICA RICHARDS OF MADHOUSE AT 9:30 CLUB *(by Leslie Clague)*, 2. JOHN STABB AND STEVE HANSGEN OF GI, 3. BRIAN BAKER, SHAWN BROWN, COLIN SEARS, AND ROGER MARBURY OF DAG NASTY, HALL OF NATIONS, DECEMBER 4, 1985 *(by Bert Queiroz)*

chapter ten, 1986-87:

waiting room

the State Of The Union

*"Another dream is broken/Like glass against a wall
I pick up a piece as a token/It cuts deep as I fall
Rising up from the ruins/Rebuilding the fallen wall
Another repeat of defeat?/Or a chance to see it all . . .
Life is so easy to spend/Dreams are so hard to earn."*
—Ignition, "Rebuilding," 1987

STATE OF THE UNION FLIER *(by Mark Andersen and Liberation Graphics)*

waiting room

Their freshman years at college finished, the members of Lünchmeat returned to find a Revolution-free summer. "We came back from school raring to go," remembered Bobby Sullivan, "and all these people were just sitting around moaning, 'Nothing's going on in DC, all the bands have broken up.'"

The Dischord bands' proclivity for breakups had become a running joke. Many fans outside Washington had grown used to buying records of bands they could never expect to see. "Where are they now? Just as soon as the interviews come out, they've already broken up," taunted Pussy Galore's Julie Cafritz from the band's new roost in New York. Band member Jon Spencer added, "That whole 'Revolution Summer' thing just fell flat on its face."

Even allies like Tim Yohannon were mystified. When he asked Chris Bald for an explanation in a *Maximum RockNRoll* radio interview, Bald patiently noted that many of the Dischord crowd had gone to high school together, that bands tended to be groups of friends who were so close that the loss of one member was fatal, and that it was because of artistic integrity and respect for each other that the bands regularly committed commercial suicide. Yet from his tone of voice, it was clear that the subject had become exasperating.

The initiators of the previous year's revival had scattered not only psychically but physically: Bald to San Francisco, Mark Haggerty to New Zealand, and Dante Ferrando, Ian MacKaye, Brendan Canty, and Cynthia Connolly on cross-country trips.

The larger DC punk scene centered rather listlessly around a new club, the Complex, that Gordon Gordon and new arrival Dave Redman had helped open in Shaw, a rough neighborhood north of downtown. Together with the Hung Jury Pub—a sometime lesbian bar in the midtown office-building district—the Complex gave many touring bands a chance to play DC for the first time since early 1985. These shows often attracted the destructive punks who made WUST shows unpleasant. In addition, the Complex's actual owner soon deserted the club, leaving massive debts that would lead to the club's closing at summer's end.

Positive Force was also adrift, although many national political issues were affecting the local punk scene. The most chilling sign of this was the death of 19-year-old Rodrigo Rojas, a recent graduate of Woodrow Wilson High School and the son of a long-exiled Chilean human rights activist. Rojas, who was friendly with such Wilson alumni as Bobby Sullivan, returned to Chile simply to learn more about his homeland and perhaps find the father he had never known. Rojas was observing an anti-government demonstration when soldiers arrived, beating the young man and a friend savagely and then pouring gasoline on them and setting them on fire.

At home, rock music itself was under attack by a bipartisan group of "Washington wives," the Parents Music Resource Center. While many of the women were conservative Reaganites like Susan Baker, the PMRC's most recognizable public face was Mary Elizabeth "Tipper" Gore, wife of moderate Democratic Senator Al Gore, who was shocked by rock videos and the lyrics to songs like Prince's "Darling Nikki."

While Gore and her colleagues portrayed themselves as opposed to censorship, their calls for rating or labeling systems for records suited the New Right agenda. One of the first blows in this campaign fell when Dead Kennedys singer Jello Biafra was charged with "distributing matter harmful to minors" because of the H.R. Giger "Penis Landscape" poster included with the band's *Frankenchrist* album.

Positive Force decided to focus attention on both the Biafra and Rojas cases, organizing a benefit for the No More Censorship Defense Fund at the Complex in August, followed by a "Concert for a Free Chile" in Dupont Circle on September 13th. Two new bands, One Last Wish and Soul Side, played the former show, with Carpe Diem and Boston's the Freeze.

Soul Side was simply Lünchmeat reunited under a new name. Although Sullivan would later discover that *Soul Side* was the name of an incendiary book on the 1968 DC riots, the name was initially chosen simply because "it sounded good." The new band kept some of its old anthems like "Fresh Air" and "Under the Glare," while adding potent new numbers like "Dreams" and "Pearl to Stone." The band soon went on extended hiatus again, while most of the members returned to school. Before splitting again, however, it recorded an album with MacKaye, Don Zientara, and Eli Janney at Inner Ear. This would be Sammich's second release; driven largely by the boundless energy of Amanda MacKaye, this label soon began to shed its image as "Dischord Jr." to earn its own distinct following for a time.

The members of One Last Wish were clearly excited to be back onstage after an eight-month absence. Their initial gig—which ended with a fiery version of the MC5's "Looking at You" climaxed by Picciotto leaping from the stage to scale the balcony—showed great promise, while demonstrating that the band did not intend to be Rites of Spring.

Mike Hampton's pop sensibility was enough to earn the band comparisons to local power-popster Tommy Keene. Picciotto remained the principal vocalist, but Eddie Janney—now playing bass—brought his wispy voice to the fore on two songs. While Janney's songs were solid, they lacked the immediacy of Picciotto's work and could slow the momentum of the band's set.

If One Last Wish's sound disappointed some Rites of Spring fans, another new band emulated Rites' style. Rain, composed of guitarist-vocalist Jon Kirschten, drummer Eli Janney, and bassist Bert Queiroz, showed the influence of its predecessor in songs like "It Is for Always" (a reference to Revolution Summer). Like One Last Wish, however, Rain tended toward the poppier side of post-harDCore.

Listening from San Francisco, Chris Bald was not impressed by these new bands. "I can't tell [them] that they're wrong, but I am looking forward to going back and doing it in a different way," he said at the time. "I love all those people, they are my life in a way, but it has come to a kind of crossroads where they are pursuing some 'brand new ideal' which to me is some stale ideal." In November 1986, *Maximum RockNRoll's* DC scene report noted that "Chris Bald is moving back to DC to kick ass on the post-punk beatnik wimps."

To the members of One Last Wish, however, the new band was not a refutation but an evolution of Rites of Spring and Embrace. Asked by *Maryland Musician* magazine how his new band compared to Rites, Picciotto said, "Our intentions remain the same."

While One Last Wish's guitars were generally more restrained than Rites', the lyrics continued the themes of songs like "Hidden Wheel." "Three Unkind Silences," "Break to Broken," and "Loss Like a Seed" meshed the personal, the poetic, and the political. As "My Better Half" put it: "I would take the world as my ally/I would take the world/Against jealous fear and bitter ambition/That only aspires to the done and the dead."

The quartet also performed the most directly topical song Picciotto had yet written, "Burning in the Undertow," which was inspired by Rojas's murder. The song's verses are pleas for engagement with the wider world, while the wrenching chorus—"They poured their malice/Down your back/And then they dropped the match"—keeps returning to the horrific reality of one person's death.

After a show at the Complex, a *Flipside* reviewer named two of the DC bands that played there as among the country's finest. The first was One Last Wish, the other Dag Nasty. The latter's *Can I Say* had appeared to much acclaim, although some reviews accused the band of covering old ground. While the band's new singer Peter Cortner lacked the experience and range of David Smalley, he worked hard and had a strong stage presence. After only a few practices with its new vocalist, the band set off on a successful US tour in a yellow mini-bus later immortalized in the song "Mule."

Shortly after its July return, the band recorded four new songs at Inner Ear with MacKaye and Zientara: "All Ages Show," "Safe," "Fall," and "Trying." The new songs showed that Dag Nasty was skillfully fusing pop melody and hardcore energy and had rebounded from its latest vocalist switch. But another crisis was looming: Descendents bassist Doug Carrion, who had become close friends with Baker, convinced the guitarist to move to LA to join a punk supergroup with the vocalist and drummer of the goofy but popular straight edge band Doggy Style.

The new band, Doggy Rock, would divest a name that was under attack by PMRC-type groups and adopt a style that might attract a broader audience. Carrion called the group "a total entertainment package. Imagine four wild animals turned loose onstage. I hesitate to call it funk or rap but it is definitely dance music."

This description suggests the influence of the Beastie Boys, who had recently hit the Top Ten with "Fight for Your Right to Party." Baker explained his interest in the band simply as a career opportunity: "What I want to do is to play my guitar." When Doggy Rock played its debut gig on Halloween—barely a month after Baker arrived in LA—it was the apparent end of Dag Nasty and another blow to Baker's punk credibility.

Dag Nasty wasn't the only local band experiencing dramatic personnel shifts. After the release of a potent single on Fountain of Youth, "Mecca" b/w "So Sad," Madhouse lost bassist Eugene Bogan and guitarist Norman Van Der Sluys. The band had also come to an impasse with Derek Hsu, owner of the label. Since neither he nor the band would pay for the sessions, the recording of the band's completed second LP remained in the possession of Hit and Run Studios.

After splitting from Fountain of Youth, Monica Richards and Danny Ingram recruited ex-

Beefeater guitarist Fred Smith and bassist Franz Kellner. By early 1987, the band had a new set of material, an increasingly sophisticated sound, a new name, and a $10,000 settlement from Prince, who had claimed the tag Madhouse for a side project. The quartet became Strange Boutique, after a Monochrome Set song.

King Face, meanwhile, overhauled its rhythm section. Mark Sullivan and Pat Bobst found bassist Andy Rapoport, drawn from harDCore's "class of '83," and Larry Colbert, an African-American drummer who had never before been exposed to punk. This varied lineup suited the band's rock-oriented direction. If King Face's music was more Van Halen than MDC, Sullivan's lyrics were consistently thought-provoking and subtly subversive, and his Iggy-like stage presence helped win an audience for the band's brainy hard punk.

DC punk's undisputed champion of personnel changes, however, remained Government Issue. Throughout 1986, GI dealt with a parade of newly departing and arriving members, as well as its own set of grievances with Fountain of Youth, to which it had returned for a self-titled LP after a two-album stint with Mystic. Fountain of Youth had entered into a distribution/financing agreement with Dutch East India, a powerful force in indie-rock distribution.

Fewer punk bands were releasing their own records, and a small group of companies like Dutch East, SST, and Caroline were becoming "mini-majors"—complete with promotional hype and sometimes sleazy business dealings. Dischord was insulated by its refusal to do PR and its commitment to release only DC-area music. Even so, many bands courted the label. In a *Maximum RockNRoll* interview, rising Orange County straight edge band Uniform Choice declared its intention of being on Dischord. The group was politely but firmly refused.

The growing division of labor between musicians and labels was a logical evolution. Bands wanted to focus on music and not be distracted by business. For the most successful, signing to major labels was the next step. This was a painful transition for idealists like MacKaye. In early 1987, he sadly noted that bands like Hüsker Dü were no longer "confederates in the same conspiracy."

John Stabb was one who defended Hüsker Dü's decision to sign with Warner Brothers. "If we could get a 'creative control' kind of contract being on a major, I'd go for it," he said. While purists denounced bands for 'selling out' to achieve mega-stardom, many punk musicians just wanted to avoid shit jobs and to be able to play music seriously.

The good intentions of little labels were small consolation. "I only looked at getting records out. Once they were out, I didn't really know what to do with them," Derek Hsu admitted years after Fountain of Youth closed. This irked hard-touring bands like GI, who found themselves playing shows in town where their records were unavailable.

The Dutch East deal improved distribution for GI's records, but the band soon decided the local label was unnecessary. "We found out that Dutch East was giving Derek money for us to record," said Tom Lyle. "He'd take some of the money and give the rest to us—for doing nothing, as far as we could tell. Dutch East was really our record company. They put up the money, manufactured and distributed the record." The band took its next record to Giant, a Dutch East subsidiary. Amid financial turmoil and wrangles over royalties with such disgruntled bands as Crippled Pilgrims, Fountain of Youth faded away.

GI soldiered on, however. In early 1986, the band lost its only other original member, drummer Mark Alberstadt, as well as bassist Steve Hansgen. A shy, unknown kid named J. Robbins replaced Hansgen, and after another drummer and Alberstadt's temporary return, the drum position was permanently filled by Pete Moffett, formerly of Dove.

No one realized it at the time, but GI had finally found its definitive lineup. Robbins and Moffet were strong players, and their chemistry with Lyle was right. Revamped and revived, the new GI entered its most prolific and popular period.

Although its lineup was one that hadn't changed, Marginal Man was facing an identity crisis. Outwardly, this was seen in singer Steve Polcari, who came to resemble Ratt frontman Steven Pearcy. He also seemed to take the songs less seriously, becoming more a showman than an impassioned punk. After two solid albums and two grueling US tours, the band had reached a plateau. While the band continued to play to good crowds in Washington about once a month in 1986 and early 1987—including a couple gigs with the venerable Slickee Boys, still plugging away in their second decade—it did not release a new record or undertake a major tour.

Creatively, the band also stalled. Although its style had foreshadowed "emo-core," the band had retreated from that approach just as others took it up. Interviewed in 1991, Pete Murray said that in music, "emotion is all that really matters to me." He complained that "the band wouldn't let me play 'Forever Gone,'" a wrenching song inspired by the suicide of a friend, "because we played it twice and I nearly lost it onstage both times. It was like they were telling me that I couldn't write about things that were important to me."

Although the band was descended from the extremely topical Artificial Peace, some of its members were uncomfortable with the activism increasingly associated with DC punk. Polcari had helped write many of Artificial Peace's protest songs during the early Reagan years, but by the mid-'80s he rejected radical—and especially anarchist—politics. "Whenever you start mixing music and politics, people will have different opinions about it," Murray said years later. "Steve didn't like it. I didn't agree, but I can't really blame him."

Marginal Man was not the only popular DC punk band to distance itself from radical politics—and the scene's most conspicuous proponent of them, Positive Force. So did GI and Dag Nasty. However, Marginal Man did play at anti-apartheid and anti-hunger benefits, as well as ultimately a pair of PF shows.

x x x

Despite some continued concern over the role of the Revolutionary Communist Party in the coalition, Positive Force chose to participate in No Business As Usual's protest against Reagan's Strategic Defense Initiative, a proposed anti-missile system nicknamed "Star Wars." This time some of Dischord's inner circle joined, including MacKaye, Mark Sullivan, and Jeff Nelson. The latter felt so strongly about the issue that he got "STP SDI" as his car's license plate.

While struggling to assemble an ambitious multi-instrumental group with Dug Birdzell, Tomas Squip remained politically active, continuing to protest at the South African embassy. He also conceived a demonstration in Lafayette Park across from the White House in response to new restrictions. In an attempt to clear the park of the group that had maintained a 24-hour Peace Vigil since Reagan's inauguration, the National Park Service banned signs above a certain size and required permits for gatherings of more than 25 people.

In response, Squip manufactured 25 signs precisely under the size limit, with a single letter painted on each. When the panels were held up by 25 people, it constituted a gigantic—but entirely legal—sign that spelled out, "YOUR PRESIDENT IS LYING TO YOU." Squip then organized a group of punks who marched silently in single file to the edge of the park directly across from the White House and held up their panels, creating the full sign.

The Park Police quickly arrived. "You could really tell they were unhappy," Squip said later, smiling. "But even by their own guidelines, there was nothing they could do."

One of Positive Force's most enthusiastic allies was Scream. The band played over a half dozen benefits between early 1986 and mid-1987, most in conjunction with Positive Force. Indeed, it almost replaced Beefeater as "the official Positive Force band." The group would even tailor its set to the relevant political issue, encouraging audience members to act.

Scream had been playing for seven years, but it hit its stride in this period. In the summer of '86, the band toured Europe, the first DC group besides Bad Brains to do so. There the musicians found a highly politicized scene, described by one observer as a "hotbed of counterculture, larger and more permanent than the Haight-Ashbury hippie experiment ever was." Energized by European punk's upfront politics and embraced by the audiences there, Scream returned to do a series of incendiary shows in Washington, including an appearance at the Concert for a Free Chile.

While in Britain, Scream recorded several songs with John Loder at Southern Studios. Combined with material previously recorded with MacKaye at Inner Ear, Scream had its next record. *Banging the Drum* was the band's most diverse and realized work yet. The title song celebrated punk percussion protests, "Walking By Myself" was a neo-Detroit rock howl, "People People" a Guthrie-esque celebration of protest music, and "ICYUOD" a claustrophobic sledgehammer dirge.

Scream's European trip was a turning point both for the band and for drummer Kent Stax. Now married and a father, Stax was reluctant to undertake long tours. Initially he had decided not to go to Europe, only to change his mind when the band began seriously pursuing other drummers. Once back from Europe, however, Stax chose his family over the band.

Scream was interested in Dave Grohl, now drumming in Dain Bramage, a Hüsker Dü–influenced band descended from Mission Impossible. Dain Bramage had begun to establish itself, and had recorded its debut album for a California label, Fartblossom. But Scream was Grohl's favorite band, and he couldn't resist an audition. Since he was 17 and still in high school, he lied about his age. To Grohl's amazement, Scream was delighted by his energy and skill and asked him to join.

Initially, he declined, not wanting to desert Dain Bramage with the record and a tour looming. When the tour was called off, however, Grohl changed his mind. To join Scream, he dropped out of high school, but was careful not to let his new bandmates realize that.

xxx

In late October, Bad Brains returned home to play a sold-out show at the 9:30 Club. "These are people who watched my transformation from boy into man," HR said. "I could never turn my back on them." Jenifer, however, noted that "I get a lot of mixed vibes sometimes" playing in Washington.

There were those in DC who questioned the sincerity of Bad Brains' reunion, but their powerful SST album *I Against I* had silenced most such critics. One of their oldest fans, Henry Rollins, said at the time that Bad Brains had "aged gracefully. It's not the same as it used to be, but I'm glad. Bands that don't change are a lie."

The band's new songs were more controlled and less intense, but they had grace and swing, topped by HR's showmanship. After the band's first burst of songs, HR glad-handed exultant fans in front of the stage like a conquering hero. Most of these admirers were likely seeing Bad Brains for the first time, as *I Against I* was selling very well for an indie record.

Of course, this Bad Brains was a different band than in the early '80s. While Dr. Know claimed the music was still meant to carry "a revolutionary vibe," the band seldom spoke in the apocalyptic terms of 1982. In one 1987 interview Jenifer said that it was important for bands to be politically conscious, "but nobody wants to get to the point where you get too wound up." Still, *I Against I* was dedicated to "all artists and supporters of the underprivileged."

Under Tony Countey's management, the band was also more professional and better publicized. Old allies Ric Ocasek and Dave Hahn—with an assist from Wilson-punk-cum-filmmaker Jem Cohen—had gotten "Pay to Cum" into Martin Scorcese's *After Hours*, and one of the album's videos was accepted by MTV. Not surprisingly, Babylon beckoned once again. This time, it was Island Records' Chris Blackwell who pursued them. Since Blackwell had signed Bob Marley and the Wailers and helped make them global superstars, his interest was taken seriously. Island's feelers became what Countey later described as "a firm, multi-million-dollar deal."

HR resisted the band's commercial momentum. While *I Against I* had gotten rave reviews, HR would later say that he was secretly "heartbroken" that producer Ron St. Germain had excluded reggae from the record. "I didn't want to put out an album that didn't have any Rasta Man identification on it," the singer said. "Prior to that everything we had put out had reggae music on it, right back to our first 45."

HR began to talk freely in interviews about Bad Brains' recording an all-reggae album—which Dr. Know and Jenifer didn't want to do. He was also becoming disgusted with punk rock itself. He was now over 30 and tired of screaming "like a madman" and playing for audiences that seemed untouched by his message. He protested that he couldn't perform the "devil's music" anymore: "Imagine playing 'Rock for Light'—'Don't want no violence/Just want some peace and love'—and all you see is madness around you? It's not easy for any godly man to take."

By now, a new word adapted from Bad Brains' Jamaican slang for dancing—"to mash it up"— had become hardcore's latest term for the slamdance: *moshing*. This couldn't have been very happy news for HR, who later told *Sold Out* magazine that "the music that [Bad Brains] play is very, very hard. People slam, people jump, and they scrape, they scream, they bite, they act very barbaric. And even me, as a man who came out of a civilized family, has become uncivilized."

For some shows on the 1987 tour, HR strapped himself in a chair with duct tape onstage. The sight of the normally hyperactive HR confined to a chair—breaking free only for the show's finale— could be a compelling if confusing drama. HR would later claim he used the chair simply because a childhood injury had flared up, but he told *Sold Out* that "I tied myself down because I was tired. Inside of my heart, to tell you what's going on would take years. The anger that I feel and the oppression of the music [was] overwhelming."

This oppressive music was punk rock, Bad Brains music. "I waited seven years and we never played reggae," HR told Cynthia Connolly in 1988. "Just one or two or three songs at the most, here and there. I'd be crying inside. I would be so frustrated. I'd want to play reggae for them and all I could play was all this screaming and hollering. They'd be thinking, 'That's the greatest thing in the world,' and I'd just be going . . ." He shook his head sadly.

The possibility of signing with Island only pushed HR further from the band. He was still suspicious of contracts and major labels, and the thought of being compelled to be in Bad Brains for several more years was devastating. On the eve of a tour, he just walked away. Once again, Earl Hudson followed. For the second time, Bad Brains had self-destructed on the verge of a major record deal.

As always, Dr. Know attempted to be upbeat: "You go with the spirit, man. If it's time for us to break up then that's what we do. You can't fight with Jah, you know?" Still, there was a hint of bitterness when he admitted, "It was a very hard thing. When I was 17, 18, 19, 20, whatever, before I had a family, I could deal with it a lot easier because it was just me. I could go sleep on somebody's couch and eat a bag of potato chips and be cool, but I can't be doing them things now."

Privately, Jenifer called HR a "traitor" and a "hypocrite." With families to feed and their band and ambitions in shambles, Jenifer and Dr. Know decided to do what had once been unthinkable: replace HR and Hudson and continue Bad Brains without them.

X X X

Black Flag continued to tour tirelessly, spending the first six months of 1986 on the road; Greg Ginn's other project, the all-instrumental Gone, opened many of the shows. It was a merciless pace, especially since SST had become a massive operation. After the tour, the band took a breather, and in August Rollins visited DC. While there, he received a curt call from Ginn: Black Flag was history.

Rollins found himself facing a wide-open future. His first step was to shave his shoulder-length hair in a return to "war footing." When he had been asked in 1984 what he would do if he weren't in Black Flag, Rollins had said, "Write, paint, be in another band, be a terrorist." Now he called on old DC allies Chris Haskett (ex-Enzymes) and Bernie Wandel (ex-Nuclear Crayons) as well as drummer Mike Green, to write and record an album, *Hot Animal Machine*. They also made *Drive-by Shooting*, an EP that would be released under the name Henrietta Collins and the Child-Hating Wife-Beaters.

Neither Wandel nor Green could commit to the next step—touring till they dropped, basically—so Rollins recruited a new rhythm section. Ironically, Sim Cain and Andrew Weiss were drawn from Gone, also now defunct. By early 1987, Rollins was on a spoken word tour, planning the first Rollins Band tour, and about to release his first two solo records on a new independent label, Texas Hotel.

X X X

"This is for Toni Young," announced the new band's singer, and the group began its first song. The sound was dense and grinding, the guitar heavy, the rhythm section slightly tentative. While the band displayed a discomfort common to debut performances, the music was powerful and distinctive. Particularly striking was "Drowning Intentions," with a chorus whose words—"The only way out is up"—matched the music's motion.

The brief set introduced an uncompromising new version of harDCore, but the music wasn't the only thing that was unusual. This band, Fire Party, was made up of four young women.

In another world, this biological fact would scarcely have been worthy of attention. Yet in DC punk, such a band was nearly unprecedented, even after Revolution Summer's anti-macho crusade. Singer Amy Pickering, guitarist Natalie Avery, bassist Kate Samworth, and drummer Nicky Thomas were ripping down an invisible sign that said "No Skirts Allowed (Onstage)." And they were doing so in a set dedicated to Toni Young, one of the few women to hold her own in the hardcore "boy's club."

Young had died unexpectedly just days before of pneumonia. She had not been seen much since leaving Dove in 1984, and had kept in touch with only a few of her closest friends from the punk community. It was rumored that the pneumonia was a complication of AIDS, but Young's close friend Vivien Greene offered another explanation: "Toni had problems with health insurance. She didn't have the money to afford doctors so she let [the pneumonia] go too long. She wasn't like most of the kids in the scene, many of whom were from the upper class. And, in a way, that killed her."

When Young died, the scene's sexual politics were changing. New arrival Kim Coletta, a Georgetown

THE RISE OF A NEW PF
by Mark Andersen

At around the same time, Positive Force House opened, not far from Dischord in Arlington. As plans for the house were being made, several people within PF (including myself) arranged for a "Fall Offensive"—a series of benefit concerts, protests, and educational events invoking the spirit of Revolution Summer and seeking to somehow maintain its fading momentum. Upon returning from his West Coast trip, Ian MacKaye—who had begun to let his hair grow out for the first time in six years after the collapse of Embrace—saw our flier and sadly told me, "You're the only ones still doing anything."

PF itself was floundering, however. Things were bleak enough that a study written by graduate student George Shaner spoke of the group in the past tense. Such a sudden rise and fall of a voluntary group was hardly unheard of; of the dozen or so Positive Force affinity groups that had sprung up across America, by 1987, DC was the only survivor. Even the original one in Reno had become a record label.

Shortly after a much smaller Positive Force relocated from the Peace Center into our communal house in January 1987, the group voted to disband once our planned events were completed. Fortunately,

University student, later wrote an academic paper that identified the "social contradiction" of the DC hardcore punk scene: "There are few women in bands, men have traditionally done most of the organization of shows and bookings of bands, and women are usually passively observing rather than dancing and getting actively involved at live shows. In joining this subculture, many women were rebelling against traditional societal roles, yet they were still contained within a subcultural ideology of male supremacy."

Such male leaders of the new scene as MacKaye, Squip, and Picciotto had already attacked this. As the latter noted, "Insurrection was way macho, ROS was way not." Moreover, Squip had encouraged women not only in words but also by bringing female musicians—among them Nicky Thomas—onstage and into the studio with Beefeater.

Women were also taking new roles within the scene. Pickering became the booker at 9:30 and Connolly replaced Claudia DePaul in that role at dc space. Under both DePaul and Connolly, dc space had "an important impact on women in the scene because they (are) willing to promote female talent," Coletta later noted.

In a letter to *Flipside*, Positive Force member Kristin Warren expressed her support for straight edge and admiration for MacKaye and Squip, but argued that "Ian's whole straight edge denial of obsessive sex was directed at women. The 'she' in his songs ruining the lives of otherwise 'free' 'cool' 'punk' men." She also criticized Squip for characterizing the downfall of punk in the 1985 *Flipside* interview as exemplified by people "dragging around little bleach blond girlfriends and shit."

MacKaye's response to the critique of female images in his songs was simply to note that "Minor Threat songs are true stories: the characters are

the events went well and meetings began to be more well-attended as word of our new location spread. With a modicum of structure added—an agenda, rotating meeting facilitators—and a more modest mission in mind, PF stabilized.

At the same time, DC was heating up. Congressional hearings on the Iran-Contra scandal, similar to those that had been so damaging to Nixon during Watergate, were planned for the summer. A massive, yet peaceful blockade at the CIA headquarters in suburban Virginia had tied up traffic for hours, effectively shutting down the Agency for most of a day and leading to nearly 600 arrests. After years of a seemingly invincible "teflon" presidency, Reagan finally appeared to be on the defensive. Some were even talking of impeachment.

The combination of our new home and new members like Melisa Casumbal, Brad Sigal, and Patrice Williams added to the political situation and the energy suddenly bubbling within the scene energized PF once again. After doing only three public events in the first half of 1987, the group mobilized to do more than two dozen different actions from June through October. In the process, we found support from many in the DC community, including non-Dischord bands like MFD, Braver Noise, and Broken Siren.

real people." He and Squip denied that their critique of obsessive sex was aimed at women: It "is directed at people who are power-tripping on their organs, boy or girl."

As for the "bleach blond girlfriends," they argued that "in this case, both parties are guilty. [We] get down on girls for playing the desirable young lady all feminine and fine and also for submitting to the role of simple-minded acquiescence. But [we] also attack the boy who puts her in this position."

Ironically, Fire Party did not address the cause of women in punk in its lyrics. "It's not that we don't want to make a statement," Pickering said. "Just the fact that we do it is a statement on its own."

"Fire Party formed around music, not around sex," she told a skeptical interviewer in 1989. When pressed, she insisted that the four of them became a band because they were close friends and because they "were on the same musical level, as opposed to most of our male friends. It was much more natural for us to get together."

For Pickering, the line between Revolution Summer and Fire Party was direct, even if nearly two years passed between her Neighborhood Planning Council ransom notes and the band's February 1987 debut. She played a major part in igniting Revolution Summer, yet neither she nor any other woman had been in any of that season's bands. By the time those groups had fallen, however, Pickering was already jamming with Avery. As a result, she didn't see 1986 as a "desolate period like 1984."

Revolution Summer, she said in 1993, "started when it needed to and then it died, as a concept on its own. But we were still left with all this input we had gotten from all these bands. [That summer] was the climax of the one thing which gave birth to the next thing. For me, it was the end of youth and that lackadaisical approach to your own life."

One of the next steps was out of parents' homes and into a series of group houses, beginning with Garfield House—where Picciotto, Canty, Birdzell, Mike Fellows, and later Natalie Avery lived—and then S Street, Kearny Street, and Positive Force House, among others. "We moved into S Street right after that summer," remembered Molly Burnham. "Garfield had just started up and there was Dischord House, but were they called 'Boy House'? No, it was 'Garfield Street.' But when we started S Street it was immediately labeled 'Girl House.'"

It was partly as a result of living together that the bonds that would result in Fire Party were created. The band was named after a birthday party at which a group that included the members of the band built a bonfire in the woods.

Since a greatly increased level of musical proficiency was now expected of local bands, Fire Party practiced diligently for months before playing out. "You couldn't just 'get up and do it,' you had to be good from the first show out or you wouldn't be taken seriously," Pickering said. Of the four, only Thomas had any real experience, having played with Lebensluste, a raggedy but earnest hardcore band, and In Pieces, an energetic but unpolished group.

Fire Party was not the first all-women DC punk band; it was preceded by the Pin-ups, the Nike Chix (a.k.a., Sybil), and the Furies. The most recent and accomplished female punk contender was Broken Siren, which showed its cool at a July 1986 Complex gig on a bill with Phlegm. The latter featured intelligent, often political lyrics and winning melodies, but it tended to attract a drunk-punk element. The show "turned out to be the most violent gig ever" at the Complex, according to Gordon Gordon.

Broken Siren defiantly played its music—recalling such British bands as Delta 5, X-Ray Spex, the Slits, and Au Pairs—to drunken shouts of "Skirt rock!" All three women shared vocal chores, but the main vocalist and visual focus was guitarist Karen Weiss. Caroline Ely played bass and sang a delightfully snotty cover of Iggy Pop's "Funtime," while Maria Jones, who had previously tried to start a band with Connolly, played drums.

Aside from writing songs about such issues as the US bombing of Libya, Broken Siren implic-itly aired another touchy subject: homophobia. All three members were openly either bisexual or lesbian. While Nuclear Crayons had played the Gay Pride Day in 1983, this stance was still unusual in the DC punk scene.

The lesbian-oriented pop-rock band On Beyond Zebra (which later became the popular and more cabaret-styled Betty) thrived on the fringes of the rock scene. But Broken Siren's harder style didn't attract the same crowd. As Ely remembered in 1994, "The dykes wouldn't come out to see us because we were too punk—and the punks wouldn't come out because we were too dykey." The trio did play some Positive Force benefits, including one opposing antiquated local anti-sodomy laws.

XXX

In the summer of 1987, the members of Soul Side decided to quit college and be full-time musicians. Bobby Sullivan later recalled the energy of the time: "Revolution Summer could have happened for three years or more. But all of the sudden the people in the limelight called it quits and everyone followed them. I really resented that, so I wrote the words, "You say the revolution is over—but the revolution has just begun."

Slightly altered, these lyrics now appeared in a powerful new Soul Side song, "KTTK"—Kneel to the King—Sullivan's sarcastic comment on the fatalism of some of the erstwhile leaders of the new scene. In a way, the song became the anthem of the revived and recommitted band.

When the band made its definitive return, however, it did so without Chris Thomson. Impatient with Soul Side's on-again, off-again nature, he had already decided not to return to school in 1986: "I didn't want to sit around and wait a whole year for those guys to come back, so I got this other thing going." He had made a connection with a kindred impatient soul, Chris Bald.

When Bald returned to DC in October 1986, he immediately set to assembling a new band that could last, embody his punk ethic, and, above all, get out and make things happen. He quickly found sympathetic conspirators in Thomson and Ferrando, newly returned from a motorcycle tour of the US. After his frustrating experiences with Embrace, Bald had decided to return to his original instrument, the guitar. With the addition of Thomson and Ferrando, all the band required was a singer.

Bald knew who he wanted: Alec MacKaye, who had not performed since Faith's last show in 1983, save for brief appearances with Bells Of and Beefeater. Bald was elated to discover that the wounds from Faith had more or less healed and that MacKaye was ready to return to the stage.

Neither knew that MacKaye was being eyed by the architect of another potential band: his older brother. After Minor Threat and Embrace, Ian MacKaye wanted a group strongly united around certain shared ideas, so that it would not self-destruct. For this, he was willing to wait and work as long as necessary.

Ian MacKaye had a lot of requirements. He still insisted on all-ages shows and low door prices. In addition, he felt the band should be self-contained and able to pursue its objectives unhindered by the distractions of drugs, alcohol, and the rock business. Artistically, he wanted to create a new music that didn't fit neatly into old harDCore categories or sidle up to the mainstream. Once the band had honed that music, he wanted to get out and play as many different places as possible.

He also intended to continue opposing punk-as-usual, speaking out against violence and machismo and regenerating the sense of community at shows. "When people actively participate, it gives the shows a purpose and unity that you don't see often now," he said in 1986.

Once the ritual of slamming had been disrupted, many were not sure how they were "supposed" to react to the music. In 1994, Jon Kirschten noted that after Revolution Summer "people stopped dancing to bands. They just stood around and watched." While this was preferable to mindless auto-mayhem, it violated the ideas of communal abandon and an egalitarian bond between audience and band. Without this connection, shows were simply a commercial transaction between creator and consumer. MacKaye hoped his new band could inspire a new and more inclusive communal release.

Where MacKaye had once disdained politics, now he was interested in pushing creative protest, in having a "militant" band that could do as many benefits and free shows as possible. In separate 1987 interviews, he spoke of "redesigning the conspiracy" and of his hope that his new band would "be soundtracking some coming upheavals. I think the time is right for people to get up off their asses and look around. And I'm not talking about the scene, I don't really give a fuck about that. I'm talking about the society we live in. If our music can elicit any kind of protest or get people thinking, that's what we're hoping for."

MacKaye had already decided that he would play guitar. Squip told him about bassist Joe Lally, who had roadied on Beefeater's US tour. Later Lally laughed when he recounted his initial qualifications for the job: "Tomas said that I was someone that you could ride in a van with for long distances without wanting to kill!"

It seemed an unlikely combination. Lally had never played in a serious band, and his main musical connection was to the drug- and alcohol-soaked metal-punk scene centered on the Obsessed. His friendship with Beefeater, however, led him to stop drinking, using other drugs, and eating meat. When the two jammed, MacKaye and Lally hit it off musically and personally, bonding over their shared love for the Obsessed.

The next step was a drummer. With Brian Baker's sudden departure to Doggy Rock, Colin Sears had been at loose ends. While neither Dag Nasty nor BMO—Sears's previous bands—had epitomized MacKaye's approach, Sears was more politically conscious than his musical resumé suggested; he had worked with Kevin Mattson at the Peace Center and was also a vegetarian. In addition, he was a skilled player and clicked with MacKaye and Lally.

The music the fledgling band began to play reflected MacKaye's scheme: a tight reggae/funk rhythm section underlying driving guitar rock built from fragments of punk, Detroit rock, harDCore, and Obsessed-style metal, yielding a powerful dance music with varying tempos. While the music seemed to be developing well, MacKaye was concerned about his ability to sing and play guitar at the same time. He had not played an instrument in any band since the Teen Idles—and then it had been bass, not guitar, and he hadn't sung.

Few vocalists could be expected to satisfy MacKaye; the most obvious candidate was his brother Alec. By the time MacKaye approached his sibling, however, Bald had already recruited him. So Ian MacKaye pressed on, working toward handling both vocals and guitar.

At the same time, a new band was forming from the remains of Gray Matter. Geoff Turner and Steve Niles had jammed with Jeff Nelson and MacKaye for a time in the fall; when MacKaye left for his other project, Nelson continued to play with Turner and Niles. Then Mark Haggerty returned from New Zealand and joined. Initially, this band too sought a vocalist. But after the musicians auditioned and rejected former 9353 singer Bruce Merkle, Turner assumed the vocals. Turner's increasingly sophisticated songwriting and Nelson's powerful, precise drumming distinguished the band from Gray Matter.

Minus Baker, the Meatmen were still up to no good. The final LP to feature Baker, *War of the Superbikes,* was released in 1985 on Homestead, followed in late 1986 by *Rock'n'Roll Juggernaut* on Caroline. Songs like "Cadaver Class," "French People Suck," and "Pillar of Sodom" were as juvenile as ever, but the band cleaned up its act a bit in an apparent bid for a larger audience. With MTV playing the video for the band's goofy stomp, "Centurions of Rome," Lyle Preslar wanted it known that the Meatmen did not perform joke-punk but the presumably more respectable—and sellable— "'70s glam-rock."

Preslar mocked "Dischord bands that break up every fifteen minutes," and indeed another such group had split after only a few gigs: One Last Wish came asunder in late '86 after recording demos with MacKaye at Inner Ear. Some in the band were very unsatisfied with the recordings; songs that crunched in live performance merely jangled in the studio. Picciotto's passion seemed fettered by Hampton's skillful but restrained approach, and the guitarist's controlling nature exacerbated such longstanding issues as Janney's unhappiness with playing bass. The collapse was so sudden that, when asked in 1994 why the group ended, Hampton could only confess continued mystification.

Two new Dischord bands were ready to play, however. Advertised only as "Steve N./Jeff N./Jeff T./Mark H." and "Chris B./Alec M./Dante F./Chris T.," the quartets that would soon be named Three and Ignition, respectively, debuted at dc space in March 1987. The show was part of a series of concerts Connolly had arranged to benefit the No More Censorship Defense Fund. She lured old-timer Root Boy Slim onto the bill for one night, arranging for Scream to be his backing band.

Scream headlined the following night, playing one of its last gigs with Stax and introducing topical new songs like "No More Censorship" and "Fucked Without a Kiss." The latter was a graphic account of prison rape inspired by the experience of a friend who as a youthful Quaker antiwar protester had been locked in DC Jail after being arrested in an act of anti–Vietnam War civil disobedience. Left unprotected by his captors, he was assaulted over 40 times in 48 hours.

While Three was impressively tight, Ignition at times threatened to fly apart. Still, the band's spirit was undeniable. As its name suggested, Ignition was meant to be a catalyst. "We're trying to start something," Bald said at the time. "We've got lots of ideas and big plans and it's up to us to make it happen. And, unlike in the past, I think everyone in the band wants to do it." Ignition soon played its second show, the Positive Force–sponsored anti-sodomy-law show with Broken Siren, Bad Pieces (a brief reincarnation of Nuclear Crayons) and Rain, temporarily bolstered by Soul Side's Scott McCloud on second guitar.

A mere month after its live debut, Ignition recorded its first single. The band had already decided to release the disc on its own label. "Dischord couldn't do it fast enough," Alec MacKaye later explained. "They were kind of backed up with other projects."

Speed was essential because the band was already booking its first out-of-town shows. For Bald, that was crucial: "DC fucking eats itself. Rites of Spring should have gotten out and toured. But they didn't want to do it without Embrace and Beefeater—one big happy family. It was completely absurd. Everyone wanted their 'safe European home,' to live under their safe roof, their safe little punk community."

Released in May, the Ignition 45 featured the band's logo, an ancient Asian symbol which Bald said meant "strength" or "long life"—his hopes for what the band would embody. The slow-motion crash and grind of "Sinker" conveyed the erosion of ideals by the workaday world, while "Anxiety Asking" assumed harDCore's musical garb to indict Bald's old comrades: "Suckers to the whole world/Killing yourself and your fighting chance/You quit when you were ahead . . . you just change for the same." The 45's centerpiece was "Rebuilding," which combined a relentless guitar riff with hopefulness—"This time could be different"—and acceptance: "Life is a one-way cycle/ You're born, you live, and you die."

x x x

Even as this song was being recorded, the regenerating scene received perhaps the biggest surprise of all. After One Last Wish's breakup, Canty, Picciotto, and Janney had doggedly returned to their basement jamming. As they sought a new direction, who should materialize but Mike Fellows. Although he planned to move to New York in the fall to attend art school, the four began to rehearse again and, surprisingly, found new common ground. The music they began to invent was far removed from Rites of Spring and One Last Wish, pulling its inspiration from an unlikely source.

Hip hop had been insinuating itself throughout the decade, but a new group had just appeared that changed the stakes: Public Enemy. Transfixed by the group's first album, the four musicians took Public Enemy's noisy funk and added their punk energy and growing art-school aesthetic. The result was the musically revolutionary Happy Go Licky.

The band's debut at dc space in April left many puzzled. This was Rites of Spring reunited, albeit with an odd new name, yet the band played jagged, danceable sheets of noise while Fellows intoned deadpan absurdist lyrics like "Get the dog—definitely," or Janney whimsically promised "Thirteen months of sunshine." At the same time, many of Picciotto's words and vocals were as earnest as ever. To some, the band seemed to surrender to arty, post-punk irony; its aloofness disappointed fans of Rites of Spring's openness and vulnerability.

In retrospect, the band could be seen as a brave if ruthless attempt to escape the image of the venerated Rites of Spring. Where the scene's musical choices seemed to be either more hardcore or a move toward mainstream pop-rock, Happy Go Licky exploded all expectations. The band reconciled passion and cynicism not by resolving the tension but by throwing it all into the mix and just playing the hell out of it. Happy Go Licky communicated not so much with words as with intense inventiveness of the music itself. The band sometimes skirted the edge of disintegration, but the precariousness was exhilarating.

With Ignition, Fire Party, Three, and Happy Go Licky in motion and Soul Side soon to return, the only major Revolution Summer players still sidelined were MacKaye, Squip, and Birdzell. While the latter two were having difficulties assembling the "big band" they envisioned, MacKaye, Lally, and Sears had been practicing zealously.

Then Sears received a call from Baker. Doggy Rock had proved a fiasco, and Baker was coming home. He wanted to re-form Dag Nasty, but with Doug Carrion on bass in place of Roger Marbury, who had been at odds with Baker in the band's earlier version. This was a dilemma for Sears, who had been rhythm-section partners with Marbury since the days of BMO. However, he recalled, "I wanted to play music for a living. Brian and Doug wanted to do something, so did Peter, and since it was me and Baker and Peter, why not call it Dag Nasty?"

The band immediately entered the studio to re-record the songs they had done the previous fall, adding a half dozen new numbers. These sessions yielded the second Dag Nasty album, *Wig Out at Denko's*, a further shift from harDCore toward pop. Shortly after recording, the band hit the road again.

At the time, Baker mused that the new songs "could take the positive thing to a new level," adding, "I don't think we're much of a hardcore band anymore, I think we're just a band. We play for a punk audience and I like playing for them. I hope they like the direction we're moving in." Rather than enforce hardcore conventions, he said, "New bands have to be more creative and not follow anybody. Take all your influences and make your own music."

This was what GI was attempting. The band had successfully toured Europe and the US and recorded a new record, *You*, that was released on Giant to positive critical and public reaction. "The last few records are the ones I've been waiting to make for three years straight," Stabb said. "I always wished we could get that melodic element with that good musicianship. The new lineup is the best we've ever had."

As GI and Dag Nasty toured, MacKaye and Lally were contemplating an appropriate replacement for Sears. None of the drummers they auditioned seemed to fit. MacKaye asked Canty to sit in while they searched for a permanent drummer. At least this way they would stay practiced, even if they were unable to escape the basement for now. The lyrics to a new song expressed MacKaye's mood: "I am a patient boy/I wait, I wait, I wait."

As he and Lally tried out drummers, MacKaye was drawing closer to Positive Force. Although his new band probably wouldn't hurt for gigs, he looked forward to playing as many Positive Force benefits and protests as possible. In 1986, he told an interviewer that the punk community had "backed off our really heavy statements." MacKaye didn't want to back off.

Positive Force organized an average of at least one teach-in, protest, or benefit a week during the summer of 1987, but venues were a recurring difficulty. New DC regulations closed the Chevy Chase Community Center to events that charged admission, and the Bethesda Community Center was hard to get. dc space was supportive but not big enough for some of the shows, while other existing spaces like the Hung Jury Pub and WUST could be expensive and a bit sleazy. Non-club all-ages spaces were needed.

With some hard work and persuasion, Positive Force was able to reopen Sanctuary Theater, closed to punk during the great harDCore bellyflop of 1984-85. The group also strengthened its relations with St. Stephen's, the church MacKaye's parents attended. MacKaye had another suggestion: "Why don't you try to reopen Wilson Center?"

It was an excellent space, and symbolically its use would reclaim lost ground. Wilson Center had been harDCore's ground zero, and its closure had signaled the end of an era. Reopening it would not be easy, however. Initial calls to the facility were not promising. But Wilson Center was a community space with a genuine commitment to social action, so a request to hold a benefit concert for a respected community group—longtime Positive Force ally the Washington Peace Center—was hard to refuse.

The July 1987 show was carefully planned. The revamped Soul Side, with high school friend Johnny Temple filling the vacant bass slot, agreed to headline the show. It was joined by Fire Party, Three, and a new political hardcore band, Christ on a Crutch, that had recently relocated to DC from nearby Annapolis.

The show went off without a visible hitch, with perhaps 250 in attendance and an upbeat, friendly atmosphere. Afterwards, Positive Force workers mopped floors, picked up trash outside, and even scrubbed the toilets. The next day, the manager held the group responsible for a broken window, although it had not been broken during the gig. This almost closed the hall to more events, but finally Positive Force was allowed one more show.

The group also used the Embassy Row ballroom of Johns Hopkins' School of Advanced International Studies for several shows, including an Amnesty International teach-in/benefit/protest march in July. Scream headlined over King Face, Three, and a potent new band called Swiz. This foursome recalled the spirit of groups like Faith and early Dag Nasty—no surprise, since original Dag Nasty singer Shawn Brown was the vocalist.

The name was taken from Peter Shaffer's play *Equus*: "You sit in front of that TV long enough, you'll become stupid for life like most of the population. The thing is, it's a swiz. It seems to be offering you something, but actually it's taking something away. Your intelligence and concentration, every second you watch it. That's a true swiz, do you see?"

COWARDICE AND COMMUNITY
by Mark Andersen

This show was personally significant in at least two ways. First of all, I shared a story from stage that had been eating away at my heart since my return from Central America in August 1985. I had stumbled across the body of a man apparently just killed and dumped by the police behind the National Cathedral in Guatemala City. As I walked between the body and the police, my gaze was first drawn to the mutilated head of the victim, and then riveted by the sight of the policemen in mirror sunglasses standing just feet away, having their shoes shined by two ragged street urchins, secure in their sense of absolute impunity. I was face-to-face with my conscience–and I blinked. Without a word, I walked away. Ashamed of my cowardice, I spoke to no one of the incident . . . until that night.

Secondly, I began to understand that PF shows were becoming significant community events, much like the old Wilson Center shows had been in the 1981-83 period. This became clear when Marginal Man's Pete Murray confronted me during a break between bands and speakers. Hurt and confused, he asked earnestly why Marginal Man was not being asked to be part of these shows. Aware of the band's past ambivalence toward us, but impressed by Pete's sincerity and palpable sense of exclusion, I apologized and promised to call on them in the future. Immensely moved by the concert, teach-in, and march, Pete wrote a powerful new song called "Stones of a Wall."

With unknowns Jason Farrell, Nathan Larson, and Alex Daniels on guitar, bass, and drums, respectively, Swiz lived up to the description of its music as "big power sounds." For those disillusioned by the trajectory of Dag Nasty and other scene elders, the rise of Swiz was cause for celebration.

That night, Swiz was followed by equally dynamic if quite different sets by King Face and Three. The former unveiled several new songs, including "Your Body Is Your

Mind" and "Television's Better," while Three both streamlined and diversified Gray Matter's sound. Turner's thoughtful lyrics reflected a broadened vision, with references to AIDS, fundamentalism, consumerism, and Reagan's Central America policy in songs like "Dark Days Coming" and "Pious and Blind."

Still, the evening's most compelling set was by Scream, playing for the first time with Dave Grohl. Only a few feet of wall separated Scream's fury from the Chilean Embassy, US outpost of those who had murdered Rodrigo Rojas. The set's climax was the closing "Hit Me," a crunching mid-tempo number about "inspiration"—inspiration from music, the written word, the spoken word. After references to the deaths of Marvin Gaye and Martin Luther King Jr., the song climbed to a crescendo, ending with a simple affirmation: "I am free."

The band screeched to a halt, but Pete Stahl continued singing the final line over and over. At his urging, the crowd picked it up and a chorus rose, the words "I am free" ringing out again and again until the band built back to full steam. As Stahl spun around the stage, the song shifted into "Solidarity," soared for a few seconds, and was gone. As a silence fell on the room, Stahl said: "Let's march for the people who aren't free."

After Scream's galvanizing performance, well over half the 300 people in the audience joined in the silent candlelight march past a dozen embassies of countries that shared only one thing: human rights abuses. The procession ended with a short rally in Sheridan Circle, where in 1976 Chile's secret police had blown up exiled Chilean dissident Orlando Letelier and his coworker Ronni Moffit with a car bomb.

While not all the summer's events went so well, momentum was building. New people began to join Positive Force and support within the broader punk community seemed to be growing. The group's deepening connection to the resurgent scene inspired an idea: Why not do a compilation record that would in effect be a vinyl version of a Positive Force benefit, spreading powerful music and messages while raising money for a good cause?

This idea came from an unlikely source. William and Azar Dagher, formerly of harDCore-linked Baltimore bands like the Bollocks and Law and Order, had formed a new Smiths-influenced group called Braver Noise. After releasing a Braver Noise LP on their Fetal label, the Daghers began work on a DC-area sampler, *FR5*. This would prove a spotty compilation, but it contained at least two gems, Press Mob's "Sundays" and Broken Siren's "Driving With the Top Down." Positive Force

House resident Lida Husik submitted the haunting "Candle," but it arrived too late. Azar Dagher suggested putting the song on a Positive Force compilation.

It seemed like the right time to make a record that could be both a documentation of the new scene and a kind of alternative State of the Union message. The American Civil Liberties Union and the Community for Creative Nonviolence were chosen as the beneficiaries for the record, and a benefit show was arranged to pay pressing costs. Ignition, Fire Party, and Marginal Man all signed on. Ian MacKaye was also approached.

He not only thought that Dischord could help with the project, but also that his new band would be ready to play the benefit as its first show. After a brief period rehearsing with Ivor Hanson, who then returned to college, Canty was again playing drums. Practices were going so well that MacKaye had decided that the new band would play out with Canty. While he publicly stressed that this was to be a temporary arrangement—since Canty was still in Happy Go Licky—it's possible that he felt he'd found the right drummer and was going forward in hopes that Canty would ultimately be available.

It was not a bad gamble. Happy Go Licky had built a strong following—including many who were not Rites of Spring fans—with unpredictable, explosive performances. The band's inventiveness and almost telepathic interplay could be breathtaking. Nonetheless, Fellows would soon leave for school. The band would try to continue, but that seemed a dubious proposition.

While planning the show, the second at the reopened Wilson Center, MacKaye unveiled a practice tape with part of a song called "Word." The sound was far closer to Egg Hunt than Embrace, with the same taut, dubby rhythm section, blunt sentiments, and crashing chords. The style would confuse the mosh-happy masses with its changes in tempo and volume, while providing ample opportunity for more flexible dances and allowing MacKaye to sing and play guitar at the same time. Asked if the band had a name, MacKaye grinned and said: "Fugazi."

A GROWING PARTNERSHIP
by Mark Andersen

References to Positive Force in the main text should not be generally read as code for "Mark Andersen"; however, in this chapter, some of the stories result from my growing friendship and working relationship with Ian Mackaye, whose encouragement was crucial in this period. "Inspiration goes round and round," he said when I told him this later; the actions of PF had also helped, to some degree, inspire him to take the next step with Fugazi.

The word was taken from *Nam: The Vietnam War in the Words of the Soldiers Who Fought There*, a book assembled from interviews conducted by Mark Baker. For MacKaye—a self-taught scholar of the '60s who remembered attending anti–Vietnam War demonstrations with his parents as a kid—it was an ideal choice. "Fugazi" evoked not only his '60s influence but also a certain militant intent. The word, MacKaye noted, "was veteran's slang for 'a fucked up situation,' which is kind of how I view the world."

With Fugazi in the wings, the city's punk standard bearer remained Scream. The band had signed to RAS (Real Authentic Sounds) Records, a well-respected local reggae label that had decided to expand into rock. Although Scream was sad to leave Dischord, Pete Stahl said, "We liked [RAS'] politics, we liked many of artists on the label, and it seemed like they could help us take our next step." With *Banging the Drum* about to emerge, Scream had already recorded its next album for RAS, *No More Censorship*.

A show at 9:30 in late August showed the band at its peak; both the musicians and the crowd seemed to sense Scream was on the edge of something. Scream had been one of the few harDCore bands to take direct inspiration from the revolt of the 1960s. Now nostalgia was turning the '60s into just another marketing opportunity, as exemplified by the use of John Lennon's song "Revolution" in a Nike ad. "It seems like this summer that some people are making a lot of money off the generation of the 'Summer of Love,'" Stahl said bitterly. As another new song, "Run to the Sun," rose behind him, he spat on the stage and exclaimed, "Revolution doesn't mean selling shoes." By show's end, when Stax came onstage for a rousing version of "American Justice/Fight," it was clear that in mid-1987 only a handful of bands from DC—or anywhere else, for that matter—could rival Scream's power.

One of the few that would opened the State of the Union benefit in September 1987. Fugazi began with an instrumental designed to draw in the crowd—which, as usual at Wilson Center shows, was outside socializing—for a short speech about the purpose of the event. Then the band opened, appropriately enough, with "Song #1," MacKaye's farewell to punk's fractious and short-sighted tendencies. The song's monster chords drove home a concise moral: "Life is what you want it to be/So don't get tangled up/Trying to be free/Don't worry what the other people see/It's nothing."

What people saw was a power trio led by a MacKaye whose long, knotty hair was held back in a ponytail. This was such a different look for him that it sparked an amusing rumor that MacKaye had adopted Rastafarianism and taken up pot smoking. Lally, meanwhile, had cut his metal-head hair short.

If MacKaye seemed a bit uncomfortable as guitarist and vocalist, he still commanded the stage. "Song #1" slid gracefully into "Furniture" before a broken string sidetracked the song. Unrattled, the band unleashed the next three songs—"Merchandise," "Turn off Your Guns," and "In Defense of Humans"—in quick succession, punctuated only by MacKaye's acerbic commentary. The songs, complete and yet open-ended, were built of butcher-block chords, dub drop-outs, propulsive bass, and terse lyrics.

The set nearly concluded, MacKaye paused to joke that "we were going to have a little diversion, we were going to have Guy"—who was watching from the crowd—"start a fight or something if we started to fuck up on one of the songs." Then he introduced the next tune as being about "what the heck we could do if we did." Lally's loping dub bass line was greeted by Canty's sharp drum cracks and MacKaye's jittery guitar. The song's tension was eventually resolved by big chords and a call-and-response chorus straight out of DC Go-Go. It was "Waiting Room," the song written amid the frustration that had led to the band's creation.

The show raised nearly $1000, so the State of the Union project could move forward, and the Wilson Center was secured as a continuing venue. While Fire Party, Ignition, and Marginal Man also gave fine performances, the words that lingered were from "Waiting Room": "But I don't sit idly by/I'm planning a big surprise/I'm going to fight for what I want to be/And I won't make the same mistakes/Because I know how much time that wastes."

"*I see you in captivity of what the world wants you to be*
I see you in captivity of one degraded destiny
But listen up—there's time to flee, follow me
Every step you drop a bit of what no longer seems to fit
Ain't no need to trail along where generations done gone wrong
Ain't no need to trail along this lost procession, millions strong
What could be worse than history? Break free
Look at me, I never die, I drop the years as they go by . . ."
—Fidelity Jones, "Fountain of Youth," 1988

"MEESE IS A PIG" GUERRILLA POSTER STRIKE, MAY 1988 *(by John Falls)*

fountain of youth

It was almost Christmas, and Washington's downtown shopping districts and suburban malls sparkled with evidence of America's biggest annual consumer festival. But on this morning—December 21, 1987—the holiday crowds were greeted by some unusual decorations. Throughout city and suburb, huge three-color posters greeted commuters and shoppers with an unseasonal message: "MEESE Is a PIG."

Passersby who didn't understand why the Attorney General of the United States was being so maligned could read the small print noting that the nation's top law enforcement officer was currently under investigation by two special prosecutors, one for his "highly suspect role in obtaining government contracts for the Wedtech Corporation," the other for his involvement in the Iran-Contra scandal. The text argued that Meese's "personal conduct and muddled testimony before Congress suggests that he is either a chronic liar or a confused man with sloppy ethics." The poster continued:

> "If a person is innocent of a crime, then he is not a suspect." Edwin Meese said that, and his policies since becoming Attorney General prove that he believes it. For Meese, the Constitution is so much toilet paper. Meese has argued that the Bill of Rights was not meant to apply to state and local governments. He has encouraged public officials to disobey Supreme Court decisions they disagree with. He supports mandatory drug testing, has argued that states should have the right to make abortion a crime, and has led the Administration's campaign to smash the hard-won civil rights gains of the 1960s and '70s. Under Meese's Justice Department, companies are free to discriminate against blacks, women, and, most blatantly, persons with AIDS. Meese has urged the Supreme Court to abolish the "Miranda Rule" which requires police to inform citizens of their rights prior to questioning. Meese has sought to abolish the "Exclusionary Rule" which protects Americans from unlawful search and

seizures by making evidence obtained in violation of the Constitution inadmissible in court. What can you do? Write President Reagan. Write Congress. Write Ed Meese. Let's make this odious little weasel resign right now.

Given the simple taunt that dominated the poster, this postscript seemed surprisingly well-informed, suggesting more political sophistication than immediately met the eye. So did the skilled execution of the strike. According to the *Washington Post*, the "mysterious posters appeared across the city overnight, pasted on walls and utility boxes all over Washington and nobody seems to know who put them up." As city workers were dispatched to remove the posters—after a complaint from "Capitol Hill," reported the *Post*—Justice Department spokesman Patrick Korten called the poster "obnoxious" and "not nice."

With Congress recessed and other political news at a low ebb, the affair became a holiday sensation; the *Post* story was picked up by papers as far away as San Francisco. Stumped, the *Post* was reduced to dropping hints that the poster might be connected to the eccentric right-wing sect headed by Lyndon LaRouche. Many theories were floated, but none came near the truth: Behind this rude but effective holiday prank were three dozen DC punks—and, in particular, Jeff Nelson.

Unlike his Dischord partner, Nelson had kept a low profile since Minor Threat split. Before Three, Nelson had not been in a serious band since 1983, focusing instead on Dischord's business operations and art direction. Nelson's graphics skills had grown dramatically as Dischord's sleeve designs progressed from crude black-and-white to—beginning with the Egg Hunt 45—elaborate full color.

This was not the only kind of progress that Nelson wanted for Dischord. Although Amy Pickering—as well as Cynthia Connolly and newcomer Jenny Thomas—did important work, the label was still essentially a two-man operation that seldom advertised, sent out few promotional copies, and didn't issue press releases. Minor Threat remained Dischord's best-selling band nearly five years after its breakup—in effect, subsidizing later releases—but Nelson freely admitted he was tired of hardcore. "I don't want to put out stuff that I don't listen to myself," he said, and he wanted "to branch out to reach more people."

The company's low marketing profile was the subject of a long-running if good-natured dispute between Nelson and MacKaye. "Ian can't stand how businesslike [Dischord] gets while I can't stand how unbusinesslike it is," Nelson said at the time.

The label had started paying royalties with *Still Screaming*, but in what Nelson termed an "erratic and ever-changing way." By 1985, he said, "We thought we were doing really well. We'd paid off $4000 or so in debts and paid most of our royalties. But then came tax time and we realized how horrible our accounting methods were." The issue was partly resolved by revamping the books, but Nelson still felt that "we don't sell enough of each record to keep the prices so low. Our problem is not selling records, it's keeping them in stock." However, Nelson added, "Ian doesn't think the problem lies in the prices—or doesn't want to believe that—and thinks it's more important to try to cut spending even more and keep prices down." Since cost-cutting often affected packaging or promotion, this difference of opinion led to some uncomfortable discussions.

Dischord's other half could hardly help but be overshadowed by MacKaye, who the *Post* dubbed "a punk rock philosopher king." But Nelson's own politics were also evolving. "There were just endless Minor Threat interviews that said, 'Look, we're not political at all—sorry,'" Nelson remembered. "We just didn't know that much and we didn't want to be hypocrites." But by the mid-'80s, "I was starting to know what I was talking about." All that was lacking was a catalyst.

That came in October 1987, when Nelson read that Meese, bowing to the National Rifle Association, had withdrawn a plan to prohibit plastic guns. Such guns could elude existing metal detectors, so banning them was supported by law enforcement groups. A Justice Department spokesman explained that the NRA had "made some reasonable arguments that deserve further attention." To Nelson, a gun-control supporter, this seemed a classic example of the influence of moneyed right-wing lobbyists. Already angered by Meese's actions in the Iran-Contra scandal and on an "anti-porn" commission, Nelson decided to go public.

The phrase "MEESE Is a PIG" materialized quickly. Nelson decided that a huge poster with that simple phrase, rendered in striking letters and colors, would be the perfect instrument. The poster's designer didn't realize it at the time, but his choice of words was oddly appropriate. For years Meese, an archenemy of 1960s protesters, had been collecting pig statues in an odd personal tribute to law enforcement officers.

Positive Force was a logical source of support. After Nelson readily agreed to add a paragraph detailing reasons to censure Meese, the group signed on. In retrospect, the whole idea seems almost mundane. After all, punks had surreptitiously pasted show fliers for years. This project just used existing skills for a larger cause. The DC scene, once avowedly "apolitical," was applying lessons learned in the DIY underground to larger concerns.

XXX

Not long before, MacKaye had been a leader of that chorus. But as Nelson's idea took shape, MacKaye was building his own soapbox, Fugazi. The band had begun with a burst of shows, most of them benefits, including one supporting a huge gay rights march. MacKaye shaved his head once again, and the band gained skill, confidence, and new material. It also appeared to have become a foursome with the acquisition of a backup vocalist, Guy Picciotto.

The latter was in an odd position. He and Brendan Canty had been a musical team for over five years. But as Fugazi was fitting together, Happy Go Licky was in danger of coming apart. Mike Fellows had moved to New York, and now Eddie Janney was considering Paris. Still, the band continued to gig whenever Fellows came to town, often performing with little or no practice.

At a September 9:30 Club show opening for Sonic Youth and Ignition, Happy Go Licky was in blazing absurdist form. Among the highlights of the barely 20-minute set was Melle Mel's anti-cocaine rap "White Lines." Later, Fellows laughingly recalled that "I played the bass line from memory and we just threw in the lyrics we could remember." Only a few jumbled lines of the original remained intact, repeated chaotically. The clash of chattering guitars was punctuated by cries of "free base," "crystal eyes," "blow away," "get higher baby," and "never come down."

"Ansol" rode a supple bass line, decorated with feedback and radio broadcasts run through the amps. Such cut-up lyrics as "every day is like nirvana" and "wooly bully"—both from '60s songs—seemed a form of sampling without machines. During the set's finale, "Suzuki," Janney climbed onto his equipment stack, coaxing screams of anguish from his guitar by pressing it directly against the amp's top. Picciotto crumpled to the stage, writhing and singing lines like "she's my man now" to Fellows's interjections of "wooly bully/wooly bully."

If many found the intent impenetrable, the performance's intensity suggested that Happy Go Licky was, in its way, just as heartfelt as Rites of Spring. "When we did Happy Go Licky the whole intent of the band was to just say 'fuck it,'" Picciotto said later. "You can sing in many different voices and you can do many different sounds and shift it around and do all this stuff [as long as] it's you that's present and on top of it and delivering."

That night the call for an encore was so unrelenting that MacKaye had to come onstage to announce that "Happy Go Licky thanks you" and ask the soundperson to "roll the music please." The buzz was building, even as Happy Go Licky's future grew more dubious. The situation made Picciotto's potential role in Fugazi all the more unclear. He had begun as a roadie on Fugazi's first out-of-town gigs; after a few shows, he started to come onstage mostly to dance and sing some backup vocals.

This signified nothing permanent, for one of Fugazi's ideas was to encompass unexpected happenings and guest appearances. Although Canty continued to play with the band, he was still officially considered "on loan" from Happy Go Licky. By year's end, a parade of persons had joined Fugazi onstage, including Ian Svenonius, the ex-singer of In Pieces, playing keyboards; Molly Burnham playing trumpet; and, in particular, Positive Force House drag-king Charles Moats shaking his booty.

The band's potential was apparent when it played dc space in October, opening for King Face. The show had a jovial feel, with MacKaye ribbing King Face bassist Andy Rapoport, who had appeared in the starring role in a play earlier that night at Catholic University. With 150 people crowded into the small room, the band began with the instrumental "Joe #1."

As Joe Lally uncoiled the back and forth notes, MacKaye talked over the tune, encouraging the crowd to dance in a creative, nonviolent way. He called Jenny Toomey onstage to give a brief plug for the upcoming "Women Take Back the Night" anti-rape week, noting that "everyone should listen to this because it involves human beings, not only women." Then the band dove back into the set with "Merchandise" and "Furniture." As this "song with no words" rose from its dubby beginning to a roaring crescendo, MacKaye sang, "That's right/It's coming from here/You can check it out/It's coming from here." The song stopped on a dime, and MacKaye exclaimed, "Right fucking here," pointing to his heart.

In the pause that followed, MacKaye encouraged "anyone who has some musical idea to come on up sometime. Or if you have something to say, come up and say that too." He prepared to start "Song #1," noting that "this song is sort of a philosophy that you can attach as much importance as you want to anything. In the end, it's all nothing. So, you should take care of each other and never put movements in front of human beings because"—MacKaye cut himself off with the song's gigantic chords and the crowd erupted.

Such powerful new songs as "And the Same" suggested that Fugazi had just begun to explore its capacity, but the biggest surprise was yet to come. MacKaye yelled "Tonight!" and unleashed a classic buzzsaw riff; then suddenly Picciotto was flying around the stage, singing lead for the first time in Fugazi. Even though the vocals to "Break In" were barely audible—apparently the sound technician had been caught off guard as well—the moment's energy was extraordinary. Barely missing a beat, the band went into "Waiting Room," which climaxed with MacKaye's exhortation—unnecessary under the circumstances—to "get up!"

As he tossed off the jagged intro to "Word," MacKaye made a series of dedications—to Ignition, King Face, dc space, and Positive Force. His words propelled by the song's acceleration, he continued: "This is dedicated to everyone here. This is a song about change. I encourage you to break down whatever fucking walls are between the band and the crowd tonight, please raise your voice and join in." As chanting from friends in the crowd rose, MacKaye spit out the words: "You got a problem?/You got a problem?/What was that word again?"

Looking out at the wildly dancing mass, he said, "Yeah, we can move. Isn't it fun to move without hurting each other? It's possible." Again the song erupted, and Fugazi finally completed the deliberately incomplete thought: "What the fuck was that word? The word is . . . change." The tension resolved, the band cooled the song down to a peaceful dub pattern and walked it home.

x x x

More and more new people began coming to see Fugazi, which quickly surpassed Embrace's draw. After one heartstopping show, Tomas Squip and Dug Birdzell dissolved their big band lineup, whose members they decided were too compromised by different lifestyles and attitudes toward the music business. They decided to strip back to the basics like Fugazi, with Squip playing guitar. Their Kearny Street group house was being displaced, so in November almost the whole group—Squip, Birdzell, Joe Lally, and friends Dana DeNike and Bobbie Brewer—moved into Positive Force House.

There, Squip and Birdzell connected with the other two members of their new band: drummer Jerry Busher and percussionist Maria Jones of the now-defunct Broken Siren. While Busher had only started playing drums a few months before, he had natural aptitude and—most important to Birdzell and Squip—the right attitude. Besides, despite his knack for twisted noise-making in Beefeater, Squip was almost as much a novice on guitar, knowing only a few chords at the time.

Ignition had released its second single by October, and had done two mini-tours and numerous weekend trips. Chris Bald played hard enough to inflict some damage to his equipment at almost every show. At a Positive Force–sponsored Native Rights demonstration in Dupont Circle, he climaxed the set by ramming the nose of his guitar straight into the ground. This explosiveness made for gripping performances, but it was hard to sustain. "We would be on the road going to the next gig and we'd be gluing the guitar together in the backseat," Dante Ferrando later recalled, wincing.

One Bald outburst nearly ended the band. At a dc space show, intermittent sound problems inspired him to smash his guitar over his amp—breaking it neatly in half—and then to attack the rest of his equipment before storming offstage. This might have been a slightly excessive if electrifying climax to a powerful set—except the band had not yet finished its second song. The rest of the band stood by in shock till Alec MacKaye matter-of-factly announced, "Well, I guess that's it for tonight. Thanks for coming."

Rumors flew that the show would mark the end of Ignition, but the band returned with a series of gigs announced by a poster with the band's logo superimposed over a mutilated picture of Elvis and the headline, "Not About to Die." The quartet was planning a US excursion with Scream when a last-minute slot opened on a European tour with Norwegian hardcore band So Much Hate. When Ignition accepted, Southern Studios offered to release a 12" combining the two singles to coincide with the tour.

At the same time, Soul Side was finally assuming an identity of its own, moving beyond Lünchmeat's style, thanks in part to the rhythmic emphasis of Johnny Temple, a huge reggae fan. Powerful new songs like "Name in Mind" and "Trigger"—as well as a cover of Bob Marley's "War"—showed both musical growth and an evolving political consciousness. Shortly after returning from its first US tour, the band played a Positive Force benefit for the Community for Creative Nonviolence at Wilson Center with Fugazi, political hardcore band Thorns, and the Hated, an intense, explosive Annapolis group. Then Soul Side entered Inner Ear with MacKaye to record its first Dischord release.

By early 1988, the scene was bustling. Swiz was touring the Northeast as Sammich prepared to release the band's first 12". The label also planned an LP by Shudder to Think, a quartet that had evolved out of the teen hardcore band Stuge and was developing an unusual style based on singer Craig Wedren's quirky outlook and operatic vocal range. And King Face had released a 12" with sharp renditions of "Lull-a-bye," "Anyone," and "Crawl Into Tomorrow."

Scream began its *Banging the Drum* tour, which included some Midwest shows with Fire Party. Now much more comfortable onstage, Fire Party had allied closely with Scream; the two groups decided to tour Europe together in early 1988. Fire Party recorded its first EP with MacKaye at Inner Ear, to be released in mid-1988, concurrent with Scream's *No More Censorship*.

Of the new Dischord-affiliated bands, only Three seemed largely confined to the Washington area. This was a source of tension between Steve Niles and Nelson, who thought Niles was too involved in his Arcane Comics company and not sufficiently serious about the group. When Niles, in a fit of romantic pique, broke his hand on the eve of a series of shows in early 1988, Nelson was incensed. The band soon fell apart, but before disbanding it recorded an album as well as basement tapes of new material. Nelson thought the basement tapes were "far, far better" than the record, but he provided a typically elegant package for the latter when it was released in 1989.

Nelson and a few carefully chosen friends were also clandestinely silk-screening almost 300 "MEESE Is a PIG" posters in Dischord House's basement. Once struck by this idea, Nelson had became, in his own words, "a total lunatic," pouring many hours and hundreds of dollars into the project. Kurt Sayenga, editor/publisher of the fanzine *Greed*, was recruited to write the poster's text.

The production process was laborious. Hanging the posters to dry outside—where they might be seen—was unthinkable, so the first two floors of Dischord House became a huge drying rack. MacKaye's piano—and more than one insufficiently agile person—was marked with the bright paint.

Then posterers were recruited and organized into teams, while Nelson tried to pick a night when the police presence was light and the weather favorable. On December 20, close to 10 teams, each with three to four people and about 20-30 posters, were dispatched. One team skirmished with Secret Service cops, but all the others—including the one that pasted a poster directly across the street from Meese's office—encountered no police. In less than two hours, over 200 posters had gone up.

x x x

As the "MEESE Is a PIG" stir faded, Happy Go Licky greeted the new year with its first headlining 9:30 Club show, with Three and an abrasive new band called Bastro. The show was mobbed, indicating that the band had unexpectedly broken out of the punk crowd to reach a much larger audience. The musicians played a blistering set, topped by a shocking but appropriate encore: Rites of Spring's anthem, "Drink Deep." Performed on the spur of the moment, the song was the band's valediction.

"It was a good way to go out," Picciotto said at the time. "Happy Go Licky never really 'formed,' it just had an idea, fell together, and played a lot of shows." He added that "I can't imagine not playing with Mike and Eddie again," but for now both he and Canty were free to focus on Fugazi.

Another important and much longer-lived group was also about to quit. Marginal Man had been doing some recording, including a version of "Stones in the Wall" that it agreed to contribute to the *State of the Union* compilation. Otherwise, however, "we were drifting," Pete Murray later recalled. Kenny Inouye was going to school and Mike Manos was getting married. The recording of the third LP had taken a long time—the album's credits say only that it "was recorded over the 1980s"—and the band performed only once in the last quarter of 1987.

Murray, in his own words, "instigated a breakup." The band ended with a packed finale concert at 9:30 in March 1988. The third LP—containing "Spirits," a tribute to Toni Young—would surface later in the year. The cover photo of a fish being released into the Potomac River was an apt symbol of the band's farewell.

Shortly after his decision to leave MacKaye and Lally and rejoin Dag Nasty, Colin Sears discovered a cyst in his arm. Needing an operation and unable to play just as the band faced a tour, Sears was replaced by punk newcomer Scott Garrett. This left Dag Nasty with only one original member, Brian Baker.

The band then recorded a single, "You're Mine," with a slick sound that further offended punk purists. "When it was written it was supposed to have a Gang of Four–meets–Clash texture to it," Peter Cortner recalled. "Then we went and spent $3000 recording this single and it sounded like Bon Jovi. We make a point to not even practice that song. We don't play it, we don't like it." Baker, however, defended the recording as an experiment: "I'm into the idea of recording singles that push the limit of what the band can do, whether it fits into what the band's supposed sound is or not."

With its new lineup—the fifth since the band started only two years before—Dag Nasty went on a US tour and never came back. Calling Washington "a little stifling," the band set up in LA and started work on a new record for Giant, *Field Day*. "I don't want to be considered a DC band," Cortner said, a sentiment roundly seconded by Baker.

The transition of Dag Nasty from harDCore to pop-rock was complete. Though some termed *Field Day* a sellout, it got good reviews outside the punk-purist fanzines and sold 20,000 copies in its first two months, quite successful for an indie release.

Among anti-commercial DC punks, the band would not be missed. "The only reason Dag Nasty exists [is] to make money," complained Alec MacKaye. "Brian Baker is the only one who is really in the band—he just hires and fires them. I guess they're talented, but at the same time, it's just about money." Bald was even blunter: "It makes everything they did before a complete lie."

"I have yet to see any band, punk or speed-metal, that has become so successful that you can apply the term 'sold out,'" Baker responded. "No matter how you slice it, we are an underground band. We just want to sell as many records as possible and expand our audience without alienating those who like us now."

Baker also attacked Washington's punk scene for being cliquish and insular. "Very few bands make it out of DC," he charged. "As of right now, we're really the best-selling thing from DC ever except for Minor Threat. I was trying to do something bigger and that just kinda goes against the grain of Washington. By the time Embrace had broken up, they had played 12 shows. In those six months we had played 62 shows. The Embrace album came out two months ago, while we are about to record our third album."

He also attacked Dischord's production values, calling the "shitty" sound of *Wig Out at Denkos* "an example of the Washington, DC ideal: 'Why go into a better studio, this one's fine. We like this studio.' That's why Embrace stayed home: 'We like this studio, this is really great,' and their record sounds really awful."

Cortner made a subtler point, noting that Dag Nasty's debut could also be considered an example of commercial calculation: "The first record is a great hardcore record, but as far as the meaning and truth that most of the punk scene gets out of it—I think that's really funny, because if there ever was a case of people trying to cater to the tastes of a certain audience in order to get their record sold, that's it. You have your ex-MT, you have your ex-DYS, you have your hardcore tunes, you have vague lyrics that point basically to being angry with society and parents."

x x x

Baker blasted DC bands for not touring, but with Scream, Ignition, Soul Side, and Fire Party on the road, that criticism was becoming outmoded. When Fugazi was offered a gig at Gilman Street, a new punk-run performance space in Berkeley, the band decided to build a tour around the date. MacKaye called the tour "a chance to refamiliarize myself with what is happening in the country. For the band as a unit, it's a chance to play, let people see the band, and since only the four of us are going I think it's a chance for us to 'become' the band." The quartet had recorded a demo in January, but decided not to release anything from the session, save one track for *State of the Union*.

This meant Fugazi would hit the road without a record to promote, a highly unusual move, although copies of the demo tape soon began circulating widely with the band's blessings. "If bands *have* to have a record out to tour," MacKaye remarked, "then definitely we are the band [that] is going to tour without a record."

The band had also decided not to sell any T-shirts or other souvenirs. "When something is for sale it becomes just another product," MacKaye argued. The message of the song "Merchandise," he explained, was "spend your dollars wisely, because your dollar is your vote."

Picciotto rejected band merchandise for another reason, his concern that punk was no longer self-generated: "When I was 16 or 17, we couldn't play in clubs, we'd just go off and play in the basement of some suburban home. Forty kids would come over and dance like maniacs, the cops would come, and then we would all go home. I didn't need 900 T-shirt designs. We just made up our own circuit. Now the kids come to our gigs and ask for our T-shirts or our fucking baseball caps."

The only thing the musicians took on the tour—besides their equipment—was a supply of free lyric sheets. Lally had designed a one-page sheet that parodied a TV advertising pitch, with the headline, "And now, a few words from . . . Fugazi." The band name—a goofy Squip-designed logo with a phony copyright symbol—continued the pseudo-commercial theme. At the very bottom was the punch-line: a fake UPC sticker with the word "CHANGE" written into the bars.

Consciously choosing to avoid the established punk club circuit, the band decided not to play venues known for violence, to require all-age shows, and not to charge more than five dollars. Promoters were also told they couldn't advertise that Fugazi contained an ex-member of Minor Threat.

"How a band carries itself, where the band plays, where it won't play, how we handle our business is very important," MacKaye said. "We try to present a show that brings feelings of community to the crowd. We literally stop playing if it gets violent because I won't play for violence anymore."

To insure the low ticket price, Fugazi took a percentage of the door receipts, not a guarantee as most bands did. This meant that the band would make less money, but it would enable it to achieve larger objectives. As MacKaye had planned, all the band members agreed on this.

The tour included shows in art galleries, record stores, basements, movie theaters, and the Sundance Saloon in Bozeman, Montana. "We could cash in on the established circuit but we chose not to," said MacKaye. "We would rather play a small show set up by an individual we trust and like."

This approach to booking, Picciotto explained, "gives people the idea that this is not a rock'n'roll circuit, that this band is moving in a different kind of network and that things can happen in a different fashion. Basically we're saying, 'Trailblaze with us, let's create.'"

x x x

As Fugazi prepared for its tour, the band played more benefits and demonstrations. One was a Positive Force–sponsored fundraiser for the Christic Institute—a group focusing attention on the Iran-Contra scandal—at Wilson Center in March with New York's False Prophets and King Face. Opening the show was a new band whose lead singer came onstage with an odd head decoration—DC Comics superhero underwear.

"Some people say punk is dead," announced the slender figure. "I don't know if that's true—but I do know for sure that protest music lives." The man turned to the band and stepped back to the microphone. Then with all the force his skinny frame could muster, he roared, "If there's anybody out there who can hear me/I'm screaming from way down here below . . ." The band kicked in behind him, raising a joyous racket.

The clown/prophet was Squip with his comrades Birdzell, Jones, and Busher, and this self-described "protest" band was Fidelity Jones. Combining the drug term "jones" (meaning "addicted") with the concept of "fidelity," the name declared a need for truth.

The songs were less experimental than Beefeater's, and despite Birdzell's powerful bass the band was not nearly so tight as its precursor. Indeed, the set demonstrated that Squip was still struggling to play and sing at the same time.

Still, the songs were energetic fragments of punk, funk, reggae, and rock, and their sincerity was obvious. Squip's message had continued to evolve in a spiritual direction, so that he was dealing in "liberation theology" as much as his original influence, Bad Brains. Where HR had focused nearly exclusively on Rasta, however, Squip drew from a variety of sources—Hindu, Buddhist, Native American, and Christian—while using both female and male images for the divine.

Squip's message made some punks uncomfortable, and the singer himself once asked if his lyrics made him look like a "religious nut." Still, he didn't see a conflict between spirituality and punk. "Once you've torn everything down you have to adopt things that make sense. More than anything, punk's just a big sponge, wiping the slate clean so that you don't get caught up in distractions, fraud, and deceit. It's just destructive to cover yourself with paint and hair spray, TV and video games, Big Gulps and cigarette smoke. Drop it all. That's my punk philosophy: Drop the bullshit."

This was the essence of Squip's vision. In 1987, he helped prepare a boycott list, encouraging people to avoid drugs including alcohol and tobacco; meat, leather, and other animal products; and companies like Shell and Coca-Cola that had not divested from South Africa. Underlying the specifics of the list was a general plea to turn away from the "deathstyle" of modern consumer culture and adopt a simple, non-abusive existence.

Almost by accident, the boycott list became part of *State of the Union*. The 10-page booklet for the album had been completed and given to Nelson, who noted that a 12-page version would be more practical. Positive Force then decided to include the boycott list, an anti-Shell handout from a recent South African Embassy protest, and an essay on the theme of "live the life." A note explained that the list contained "suggestions, not rules to divide us into the 'righteous' and the 'unclean,'" yet it was widely misinterpreted as a neo-Puritan rulebook. It generated more controversy than any other aspect of the project—even the full frontal nude photo of Squip with "Lord let me do no wrong" scrawled across his chest.

Squip's plan to "drop the bullshit" was also expressed by the song "Fountain of Youth," which presented punk as an opportunity for open-ended growth. "At the time, it seemed like a lot of people [in the scene] were passing into 'adulthood,'" the singer noted. But "if you want to grasp onto youth, you can. You don't have to pass into the stages of decay that people go through, from spiritual death to physical death. A youth is someone who's growing, who's wild at heart. If you are in growth and furtherance, it's got nothing to do with chronology or calendars."

Among the other early Fidelity Jones songs were the pro-vegetarian "Gorilla Gorilla," the apocalyptically funky "Purifire" and "Mountains of the Moon," and "Long Sexy Showers," a sensuous yet spiritual "livication" written for Toni Young. Aside from "Fountain of Youth," however, the set's highlight was the bleak "Blood Stone Burn," which the band had already recorded for *State of the Union*. As the music shifted from folky rock into an extended reggae coda, it countered images of rape, drunkenness, war, AIDS, and murder with the repeated assertion that "today is the aphelion"—meaning that earth was about to turn in its orbit back toward the sun, symbol of light, warmth, and life.

In part, the song was an acknowledgment that Washington was fast becoming a particularly gory region of the "blood stone." In 1985, there had been 148 murders in the city; by April 1988—the time of Fidelity Jones' second show—100 people had already been slain, a fact Squip noted onstage during "Blood Stone Burn." At this rate, more than 300 people would be murdered in DC in a single year, a new record.

x x x

As Meese's troubles mounted, Nelson conceived an even more ambitious poster campaign. With his friend Peter Hayes, a graphic artist who had also played with Mourning Glories and Wonderama, Nelson designed a new version of the poster. This time the text at the bottom was eliminated in favor of blazing yellow bar across the top. Within the bar were the words, "Experts Agree!"—a gleeful reference to the mounting call for Meese's resignation.

The design looked so good that Nelson decided to make T-shirts as gifts for those involved. As the dimensions of the new campaign became clear—twice as many teams and posters—and Nelson poured hundreds of dollars more into the project, he began considering selling some shirts to cover some of his expenses.

While the team silk-screened 800 posters—this time with four colors—and recruited "poster guerrillas," once again with the help of Positive Force, Fugazi was making final preparations for its tour. Nearly every show seemed to bring the debut of another powerful new song. Two of them, "Burning" and "Give Me the Cure," were sung by Picciotto. Although they clearly carried his mark, both songs fit Fugazi's topicality.

While "Burning" evoked the dangers of the databank age, "Give Me the Cure" was even more timely. "Ian suggested that we write a song about AIDS and I had some ideas about it," Picciotto said. "Generally, AIDS has been approached as a 'sinner's plague' or a plague among people of lesser value," MacKaye noted, "where in fact it is a disease like any other. Until people can confront AIDS on that level, I don't think the energy can be found to find a cure." Appropriately, the song debuted at an April AIDS benefit.

Perhaps the most striking new song was inspired by an intense exchange MacKaye had with a friend right after she had been accosted on the street by a man. MacKaye wrote, "Why can't I walk down the street/Free from suggestion?/Is my body my only trait/In the eyes of men?" which would become the opening lines of "Suggestion." The band first played the song at dc space in December '87.

"Of all the music I've done in my life, it does more to me than any other," MacKaye later told *Maximum RockNRoll*. "Rape gets the most attention, but there's also the constant intimidation and harassment which every woman I know has been confronted with. It created such an anger inside of me and I really wanted to write about it, but it didn't come out right, because of my perspective, a male's perspective. So I tried to write the first half of the song the way a woman might see it. The second half I wrote as a human being, an observer of the situation."

The song provoked criticism, mostly from men threatened by the subject but sometimes by women who felt MacKaye had no right to assume a woman's voice. One way to resolve this tension arose when Amy Pickering asked to sing the song's opening part at a show in Annapolis. The band quickly agreed, and the result was riveting. She would continue to join Fugazi onstage often when the band played "Suggestion" in the DC area.

The final show Fugazi played before hitting the road was a May Day demonstration "in concern over teenage pregnancy" organized by former dc space booker Claudia DePaul in Lafayette Park, across the street from the White House. Picciotto sang another new song, "Glue Man," inspired by a film MacKaye's high school friend Jem Cohen made about a glue addict lost in poisonous reveries. To some, the song evoked past harDCore anti-drug anthems, but Picciotto was careful to describe it as "a song about obsession."

MacKaye would occasionally explain one of Picciotto's lyrics to the crowd, not always to the writer's satisfaction. At the AIDS benefit, MacKaye described "Cure" as "a song about AIDS," while at the May Day show said "Break In" was "about teenage pregnancy." In an interview after the show with the fanzine *Nomadic Underground*, Picciotto clarified that "when Ian said 'Break In' was about teenage pregnancy, he probably should have said, 'This *could* be about teenage pregnancy,' because it could be about a lot of things. It certainly means a lot of different things to me."

Picciotto would often offer his own comments on his songs, but they tended to be evocative rather than concrete. Once he introduced "Cure" with, "Every lover is a scientist and everyone has tainted love," and prefaced "Lockdown" by saying, "There is no peace as long as there are people in prison." Some interpreted these comments to mean that Picciotto was uncomfortable with political content, but he denied it. "Everyone thinks that Ian is the 'political' one, but that's not true," he said. "I care very deeply about these issues—I just have my own method of expressing it."

On the road, Fugazi ran into some expected incomprehension, but generally dealt with it effectively. In Spokane, for example, "four or five kids who were really drunk kept hitting everyone else who just wanted to dance and get into it," Picciotto recalled. "So we said, 'Everyone who wants to dance how they please, come up onstage.' Everyone came up onstage and me and Ian went out on the floor and faced the stage, Ian playing guitar and those four or five guys thrashed all around us and I just danced with them and they were trying to figure out what the fuck was going on. It just shattered the whole mystique [of the pit]. After that song, everyone went back on the floor and the show changed."

Ironically, perhaps the tour's most confrontational show awaited the band at Gilman Street. This volunteer-run warehouse space had been financed by $40,000 from *Maximum RockNRoll*, which was prospering despite its resolutely anti-commercial stance. On the walls were such messages as "Frontiers Divide People" and "Check Racism at the Door," and a membership pledge was posted by the door: "I recognize that I am personally responsible for my actions and that cooperation with others is in my self-interest. I agree to respect the right of others to express themselves." No alcohol was allowed in order to keep the space open to all ages, leading the *Wall Street Journal* to (inaccurately) call it the "mecca of straight edge."

In its way, Gilman Street represented the same kind of idealism as Revolution Summer. But those who attended shows there did not necessarily think of punk as anything other than rowdy entertainment.

With an "Experts Agree! MEESE Is a PIG" poster displayed prominently behind him, MacKaye began the show with his usual matter-of-factness: "Good evening, ladies and gentlemen, we are a band called Fugazi and we are from Washington, DC." He then praised opening bands Crimpshrine and Yeastie Girls, noting of the latter that "it's important for women to have a voice in a community where their voice is put down so much. One big way this is done is on the dance floor. Now, I know that everyone loves to run in circles, but actually it's not everyone—it's mostly boys. So do us a favor, do yourselves a favor, do everyone a favor and let everyone come to the front of the stage and move around and dance. Let's take the violence out of the scene, let's take the violence out of this show, there will be no big-bully-boy bullshit tonight!"

Despite MacKaye's words, a circle pit started up and divers soon started to swarm the stage, slamming into the band, knocking instruments out of tune, and at one point snapping MacKaye's guitar cord. As a replacement was found, MacKaye told the crowd, "We played a show in Bozeman, Montana, and people there were pretty receptive to the concept of dropping their macho facades. We played a show in Spokane, and people there were receptive to the idea of dropping their macho facades. We played at Evergreen State College in Olympia, Washington, and people there, likewise, were willing to drop their macho facades. Now, here we are, in the beautiful Bay Area, and I hope people will also be receptive to this concept."

Unmoved by the resulting chorus of complaints from some in the crowd, the band responded with the high piercing whine that announced "Burning." The band slid into "Give Me the Cure" and Picciotto sang, "I never held the hand of dying before/I never walked with the dying" to the Bay Area, one of the US communities hardest hit by the AIDS epidemic. The number of stage-divers grew again, and one ran straight into Picciotto, ramming the mic into his mouth and causing it to cut out.

Undeterred, the band pushed forward. When the bass line of "Suggestion" began, MacKaye requested, "I hope you will especially listen to this next song. If you think you're so tough, well, let me tell you, men don't know shit, they don't know nearly as much as women about how it's like to be raped . . ."

As the song rolled toward its end amidst continued clichéd responses from some on the dance floor, MacKaye motioned to the audience, calling out, "Hold on one second! Do me one big favor. For the next two minutes don't jump up and down and run around. Just give me a little of your attention please, just two minutes, then you can do what you want." The crowd's attention recaptured for a moment, MacKaye jumped back to the song: "He just wants to prove it/She does nothing to remove it/We don't want anyone to mind us/So we play the roles that they assigned us."

It was clear that MacKaye had the role-playing of punks as well as other parts of society in mind—and his point was received. With some in the crowd chastened by the confrontational performance, the band rolled through the rest of its set. During a closing "Glue Man," Picciotto once again was hit by a stage-diver. He stood pointing at his split lip as MacKaye wrung squeals from his guitar.

"People say, 'Oh, they're anti-dance,'" said Picciotto afterwards. "We're not. I'm tired of one or two tough guys ruining the atmosphere of the show. It's my show, too, and I'm going to get involved and find out what's going on."

x x x

On May 15, the second round of "MEESE Is a PIG" posters went up. This time, several people were stopped by police in both Washington and Arlington and given $50 tickets. A few days later, the FBI began investigating, allegedly because of fears for Meese's life. Before the bureau got very far, however, the *Washington Post* reported that federal agents were investigating a case that was legally classified as "littering." The FBI quietly dropped its inquiry.

There was one more chap-

PUNKS VS. POLICE, PART ONE
by Mark Andersen

This was one of more scary weeks of my life.

Positive Force House was the coordination center this time, since Jeff Nelson was concerned that Dischord House not be implicated in case of trouble. Nearly 70 punks were split into a dozen teams, each with specific territory, aiming to get out, get the posters up—including in high-visibility, high-risk locations—and get off the streets as quickly as possible.

If luck had been with us the last time, it was not that night. Two teams were caught; one fined and let go, the other—which included Jeff—warned and released after taking down a few posters. My own team had numerous close scrapes with police, but emerged unscathed. When I took a friend home afterwards, however, I foolishly stopped to recover supplies abandoned in an earlier escape from police.

Just as I picked up the lost bucket and brushes, a dark-blue Secret Service cruiser pulled out of the alley; they followed us several blocks down 16th Street before pulling us over for faulty brake lights. After my night's work, I was a laughable-looking mess covered with slowly stiffening wheat paste. The policeman took one look at me, the posters, and other contents of my backseat, and went back to his car radio. As I cursed my stupidity, I heard him say, "It looks like we've just solved the 'MEESE Is a PIG' mystery."

In short order, we were surrounded by five more police cars and a motorcycle cop, all with their lights flashing. While they let my friend go, I sat there for nearly two hours, watching the sun rise as

ter in the saga. Common Concerns, a leftist bookstore near Dupont Circle, was selling Nelson's "MEESE Is a PIG" T-shirts. With the new publicity, the shirts became a hot item; Nelson could barely keep up with demand. About a week after the *Post* article turned police harassment into police embarrassment, bicycle messenger Christopher Stalvey took a package to the Justice Department. He was wearing a "MEESE Is a PIG" T-shirt.

The Justice Department guards looked at his shirt and refused him entry. When Stalvey appealed that he be allowed to do his job, they called their superior and were told that the courier should not be admitted. Ultimately, Stalvey had to summon another messenger to do the job.

Justice Department spokesman Korten insisted that Stalvey was barred for not being "appropriately attired." The irony—and outright illegality—of this position was not lost on Stalvey, or the American Civil Liberties Union, which soon came to his aid. Ultimately, the Justice Department was forced to admit it had erred. By then, the story had been reported around the globe.

With this latest burst of promotion, T-shirt sales boomed. Nelson was forced to hire another shirtmaker—punk artist Andy Gore—and began almost nonstop production. Common Concerns went on to sell over 4000 of the shirts, making it more than three-fold the best-selling item in the store's history. Nelson cleared enough money to cover all the posterers' fines and other expenses; he used the rest of the proceeds to buy more silk-screening equipment and art supplies for other projects.

police of all types came and went, speaking into walkie-talkies, trying to question me, and engaging in vigorous discussions about my fate.

Finally, the cop who stopped me asked me to get out of the car. Fully expecting to be arrested, I was surprised to see the whole parade pulling away. I was even more surprised when the cop handed me two tickets—one for driving without brake lights, the other for not wearing my seat belt. While I wasn't about to complain, it didn't seem to make much sense to release me with only a couple simple tickets after all this commotion.

The drama was not yet played out, however. Just few hours later, my car was suddenly towed away from a legal parking spot. I spent the rest of the day reclaiming it from the impound lot. The following day, my car was broken into and ransacked. Although my steering column was vandalized, apparently to make the break-in look like an attempted car theft, my ratty old 1977 Gremlin was hardly a likely target for any real car thief.

That these were not coincidences, but part of an orchestrated campaign of harassment, became obvious when I learned that Jeff had been served an arrest warrant at 1 a.m. that morning, followed shortly thereafter by the rest of his team: Michelle Cochran, Peter Hayes, and Heather Johnson.

As Michelle recounted later, "The officer said that he knew that he had told us it would be the end of it if we removed the posters, but that his superiors had been mad at the first round of posters in December and now they were really mad." The four had been charged with "displaying political posters on county buildings or land," a misdemeanor that carried penalties of a $50 fine and ten days in jail. Given the circumstances, it seemed clear that they were being singled out for political reasons.

On July 6, Meese resigned.

x x x

Back from the West Coast, Fugazi played a 9:30 show opening for Fire Party, which had returned from its European tour a much tighter unit. Such songs from its soon-to-be-released Dischord EP such as "Drowning Intentions" and "Engine" showed the band's growing power and assurance. One of the session's best songs, "Pilate," was saved for *State of the Union*.

The band still felt pigeon-holed. "People say, 'You're good for a girl band' or, 'You sure have broken the stereo-type for a girl band,'" Natalie Avery griped. "Why can't we be a band like any other band?"

Fire Party was one of the inspirations for Jenny Toomey, who founded Geek with long-time friend Derek Denckla (formerly of Carpe Diem), Lillian Daniels, and Ivor Hanson, back from school and now a Positive Force House resident. Songs like "Herasure" and "Shoelaces" were informed by Toomey's work in Women's Studies at Georgetown University. Soon Kim Coletta and Jenny Thomas would form a band

Two days later, the stakes were raised dramatically; I received a call from Special Agent John Kerr of the FBI. He had been briefed on my early morning police tryst on 16th Street and wanted to question me further about the "MEESE Is a PIG" affair. With help from Lisa Fithian of the Washington Peace Center, I quickly retained a dynamite pro-bono public-interest attorney, Jonathan Smith, who advised me not to talk to the FBI again, that any questions should be submitted in writing. He then called Special Agent Kerr, who said he had been instructed by the Justice Department to "investigate and report on the source of the posters."

This was simple political intimidation. When I called to tell Jeff what happened, we suddenly realized that our phones might well be tapped. Outraged, Jeff—who considered himself "a reasonably law-abiding, tax-paying citizen"—lost his temper and yelled into the receiver: "If you're listening in, well, fuck you! This is America—it's supposed to be the land of the free! Fuck you!!" We stopped our conversation, agreeing it would be best to talk in person from now on.

Fortunately, James Rupert at the *Washington Post* had caught wind of our plight. Once Rupert's story detailing the campaign of intimidation against us appeared on the front page of the *Post*—next to an article suggesting that Meese had helped to quash an investigation of the corrupt Wedtech Corporation—the tide turned. Suddenly we were the heroes and Meese the villain; both Arlington County and the FBI quietly dropped their inquiries.

After the FBI call, I had little to lose and was able to speak freely. Between the *Post* story and subsequent articles in the *New York Times, Seattle Times, Newsweek, San Francisco Chronicle*, and more, our story went out across the country. The heavy-handed tactics of the FBI, police, and Justice Department rebounded against them, spreading our message much further than we could have ever hoped to on our own.

called Twister with GI bassist J. Robbins; it would debut in early '89 at Positive Force's first Women's Festival.

Ignition now joined Fugazi and Fidelity Jones in supporting women in the punk scene. Bald's new "One-Sided" critiqued male would-be revolutionaries, including himself: "A man onstage/Giving issue to his rage/I'm only telling one side of the story/Humanity is a double-edged sword/We must give equal billing to her words." When Bald started a side project, 96, the following year, the bassist was a quiet young woman named Christina Billotte who would be an important force in the future.

It was fortunate that Fire Party was in top form at the 9:30 gig, for the quartet had the unenviable task of following Fugazi, whose set included another blazing version of "Suggestion" and a confrontational anti-macho song called "Bulldog Front," inspired by a run-in with boneheads while on tour in Atlanta.

Soon after the show, Fugazi recorded seven songs at Inner Ear with ex-Razz bassist Ted Niceley providing production assistance. This session would become Fugazi's first EP. The following month, the band headlined a Positive Force–organized Greenpeace benefit at Wilson Center. During the most scorching, polluted DC summer in years, the band debuted "Burning Too," a call to arms that furiously invoked the environmental crisis.

The crowd numbered around 500, considerably larger than the average Positive Force show. This reflected Fugazi's growing grassroots pull. Also on the bill was another Annapolis band, Moss Icon, as well as Ulysses, a new group composed of Ian Svenonius and Steve Gamboa—the remnants of In Pieces—with James Canty on drums and Steve Kroner on guitar. Some were bewildered by Ulysses' blur of noise. Observers claimed that in its first half dozen performances the band never played the same song twice; others suggested it had not yet played what might fairly be termed a song.

Ignition, which also played the show, had finished recording its *Machination* album as well a new version of "Anger Means" for *State of the Union*. The song, Alec MacKaye noted, was "about growing up in America and living a life that is supposedly the greatest thing you could ever be blessed with, but that, in reality, is just as much a prison as any other." It would be the second song on the album, following Scream's "Ameri-dub," a haunting track with samples courtesy of Ian MacKaye.

During another mini-tour in June, Ignition played with a reconstituted Bad Brains. The band's sound was familiar, but the look was a bit different, for it lacked both HR and Earl Hudson. In their places were Taj Singleton, former singer for the Swiss band People, and Mackie, a drummer who had played with Darryl Jenifer and Dr. Know in projects dating back to 1983.

After defecting from Bad Brains, HR and Hudson returned to working with old allies like Dave Byers and Kenny Dread. Despite HR's predilection for reggae, pop producer Oscar Brown made the singer's *Human Rights* LP a weak synth-pop dance record. Even songs like "Life After Death," which had burned in live performances, sounded mild-mannered. The follow-up, *Singin' in My Heart,* had more reggae but was also a disappointment.

HR's erratic vision seemed best realized in the company of Jenifer and Dr. Know. As if to make this point, SST released a powerful live Bad Brains album. Still, the two factions continued apart.

x x x

The violent DC skinhead scene had withered, in part because Lefty was in prison for helping steal someone's boots at knife-point. Elsewhere, however, a new racist skinhead movement was being organized by a middle-aged white supremacist, Tom Metzger. He had known nothing about skinheads or punk until meeting some British skinheads affiliated with the racist National Front during a visit to the UK. Learning that the US had a similar if less organized subculture, Metzger saw an opportunity. While American skins tended to be more interested in beer parties than political parties, Metzger and his son John decided to make them "frontline warriors" for the White Aryan Resistance (WAR).

On an American tour, Government Issue would encounter the new Nazi skins. The band had survived a tough year of touring, including a serious van accident in Britain, and had recorded what many considered its best album, *Crash,* while undergoing some philosophical shifts. John Stabb had become a vegetarian, and had unexpectedly joined a Positive Force–sponsored demonstration at the Tenleytown McDonald's. After the protest, Stabb committed GI to playing at an upcoming Animal Liberation Front benefit.

First, though, GI would have two unpleasant encounters with Nazi skins, beginning with one at a gig at a reservoir outside Las Vegas that Stabb described as "this huge sunken area graffiti'd with such pleasant thoughts as 'Niggers Suck,' 'Death to Jews,' and 'White Power,' with swastikas painted all over." In this isolated setting, the band was intimidated when a group of Nazis started chanting, "White Power!"

"I hated every minute of our set," Stabb later recalled. "I wanted to kill [the Nazis] and leave their bones rotting in the dust." When one Nazi skin complimented the band after the gig, Stabb refused to shake his hand. "Go home and burn all your GI records," he said, "'cause I don't want you to like us." As the skin stomped away looking for backup, the band split in a hurry.

When GI encountered more Nazi skins at a gig in Memphis, the band fought back. "This skin-head started giving me this sieg-heil sign right in my face," Stabb said. "I cut loose on his ignorance in a very verbal manner: 'Why do you come here, why do you exist? Why do you hate human beings for their color or race?' They were yelling stuff back to us but we stood our ground." After the show, the Nazis waited outside to attack the band, but left when police were called.

Despite these incidents, it was otherwise a successful tour. Still, the band's slow career growth was pulling it apart. After a huge argument in Detroit turned into a discussion of their fraying friendship, Stabb and Tom Lyle came to an understanding: "We agreed that if the new record didn't make it for GI," the singer later wrote, "then we were *kaput*."

As GI headed home, Fugazi was in Europe, garnering more press, confronting audiences, playing hard and often. "We don't mind shows that are uncomfortable, where the audience is shouting out and taking swings at us," MacKaye told British music weekly *Sounds*. "With this band the audience doesn't dictate the menu." Like other DC bands before it, Fugazi was impressed by the network of squats, youth centers, and other underground institutions in Europe.

The combination of punk and politics was compelling, and Fugazi wasn't the only DC band that realized it. Soul Side recorded two songs that revealed a newly pointed outlook. The fluid yet dissonant "103" challenged "The selling of lives/To feed our country's foolish pride," but the real story was "Bass." Nimble bass, martial drums, and an ominous guitar whine propelled the verse— "Nation's capital like little South Africa/Look further on down the road/Every major city pushing down the poor"—into the rousing chorus: "I'm calling for action/So rise people rise/Rise and revolt/Burn the eyes of rulers/Burn it down."

On a bitterly cold day soon after, Ignition played the Safari Club, a venue in a long-neglected section of the Shaw neighborhood. Alec MacKaye described how two homeless men had burned to death while trying to keep warm by building a fire in an abandoned building across the street just days before. Then the band exploded into the crash'n'grind blues of "Lucky 13," which addressed the plight of the homeless. The aching verses led to an angry question: "How come the cost of living is so high/When the price of life is so cheap?"

Bald was now sharing a group house with Squip and Birdzell. As a result of this physical and spiritual proximity, Ignition and Fidelity Jones had grown close. Bald and Squip made a huge banner with the word "STOP" and they used it as a backdrop when they played the Animal Liberation Front benefit with GI and Blind Ambition at Wilson Center. During Ignition's "Wrenching," a song inspired by author Edward Abbey's eco-sabotage ideas, Bald tore loose from the song, confronting the crowd, screaming "STOP!" over and over, pointing at the banner.

GI played well, showing the precision of a well-oiled touring machine. Thanks to the band's presence on the bill, close to 500 people attended the show. Many were from the more mainstream punk community, making for a somewhat uneasy mix of cultures. Squip and Bald messed with the crowd's diving and dancing rituals by stage-diving nude.

Banned in DC, a beautifully designed photo-history of the early DC punk scene created by DC punk veterans Cynthia Connolly, Sharon Cheslow, and Leslie Clague appeared late in the year. While the book was a powerful document, what was happening now was strong enough in its own right to make it almost seem like old news.

PUNKS VS. POLICE, PART TWO
by Mark Andersen

Although our satisfaction at Meese's fall was real, George Bush soon became our new president. Despite the criminality of Iran-Contra and growing poverty and violence in the USA, four more years of grim conservative rule loomed; Ian suggested to me that we might have to adopt some version of the "self-defense" techniques of the Black Panthers to protect our punk community in the dark days ahead.

One small test came with the '88 Alternatives Festival. Inspired by the rebounding energy of the scene, Jenny Toomey had returned to the fringes of PF. Just before heading off to study in the UK for a year, she helped to organize the annual festival. When one of the two days of poets, speakers and music in Dupont Circle—on which Fugazi, Fire Party, Geek and the smart, passionate punk/metal band Parasite were to play—was rained out, Jenny called the Park Police to arrange for a rain-date permit the following week on September 11. Assured over the phone that she could pick up the permit on Friday, Jenny merrily went on her way, calling the bands and publicizing the event widely.

Jenny arrived late Friday afternoon, only to be gruffly told that no such permit existed and none would be issued. In other words, PF had a gathering planned for the next day sure to draw hundreds of people—and no legal way to hold the event. Angry about this rude brush-off, I volunteered to manufacture

Positive Force had decided to do a homeless benefit because the onset of winter was increasing suffering on the streets and because the city government was refusing to honor the right-to-shelter law approved in a popular referendum. Days before the late-December show, Fugazi returned from Europe, where it had recorded a new EP at Southern Studios and a John Peel session. Picciotto was now fully integrated into the band, and beginning to experiment with playing second guitar.

Longtime DC punks Lydia Ely, who now worked for the National Coalition for the Homeless, and Donald Keesing helped organize the event. Keesing's band, Rain Crow, opened the show, followed by inventive Rhode Island hardcore band Verbal Assault and then a pumped-up Soul Side, which performed "Bass" and "103."

As Soul Side played, PF workers at the front door were nearly overwhelmed. Over 1000 people had shown up, the largest Wilson Center punk crowd ever. While both Verbal Assault and Soul Side had sizable followings, the vast majority of people came to see Fugazi. In its first DC show since the release of its EP, the band had unexpectedly doubled its audience.

a counterfeit permit. After consulting with Fugazi and the other bands, we decided to go forward with the event; with some creative use of white-out, a typewriter, and a Xerox machine, I came up with a reasonable facsimile of a new permit.

With our "permit" in hand, we arrived early and got the equipment set up as quickly as possible, knowing that once our crowd was there, it would be difficult to shut us down without risking a riot. By noon, as we prepared for soundcheck, a motorcycle cop came by. We held our breath as he examined the permit at great length—only to hand it back and go on his way. The event was soon underway, but tension continued; twice, more police officers stopped to examine the permit, one going so far as to call it into headquarters. Both times they left and we went on with our event.

By the time Fugazi climaxed the day surrounded by a crowd hundreds strong, our sense of triumph was palpable. Afterward, a satisfied Ian commented that the day had been "good exercise." In a later interview, Ian explained his concept: "We've done all these percussion protests, marches, and other stuff . . . on the surface you're going to think, 'Well, this is stupid, us banging a drum outside the South African embassy, what's that gonna do about apartheid?' But what's important is that you're exercising your protest muscle and the time will come when this muscle had better be in shape because a lot more bad shit is gonna happen and we have to be prepared to deal with it."

Before Fugazi began to play, MacKaye noted the audience's unprecedented size to a roar of approval. "But now at the risk of being a real asshole—and I don't really care, that's all right—I'm going to beg, cajole, plead with the people up front to be a little more caring of each other because all night I've been watching people get their heads smashed right about here"—pointing to the front of the stage. "Now I know we live in a democracy—or what you might think is a 'democracy'— so I'm sure some people will say, 'Hey, man, it's my right to jump and land on people's heads all night long.'" He paused, considering this for a second. "Fair enough. But how many people would just as soon they didn't jump on their fucking heads all night?"

As the crowd cheered, MacKaye continued: "So listen, let's get everyone up front, let's make sure it's not only boys, right? Let's make sure that everyone can have a good time. And I can tell you now that if I see you come up more than two times, swimming your way up here, I'll say, 'Hey, man, get the fuck off the stage!'" As the audience erupted again, the band began "Provisional," a new song written by Picciotto after a visit to Dachau, the Nazi concentration camp. When his amp fizzled, Picciotto discarded his guitar and the band reignited the song. From that point on, the set's momentum would be ferocious and uninterrupted.

After "Provisional," the band rushed into "Song #1." As MacKaye hit the chords, the room erupted into intense (and non-slam) dancing. When he began to sing, the crowd nearly drowned out his vocals; the song's gaps were filled with joyous screams from the crowd. A sucessive song, "Bulldog Front," was the most deafening DC singalong since Minor Threat days.

Soon Pickering moved in from the side of the stage, where she had been dancing, to take the mic. As she hit the lines, "I've got some skin/You want to look in," she pulled up her T-shirt, screamed, and whirled to face the drum set. She spat out the words: "You spent yourself, boy/Watching me suffer/Suffer your words/Suffer your hands/Suffer your interpretation/Of what it means/To be a man." On that final line, it seemed the whole room joined in.

As the music dropped back, MacKaye inched forward, with something specific on his mind. About a week before the show, the *Washington Post* had published an article on DC skinheads. These skins vigorously denounced the new Nazi skinheads, even bragging that they had "beat up quite a few" Nazi recruiters. They went on, however, to strenuously defend attacks on gay people. Indeed, at the time one of the skins was under arrest for a near-fatal P Street Beach assault on a gay man.

MacKaye saw his music as "an action," and as the band continued the sinuous rhythms of "Suggestion," the singer put the tool into motion: "You know, I read in the paper the other day about some young men, some 'boys' who were beating up homosexual men in a park." A voice in the crowd yelled, "Fuck that!" MacKaye repeated, even more scornfully, "I read in the paper about some young men, some 'boys' who were beating up gay men in a park. Well, I don't give a fuck what you are, you do not beat up people for being gay"—a huge cheer from the crowd—"you do not beat up people for being black"—an even larger cheer—"you do not beat up people for being women"—more cheers—as MacKaye's voice rose, cutting off each word sharply—"YOU . . . DO . . . NOT . . . BEAT . . . UP . . . PEOPLE . . . PERIOD."

MacKaye paced away for a second, shaking his head. Then as the band continued to push the song forward, he returned to the mic: "So, usually, this is a song about rape, but tonight it's a song about"—now he was softly singing—"beating up gay men . . . in the park at night." The emotional electricity crackled as MacKaye jumped from song into speech and back again: "He did nothing to deserve it/We sit back like they taught us/We keep quiet like they taught us." The singer asked, "How many people out there know someone who has beaten up a gay man, a black man, a black woman, a gay woman, a white woman? Everyone."

The band hit a dead stop at the word "everyone." With the identity of the song's protagonist changed to a gay man, the song yielded new meaning: "They assign us roles of passivity, they assign us roles of fear, they say, 'Don't get involved.' Well, that's bullshit!" As the audience's thunder rose again, MacKaye continued, "Because someday you and you and you"—pointing to members of the crowd and then to himself—"and you and you and me will get beat up for some reason which is equally insane, equally idiotic." The music returned, heading for its crescendo: "He does nothing to conceal it/He touches him because he wants to feel it/We blame him for being there/But . . . we . . . are . . . all . . ." The music dropped away, and the whole room shouted: "GUILTY!"

After an airless, silent second, wild applause broke out. With his head hanging and dripping with sweat, MacKaye walked back to his amp. The moment's weight was resolved by a glissando of barbed notes from his guitar, and the band was into "Lockdown," followed quickly by "Give Me the Cure," "Waiting Room," "Burning Too," and the final "Glue Man."

Now Picciotto was on his knees, beating his chest with the mic as he sang. He rose only to fall backwards into the drums; he hung onto a cymbal for a moment, then lurched onto the crowd. Tossed back to the stage, he screamed the song's final words—"I'm alone/I'm alone"—and the music accelerated to its climax. As Picciotto, Canty, and Lally staggered offstage, MacKaye conjured a soft guitar lullaby and delivered a closing benediction: "Do drive home safely. Thanks so much for coming out, we'll see you again soon. And it's nice to be home."

Clockwise from top left: 1. AN INCOGNITO JEFF NELSON (WITH A SOCK TAPED OVER HIS EYES) WITH FIRST VERSION OF POSTER *(by Theodore Nelson)*, 2. MEESE POSTERS DRYING IN DISCHORD HOUSE *(by Jeff Nelson)*, 3. LIDA HUSIK (A.K.A., RED EMMA) AND CLAUDIA DEPAUL AT P STREET BEACH *(by Mark Anderson)*, 4. LESLIE CLAGUE, SHARON CHESLOW, CYNTHIA CONNOLLY; AUTHORS OF *BANNED IN DC*

Clockwise from top left: 1. POSITIVE FORCE LOGO *(by Seth Tobocman, James Miller, Mark Andersen)*, 2. POSITIVE FORCE IN FRONT OF PF HOUSE, INCLUDING MELISA CASUMBAL, JOSH, JENNY TOOMEY, MARK ANDERSEN (IN X-RAY SPEX SHIRT), ANDREA, SEAN KNIGHT, (IN "UNION YES" SHIRT), LARRY KEITZ, JIM MILLER, DEBBIE LEWIS, BRAD SIGAL (PARTIALLY OBSCURED), GEOV PARRISH, ERIC FUERTADO, AND OTHERS, SUMMER 1989 *(by Darrow Montgomery)*, 3. PORTION OF PPP GROUP FROM MARCH FOR WOMEN'S LIVES, APRIL 1989, 4. JENNY TOOMEY AND JULIANA LUECKING AT P STREET BEACH *(by Mark Andersen)*

Clockwise from top left: 1. FRANZ STAHL, DAVE GROHL, SKEETER THOMPSON, AND PETE STAHL OF SCREAM *(by Tomas Squip)*, 2. JERRY BUSHER, MARIA JONES, TOMAS SQUIP, AND DUG BIRDZELL OF FIDELITY JONES, STATE OF THE UNION PHOTO SESSIONS *(by Bobbie Brewer)*, 3. IAN MACKAYE AND BRENDAN CANTY, THE ORIGINAL LINEUP OF FUGAZI *(by Bert Quieroz)*, 4. KATE SAMWORTH, AMY PICKERING, NATALIE AVERY, AND NICKY THOMAS OF FIRE PARTY, STATE OF THE UNION

Clockwise from top left: 1. MARC LAMBIOTTE AND JOEY ARONSTAMN OF HOLY ROLLERS, DC SPACE *(by Naomi Peterson)*, 2. BOBBY SULLIVAN AND JOHNNY TEMPLE OF SOUL SIDE *(by Amanda MacKaye)*, 3. GEOFF TURNER, STEVE NILES, AND MARK HAGGERTY OF THREE *(by Naomi Peterson)*, 4. JOE LALLY, THE ORIGINAL LINEUP OF FUGAZI *(by Bert Quieroz)*

Clockwise from top left: 1. CHRIS HASKETT AND HENRY ROLLINS, 9:30 CLUB *(by Pat Graham)*, 2. IAN MACKAYE, ANTI-GULF WAR PROTEST AT WHITE HOUSE, JANUARY 12, 1991 *(by John Falls)*, 3. GUY PICCIOLO, BRENDAN CANTY, AND JOE LALLY OF FUGAZI, ANTI-GULF WAR PROTEST AT WHITE HOUSE,

PUNK PERCUSSION PROTEST

The world is teetering on the edge of war in the Middle East, a war that will surely cost thousands upon thousands of lives and could escalate into nuclear or chemical warfare. Join us in protesting both the Iraqi invasion of Kuwait and the Bush Administration's rush towards war. Call the White House (456-1111) to voice your opposition to a war based more on oil than protection of democracy and join us in calling for a peaceful solution to the Middle East crisis. For more info, call Mark (703-276-9768) or, better yet, help us plan our demonstration at our next meeting, 1:30pm, Nov. 17, 3510 N. 8th, Arlington (very near Virginia Square Metro) -- we could use your energy and creativity!

OPPOSE US WAR
IN THE MIDDLE EAST
*Noon to 2 pm/Saturday, Nov. 24/the White House

Clockwise from top left: 1. SHAWN BROWN AND JASON FARRELL OF SWIZ *(by Amanda MacKaye)*, 2. MARK SULLIVAN, ANDY RAPOPORT, AND PAT BOBST OF KING FACE *(by Amanda MacKaye)*, 3. 1990 PPP FLIER *(by Mark Andersen)*, 4. KIM COLETTA, ADAM WADE, AND J. ROBBINS OF JAWBOX, PF BENEFIT AGAINST THE

Top to bottom: 1. SEAN COLEMAN, RYAN NELSON, AMANDA MACKAYE, AND TODD MCDONALD OF JURY RIG, 2. IGNITION PLAY "LUCKY 13" AT P STREET BEACH WITH CHRIS THOMSON ON SAX, JON K. ON BASS, ALEC MACKAYE ON VOCALS, AND CHRIS BALD ON GUITAR *(by Mark Andersen)*

long division

*"It's a long time coming/It's a long way down/It's long division/Crack and divide
This is a parting/Some separation/We lay in pieces/Cracked to survive . . ."*
—Fugazi, "Long Division," 1990

FROM COVER OF *WDC PERIOD* *(courtesy of Gordon Gordon)*

long division

"Murder Wave in the Capital: Crack-related violence explodes in Washington, putting the city—and Mayor Barry—under siege." The headline was from *Newsweek*, but it could have been any of a dozen different publications. With homicides up 151 percent in 1988, DC had the highest murder rate of any major American city. In addition, rumors that Mayor Marion Barry was using drugs were widely circulated.

The notion that Washington is the most corrupt and violent US city has timeless appeal. It bolsters both international anti-Americanism and American racism, since the city has had a large African-American population since its founding, and became majority black in the 1950s. In fact, *Newsweek* first dubbed DC America's "murder capital" in 1941. Washington's high murder rate was in part a statistical fluke: It is a relatively small jurisdiction that serves as the vice market for a much larger metropolitan area. Still, there was no question that something had gone seriously wrong.

The drug market was booming and prisons overflowing. *Newsweek* reported that there had been more than 45,000 drug-related arrests in the past two and a half years, and that prison costs had soared nearly 400 percent. The ease with which guns of every description could be purchased in nearby Virginia made a mockery of DC's stringent gun laws.

In Britain to mix the next Fugazi EP, Ian MacKaye told *Sounds* that "Washington, DC is the lie, the city itself is an untruth. It appears to be this beautiful city of white marble, the seat of power in the 'free world.' In fact, it's a very troubled town. There are a lot of poor people here. We've already had the 100th murder of 1989 which is unbelievable. There's no real culture here. There's a rich man's culture and that's about it—no one gets help or support from the powers that be."

Against such inequities, music seemed a flimsy catalyst for change. Still, in little more than a year, Fugazi had become one of the city's most potent artistic forces. And the band was not alone. It was at the forefront of a political-artistic punk community that had dramatically matured.

Fugazi's role generated some resentment—Chris Bald griped that "it seems like people can only accept one band from DC at a time and it's always the band Ian is in"—but the group's ascendance came in the context of a community also represented by such powerful bands as Ignition, Soul Side, Fire Party, Scream, King Face, Swiz, Fidelity Jones, and Shudder to Think.

The scene's camaraderie persisted amid growing musical diversity. "There's no DC sound now at all," Guy Picciotto noted. "It's really varied, the artistic levels are totally diverse. The things that hold the scene together are like connections between friends rather than some code of ethics or sound. I think that is really healthy."

"There are political people, folks working on books, other kinds of performances or artwork," MacKaye added. "People are getting to the point where they branch out and do all kinds of stuff, which I totally encourage. That's part of creativity and from that comes energy."

The momentum continued into the second half of 1989, as Fugazi headlined a Positive Force–organized Peace Center benefit at Wilson Center. The show introduced another vigorous new band, the Holy Rollers, an alliance of Joey Aronstamn and Marc Lambiotte, formerly of Grand Mal and Law of Fives, and ex–Fidelity Jones drummer Maria Jones. The Rollers' kinetic punk-funk and passionate, message-driven songs suggested Fugazi at times, but with all members trading vocals.

The Rollers were followed by Edsel, another new band. These musicians were former members of teen-core bands Kids for Cash and At Wit's End, but they had moved beyond that aesthetic to create a Wire-y art-punk style with spare lyrics.

The most traditionally harDCore of the evening acts was Swiz, whose debut EP on Sammich included singer Shawn Brown's slap at former bandmate Brian Baker: "Lies aren't exercises," charged "Wash." The disc received good reviews in punk circles, with New York fanzine *Dear Jesus* judging it "the absolute best record of 1988." The band had since introduced a pair of powerful new songs: "Godspeed," a harrowing account of life from a streetwalker's point of view, and "Tylenol," Brown's assertion of pride in his African-American heritage in the face of the rising tide of Nazi skinheads.

Fugazi's set showcased its latest creative spurt. Now two guitars drove songs like "Sieve-Fisted Find," "Greed," and the polyrhythmic instrumental "Brendan #1." Perhaps the best of the new material was the chilling "Shut the Door." The song—which MacKaye dedicated to his brother Alec—had been inspired by the death of longtime DC punk Catherine Brayley, formerly of the band Sybil (born out of the Nike Chix). Brayley and Alec had lived together, and after they split Brayley—struggling with depression and a heroin addiction—continued to live in a MacKaye family apartment until her death by overdose.

Underpinned by a spare dub foundation that erupted into raw anguished noise, the verses expressed the no-exit logic of addiction, while the chorus switched to the horrified voices of Brayley's parents breaking into the apartment to find their daughter dead. Like "Glue Man," the song conveyed not moral condemnation but empathy and a sense of immense loss.

The show was so packed that it attracted the attention of fire marshals, who arrived at the very end of the band's set and cited Positive Force for overcrowding. The $400 fine was confirmation of what was already obvious: Fugazi had outgrown the city's existing underground venues.

Soon after, Fugazi went on a mini-tour of the Northeast, talking up a big pro-choice march as it traveled. Positive Force organized a punk percussion protest contingent for the march that Aronstamn deemed "incredible! There were at least 200 of us dancing and drumming."

The long-delayed *State of the Union* finally appeared in April 1989. The compilation documented the evolution of DC punk both musically and politically since Revolution Summer, while spreading Positive Force's ideas across the country. Organized radical politics were now an essential element of the DC punk mythos, inspiring kids elsewhere to form activist groups.

As the city's crack/murder crisis reminded punks who were mostly offspring of the white middle-to-upper class, there was still a major issue that hadn't really been faced: bridging the gap between Washington's privileged and disenfranchised. Positive Force sought to hold its shows in churches and community centers within low-income areas, so the rent money would benefit that community and the mostly white suburban audience would gain experience with—and, perhaps, empathy for—the inner city. Fugazi and some other bands began to target their benefits increasingly toward organizations that assisted the poor, including the Washington Free Clinic, Washington Inner City Self-Help, Roots Learning Center, and various tenant groups.

Some longtime punks confronted the dilemma by going to work in the inner city. Tomas Squip and Lydia Ely worked with the homeless through, respectively, Victor Howell House and the

National Coalition for the Homeless. Aronstamn worked for a public-defender office, venturing into locales such as the Capital City Inn shelter for homeless families, a "hell on earth" experience that yielded the song "Cross the Line."

In June, Fugazi played a Wilson Center benefit for the Washington Free Clinic; the hall was so hot, packed, and humid that ceiling tiles became unglued and began to fall on the crowd during the band's set. Also on the bill were Ignition and a revamped Fidelity Jones. The latter had added guitarist Andy Charneco (formerly of On Beyond Zebra and several other bands), which freed Squip to bound about the stage. Birdzell and Busher were now a solid rhythm section, having jelled during a series of shows at dc space and a new Logan Circle club, BBQ Iguana.

Ignition did not disappoint either, playing ferociously in front of a lighted metal sculpture of the band's logo. At one point, Alec MacKaye paused to make sure the crowd knew why the band was there: "Feeling all right? Well, that's good because it costs a lot these days to be sick. It costs so much, that if I were to get hurt now, I'd be in debt for the rest of my life." (Incredibly, while MacKaye was riding his motorcycle home after the show, he was broadsided by a car running a stop sign. He eventually recovered fully from his injuries—but not before piling up just the sort of the massive bills he had warned the crowd about.) The show would prove to be Ignition's last.

A month later, Fugazi played two sold-out shows at the 9:30 Club with Bad Mutha Goose, a politically pointed Texas funk band led by former Big Boy Tim Kerr. On the second night, Fugazi debuted a new song, "Repeater." With its fierce twists and turns, careening guitar, and sturdy rhythmic backbone, the song recalled the wide-open spirit of Happy Go Licky.

THE MOUNTING MURDER CRISIS
by Mark Andersen

The same day that *State of the Union* came out, a *Washington Times* headline noted that over a dozen people had been shot in the last 24 hours, DC's single most violent day to date. Shaken by the mounting crisis, I left my job at the Washington Peace Center to become an outreach worker for a small nonprofit, Emmaus Services for the Aging, that worked with inner-city seniors in the Shaw neighborhood. This job would catalyze a deeply demanding but transformative journey.

"Repeater" was a stark vignette of the murderous atmosphere on Washington's meaner streets in 1989. Its hurtling pulse captured the heedless tumult of the drug and gang wars that had even reached the steps of Woodrow Wilson High School, where a January drive-by shooting left several students wounded.

Now making more money than they had ever imagined possible with such a staunchly anti-commercial enterprise, the members of Fugazi resolved after the 9:30 shows that for the foreseeable future they would play only benefits, free shows, or demonstrations in the DC area. They also decided to work consistently with Positive Force on such shows. This partnership did not mean—as some would infer—that Positive Force and Fugazi held identical positions, but it did show trust and kinship.

x x x

While Fugazi accelerated, other DC bands were slowing down. The once unstoppable Scream now seemed adrift. The band continued tirelessly crisscrossing North America and Europe, but could barely support itself. *No More Censorship* had sold more than 10,000 copies, a respectable showing for an indie-label punk album, but significantly less than either the band or RAS had expected. Soon the label and Scream agreed to part.

Ignition was also nearing burnout. Ferrando often found himself at odds with Bald over money issues, and was growing tired of the constant grind. Meanwhile, Food for Thought was in danger of losing its lease. Concerned about the void that would result if this fixture of DC bohemia folded, Ferrando wanted to get off the road to start his own place. Chris Thomson was also tired of touring, wanting more time for a personal relationship and to return to school.

Alec MacKaye and Bald wanted to continue with a concept called "Ignition Services." The band could persevere with two new members, some of the same songs, and almost the same name. While MacKaye and Bald supplied Ignition Services' music, Ferrando and Thomson would run the "food" and "education" branches. It was a clever idea, but would prove impossible to realize.

Soul Side also faced internal dissension. While *Trigger* and "Bass"/"103" had proven successful and the band was a strong draw, Bobby Sullivan's increasingly topical lyrics were not endorsed by all the members. In addition, some in the band saw Sullivan's rhetoric as hollow, not backed by action. Not wanting to feel hypocritical, they pressured him to write more opaque lyrics and he reluctantly agreed.

During a marathon three-month European tour, Sullivan worried that Soul Side had become a "party band," blunting the boredom and grind of the road with chemicals. The group recorded a musically compelling new record—with extremely oblique lyrics—while in Europe, but the tour left the group exhausted and increasingly at odds. The group played a few more gigs after its return, but soon folded.

HR had an even tougher time in Europe. While Human Rights had coalesced musically, the band's tour was a financial failure. Stranded penniless in Europe, the singer swallowed his pride and called Tony Countey. "It was cold on the street and I and I had to deal with survival," he later explained.

It was an opportune moment, for Bad Brains were at a costly standstill in the studio, recording a new album for Caroline. Darryl Jenifer and Dr. Know had written powerful new material on the foundation of *I Against I*, but singer Taj Singleton was not working out. With the success of Beastie Boys, Living Color, Metallica, 24-7 Spyz, and the Red Hot Chili Peppers, Bad Brains felt they had sparked something only to see it pass the band by.

Jenifer and Dr. Know were naturally skeptical of HR, but the band was in no position to turn him away. At Countey's insistence, the singer agreed to return to the band for a minimum of two years, bringing along his brother Earl.

With all the music already recorded, lyrics had to be written and vocal tracks done immediately. "When I got back, I had one week to listen to the music before it was time for me to go into the studio and lay down my vocals," HR recalled. "I locked myself away in the hills of Woodstock and listened to that music continuously, not even really sleeping. I totally engulfed myself to come up with the lyrics, inspired by Jah's spirit."

Considering its jumbled heritage, the resulting LP was extraordinary. If *Quickness* was not the quantum leap of *I Against I*, it was a worthy successor. Once again produced by Ron St. Germain, the album took Bad Brains' hardcore roots—"Don't Bother Me" was reprised as part of "Gene Machine" and the "PMA" concept returned in "Don't Blow Bubbles"—to a new level of accessibility.

Some of the lyrics would later spark great indignation, but at the time of the album's release most of the attention was focused on the music's energy and craft. A *Sounds* reviewer wrote that "only Metallica can compete with Bad Brains on their terms, welding overdriven stick ferocity and riff pileups to a superfluid suppleness."

The title track exemplified the band's virtuoso hybrid of metal, funk, rap, punk, and dub. "The song itself is a documentary of the past 40 years of rock'n'roll, right back from bebop and jazz through to hip hop and the music of the future," HR said. "The title is a slogan I picked up on the streets of New York, the steadfastness to leave the system and get Babylon out of our lives."

The singer had moderated his view of *I Against I*. "Even though there was no reggae [on the LP] the message was still there. The Father was working in His own way. I see it as a door opening for us to reach people with the Rasta message. [Initially] I was apprehensive but it's not up to me to decide. I am a musician and God uses me. Kids would come up to me and say that they liked the album a lot. So it felt a mission had been accomplished. I didn't get what I wanted, but if I had, I would have been standing in the way of the mission God had for the Bad Brains."

While Bad Brains attempted to reach out, Henry Rollins walked warily on the edge of the commercial rock world. While physically transformed by myriad tattoos and years of bodybuilding, he still believed that "the mainstream is a bunch of asswipes. I don't want those people into me. I want them to hate and fear me. I'm a free-thinking person and I'm a destroyer of God and those people live in darkness and fear and chains and they should fear someone who walks freely like me."

Such statements existed uneasily next to the sight of Rollins in a Gap ad in *Rolling Stone*. Rollins later said that he did it for "fun" and to outrage people. "I take the money and put into my other projects, that's it," he explained. "That's why I seized as much control as possible. I'm not going to sell anyone out. The profit on this is really minimal and it's always put back into the company. The whole capitalism parade is only done to put out the art."

Rollins had founded a publishing company—2.13.61, named after his birth date—and continued to do spoken-word tours, offering "a spoonful of sugar to make the napalm go down." Ian MacKaye produced Rollins Band's 1988 album, *Lifetime*, which showed the road-tested group's gripping punk-blues style.

Major labels were beginning to court the "punk Renaissance man." By late 1988, Rollins decided to do an EP with bassist Andrew Weiss under the name Wartime for Chrysalis Records, a project he laughingly described as "Trouble Funk meets Satan. It's definitely assault rock. It's not pretty. It's perfect for a major label. It's totally slagging off everything they stand for." At the time, the singer said that "I wouldn't want Rollins Band on a major label, not now at least."

Angry at the lack of royalties paid by SST for his Black Flag recordings and now convinced that the proprietors of Texas Hotel were "hippie scumbags," Rollins would soon reevaluate major labels. "I'm tired of putting out collector items," he said on the verge of departing the indie world.

x x x

Sitting in a Princeton cafeteria after a gig, arguing over the guarantee their booking agency had gotten for some upcoming dates, the members of one of harDCore's longest-running bands decided to dissolve. Government Issue "had planned to do a few more East Coast shows and another European tour," John Stabb said, "but we all agreed that our hearts weren't in it."

The band's massively sold-out final show at the 9:30 Club demonstrated both its musical power and internal tensions. "We're breaking up because I wanted to do something new and creative and [Tom] didn't," Stabb told the crowd. Such gibes aside, GI's farewell was a mostly upbeat affair.

Stabb was already developing a new band, Weatherhead, with his friend Frank Love. Although the group was voted "best new band" in *Flipside*, Weatherhead's twisted pop alienated many GI fans. The final GI lineup had been Stabb's ideal foil; it would not be easy to assemble such a combo again.

Relieved to be free of GI, J. Robbins concentrated on his new band with Kim Coletta. Original drummer Jenny Thomas left, replaced by Adam Wade, although the group retained the best of the songs initially written with Thomas: "Tools and Chrome," a sharp analysis of traditional sex roles. The trio took the name Jawbox from a derisive term for TV, and prepared for its first gig, a Positive Force benefit for a tenants group with Shudder to Think and Fugazi at the reopened Pierce Hall at All Souls' Unitarian Church.

Robbins proved to be a strong frontman and the band's sound—somewhere between Fugazi and Holy Rollers—meshed melodic guitar riffs with the message-oriented lyrics of songs like "Foot Binder" and "Bullet Park." Following the new band onstage, Shudder to Think displayed its increasingly sophisticated sound, soon to be documented by a new Dischord LP, *Ten Spot*.

Major labels were now eying Fugazi, and a CBS A&R man reportedly came to see the band at the All Souls show, even after MacKaye encouraged him not to waste his time. The band's only apparent response was a blistering new song, "Blueprint," that suggested Fugazi would not be playing the majors' game.

Two weeks later, Fugazi played the annual Positive Force Alternatives Festival in Dupont Circle. Despite a hostile police presence, the event went well, highlighted by powerful performances by Baltimore's Lungfish (whose lead singer Daniel Higgs had been in Reptile House), Fidelity Jones, and charismatic spoken-word performer Juliana Luecking. Since Fugazi's following could have overwhelmed the park, the band was advertised as "Gazebo Front." When the band began at 5:15, six police cars and a police-dog van stood by to insure that the event ended no later than 6 p.m., as the permit specified. Fugazi played a ragged but defiant set, ending exactly at 6 p.m. with MacKaye's acid comment, "Now go home before you all get arrested."

In the crowd was Kent McClard, visiting from Santa Barbara. He published a fanzine, *No Answers*, that sought to tease out the revolutionary implications of straight edge. The 'zine carried a heavy moral tone, but was already becoming influential across the country. While obviously inspired by harDCore, McClard was not uncritical of the scene. A big supporter of Swiz, he felt that it and other harDCore-style bands were being unfairly excluded from the Dischord/Positive Force axis.

The members of Swiz did feel excluded, but there was no bias against them. The band wasn't invited to appear on *State of the Union*, but that was solely because space was limited. Swiz had been asked to play several Positive Force shows, including two with Fugazi. Still, the band was most popular locally with the teenage hardcore fans who frequented the Safari Club's Saturday afternoon matinees. Positive Force members rarely attended Safari Club matinees simply because they happened at the exact same time as the group's weekly meetings.

Despite his concern over divisions in the scene, McClard was left energized by his encounter with DC punk and noted one of its particular strengths: "What makes DC unique is that many of the early scenesters are still kicking, still struggling against the 'maturity' of the mainstream," McClard wrote. "Friendships, histories, ideals, and commitments that began in the early '80s have grown stronger and more focused. Their words of protest are backed with strong political actions. Punk rock has not been sold to society. In DC, it exists in spite of and as an alternative to mainstream society. HarDCore lives on. Let it be an example and an inspiration."

Under Cynthia Connolly's guidance, dc space had become central to the punk community. She organized an ambitious week of concerts whose highlights were preserved on an album, *Pre-Moon Syndrome*, which benefited the Free Clinic. The shows captured the growing diversity of the DC scene. Led by Teenbeat label founder Mark Robinson, Unrest was "delving into more musical styles than actually exist." Velocity Girl and Whorl (formerly Gotterdamocrats and Big Jesus Trash Can, respectively) were affiliated with a new local label, Slumberland, inspired by the British "dream-pop" scene. Kim Kane's new band Dait Bait continued "The Brain that Refused to Die" side of the now-defunct Slickee Boys. The shows also included out-of-town groups like Richmond's Butter Glove, Olympia's Go Team, and New York's Honeymoon Killers.

The scene's cohesiveness was still threatened by adulthood, as both musicians and fans tried to support themselves within punk and without. Former editor of the *Thrillseeker* 'zine and current law student Steve Kiviat took exception to Squip's blanket dismissal of "punks who became lawyers." As he recounted later, "I wrote to Tomas and said, 'What are we supposed to do, work shit jobs for the rest of our lives?'" It was a hard question, since the act of diversifying and pursuing one's own path—surely a punk ideal—often brought people back into the mainstream. As people left bands or college and began to question the wisdom of making the scene the center of their lives, the community inevitably unraveled a bit.

Law school was hardly the only route to becoming a professional, however. Brian Baker continued his career odyssey by joining Junkyard—a band that drew liberally on '70s Southern hard rock—three weeks before the group began recording its Geffen debut in late 1988. It seemed an unlikely step for someone who had once made a comic book ridiculing rednecks and Southern rock touchstone Lynryd Skynyrd. In fact, Baker told *Sounds* that "I hate the concept [of Southern rock]. I like some of that music but I'm not into the rebel flag or the throwing up in your pickup truck."

Ex–Big Boys guitarist Chris Gates—who recruited Baker to the project—compared his new band to Guns N' Roses and Tracy Chapman "'cause they're real. Guns N' Roses and Metallica have kicked down the walls for anyone who can play good music and mean it." From the "hot rods and hell-raisers" band logo to the longneck beers prominently displayed on the back cover, Junkyard came on as if punk—let alone straight edge—never happened.

Interviewed by McClard for *No Answers*, the members of Fugazi declined to criticize Junkyard. "There was a point in my life where this was the end all: the punk scene," MacKaye said. "Anyone who would go against it, to me that was like the cardinal sin. But then down the road I found that we have more important things to talk about than other people." Picciotto added that "there are worse things on earth than another rock'n'roll band."

Three harDCore stalwarts, SOA and Faith's Mike Hampton and Ivor Hanson and the Untouchables' Bert Queiroz, also made a move toward the mainstream with a new band, Manifesto. Its polished, tuneful pop-rock, which employed both live and synthesized drums, was a logical step from One Last Wish. It carried little of punk's raw energy or rebellious spirit, but Hampton argued that "all the bands that I've done have seemed like a natural progression to me." As with an increasing number of punk veterans, these three hoped that music could eventually become a paying career.

Jeff Nelson liked the band's work and arranged for it to record a single for Dischord. When MacKaye heard Manifesto's tape, however, he blocked the single's release. This further frustrated Nelson, who was coming to prefer melodic pop-rock to punk. He began to plot a new label, Adult Swim—the name playfully expressed its owner's dwindling interest in teen-angst music. In this period, Nelson played with two harDCore-rooted pop-rock bands, Senator Flux and the High Back Chairs. Only the latter band, which was fronted by Peter Hayes, recorded for Dischord.

Nelson was one of the many Dischord veterans who seldom went to shows anymore. Even Fugazi began to see fewer of the older crowd at its gigs. MacKaye's thoughts about this change surfaced in "Long Division," a song he began to write on the band's '89 European tour. It was the quietest song Fugazi had ever done, and it seemed to echo "Long Time," one of the Manifesto songs intended for the Dischord single. (MacKaye later said that any similarities were entirely coincidental.)

In Europe, Fugazi wasn't allowed to forget about harDCore's early days; the band was peppered with questions about straight edge. Although the musicians hadn't changed their attitude toward drugs, they were tired of talking about such non-musical topics as straight edge, low door prices, all-ages shows, slamdancing, and the *State of the Union* boycott chart.

In the US, the straight edge (or "SE") scene now existed as an almost separate entity. One day, MacKaye saw a flier for a six-band bill of "DC SE—the new school" at the Safari Club (often booked, ironically enough, by a hard-working female punk duo, informally known as "Pam 'n' Shawna"), and he recognized none of the bands. Asked by one straight edge fanzine about Minor Threat's "SE hardcore," MacKaye responded, "What exactly is 'SE Hardcore'? Minor Threat wrote songs about the improvement of life."

Ray Cappo of Youth of Today, a popular band that began as an almost cartoonish version of harDCore, was also attempting to leave straight edge clichés behind; he wrote new songs attacking racism, blind patriotism, and the abuse of animals. Cappo's direction became an issue of its own, however, when he joined the International Society for Krishna Consciousness, commonly known as the Hare Krishnas. With a new band, Shelter, Cappo set out to spread the message. *Maximum RockNRoll* printed a contentious discussion between Cappo and Tim Yohannon, paired with an exposé of ISKCON corruption.

Such developments inevitably reflected on MacKaye, the author of "Straight Edge." He was no fan of organized religion, much less the Hare Krishnas, and was unhappy to see his idea contribute to this evolution, however indirectly. A related controversy arose after a California label, No Master's Voice, released an Animal Liberation Front benefit LP which featured Beefeater (with a guest appearance by MacKaye) and British bands Chumbawamba and Oi Polloi. It turned out that the label founder's militant animal rights/straight edge stance also incorporated homophobia, rabid anti-abortion sentiments, and worship of discipline bordering on outright fascism: "It's survival of the fittest and it's gonna be the straight-up vegan who comes out on top." This label—soon renamed Hardline, with two automatic rifles superimposed on the SE "X" as its logo—spread this vision through bands such as Vegan Reich.

Bad Brains were again controversial, as some listeners interpreted "Don't Blow Bubbles" as celebrating AIDS as a punishment of gays. The supposedly objectionable lines were, "In time before there was no cure/Now through His will it's healed for sure." HR later said that the song meant "don't shoot heroin. The bubble is at the end of the hypodermic syringe." HR was himself an admitted former smack user, and the band's friend and ex-manager David Hahn was then mortally ill with AIDS contracted via IV drug use.

Jenifer later noted sardonically that "if we had just said 'wear a condom,' no one would have been mad." The band members, however, frequently said things to make people angry. Even the easygoing Dr. Know once explained that the song's message was, "Don't be a faggot."

On tour in Europe, Bad Brains shows were garnering rave reviews. If HR was not quite so frenzied as in earlier days, he was still incredibly energetic, while now carrying an almost regal assurance—as well as often a Bible—onstage. The singer led the band through new and old songs, making up for any loss in savagery with grace and fluidity. In London, he even climaxed the show-closing "At the Movies" with one of his trademark back flips.

In interviews, however, HR had begun to say that "I am not a 'Bad Brains,' I am a 'Human Rights.'" Jenifer was the leader of the new Bad Brains, and HR was not inclined to take orders from anyone. "HR likes having his band Human Rights because he can hire and fire anyone he likes," Dr. Know said in 1993. "Bad Brains is not like that." The tension came to a head after a show in West Berlin, when HR jumped Jenifer on the tour bus. The fight was broken up and HR leaped from bus while it was still moving. "HR just jumped right off and rolled on the pavement," Countey recalled with a wince years later. "He could easily have been run over by the bus wheels."

This was just days before the Berlin Wall would fall, but at the time the band was on the only road that linked Berlin to West Germany, surrounded by tall fences on either side. Despite the unpromising surroundings, HR refused to return to the bus. Eventually, Jenifer got off and walked with HR, trying to reason with him as the rest of the band went to the next show.

The two managed to come to an agreement that saved the tour and even that night's gig. Once back in the US, however, Bad Brains were defunct yet again. Despite HR's agreement to stay for two years, he and his brother were gone.

In a symbolic rebuke, Jenifer cut off his dreads, pub-

TALE OF TWO ARTICLES
by Mark Andersen

After the release of *SOTU*, Positive Force was thriving—and, as massive features in the *City Paper* and *Washington Post* suggested, we were becoming seen as a central part of the DC punk story. Alan Keenan's *CP* article was a blessing; mixing quotes from Jenny Toomey—who had returned from Europe to rejoin the group—Brad Sigal, Melisa Casumbal, and myself, it discussed our efforts to create a self-challenging "revolutionary" ethic that included an anti-drug stance, vegetarianism, voluntary simplicity, commitment to ecological imperatives, and radical democracy, while opening our home not only to activism but directly to those in need.

As Alan wrote, "Punk rock was a rebellion against mid-'70s complacency but it quickly became just haircuts, fashion, and posturing. PF wants to reclaim punk's ideals and spread the word . . . Essentially, PF functions as the unofficial political wing of Dischord Records, translating into action the do-good, be-responsible message of such past and present Dischord 'harDCore' bands as Minor Threat, Beefeater, Soul Side, Fire Party, and Fugazi."

State of the Union had spread these ideas far beyond the Beltway. Alan: "The sense of punk's potential pervades the music on *State of the Union* which has received friendly reviews from such publications as *Rock'n'Roll Confidential* and the British music weekly *Sounds* . . . The sense of purpose is everywhere on the record." A simple statement in *SOTU* read: "This album was made by people very much like you . . . you could make a record . . . write a song . . . organize a demonstration . . . etc. . . . so why don't you?"

Judging by the mail we were receiving, a good number of people were taking us at our word but wanting just a bit of assistance. Jenny—who, together with Kristin Thomson, had assumed responsibility for answering the letters—came up with the idea to make a packet of information that could help respond to regularly asked questions about setting up activist groups, putting on benefit shows, making a record, and more.

licly denouncing his former friend as a "hypocrite." Without HR, the band's two stalwarts had to go on public assistance. "I'm in line talking to people telling them, 'I'm a musician, I've got a video on MTV,'" Jenifer remembered. "They'd just laugh and tell me, 'Well, you got your ass in the welfare line just like us, don't you?'" This time, the bassist vowed, HR would not return.

x x x

In the *CP* article, Alan compared our informal partnership with Fugazi to that of the MC5 and the White Panther Party of the late '60s. While neither Fugazi's nor PF's politics were of the "dope, guns, and fucking in the streets" variety, Keenan's remark was intended and taken as a compliment. As Alan noted, in a way, Fugazi and PF had joined forces in an experiment to push the bounds of punk rock as a genuine force for social change.

Alan pointedly noted, however, just how difficult it would be to translate this idealism and energy into lasting change without more serious efforts at institution- and coalition-building: "Though they currently help support, through their benefit concerts and their own labor, alternative institutions that embody many of their political ideals, they have not so far concentrated on finding ways of making it easier for others to emulate a PF lifestyle . . . Without the support of institutions beyond group houses and food co-ops, it will always remain hard for anyone but a few (most often young) free spirits to live the communal anti-materialist life of PF group members." It was a fair and insightful challenge.

Our experience with Todd Kliman of the *Post* was not nearly so pleasant. While he did feature other key PF members like Sean Knight, Jim Miller, and Larry Keitz, his cynical, error-filled article falsified our beliefs and made us look like fools. A cutting letter by former ally Kevin Mattson—now a history graduate student who had no contact with PF for over four years—applauding the article only made it worse.

Although Todd didn't use the term, the article was a precursor to what would become a veritable flood of attacks on "political correctness." While it was true that some on the Left went to ridiculous extremes, soon all one would have to do to dismiss any radical critique was to label it "politically correct"; no further thought was necessary. It was a nice bargain for small minds; fortunately, however, we had allies like the Nation of Ulysses to retaliate against the running dogs of the media.

Back in Washington, there was no shortage of new bands. At a Christmastime Positive Force show to raise money for striking coal miners in southwestern Virginia, Fidelity Jones, Swiz, and a revamped Ulysses were joined by a new outfit, Hazmat. This quartet offered a brittle and tuneful sound, and a reversal of traditional rock lineups: a female band—bassist Christina Billotte, drummer Melissa Berkoff, and guitarist Kathy Cashel—backed male singer Charles Bennington, who had most recently played in Blood Bats with old BMO comrades Colin Sears and Roger Marbury. Hazmat recorded a demo with Geoff Turner, who resurrected his WGNS studio in a new location with more sophisticated equipment. The group would soon self-destruct, but

Billotte and Berkoff then joined newcomers Nikki Chapman and Mary Timony to form an even more promising band, Autoclave.

Ulysses had now become the Nation of Ulysses, with its own embassy—the band's name for its group house, one of several new punk homes in the ethnically diverse Mount Pleasant neighborhood. The addition of guitarist Tim Green, formerly of raucous garage punks the Vile Cherubs, helped spur the unit's evolution from mere band into a "terrorist group/political party."

Ian Svenonius admitted that "we still can't play our instruments," but the group's concept was progressing nonetheless. "The Nation of Ulysses is basically a shout of secession," he announced in an interview with Sharon Cheslow for an new 'zine called *Interrobang*. "We don't want to be involved with the United States and the structure that exists. I think you have to try as hard as possible to be underground and not be assimilated. The Nation of Ulysses is the establishment viewing their own mortality. The Nation of Ulysses spells the end for life as we know it, society as we know it. The Nation of Ulysses is the apocalypse."

Svenonius and his conspirators plucked elements of their identity from Dada, the Nation of Islam, Futurism, Situationism, the Black Panthers, and Filipino and Latin American guerrilla groups. "Ulysses similarly might not be appreciated in our lifetime," conceded its frontman, "but that's all right."

One of those impressed by the group's verve at the miners' benefit was Calvin Johnson, back in Washington for the holidays. After the show, he approached the band about doing a single for K Records. "The Sound of Young America" b/w "Atom Bomb" came out in mid-1990 on "DisKord," a combination of K Records and Dischord. The band began playing with a DC flag flying proudly behind the chaos. "We basically want to create a new sense of who we are community-wise, a nation of youths under one groove," Svenonius proclaimed. "In the '90s, righteousness will prevail!"

In October 1990, the band's program would be spread nationwide by a tour and *Sassy* magazine's selection of Svenonius as the "Sassiest Boy in America." Besides printing much of the Nation's "Syllabus Ulysses," the magazine allowed Svenonius to project his vision for DC to the world: "I'm very devoted to my mother city, Washington, DC. I think DC will define the '90s. It'll be the youth mecca, like San Francisco in the 1960s."

But as the '90s dawned in Svenonius's beloved "Chocolate City," there was more bad news. With 437 murders, 1989 had been the bloodiest year in the city's history. And on January 14, a FBI sting operation busted Mayor Marion Barry after videotaping him smoking crack.

Positive Force responded with a benefit featuring Fugazi, Fidelity Jones, and Lucy Brown, a rising funk-metal outfit. The show reopened the school gymnasium of St. Augustine's, the oldest black Roman Catholic church in America. Closed to punk after a chaotic Black Flag show, St. Augustine's was potentially large enough to handle Fugazi's swelling audience. A sell-out crowd of nearly 1,200 people packed every available inch of space.

Playing before the largest crowd of its career, Fidelity Jones took the bold step of performing almost nothing but new songs. The set peaked with a riveting Squip rant inspired by the Bush Administration's recent invasion of Panama. As he hit the rap's crescendo, the band segued into a clenched-teeth version of Stevie Wonder's "Misstra Know-it-All." Then Charneco hit the quiet opening pattern of the anti-drug anthem "Venus on Lovely," a song inspired by Squip's encounter with a delirious, partially clothed female crack addict while working the volunteer overnight shift at the infirmary of the Community for Creative Nonviolence's homeless shelter: "Fight for life child, fight for life/I'm staying up with you tonight."

While the band's potential was obvious, its members were increasingly disappointed by the lack of diversity in its audience. The group initially planned as a multi-racial, multi-gender, militant worldbeat punk band had ended up the same old alignment: four white men playing for mostly middle-to-upper-class white boys. In an interview with *Maximum RockNRoll*, Squip said, "I don't blame black folk for not coming to punk gigs because it's loud and stupid and everybody onstage or in the audience is white skate kids in big tennis shoes. If I were black, I'd stick my head in the door and turn around and go back home because punk doesn't concern me."

Squip was not the first to note this cultural divide. In the early '80s, a string of punk/Go-Go fests with Minor Threat, Trouble Funk, GI, and others tried but mostly failed to bridge it. Meanwhile, Fidelity Jones was pulling further way from its original design: Charneco's influence was shifting the band's music toward hard rock, and the musicians were becoming uncomfortable with Squip's militant views and his strident expression of them.

Fugazi, however, remained committed to confrontation. In its first show since returning from Europe, the band dedicated "Blueprint" to the "young idea" and its latest exponents, the Nation of

Ulysses and Hazmat. Then it played a Pickering-powered "Suggestion" and a galvanizing new song, "Turnover," which that night featured MacKaye's shouts of "Better wake up/Better wake up/WAKE UP!"

After another new song, "Two Beats Off," MacKaye returned to the mic: "You are currently in Washington, DC. I tell you that because if anybody's been following the papers or the politics, you know that there's been a lot of ballyhoo about our mayor who has just been arrested. This song is sort of dedicated to him. In Washington, DC last year, over 400 people were killed in the streets. This year possibly even more will be. People are talking about a 'war on drugs' but we need to get on to a 'war on poverty.'"

Those words prefaced a fiery version of "Repeater." Lines like, "Did you hear something outside?/Sounds like a gun/Stay away from that window/It's not anyone that we know," rang out just a few dozen feet from W Street, a notorious drug market and site of numerous shootings.

x x x

While Fugazi remained resolute, it was time for another shakeout. Fire Party returned from Europe with a slew of new songs, but soon quit. Bald tried to make a serious band

EDUCATION ON W STREET
by Mark Andersen

I worked on W Street in one of the most scary buildings; with front and back doors broken, the building was a full-service 24-hour-a-day drug market and shooting gallery, notorious enough to be featured on the TV program *City Under Siege*. One of our seniors lived next to a basement hallway where junkies congregated to inject their drugs; blood splattered the walls where they sprayed the gory backwash from their syringes. Users nodded out on the basement steps. Dealers crowded the front steps and hallways of the building. Shootings–and raids–were commonplace. Needles littered the grass outside, including a playground used by kids from the soup kitchen around the corner.

The immensity of the problem was undeniable. Unfortunately, a major culprit in the mayhem were the ill-considered, counterproductive drug laws. Billboards that loomed on either side of the intersection of 14th and W Streets at the time neatly captured the contradiction. One portrayed a hooded Grim Reaper skeleton, a syringe, and the words, "SAY NO TO DRUGS"; the other, a giant Schlitz Malt Liquor bull.

Everywhere in DC's low-income neighborhoods there were liquor ads full of sexy, affluent men and women, taunting the poor who walked by. "Feel the Power," the ads said, "Ride the Bull," selling high-potency malt liquors with names like "Power Master" and "King Cobra" to disenfranchised and hopeless people. Statistics tied horrifying acts of violence to alcohol, the drug that the Harvard Medical School health letter called in 1978 the most "devasting socio-medical problem faced by human society short of war and famine." How were the corporate pushers of alcohol–or tobacco–any different than the dealers on the corner? Only one arbitrary distinction was obvious: alcohol was legal.

Supporters of legalization included Ian MacKaye, who noted in one interview that "most of the murders in DC are not 'drug killings' but 'money-killings,' it's capitalism at its best. I think drugs should be legalized. I'm not into any dope, I think it's stupid shit, but I know about economics. I know about people who are poor and I know about people wanting money quick. It's the 'American Way,' isn't it?"

of his side project, ChrisBald96, recording an LP in Germany, but the band soon fell apart and he withdrew from the scene. Swiz and King Face split after making personnel changes that didn't quite work out. Gray Matter had reunited, but only on a part-time basis, for all the members were involved with other projects, notably Ferrando's restaurant and Turner's WGNS recording studio.

Fidelity Jones splintered after a mini-tour of Eastern Canada in mid-1990. Deciding that punk was a lost cause, Squip withdrew to his spiritual pursuits and his work with homeless men at Victor Howell House, never to return to the scene. While he feared that Fidelity Jones had become mere entertainment, other scene veterans like the members of Strange Boutique and Manifesto hoped to reach the mainstream audience Squip disdained. Strange Boutique was chosen "DC Band of the Year" by the pop-oriented Washington Area Music Association, and Manifesto signed a contract with Fire Records, a UK indie label.

The saddest fate befell Scream. The band recorded a strong new LP in fall 1989, but had no label. (They did, however, release a 45 on John Fox's DSI label.) Moreover, the band was undermined by bassist Skeeter Thompson's increasingly serious cocaine use and ensuing erratic behavior. Thompson quit Scream while in Europe, and the band had to hurriedly recruit a replacement to finish the tour before limping back to Washington. Another bassist defected during a US tour, which the band continued with J. Robbins filling in.

After the tour, Robbins returned to Jawbox and Thompson resumed bass duties. Facing eviction from its house, Scream booked an impromptu tour to California and moved in with relatives, playing gigs up and down the coast. At a Santa Barbara show, Thompson hassled the promoter—who happened to be straight edge crusader Kent McClard—for cocaine as payment. Such incidents cast a pall over the once highly regarded band.

Then Thompson got a desperate call from his ex-girlfriend, who was living with a cocaine dealer and was lost on a crack binge. Worried that she was in danger, Thompson listened to a Bad Brains tape over and over for guidance, finally concluding that he must return home to help her. Scream was stranded on tour with no bassist for the third time in less than a year.

Dave Grohl waited for a time, but finally called Buzz Osborne of the Melvins for the number of a group that had seen Scream in San Francisco. Nirvana was a rising punk band whose members had been so impressed by Grohl's playing that they immediately tried to recruit him. After talking to bassist Chris Novoselic, Grohl headed to Olympia, where he stayed on a tattered couch in the apartment of singer-guitarist Kurt Cobain. With no rhythm section and no money to return home, the Stahl brothers stayed at their sister's house in LA.

x x x

The largest of Positive Force's 1990 shows was a March "Freeze the Drug War" benefit with Fugazi, Sonic Youth, and a revamped version of Jenny Toomey's band Geek. About 1800 people attended the show, held at Adams Morgan's Citadel Center, a former skating rink now used as a movie and TV soundstage.

Toomey had been in and out of Positive Force over the past several years, and was now thinking about a vehicle to release material by Geek and other bands unlikely to find a home at Dischord. She brainstormed with Brad Sigal, who had some money to invest in such a project. Initially they proposed continuing the PF-connected Homeless Records label created for *State of the Union*. They wanted to control the project, however, so they decided to strike out on their own.

Toomey and Sigal's new concept was a label that would issue a series of compilation 45s named for each of the six "simple machines." The initial *Wedge* 7"—released in time for the "Freeze the Drug War" show—contained Geek's "Herasure," Lungfish's "Nothing Is Easy," Edsel's "Feeder," and

AN INCREASINGLY HOLLOW TREE
by Mark Andersen

This period was becoming shrouded in darkness. My work was consuming me, and a huge psychic blow came with the suicide of CCNV activist Mitch Snyder in July 1990. The loss of longtime comrades like Tomas, Chris Bald, Lydia Ely, and Sharon Cheslow (the latter two having moved to the Bay Area) was also deeply disheartening. Ian had an apt metaphor: "The punk movement is like when a tree grows, there are rings in the tree and every ring is like another generation. At one point, this makes for a really solid, large tree . . . But then, at some point, these inner rings, these people from the beginning, become disillusioned with these outer rings and they said 'fuck it' and they dropped out . . . What you ended up with was this big body without a soul, a hollow tree, big and tall, but empty."

DC punk's special power was partly traceable to a core group that had remained far beyond the time usual to such scenes. With this continuity, the scene had the chance to actually grow—not just increase in size, but actually rise to new levels of understanding and action, instead of constantly running round the same "rite of passage" cycles. Now, as so many of the Revolution Summer stalwarts faded away, that seemed to be changing. For me, it made it hard to go on—as did a growing divide between Jenny and me that surfaced first over her championing of major label artists Sonic Youth to play the anti–Drug War benefit.

Jenny was now moving in her own direction, influenced by Washington State labels Sub Pop and K. While Jenny felt that DC, as a scene, had much affinity with Seattle—the cast of characters shifting the Hated's version of Simon and Garfunkel's "I Am a Rock." Soon Derek Denckla and Kristin Thomson joined the Machines team, while Sigal departed to focus on student activism.

Geek didn't last long, but Toomey started another band, Tsunami, with Thomson and former Positive Force House residents John Pamer and Andrew Webster. This group showed the influence of the playful Olympia scene centered around K Records—an aesthetic then largely absent from the DC scene. In the space of a few years, Toomey moved from being Geek's lyricist to writing most of the music and lyrics and singing and playing guitar in Tsunami.

Thanks to hard work, a personable style, beautiful packaging, and a sparkling, creative spirit, Simple Machines would develop a national cult following unlike any previous DC label except Dischord. With Teenbeat and Slumberland, the label began to generate a new scene in the spirit of K's "international pop underground." Toomey, Thomson, and Denckla held strong leftist views, but this new community's politics would be less explicit.

The members of Fugazi did not renounce any of their political views, but they worried that the hoopla around the band's message and business practices sometimes overshadowed the music. The group continued to play Positive Force benefits, while earning raves for *Repeater*, a new LP which came closer to capturing the band's live power in the studio—and which entered the *New Musical Express'* independent charts at #1.

In an era of carefully choreographed rock shows that relied on backing tapes, Fugazi never used a set list,

back and forth betweeen bands, its communal feel, and more—I saw Seattle, and Sub Pop (with its boozy '70s-rock revivalism and hype-mongering that had already resulted in trend-mad UK music rags heralding the city as the birthplace of a mysterious entity called "grunge") in particular, as nearly the antithesis of DC and Dischord. The Sub Pop "Singles Club" epitomized the collector record phenomenon. When Fugazi did one of these singles and put out the same music on Dischord at the same time with only a different cover, the Sub Pop version nonetheless became immediately "collectible," commanding ridiculous prices.

If Sub Pop struck me as apolitical, retro, and consumerist, K seemed almost as vapid in the face of the new reality I was encountering in DC's inner city. While I respected K's DIY spirit and creativity, I wanted punk on the barricades, not punk on "a secret teenage picnic." Florid, cutesy ramblings like "the K cassette revolution is exploding the teenage underground into passionate revolt against the corporate ogre" struck me as about as relevant or threatening as your average Boy Scout oath.

Jenny disagreed, telling me that I was being too literal, too caught up in past forms and approaches, insisting that "we need to look for different signs for rebellion now." Both of us had valid points, and there still was much common ground, but my all-too-arrogant critique of Jenny's new direction was destroying it—and our friendship. In retrospect, it should be no surprise that Jenny soon left PF, if not yet the house itself.

choosing songs on the spot. The band remained ready to confront its own audience. Picciotto devised unexpected techniques for disarming punk ritual, including hugging or kissing those who invaded the stage. "We have two kinds of shows," he said, "one that's totally confrontational, one where everyone sort of comes together. I'll play both, they're both important."

Despite low door and record prices, the absence of merchandise, and playing scads of benefits, Fugazi was making enough money that it incorporated for tax purposes in February 1990. Nonetheless, it remained self-managed, which was unprecedented for a band of such popularity.

As the quartet left for its third European tour in as many years, MacKaye came to Positive Force with two challenging ideas: a mid-winter outdoor concert across from the White House to dramatize the plight of the homeless, and a show at DC's prison in Lorton, Virginia.

Events would overtake these plans. Iraq, a country armed by the US for war against Iran, invaded Kuwait; the US began to mass troops in Saudi Arabia. Positive Force organized a punk percussion protest against the imminent war outside the White House in November, and began working with groups like the Peace Center on other actions.

Before ever larger crowds in Europe, Fugazi played 60 shows in 66 days. When the power went out during "Waiting Room" at a squat in Italy, the crowd took over singing the song all on its own. Two-guitar reworkings of old songs "And the Same," "Merchandise," and "Promises Are Shit" were lean, tight, and hungry, while "Provisional" and "Glue Man" sounded positively expansive with chaotic near-jam sections added. The band earned the title bestowed on it by *Sounds*: "America's Clash."

Fugazi continued to try to destroy barriers between band and audience, but new ones were arising. The fans were now much younger than the musicians, and as the audience grew, more and more followers came from mainstream punk, bringing with them a predilection for slamdancing and crowd-surfing. The band members had to accommodate this new reality or spend their whole set yelling at the crowd. This shift would alienate some of Fugazi's earliest supporters, but it was hard to see what else the band could do.

Fugazi seemed ever more intent on denying audience expectations, especially of the musicians as leaders. In Bremen, Germany, one person—apparently curious why the band had not been as outspoken as usual—called out, "What are you believing in?" MacKaye responded simply, "What are you believing in, sir?"

The answer should have been clear in Fugazi's actions: the songs they were singing, the way they had set up the show, the fact that despite selling over 100,000 copies of *Repeater* they still spurned major label offers. The band remained self-booked and continued to insist on low-priced, all-ages shows. Still, the musicians did frustrate interviewers by increasingly refusing to define themselves in sloganistic terms. After one such discussion, *Rock Against Sexism* fanzine called them "reticent" and "apolitical."

The cassette version of *Repeater* contained a quotation from Spanish philosopher Jose Ortega y Gasset: "Revolution is not the rising up against pre-existing order, but the setting up of a new order contradictory to the traditional one." Fugazi seemed to be challenging people to do that for themselves rather than pay homage to a band.

On the group's return to DC, *Washington City Paper* dubbed 1990 "the year of Fugazi," noting that the musicians had "taken the world by storm—and on their own terms." The band played the Lorton Prison gig and a benefit with Unrest and Autoclave at the 9:30 Club for the Whitman Walker Clinic, which was battling AIDS. Then came the biggest event Fugazi and Positive Force had ever attempted: the protest in front of the White House in Lafayette Park in support of the homeless. The January date turned out to be the Saturday before the deadline President Bush had set for Iraqi withdrawal from Kuwait.

The focus of the event was expanded to make a direct antiwar statement, connecting extravagant military expenditures and inadequate domestic spending. Along with Fugazi's set, a rally and punk percussion protest were planned. An earlier Positive Force–organized percussion protest had helped to inspire a 24-hour-a-day antiwar drum vigil, and the group took great satisfaction when Bush complained to the press that "those damned drums are keeping me up all night."

The day before the event, a heavy snowstorm hit the city. The next day, temperatures nudged into the 40s and the snow melted, but it was cold and rainy. With the country preparing for war, police blanketed the White House area. Despite the weather, around 3000 people showed up, including rarely seen old allies like Squip. As the protesters beat on oil barrels, drums, tin cans, and kettles, the organizers wondered what to do about the show. Playing on an unprotected stage in the rain could expose musicians and crew to potential electrocution. At one point the rain stopped, only to begin again just as the band was ready to go. Organizers and musicians huddled on the stage, trying to decide what to do. Finally, feeling the gravity of the political moment, MacKaye said simply, "Let's fucking do it!" All available hands scrambled to uncover the gear and prepare for the chancy performance.

As the portion of the crowd now clustered tightly by the stage cheered, MacKaye spoke: "Initially, this was supposed to be a concert in the park, figuring that if people had to live out in the cold, we sure as fuck could come out and play for an hour and a half, do a little bit of a protest in support of the homeless groups who are working to give people shelter. In DC, there are thousands of people living on the streets. If you live here, you just start to walk by them after a while. It's inconceivable to me at least, that with the billions and billions of dollars that are being spent in the Middle East, that we can't spend more for the people who are dying in the streets here!"

As the crowd applauded, MacKaye continued: "In effect, there is a tie between the homeless problem and the healthcare problems and everything else. As this country begins to fold up on itself economically, we throw ourselves into yet another war to divert people's attention from the problems here in America. Everything ties together, there is a connection. We are Fugazi from Washington, DC, thank you very much for coming out." As the band slid into "Brendan #1," the percussion protest finally ended and many of the drummers joined the crowd by the stage.

The stage quickly became the source of concern. It was sturdy, but rested on three layers of milk crates; park regulations barred affixing the stage to the ground. As the crowd surged, the pressure began to force the stage slowly southward. Divers also began to mount the stage, further stressing the structure. MacKaye asked the crowd not to stage-dive, encouraging them to instead "give us some help with the words." The band played a confrontational new song, "Reclamation," built on a titanic, rolling riff. The lyrics had been inspired by anti-abortion extremists, but lines like "These are our demands/We want control of our bodies" took another meaning in the shadow of war.

It was so chilly and wet that MacKaye later said his hands "felt like blocks of wood," but the band was hot, feeding off the energy of the situation. As the stage continued to shift, appearing to begin to split apart at one point, the musicians adjusted their songs to reflect the political situation. Picciotto added a line exhorting the crowd to "take it out into the streets" to "Two Beats Off." MacKaye stopped to note the presence of Park Police filming the assembly "for a new MTV special, I guess."

Picciotto hit the Buzzcocks-like two-note opening of "KYEO," revamped specifically for this show. The newly streamlined song led into "Long Division," with a mournful evocation of fragmentation that led to MacKaye's comment that "if George Bush wants one America, he better get out of the business of oil and war." By this point, the heat of the tightly packed audience had created a gigantic human smoke machine, sending thick clouds of steam over the stage.

Fugazi concluded with "Repeater" and "Burning Too." MacKaye prefaced the former with a comparison to DC's own war and the wish that while "we seem to have become accustomed to the hundreds that have died here, I hope we can never become accustomed to the tens of thousands that might die in the Middle East." The crowd joined MacKaye in counting off the chorus' "1, 2, 3." The song's desperate screech led to a lonely exhortation to "keep count." As MacKaye methodically recited "10,000 . . . 20,000 . . . 30,000 . . . 40,000 . . . 50,000 . . . 60,000 . . . 70,000 . . . 80,000 . . . 90,000 . . ."—the potential body count in the adventure about to erupt—the song rose to its painful climax.

Amazingly, nothing had gone wrong—with the police, the stage, or the rain. As armed agents watched from the top of the White House, Fugazi had played one of its greatest performances. Four days later, the bombs began to rain on Baghdad, the most intense bombing in human history.

x x x

As the war began, Fugazi was in Inner Ear recording its next LP. Its stark style seemed to reflect the grimness of the times. The deceptively sweet "Nice New Outfit" included references to "smart bombs" and lines like, "You're number one with a bullet/That's money well spent." The revived "KYEO" ended with defiant vow: "We will not be beaten down."

Some Positive Force members from Whitman High School helped organize an antiwar benefit at Sanctuary Theater with Jawbox, Holy Rollers, Shudder to Think, and a new band, Desiderata, that included MacKaye sister Amanda on vocals. With over 800 people, it was the group's biggest non-Fugazi event ever.

The Latin Investment Corporation, an unchartered DC "bank" that had no insurance, collapsed in December 1990, taking the savings of several thousand Salvadoran immigrants. Some of them faced a double crisis, having been evicted from apartments along Columbia Road when the buildings were found to have massive fire-code violations. Faced with this emergency, Positive Force quickly organized a benefit at Sacred Heart Church, an important institution in the Latino community that had a mammoth auditorium.

Fugazi headlined over the Nation of Ulysses and Pennsylvania band Admiral. MacKaye introduced "KYEO" by commenting, "As you may have noticed there is war in the Middle East. As you may also have noticed, there is a war here as well." Picciotto added a new intro to "Two Beats Off"—taken from the Jam's "The Place That I Love"—that ended with the plea to "take a stand against the world." The set climaxed with an ominous feedback jam, MacKaye eerily intoning "A thousand sorties everyday" over and over, a reference to the merciless US bombardment of Iraq. Over $5000 was raised for food, clothing, and other direct aid for the victims of the bank collapse.

As the Gulf War went well for the US, initial public skepticism became what Rollins called "getting high on war"—a virus that infected even the punk scene. At a Fugazi show at a club in Richmond, Virginia, Positive Force activists handing out antiwar fliers were physically intimidated and nearly ejected from the premises; only the band's intervention stopped the confrontation. When Fugazi played a benefit in Philadelphia, MacKaye noted that "a lot of people" were not happy that the gig supported conscientious objectors. Stephanie Atkinson, the first female soldier ever to become a war resister, spoke at the show, crediting Fugazi's music with helping her make the decision to resist.

The Army's media management in Panama had been great practice for the Gulf War, which Americans seemed to view as a conflict in which no one got hurt. It was unclear how many Iraqis had died, and few seemed to care. Months later, a US Census employee nearly lost her job when—required by professional demands to calculate Iraq's population—she estimated 150,000 dead. Obviously, the public was not supposed to know this.

In response, Positive Force organized an Alternative Media benefit at Sacred Heart to raise funds for Fairness and Accuracy in Reporting and the Washington Peace Letter, the monthly publication of the Peace Center. After Cringer, Autoclave, and Britain's Citizen Fish performed, Fugazi played its entire forthcoming album, *Steady Diet of Nothing*, which had pre-orders of 160,000.

Among the new songs was "Dear Justice Letter," inspired by the loss of Supreme Court liberal stalwart William Brennan. The song mourned Brennan's passing as "the last fair deal going down"—a line from a blues standard—and defiantly barked, "I won't go die politely." MacKaye dedicated "KYEO" to Rodney King, the recent victim of a brutal LAPD beating.

Fugazi was obviously still up for a fight—but how much of the rest of the community was? A recent transplant from California, Agent 86, now billed itself as the "only political hardcore band in DC." This was hype, but it was true that of the bands on *State of the Union*, only Fugazi and Shudder to Think remained. More and more DC punk radicals seemed to be retreating from militance or taking their politics outside the music.

As if to mark the final passing of harDCore, Wilson Center's stage was dismantled and the space transformed into a Latino youth center. Yet there was still considerable strength in the DC punk community, which was about to begin another upturn. This time, women—or grrrls—would lead the way.

chapter thirteen, 1991-92:
revolution girl style now

*"Hey girlfriend/I got a proposition/Goes something like this
Dare ya to do what you want/Dare you to be who you will/Dare you to cry right out loud . . ."*
—Bikini Kill, "Double Dare Ya"

KATHI WILCOX AND TOBI VAIL OF BIKINI KILL, PF PRO-CHOICE BENEFIT, SANCTUARY THEATER, APRIL 1992 *(by Pat Graham)*

revolution girl style now

The dark-haired young woman, clad only in black bra and miniskirt, seemed nervous. Onstage at dc space, she glanced repeatedly toward the other band members: a bleach-blond bassist, a wavy-haired drummer, and a close-cropped guitarist, the band's only male member. She turned back toward the crowd and at first spoke softly, almost tentatively—"We're Bikini Kill . . . and we want"—turning up the volume dramatically—"REVOLUTION GIRL STYLE NOW!"

Jagged garage punk swelled behind her outcry. In a commanding voice, Kathleen Hanna delivered a challenge: "Hey girl friend/I got a proposition . . ." As bassist Kathi Wilcox, drummer Tobi Vail, and guitarist Billy Karren played a wiry pattern, Hanna transformed the child's game of "double dare" into a call to confront centuries of misogyny and oppression.

A smile flickered across Hanna's face as she crooned, "You're a big girl now/You've got no reason not to fight/You've got to know what they are/Before you can stand up for your rights . . ." Then her body went taut and she screamed: "RIGHTS . . . RIGHTS . . . YOU . . . DO . . . HAVE . . . RIGHTS!"

As this outburst ebbed, the band decelerated jerkily, only to spring back to full fury. Hanna tossed off rapid-fire taunts that again evoked childhood—"Liar, liar/Got your pants on fire"—only to switch to grownup matters: "You profit from the lie/Eat meat/Hate blacks/Beat your fucking wife/It's all the same thing/You live your life in denial." As this song dropped to drums only, Hanna turned to Wilcox and they struck up a chorus of "Give Peace a Chance," the utopian sentiments contrasted by Vail's backup screams. Bass and then guitar re-engaged, driving "Liar" to an unforgiving conclusion.

It was June 1991. In its first Washington appearance, Bikini Kill's confrontational yet charismatic mix of feminism and punk was a rush of fresh energy. The band's arrival from Olympia—at the end of its first US tour, accompanied by the Nation of Ulysses—would have a resounding impact.

Despite the loss of numerous Revolution Summer stalwarts, the punk scene retained a strong infrastructure, with Dischord and Positive Force bolstered by new additions like Simple Machines. According to one longtime observer, *Jersey Beat's* Jim Testa, "DC is one of the most amazing musical centers in the country . . . in the shadow of the White House, more than anywhere else in the country right now, punk lives." Now Bikini Kill and its allies, the Nation of Ulysses and another Olympia-related band, Bratmobile, would empower women as never before in DC punk history.

Bikini Kill and Bratmobile's arrivals were the result of complicated links between Washington State and Washington, DC. The two distant scenes had begun swapping players: While Dave Grohl joined Nirvana, punk-folkie Lois Maffeo moved to DC, playing out with drummer Pat Maley as "Courtney Love"—a name jokingly borrowed from a then-unknown denizen of Portland's punk scene. Brendan Canty had befriended Maffeo, Johnson, and others while visiting his sister in Olympia. Jenny Toomey knew Hanna from high school in Bethesda, had toured in Geek with Tacoma's Seaweed, and had briefly played with Vail in My New Boyfriend.

One of the earliest connections existed between K Records co-owner Calvin Johnson and Ian MacKaye, who had met in 1980. Though their music was aesthetically at odds, both were action-oriented punks with a deep commitment to the DIY ethic. The bond was reinforced by Connolly's bookings of Beat Happening and Go Team at dc space, Johnson's frequent trips to visit family in DC, and his production of several Fugazi gigs in Olympia.

When K Records allied with Dischord to release the Nation of Ulysses' first single, it further united a new generation of DC and Olympia punks. One of the people who bought the 45 was Vail, the creator of *Jigsaw*, which was among the first of what she dubbed "angry grrrl 'zines" in 1990-91, including *Sister Nobody, Chainsaw*, and *Girl Germs*. Vail intended the word "grrrl" as a half-serious parody of the alternative spellings of "women" (wimmin, womyn, etc.) she encountered as a student at Evergreen State College, as well as a way to reclaim the word "girl."

Vail's feminist analysis of punk upset some of her fanzine's readers, but she was unrepentant. She had spent a lot of time in "male-dominated punk rock scenes," which she found prevented people from creating "real alternative communities that are based on something other than consumption. I feel completely left out of the realm of everything that is so important to me. And I know that this is partly because punk rock is for and by boys mostly and partly because punk rock of this generation is coming of age in a time of mindless career-goal bands."

Jigsaw called for "resistance" and "revolution," words that were also crucial to the Nation of

Ulysses. Vail first read about the band in Sharon Cheslow's 'zine *Interrobang*. "I never thought that I would ever get to see them play since it seems like I always hear about these DC bands right as they are about to break up," she wrote—only to learn that the group was headed her way.

Vail was astonished by the Nation in action. By this time, the quintet had honed its performance chops, generating raw energy of startling power. "Liberation for this room" was the first principle of their shows, which at their best became whirlwinds of abandon. "Words can do no justice to the way I feel about this group," Vail wrote. "After I saw the Nation of Ulysses, I knew I had to get in a band, and that's exactly how it should be when you see a really great band."

Historically, Olympia had one of the more gender-balanced punk scenes; macho hardcore had never seized control there, and the creative feminist aesthetic of early punks like Stella Marrs had helped to set the tone. Many associated K Records and Beat Happening with Johnson, but Candace Peterson was the label's co-owner and Heather Lewis shared vocal and instrumental chores in Beat Happening. "From the moment I set foot in Olympia in 1981, it was clear to me that girls ruled this town," said Maffeo, who had an all-girl radio show on Evergreen State College station KAOS.

By 1991, women were taking the stage in record numbers. Vail was inspired by female drummers like Holy Rollers' Maria Jones, as well as the Lunachicks, Babes in Toyland, STP, L7, and Frightwig. Yet she recognized that there were still pressing feminist issues in what was purported to be the "post-feminist" era.

In nearby Portland, Hanna was coming to similar conclusions. She carried the legacy of vicious sexual abuse, teen pregnancy, and subsequent stigmatization as a "slut." She recalled that "I was really super into my relationships with men until I was 17 or 18. I was really fucked over by this guy and I started thinking, 'I can't give all this control [to another person].' During that time, my best friend also was assaulted in our house. I had a lot of issues to do with sexual abuse and domestic violence that I hadn't grappled with. I wasn't going to shut it out."

At first, Hanna did spoken-word performances inspired by confrontational artists Kathy Acker and Karen Finley. Then she turned toward music, in part to reach "younger punky girls. I was on a mission to, like, make feminism cool for younger girls." The result was Viva Knievel, a quartet that managed one US tour before disbanding.

At the time, Hanna was working in a domestic violence shelter. "That totally influenced my work. We had a lot of songs about gang rape and stuff. We'd go to towns and girls would hear it and afterward they'd tell me their stories. It was good that I had experience with crisis counseling. I kind of knew what to say. Essentially, I was doing the same work that I did at the shelter."

By late 1990, Hanna had met Vail. "I read *Jigsaw* and it made me so happy," said Hanna. "I felt we were trying to do some similar type things and I just decided she and I were going to be friends." They planned a band that would have a strong feminist punk vision and also be sexy and life-affirming—more Madonna than Andrea Dworkin.

This drew fierce criticism from some feminists, in part because Hanna sometimes worked as a stripper. Stripping, Hanna later wrote, "is a job and like all jobs, it fucking sucks. I personally decided to be a sex trade worker 'cause I feel a lot less exploited making $20 an hour for dancing around naked that I do getting paid $4.25 an hour (and being physically, psychically, and sometimes sexually exploited) as a waitress or burger-slinger. Why do certain feminists wanna penalize me for choosing an obvious form of exploitation instead of a subtle, lower-paying one?"

Another concern for some feminists was the use of the word "girl." Hanna responded that "each person can call themselves whatever they want. If I choose to call myself 'girl,' then I would want that respected"—although she was quick to add, "Who gives a shit if I'm called 'girl' or 'woman' compared to the fact that women are being raped everyday, that women are being murdered by their boyfriends?"

Hanna and Vail studied the anti-capitalist feminism of African-American activist-writers bell hooks, Audre Lorde, and Angela Davis. Their criticism of the original feminist movement for rarely reaching beyond the white middle class could apply to punk as well.

"I'm really interested in a punk-rock movement/angry-girl movement of sexual abuse survivors," Hanna said. "And it's not just angry girls, it's everyone, because I've had so many people come up to me with their stories of sexual abuse, of being beaten up by their parents and stuff. Even if it's not getting punched, it's the emotional violence and hierarchy in the family—which is the same hierarchy that puts man over woman, it's the same fucking shit that is white over black, human over animal, boss over worker."

Vail and Hanna called their synthesis "Revolution Girl Style Now." Joining them in attempting to integrate these inspirations into a band were Evergreen film student Kathi Wilcox and, later, Billy

Karren, formerly of Go Team and Snakepit. The name Bikini Kill was borrowed from a one-off project of Maffeo and her friend Rebecca Gates.

The name was inspired by a Frankie Avalon movie called *The Million Eyes of Sumaru*, in which a female supervillain recruits a corps of beautiful women to become the wives or mistresses of all the world's leaders. Eventually, the women are supposed to assassinate these leaders, but one of the women falls in love with her potential victim and decides to reveal the plot to him. So a group of bikini-clad minions is sent to eliminate her.

Silly as the scene was, Maffeo later recalled, "It had this kind of feminist idea of taking over the world in one day. We always had this idea, like, 'What if all women decided for one day to not do anything, to go on strike? Let's watch the world fall apart.'"

To Hanna, the name conjured "girls in bikinis with guns. It's taking over that whole stereotype of what [female] sexuality is. This is ours and this is powerful." The name also evoked the devastation visited upon the native population of Bikini Atoll by US hydrogen bomb tests in the 1950s.

x x x

In nearby Eugene, Oregon, Olympian Allison Wolfe and DC native Molly Neuman were also forming a band. They already worked together on a radio show and published *Girl Germs*, a 'zine inspired by the examples of women like Vail and Maffeo. In the first issue, Neuman wrote, "My brother who is two and a half got a toy rock'n'roll drum set for Christmas this year. I got a guitar when I turned 18. I had this idea that I might want to be in a band. But nobody told me that I could or encouraged me to. There's a fundamental difference in the way I was socialized and the way my brother is being socialized. He is being given the tools to create. I must seek out those tools."

Like Bikini Kill, *Girl Germs* and their subsequent band, Bratmobile, proposed a new punk feminism. Their 'zine, Neuman and Wolfe wrote, was "pro-girl, pro-punk rock, pro-underground. We are pro-people without voices, who have consistently been denied their voice, and we are pro-people."

Bratmobile initially specialized in impromptu "guerrilla" a capella performances. At an October 1990 Unrest show in Eugene, the duo "made a surprise protest/appearance" to counter "a bunch of drunk dummies." Things got more organized, however, when Johnson called and asked the group to play a Valentine's Day show with the recently formed three-piece Bikini Kill. The show tightened the bonds between the two, but didn't quell local hostility to both bands. Wolfe: "We were always hearing our names dissed around town."

Like Bikini Kill, Neuman and Wolfe were inspired by the Nation of Ulysses. While home for Christmas 1990, Neuman had seen the band at dc space with Little Baby, a short-lived unit that included Mike Fellows and a significant remnant of Soul Side. At this show, Johnson introduced Neuman to Erin Smith, who initially preferred Beat Happening's "love rock" but had been won over by the Nation. "I wasn't around for Rites of Spring or [early] Fugazi, so to me Nation of Ulysses was the greatest thing that I had ever seen," she said. "Besides their energy and songs, it was all the DC nationalism, all the 'make [DC] a youth mecca' type thing. This was really exciting to me because growing up, I never felt that anything like that was coming."

Smith and her brother Don published *Teenage Gang Debs*, which celebrated the siblings' '70s-pop-culture fixation. There was no revolutionary punk-feminist element to this 'zine, but Smith agreed with Neuman that "it's time more girls had a voice" in punk. Smith's college essay, "The Liberation of Marcia Brady," appeared in *Girl Germs* #2.

Excited by the DC scene, Neuman and Wolfe visited the city together over spring break. Toomey arranged for them to play a show with Desiderata and Severin—a new band with Alec Bourgeois, Eugene Bogan, Alex Daniels, and Mark Haggerty—at Abi's, a Salvadoran restaurant with unusually strong ties to the punk community. (The original Abi's was very near Dischord, PF House, and Inner Ear Studio and became a favorite haunt of hungry punks.) The duo stayed at the NOU Embassy, where they met a crucial ally, Jen Smith.

With Neuman and Erin Smith on guitar, Christina Billotte playing drums, and Wolfe and Jen Smith singing, Bratmobile (DC) was born. In a few weeks, Neuman recalled, "We practiced three times, played the show, went up to New York and saw some Beat Happening and Ulysses shows, and Tim Green—who had set up a four-track in the basement of the Embassy—recorded us." Bratmobile (DC) went on hiatus with Neuman and Wolfe's return to Eugene, but planned to reunite for the summer. They heard that Bikini Kill was touring with the Nation of Ulysses in May and June, so the whole crew would be in DC for the summer.

The larger DC punk scene knew little about this alliance. While the Nation had won some ardent fans, it also had plenty of skeptics. The band's girl-punk tie was considered ironic by some older female punks who associated the group with the same kind of male-bonding hijinks once linked to DOD. Still, the city would soon resound with the Nation's "Sound of Young America," while the music received a boost from a unrelated conflagration.

x x x

In early May, Mount Pleasant erupted following an incident that showed the growing complexity of Washington's ethnic politics: An African-American policewoman had shot a Latino man. The officer said the man had lunged at her with a knife during an arrest for public drunkenness, but rumors spread that the man had been shot while handcuffed. The shooting sparked three days of the city's most intense civil unrest since the 1968 riots. On the first night, hundreds of youths fought police in the streets, destroying more than a dozen squad cars before tear gas and massive police mobilization contained the disturbance. The second night brought more of the same, but with more people arriving from outside the neighborhood to join in the looting and battles with police.

Fresh from recording their first album, *13 Point Program to Destroy America*, members of the Nation of Ulysses and other DC punks hit the streets, taking aim at the police amid the chaos. Some seemed to view what was happening as "The Revolution," but others criticized their fellow punks for appropriating a struggle that wasn't theirs. While most punks who lived in such neighborhoods said they opposed gentrification—that position was even in the Nation of Ulysses' program—it could be argued that they were part of the process of displacing poor people simply by being there.

The same month, the Supreme Court upheld the Bush Adminstration's gag rule preventing federally funded clinics from offering abortion counseling. Thanks to appointments made by Reagan and Bush, the Court seemed now only one vote away from overturning *Roe v. Wade*, allowing states to outlaw abortion again.

Positive Force and Fugazi collaborated on another benefit for the Washington Free Clinic—which was among the institutions affected by the gag rule—at Sacred Heart Church, attracting a crowd of around 1500 only a month after the riots. The show also included two out-of-town acts, Dutch anarchist band the Ex and Canada's No Means No, which opened its set by observing, "This is a benefit that shouldn't have to be. Healthcare should be free."

If the performance was particularly furious, that reflected the mood of the times. "I don't think I've ever been more angry than I am now," Picciotto said at the time. "The past six months in this country have probably been the worst in my life. I've never felt quite as marginalized or freaked out by a situation. I feel like there are things going on in this country that are just unbelievable, really frightening."

The band was bitter about the Gulf War and the recent Victory Celebration, which displayed military armament on Washington's Mall at a cost of $12 million. "That's pretty sad when you think that we'll raise maybe $4000 tonight," MacKaye told the crowd. "Imagine what something like the Free Clinic could do with that kind of money."

Positive Force and Fugazi were doing what they could. Including Sacred Heart, most of the halls used for benefits were either in or adjacent to the riot zone. Despite pressure to relocate the shows—one white male suburban 'zine writer complained that the gigs were in "Verminville DC, invariably drug-infested and Metro-inaccessible neighborhoods"—Positive Force continued to organize shows in the inner city, hoping to bring money into needy neighborhoods and break down the walls that separated the mostly white suburbs from the city.

Jen Smith had criticized some of her friends' enthusiastic response to the riots, yet the sense of possibility that came with such a rupture in the social fabric had energized her. "She wrote a letter in that amazing style of hers, where she can write really idealistically but still not have it sound corny," recalled Neuman. "It was right after the Mount Pleasant riots and she said, 'This summer's going to be a girl riot.'" The phrase named the energy that was building.

When Bikini Kill made its DC debut soon after the riots, the musicians were taken aback by the immediate support they found. The band's show generated uncommonly intense and positive word of mouth, and Ian MacKaye produced and paid for a session at Inner Ear.

A permanent version of Bratmobile debuted in July, opening for Tsunami at Fort Reno. Neuman picked up drum sticks, while Erin Smith (just returned from an internship at *Sassy*) became the lone guitarist. Some scoffed at the trio's defiant amateurism, but Bratmobile played ragged punk with a good humor that suited songs like the playfully obscene "Kiss and Ride," inspired by the husband-and-wife ritual enshrined by signs at suburban Metrorail stations.

Inspired by Jen Smith's letter, the Bratmobilers decided to start a new fanzine. "We'd been trying to figure out a name," Neumann recalled. "We had thought about *Girl Riot* and then we changed it to *Riot Grrrl* with the three 'r's,' as in growling. It was a cool play on words, and also kind of an expression about how there should be some kind of vehicle where your anger is validated." Erin Smith credited Neuman with coining the phrase.

Neuman, Hanna, Wolfe, Vail, Erin Smith, and Jen Smith worked on the new 'zine. While Neuman recalled the first issues as "mostly little bits, gossipy and fun," they also carried an attack on Supreme Court nominee Clarence Thomas, an essay on heterosexism called "Fear of a Queer Planet," and tips on police car sabotage.

At a Positive Force benefit for a low-cost women's self-defense training, Hanna, Wolfe, and Neuman passed out copies of *Riot Grrrl*, making connections with punk girls outside the Mount Pleasant scene and building a phone list—in Neuman's words—"so that we could have a chance to hang out with other girls who weren't necessarily scenesters but who were cool nonetheless." The show featured Quicksand, Desiderata, and Circus Lupus, an angular, noisy band fronted by Ignition expatriate Chris Thomson and featuring strong female drummer Arika Casebolt.

The presence of Quicksand—a New York band descended from Youth of Today and Gorilla Biscuits—made the show a little uncomfortable. Although the group didn't encourage it, slamming was likely during its set. Given that the show was protesting violence against women and many women were alienated by slamdancing, Positive Force decided to hand out pamphlets asking people not to slam at the show. Positive Force members who didn't oppose slamming also stated their position.

Although widely associated with the Dischord scene, Positive Force actually included people of diverse ages and tastes. In some ways, Positive Force felt more in sync with militant hardcore bands like Born Against, Downcast, and Shelter than with increasingly professional and apolitical post-hardcore bands. Yet the group also sought to challenge such punk rituals as slamming and control the destructive behavior of some hardcore fans that endangered the use of various performance spaces.

These goals were not universally appreciated. One band, Aggressive Behavior, wrote a song named "Positive Force, Blow Me." Rumors circulated that the Quicksand show flier had labeled all slammers "rapists." When the political hardcore band Four Walls Falling had to cancel a Positive Force show on very short notice because its drummer found himself in jail, a tale went around that the show was stopped because it was hardcore—that Positive Force was "banning hardcore."

Part of the problem was that Positive Force was still pursuing a radical critique of American society. As Matt Berger, singer for DC political hardcore band Worlds Collide, said at the time, "You can't expect them to like Positive Force—most of the hardcore scene is in love with America." If this was so, Positive Force was definitely out of step.

For Positive Force veterans, one of the inspiring things about the angry girl scene was that it was not afraid to challenge both the form and the content of punk—and didn't care when told that "you're taking things too seriously." Music and politics again mingled freely, combining with the simple excitement of the community centered on Mount Pleasant group houses like the Embassy and Pirate House.

While Wilcox was on vacation in Europe, Hanna formed two new bands, the Mecca Normal-ish Wonder Twins with Tim Green, and Suture with Sharon Cheslow on guitar and Dug Birdzell on drums. Like other short-lived units formed that summer, both recorded in the Embassy basement.

Riot Grrrl's third issue called for "an all girl meeting to discuss the status of punk rock and revolution [and] ways to encourage higher female scene input and ways to help each other play instruments and get stuff done." Hanna noted later that she "didn't necessarily have any big agenda of taking over the world. I was just, 'Let's go and find out.'"

Almost two dozen women and girls showed up at first

INTRODUCTION, INSPIRATION, MURDER
by Mark Andersen

I first picked up a copy of *Riot Grrrl* while visiting my then-partner, Claire McBride, at Edison Street, a new PF-related Arlington group house, in July 1991. What I found inside was a delicious alternative to the bonehead macho, predictability, or cynical cool that dominated much of the punk scene. I was especially taken by "THE REVOLUTION STARTS HERE AND NOW (within each of us)" list which I later learned was written by Kathleen.

I was equally impressed by the women and girls behind the 'zine, who I met at PF House. Practically, beyond a forum for support, what was evolving via the RG meetings was an organized female political force that could wield power within the scene and insist that long-silenced voices be heard. Eager to promote their work, I did an interview with Allison, Kathleen, and Molly after the second RG meeting for a local underground paper. I have never had a more inspirational conversation in my life.

All three shared similarly deep ideas and emotion. After the darkness of the past year, I had found people willing to speak of revolution and punk in the same sentence, while backing it up with action, providing the spearhead for a long-overdue feminist revolution within the punk community. Although some of their critique could—and soon would!—be applied to my own "first-among-equals" role within PF, I was generally glad for the challenge.

As a band, Bikini Kill was a revelation. Every one of their shows that I saw over 1991 and 1992 held at least one moment of genuine emotional epiphany—for me, a trail comparable only to my experience with Rites of Spring in 1985. Bikini Kill not only had the songs, the concept, and the charisma, meeting, including Neuman, Wolfe, Billotte, Vail, Cheslow, Hanna, Toomey, Kristin Thomson, and many younger girls. Held in July at Positive Force House, the conclave drew many women who ordinarily might never have met. Topics included slamdancing, sharing skills, and personal experiences of sexism or abuse. "It turned out that a lot of the girls had things they wanted to talk about," Hanna said afterward. "So we decided to keep doing it." Given the intensely personal and often painful nature of much of what was shared, the group was to remain all-female.

This was not the first time that there had been an exclusively female punk meeting in DC, but now the idea caught hold. "Basically, it's an issue of support, where women and girls can be creative together and talk about things," Hanna said. "We've all had help to not feel so isolated."

For Hanna, Revolution Girl Style Now went far beyond simply getting girls into bands. She wanted a movement "that includes where people can be really caring and considerate and not be thought of as jerks or dorks or bleeding-heart liberals or wimps. Revolution doesn't have to be a real macho thing."

There was antagonism toward Riot Grrrl within the punk scene, but it was muted. "Personally I haven't felt that anyone doesn't want us to do it," Wolfe said. "I find that opposition is quite hushed up because they know that what's going on is really cool and it'd be really uncool to be too overtly sexist about the whole thing. So, there's lots of subtle shut-me-ups."

but, most crucial of all, they seemed to have the heart. I felt it when Kathleen performed an intensely vulnerable solo song—on the edge of tears—at Wetlands in NYC, again when she did a psychically naked spoken word before an unsympathetic hardcore crowd at a St. Stephen's benefit, and yet again during the debut of an amazing new song, "Rebel Girl," before a largely female crowd at the Peace Center.

Although I didn't agree with all they said or did, after every show, I had learned or felt something deep. Bikini Kill did for me what all great punk bands do—in the rush of music and emotion, day-to-day reality faded, all verities were thrown into question, and the world seemed to roar with possibility. For punk seventeen years on, it was pretty fucking good.

Kathleen once told me that she often felt in physical danger during live performances. The band's vulnerability was real, as was made clear by an incident at a show in Boston. As Chris Bald—who, together with Laura from the *Sister Nobody* 'zine, was then roadying for the band—later recalled, "Bikini Kill was playing a show headlined by an old-line Boston band, the Freeze, and some real boneheads were in the crowd. This one guy was really drunk and obnoxious and kept harassing Kathleen." When Laura tried to calm the muscle-bound heckler, he savagely attacked, knocking her out. Chris and Kathleen intervened and succeeded in ejecting him from the show.

The man was Michael Cartier; he was then stalking ex-girlfriend Kristin Lardner, who had been part of the mid-'80s DC punk scene. Less than a month after this encounter, Cartier came up from behind and shot her to death on a crowded Boston street.

Indeed, feminist punks like Bikini Kill found more support in DC than in Olympia. "Nobody gives a shit about us in Olympia," Hanna said at the time. "No one reacts to us except for five or six girls who stand in the front and support us. We don't get a really overtly positive response in our own community. To come here to our first show in DC and have people react so positively was kind of frightening," she laughed.

The band began to consider moving to Washington, DC, for both political and personal reasons. "In Olympia, I just felt politically isolated. There was music everywhere but politics, no," Hanna said. In DC, she noted, she felt a kinship with Positive Force, Simple Machines, and Dischord.

MacKaye was one of Riot Grrrl's early supporters. Besides working with Bikini Kill at Inner Ear, he arranged for Bratmobile to play an unannounced dc space gig with Fugazi to help raise money for the struggling club. But while support from Fugazi, the Nation of Ulysses, and other males was nice, the real story was that women were stepping into the lead, not following it.

Not all the women involved with angry-girl 'zines followed Riot Grrrl in its evolution toward becoming a formal group. "I didn't go to the meetings," Erin Smith later said. "There were a bunch of girls who felt the same way, that we were just going to speak louder with our actions. Although I was interested in all the things they were standing for, [the meetings] just weren't my thing."

The group soon experienced a generation gap. Neuman recalled being astounded at the level of understanding of many of the younger girls, but others who supported the group felt it was irrelevant to them personally. "The level of discussion was not really what I was interested in," Toomey said. "I could see how important it might be for the younger girls, but I had a college degree in women's studies and just wasn't that interested in talking about boyfriends, slamdancing, or stuff like that." Billotte and Vail didn't return after the first meeting, and the group quickly shifted toward a younger suburban crowd.

Revolution (Summer) Girl Style Now—as it was in dubbed in *Riot Grrrl* #4—was fading. The Olympia crew prepared to journey to K Records' International Pop Underground convention, as did Fugazi, the Nation of Ulysses, Tsunami, and others. *Riot Grrrl* issued a sign-off challenge: "Those of us who have been working on these issues might not do them again, but this name is not copyrighted. So take the ball and run with it!"

While DC had its girl revolution, punk continued to drift toward the mainstream. Not all its established performers were comfortable there, however. Henry Rollins, who had described himself as "not very political," tried to start a record label called High on War that would donate proceeds to abused children. He also published *Human Shrapnel*, an antiwar book by Vietnam vet Bill Shields, and helped distribute Ken Jaurecke and Exene Cervenka's wrenching Gulf War photo album, *Just Another War*.

In the aftermath of the Rodney King beating and the police killing of the singer of the old LA punk band Circle One, Rollins called for "a righteous investigation into the workings of the American police." On the college lecture circuit, Rollins debated Jack Thompson, the Florida official responsible for the prosecution of 2 Live Crew on obscenity charges. Rollins called the group's Luther Campbell "an American success story" and charged that "America doesn't like a black man with money."

Yet Rollins now recorded for Chrysalis, which he hailed as "the only label that I've been on that has done what it said it would." When Chrysalis' former owner started a new label, Imago, distributed by multinational conglomerate BMG, Rollins Band signed on. The title of the first LP *End of Silence*, was a slap at indie incompetence. "I flat out refuse to work with an independent record company again," he said.

In spring 1991, Rollins was sharing gigs with the rising LA band Jane's Addiction. The group's manager asked him to join an ambitious summer tour, Lollapalooza, that would mix different cultures and music with political booths and side-show attractions. While these stadium gigs were far from early punk and Rollins was allotted the tough opening spot, he and the band embraced the challenge.

At a time when more established acts experienced disastrous tours, Lollapalooza's lineup—which also featured Siouxsie and the Banshees, Ice-T and Body Count, Nine Inch Nails, and Living Color—became the summer's surprise hit. Organizer Perry Farrell claimed that "this is as close to a revolution as this generation gets," but Rollins called it "just another gig." Still, he admitted, the tour proved that "there's a real interest in what could be called 'underground music.'"

In Olympia, the International Pop Underground was considerably more intimate—and untouched by what K called the "corporate ogre." No performers signed to majors were allowed, and no passes were issued to major-label A&R people. Beyond this anti-major stance, the event's politics were not exactly hard-edged, manifest in characteristically K touches like a pet parade, a *Planet of the Apes* film festival, and the slogan, "Make Love Rock Not War."

A wide variety of 'zines and tape compilations were prepared for the fest, including *A Wonderful Treat*, which documented much of the Mount Pleasant summer scene. One of the more impressive audio documents was a full-length vinyl compilation, *Kill Rock Stars*, prepared by longtime Olympia scenester Slim Moon; it included not only Bikini Kill, Bratmobile, and other Olympia-related acts but also DC punks both young (the Nation of Ulysses) and not-so-young (Jad Fair).

One of only two bands on the compilation that did not perform at the convention was Nirvana. In 1989—shortly after recording its first album, *Bleach*, for $600—the band relocated to Olympia. While bassist Chris Novoselic soon moved to Tacoma, the almost pathologically withdrawn Kurt Cobain seemed to flourish in Olympia, even getting a homemade K tattoo. Instinctively anti-macho thanks to his painful experiences with roughnecks in Aberdeen, the logging town where he grew up, Cobain gravitated toward Vail, Hanna, and the others developing what would become the angry girl scene.

Cobain had first been radicalized by a *My War*–era Black Flag show and a compilation tape passed on by a friend that included bands like Flipper and MDC. Nirvana's music bore the mark of that dirge-y metallic punk, tinged with underground pop flavorings.

The addition of dynamic drummer Dave Grohl re-galvanized the band, and by 1991 it was extremely popular in underground circles. After waiting while its label, Sub Pop, teetered on the edge of bankruptcy, Nirvana finally followed the example of Sonic Youth and signed to major-label DGC. This meant it couldn't play the festival, but Cobain had planned to participate as a member of a one-off project called the Israeli Donkeys. To his consternation, however, Nirvana's management booked the band to play Britain's massive Reading Festival at the same time as the convention.

The conference began with "Girl Day," officially titled "Love Rock Revolution Girl Style Now." Johnson accepted Vail's original idea of a show for women and girls only, he said, "but then it kind of evolved in the planning and finally boys were allowed in the club and onstage too. The important thing wasn't that it was just girls doing it, but that it allowed people who don't normally make music to do something."

The bands included Bikini Kill, Mecca Normal, L7, and the Spinanes. The latter's Gates was playing only her fifth public performance, but "I came out of that show feeling like a musician." According to one estimate, almost 90 percent of all the festival's acts contained at least one woman. As the days passed, it was clear that the event was generating a powerful energy; an ebullient Guy Picciotto called it "what every day will be like after the revolution."

Fugazi was scheduled to be the climax of the convention. According to *Option*, the band's appearance was "enshrouded with intense excitement." Yet the musicians had not been keeping their distance; MacKaye spent one night taking tickets at the door of the Capitol Theater.

With more than 600 people packing the theater, it was by far the week's biggest show. Before joining Picciotto in coaxing feedback from his guitar for the intro of "Exit Only," MacKaye asked people to "have a good time and . . . you know." It was MacKaye's almost ritual plea for the fans to care for each other, one he clearly hoped might not be necessary here.

Some nonetheless insisted on slamming and diving, but tonight—as sometimes happened at Fugazi gigs—other elements of the crowd were not willing to accept this. During a tight version of "Merchandise," a stage-diver attempted to jump, only to be stopped mid-leap and thrown back onstage by people at the front row. There were many similar incidents before the show ended. This must have been heartening for the members of Fugazi, who sometimes felt their audience looked to them to work everything out.

Before the show, Hanna and several other women had circulated a flier about an alleged serial date-rapist attending the event, and approached Fugazi about speaking during the band's set. MacKaye had asked to take care of it in his own way, and as the band paused to tune, he did: "I don't know if you've noticed but there are fliers about date rape being passed out. In this town, like anywhere else, there is someone involved with assaults on people. A lot of people were really concerned about it because here they were coming to this convention, this really exciting thing, yet they were struck by the fact that there were people going around who were raping people. So they really wanted to do something about it, they wanted to say something. This is kind of a weird forum for it but . . . tough shit."

The clipped guitar of "Suggestion" began, and MacKaye continued: "Some people say that music should have no meaning, or that politics don't belong in music, that music is just supposed to be fun. Well, that's fair enough—for them. This song is called 'Suggestion' and anybody who feels that they should be the one to sing this should come up and sing whatever they want. Meanwhile, I'll begin it." With that, he sang the opening lines.

It seemed unlikely that anyone would accept the invitation. As the song dropped into a quiet rhythm, however, a young woman with long, braided hair—who Hanna and the others recognized as someone who had been assaulted—emerged from the crowd and nervously took the mic to screams of support. Shaking, she sang, "Is my body my only trait/In the eyes of men?" Even a usually hardboiled *Flipside* writer was moved, writing that "she only lasted a couple lines and then she broke down and cried. MacKaye looked nearly as shaken up. Everyone in the crowd looked really freaked out as well. It was as emotional [a moment] as I've ever seen." The whole house seemed to join her as she sang, "I've got some skin/And you want to look in." With tears running down her face, she returned to the crowd amidst massive cheers.

MacKaye stood back and motioned to the mic, inviting other people to come forward. When no one did, the crowd responded by carrying the song on its own. At a break in the sound, an anonymous female voice yelled the name of the alleged rapist, who apparently was in the crowd. As she did, MacKaye returned to the song and the singalong continued.

"We've done this song many, many times," MacKaye noted, "and people say to us, 'Yeah, do that really cool song about rape!'" Behind him, the music was just barely pulsing. "But it's really not a very cool song, there's nothing very cool about it at all. [The song] is more like a wrestling match. It's man or a boy who is wrestling with a situation that he feels he has very little control over yet is directly responsible for. So he puts some words together, and he pretends that this is how someone else might see it. This someone else is a woman or a girl. And he is neither."

The room had grown totally silent. Singing in a near whisper, MacKaye returned to the song: "She did nothing to conceal it/He touches her because he wants to feel it . . ." Over MacKaye's gentle vocals came Picciotto's sandpaper tones: "We don't want anyone to mind us/We play the roles they assigned us . . ." Then MacKaye's voice leaped to the top of music, turning finally to a raw, riveting scream: "WE . . . BLAME . . . HER . . . FOR . . . BEING . . . THERE."

Echoing a common reaction, Vail later noted that she cried during the song's performance. *Option* called Fugazi's set "the apex of the IPU. By the time [the band] ripped into 'Provisional,' the auditorium felt as if it had lifted itself off the planet and beamed to some far better place."

The release of *Steady Diet of Nothing* and the rest of the band's very successful American tour elicited a deluge of laudatory features. The attention seemed a bit "sick" to MacKaye, and the band refused to grant interviews to magazines like *Rolling Stone, Spin*, or *Details*—even as the musicians spoke freely to fanzine writers and audience members. Despite this rejection, many magazines ran stories anyway; *Spin* used quotes that were surreptitiously taped.

The band members wrestled against their new image as "indie superstars." Indeed, some of the gushing praise even made them angry. "It's not enough that you're playing in Fugazi and you're trying to write music and put yourself on the line like that," MacKaye complained. "But now you gotta do it with somebody else's agenda placed on you—you have to be 'the moralists of the '90s' or 'the last true spirit of rock'n'roll.'"

"We'll keep on putting out our own records, managing ourselves, booking ourselves, and staying supremely autonomous," said Picciotto. "We never got in a band to be popular. Basically we like to play our music. We considered ourselves a success from our first show just because we played. I consider the band to be getting better because we're getting along better. Those are the kind of things I'm interested in as opposed to how many people are coming to the shows or how much the records are selling."

The musicians also rejected the notion that they were keepers of a punk code of ethics. "We probably appear dogmatic, but there is a difference between doing only what you want to and telling other people what they should be doing," MacKaye explained. "We've only ever told ourselves that we should charge five dollars for gigs." The band became more reticent about the specifics of its songs, preferring that listeners grapple with the meaning for themselves.

Fugazi had achieved MacKaye's vision for Minor Threat nearly a decade before: becoming a big band without the bullshit. Fugazi was now pushing past the old limits. As the major labels pursued the style now called "alternative rock," Fugazi wanted not to escape the underground but—as MacKaye put it—"bring the underground up with us."

Many felt Fugazi would not be able to continue as it had, but the band members disagreed. "If we were worried about the future we would have broken up this band long ago," Picciotto said. "People have been telling us for years that we're going to have to do the things that all the other bands do, [but] we haven't done it and we've managed to survive."

"It's fun to say 'fuck you,' not to individuals but to something that has been carved in stone," MacKaye noted. "'This is the way you're supposed to do things'—that's bullshit." Johnson called this "the Meatmen part of MacKaye. Like Tesco Vee, he likes to say 'fuck you,' but in a different way. Ian enjoys making the folks in LA squirm, doing shows for six dollars."

In DC, the five-dollar shows continued to be benefits for grassroots community groups. "Even though we think things like Greenpeace or Amnesty International are really important," MacKaye noted, "we try to do our benefits for smaller, more local groups where the money will have more impact and will be directly used—food for a soup kitchen, bedding for a shelter, that sort of thing. We're trying to take care of our home."

Ironically, as Fugazi stayed true to its roots, some former allies decided the band was insufficiently pure. When the band played with the Nation of Ulysses, Bikini Kill, and the dyke-punk Tribe 8 at Gilman Street, the musicians were denounced as "rock stars" by some of the volunteers—even though the band played the show for free to raise funds for the financially strapped space. They faced similar disapproval from some squat punks in Europe. In *No Answers*, Kent McClard openly encouraged the members of the outspoken band Born Against to attack Fugazi for its success, which they declined to do. When the band played New York's Palladium for five dollars—having forced the club to agree to its terms after three years of not playing in the city—some muttered that, with Ticketmaster charges, tickets were "actually" $6.50.

Such gripes were hard to understand, for Fugazi appeared not to have changed. The band still didn't use guarantees, working off a percentage of the door, and every US gig had been all-ages and five dollars, save for LA where the band had consented to a six-dollar price. The band now traveled with roadie Mark Sullivan and soundman Joey P. in two rented U-Haul trucks instead of one, but still sold no merchandise. Dischord had a small staff of salaried workers—among them Amy Pickering, Cynthia Connolly, Amanda and Alec MacKaye, Kim Coletta, Renee Tantillo, and Seth Martin, all longtime friends—and had moved its distribution wing, Dischord Direct, to its own office across the street from Dischord House, but CDs, cassettes, and LPs remained nearly half the price of the majors'. All the band members still lived in group houses, and much of the money either went back into Dischord to underwrite releases by other underground DC bands or to fuel other community projects.

Rising popularity had inevitably brought Fugazi more into the rock'n'roll circuit, dealing with promoters and spaces outside the punk underground. While the band members enjoyed making such folks walk their line, they could not always control exactly what went on at shows. Some fans asked them to play smaller venues, but MacKaye responded that they didn't want to exclude anyone. He noted that "in order to keep the door price down at larger venues we're actually taking less money to play since the overhead is so incredibly high."

Much of the criticism seemed to reflect simple jealousy or the elitist notion that anything popular must be bad. "The underground eats their own," said Brendan Canty in a moment of anger. "If you don't leave, they kick you out." Fugazi's purported "sell-out" to popularity, however, was about to be upstaged with the release of Nirvana's *Nevermind*.

While the album had a much richer, more sophisticated sound than *Bleach*, its attitude certainly hadn't been disinfected for the mainstream. "Territorial Pissings" was inspired by Valerie Solanos—founder of the Society for Cutting Up Men and the woman who tried to kill Andy Warhol—while the title of "Smells Like Teen Spirit" came from Hanna. After a night of spray-painting phrases like "god is gay" on the walls of downtown Olympia, Hanna wrote, "Kurt smells like Teen Spirit," a reference to the female teen deodorant. Even the album's title seemed to reflect the angry girl milieu: In *Jigsaw*, Vail had written a poetic indictment of her generation that called it "tame misguided no direction stuck inside of nevermind."

"We are always associated with Nirvana and Nation of Ulysses and Fugazi," Hanna said later, "and we're lucky to have [their support]. But the thing is, those bands have been equally influenced by us, by our conversations and our music. If anything, we're giving more than we're taking."

According to one account, members of Bikini Kill and Bratmobile were initially invited to portray rebellious cheerleaders in the video of "Teen Spirit." The clip showed the most hated high school institution—the pep rally—descending into chaos as Nirvana played. By the end, the cheerleaders (who had sprouted tattoos and anarchy symbols), the crowd, and the band had become indistingushable, while the principal was left bound and gagged.

Youth insurrection, punk egalitarianism, communal release, girl revolution—it was all there in a four-minute video package. In 1992, Grohl said that "Smells Like Teen Spirit"—and, in particular, its couplet, "Our little group has always been/And always will until the end"—came "straight out of the offices of K Records and Dischord Records." The video, however, would take the song somewhere very different.

x x x

As *Nevermind* loomed, Bikini Kill was on the road with the Nation of Ulysses heading east, having decided that DC was—as Hanna wrote at the time—"the new youth mecca for real!" After a dc space gig at tour's end was scrubbed due to van troubles, Bikini Kill and the Nation agreed to play a Positive Force benefit for a Philippines human rights group. The Nation had long trumpeted the doctrine of "P-Power," apparently drawn from the "people power" slogan of the nonviolent grassroots movement that overthrew the Marcos dictatorship. For the Nation, however, the phrase supported the New People's Army, a Communist guerrilla group then fighting the Philippines government.

Bikini Kill lived up to its buzz with a confrontational set. Besides fervent renditions of "Feels Blind" and "Double Dare Ya," they debuted confrontational tunes like "White Boy," a song inspired by Jane Caputi's *The Age of Sex Crime*, a book that analyzed the misogyny in the modern phenomenon of serial killings of women.

By this time, Riot Grrrl was thriving, having been taken up by such women and girls as Erika Reinstein, May Summer, Mary Fondriest, Sarah Stolfa, Jasmine Kerns, Laura Solitaire, Tiffany Fabian, Ananda LaVita, Claudia Von Vacano, and others—many of whom had been or still were Positive Force members. Hanna was the only Bikini Kill member still involved in Riot Grrrl, but the band's performances remained an inspiration.

The Nation of Ulysses headlined the show, wearing the suits that had become the band's latest uniform. Ian Svenonius was typically hyperactive, leaping off James Canty's bass drum, invading the crowd, rolling around on the stage, and twisting his body into all manner of poses.

The band's new songs showed a jazz influence. A snippet of John Coltrane's "A Love Supreme" was heisted for the intro of "The Sound of Jazz to Come," while Svenonius introduced "N.O.U.S.P.T.D.A." as "our plan to destroy America—mumbled in hard bop dialect." These songs were somewhat slower and even more discordant. The show ended with Steve Kroner flinging off his guitar partway through "Mockingbird Yeah." The guitar flew through the air and bounced off the back wall, and Kroner deserted the stage to systematically smash it into bits while the band finished the song.

Even Don Zientara, who described the Nation members as "prima donnas" in the studio, agreed that the band had "something special. You could tell they were creating something new." *13 Point Program to Destroy America* was getting rave reviews; in *Sassy*, Erin Smith called it the "punk rock record of the year."

Fugazi and the Nation weren't the city's only punk attractions. In its eleventh year, Dischord released records by the Holy Rollers, Jawbox, Shudder to Think, Circus Lupus, Severin, and the revived Gray Matter. These bands were active throughout 1991-1992, as were the High Back Chairs, Lungfish, Velocity Girl, Unrest, and Girls Against Boys. The city's three underground-pop labels, Simple Machines, Teenbeat, and Slumberland, sponsored a successful festival, Lots of Pop Losers (a parody of Lollapalooza). Still, the scene's cutting edge—politically and perhaps musically as well—was the Nation of Ulysses/Bikini Kill/Riot Grrrl subset.

x x x

The year had been DC's most deadly yet, with 483 slain, but murder rates were climbing throughout the country. In December '91, Rollins and his best friend, Joe Cole, were jumped in Venice, California, and Cole was shot dead. The loss was devastating for Rollins, but he dealt with it as he did everything else—he went to work. "Now would be the perfect time for me to just give up everything I'm doing, retire, go into seclusion," he said. "But everybody has their hard times. You just dust yourself off and keep going."

As Rollins mourned, the first club he had ever performed in was closing. dc space's new owner, the Pennsylvania Avenue Development Corporation, deemed the structure unsafe, and wasn't about to renovate it since the block was slated for redevelopment. (In fact, a real estate crash ended those plans, and 12 years later the building remains empty.) The club went out with a month-long celebration that included an unannounced Fugazi performance.

Ideas for a new club were floated but proved slow to realize, so Positive Force got access to a room at the Washington Peace Center. The room was not soundproofed, had no stage, was only erratically available, and could hold only 100 or so people, but it did fill a bit of void. The first band to play there was Bratmobile, reunited briefly over the holidays for a show originally scheduled for dc space.

The same week that Bratmobile played before 50 people at the Peace Center, Nirvana's *Nevermind* bumped Michael Jackson's *Dangerous* from the top spot on *Billboard's* chart. The 45,000 copies of the album that DGC had shipped—one-third of the pre-orders for *Steady Diet of Nothing*—were gone in days.

The source of the turnabout was obvious: MTV had grabbed hold of the "Teen Spirit" video and was playing it nonstop. Nirvana had been skeptical of their longevity on a major—Cobain predicted, "I imagine we'll get dropped"—but thanks to MTV, they were becoming a pop-music sales phenomenon.

A Bad Brains T-shirt was repeatedly glimpsed in the "Smells Like Teen Spirit" video, but punk's breakthrough did nothing for the struggling band. The quartet's latest incarnation featured Chuck Mosley, former singer of the now-popular Faith No More, with Mackie back on drums. In an interview with *Cake*, when Dr. Know tried to address a question about HR with his usual tact, Darryl Jenifer cut him off: "Fuck him. I have no respect for him, because of his ignorance and inconsideration for others—his brothers." He referred to HR's repeated exits from the band as "freak-outs." Even Dr. Know suggested that HR's actions stemmed from "wanting to play the rock star," not his artistic integrity.

HR was back with Human Rights, playing roots reggae. Paul Cornwell, a new manager who knew the singer from the Madams Organ days, had gotten him onto the reggae circuit. He was as magnetic a performer as ever, and Earl Hudson's drumming remained powerful. But where Bad Brains had once been musical trailblazers, Human Rights was trodding familiar ground.

HR was still being criticized for homophobia and intolerance, and new stories about his instability were circulating, leading former friends to speculate that he might have returned to hard drug use. Hudson's wife Susan, however, suggested that he was in fact "manic depressive."

The singer had assembled a crackerjack band that at one point included former Wailer Al Anderson, but couldn't keep it together, hiring and firing with abandon. At one 9:30 Club show he appeared with a nine-member band, including three guitarists and two keyboardists. "HR can't possibly afford to pay that many people," a source close to the band noted at the time.

Backstage, things were even more anarchic. Although Cornwell was his manager, HR apparently signed management agreements with other people whenever he was short on money.

Cornwell couldn't stop the singer from dealing with others, which greatly complicated his ability to do business for Human Rights. HR's connection to James Keene was particularly troublesome. In 1993, Cornwell described Keene as a "little Brooklyn Mafia dude who has threatened to kill me."

This description seemed to be supported by events that night at 9:30. Keene suddenly appeared at the club, claiming that HR owed him money and that he was taking the proceeds from the gig as payment. When the road manager hired by Cornwell objected, Keene pulled a gun. The road manager resigned on the spot, Keene collected the money, and HR did nothing.

With HR growing more unreliable, Hudson wanted to return to Bad Brains. HR refused to go with him, however, and Jenifer and Dr. Know would not allow him back without his brother. Angry and short on money, Hudson and his wife turned up at a Bad Brains gig in Baltimore to sell Bad Brains shirts they had made. According to Susan Hudson, this angered Tony Countey, who ordered security to stop them. The conflict was resolved and Hudson appeared onstage briefly during the band's set, but the drummer remained bitter. Asked for an interview during this period, he offered to tell the "real story of the Bad Brains"—for $25,000.

x x x

Bikini Kill was settling into its new home, Mount Pleasant. The band had yet to release anything beyond its *Revolution Girl Style Now* tape and tracks on compilations like *Kill Rock Stars, Give Me Back,* or *There's a Dyke in the Pit*, yet was attracting much attention. After the breakthrough of "Smells Like Teen Spirit," Hanna told *Option*, "It's been easy to get publicity, it's been easy to be punk rockers and get away with a lot of shit in society without losing your dignity or selling out."

Still, much of Bikini Kill's support continued to be word of mouth. The band was reaching teenage girls who came to believe, perhaps for the first time, that punk was their story, their drama. Riot Grrrl had decided to do a convention, an event that promised to further focus girl-punk energy.

As it gained popularity, Bikini Kill refused to cooperate with big rock magazines like *Spin*. When an *Option* article appeared to pit them against other female rockers, the musicians denounced the piece from the stage at a New York gig and destroyed a copy of the magazine. In DC, the band members chafed at playing in churches—Positive Force's principal venues—and declined to perform with one local band who had a member accused of abusing a girlfriend. They made a similar decision about an out-of-town band when one of its members wrote an article that appeared condescending toward women.

DC was now home to what were arguably the two most important American punk bands, Bikini Kill and Fugazi. Positive Force brought them together for a benefit to support the upcoming March for Women's Lives in April 1992. Also booked were Ohio's Scrawl and LA's L7, which had helped organize Rock for Choice with the Fund for a Feminist Majority on the West Coast. Some of the money was to go to the Fund, but part would benefit two local pro-choice groups that assisted low-income women, the Planned Parenthood Justice Fund and the Washington Free Clinic.

The show was scheduled for the Citadel Center, but the city revoked the venue's performance license after neighborhood complaints about rowdiness following commercial events there. At the last minute, the benefit had to be split into two nights at the much smaller Sanctuary Theater.

Both nights quickly sold out, and MTV called, asking to cover the event. Most Positive Force members did not want the network's cameras there, but the decision was left to the bands. With the exception of L7—whose representative became angry at the mere suggestion that MTV might be barred—all the bands declined to give permission to film them. Thus rebuffed, MTV did not attempt to cover the show.

On the first night, Scrawl, L7, and Fugazi played strong sets to an crowd that included Joan Jett, by now a Fugazi fanatic. Bikini Kill opened the second show with Hanna—clad in a Riot Grrrl T-shirt—offering a mic to the audience; Reinstein took the invitation and leaped onstage to speak on behalf of Positive Force and Riot Grrrl. With Hanna on bass, Karren on drums, and Wilcox on guitar, the band launched into "Hamster Baby." Over a jagged surf tune, Vail's Yoko Ono-ish screech needled British rock writer Everett True.

Hanna removed her T-shirt to reveal a striped mini-skirt and sheer white nylons. As the band rumbled into the new "Lil' Red Riding Bitch," Hanna acted out the words, grabbing her breast as she sang "these are my tits," turning around to moon the audience for the line "this is my ass."

Hanna was a disturbing yet riveting presence, defiantly touching her crotch as she sang, then slipping into a semi-ironic go-go dance. There was a palpable sexual charge to her movement, but it didn't seem coy or exploitative. It was as much a part of her as her political conscience.

"Don't Need You" disavowed male approval, but tonight—as at many shows—it became a rallying cry for numerous disenfranchised groups. As explained by a lyric sheet the band handed out, the song was also aimed at "dumb corporate rock magazine" *Spin*, which had attacked Hanna after she declined to be interviewed. "Does it scare you, *Spin?*" the singer asked, "That we don't need you?/Us punks/We don't need you."

After smiling broadly at a woman who threw a flower to the band, Hanna played a tape of a man blaming "dumb hos and butt-rocker bitches" for provoking street harassment and rape. (Part of this tape later turned up at the beginning of the Embassy version of "White Boy.") "This song is dedicated to him," Hanna exclaimed, and tore into "Suck My Left One."

"Rebel Girl" was plagued with guitar breakdowns. When Karren—wearing a long black dress that night—threw down his guitar in frustration, Hanna slid into a sardonic bit of Hall and Oates's "Maneater" that led to a short rap. After "Jigsaw Youth," Karren came to the mic to sing a new song that included the lines "George Bush ain't no hero/George Bush is a pig" screeched over and over. The final "Thurston Hearts the Who" was prefaced by Vail's statement that "if abortion is made illegal, it shows not only that we live in a fucked-up, white-male-dominated, patriarchal society, but that they don't even care if we live or die."

As Karren's guitar emitted unearthly feedback, Neuman began to read from an article that called Bikini Kill "confused and contradictory," "activists not musicians," and "man-haters." At the same time, Vail attacked indie cool-mongers and their devotees. Then Hanna leaned over to Reinstein at the front of the stage, who filled the air with high-pitched screams. The song re-materialized out of the chaos, gathering momentum before disintegrating as Karren tossed his guitar into the air and let it crash. Reinstein's screams carried past the music, then faded.

If this spectacle wasn't exactly music, it was obviously something potent and true. Even the shifting of players and instruments—which sometimes could slow the momentum of a set—had only added to the power. Chris Bald, who had been drawn back to the punk scene partly by Bikini Kill, later called the night "one of the two best shows I've ever seen."

For all of Hanna's magnetism, the set demonstrated that the band's totality was its strength. As

Vail later wrote, "We have problems with making clear-cut distinctions between form and content and therefore recognize Bikini Kill's total aesthetic as something which comes together when we play: music, lyrics, lipstick, etc."

The next band, L7, sought to beat the boy-rockers at their own game. The quartet played a metal-tinged set that climaxed with a fire dance by a member of theatrical Richmond metal-punk band Gwar. L7 had an unenviable position, however: following Bikini Kill and preceding Fugazi.

Fugazi was even more jacked up than the previous night. "I think we all know why we are here," MacKaye said, introducing "KYEO." "This is a song about fighting, this is a song about being lulled into a false sense of security. KEEP . . . YOUR . . . EYES . . . OPEN!" After several songs, Picciotto spoke: "Kids are out there fucking—and that's cool, fucking is cool—but when you get into trouble, there are people telling you that your body is your prison. That's bullshit. This is a song about being young, and it's for Bikini Kill." The band ignited "Runaway Return," building to a new song Picciotto called "Rend My Body Politic."

A portion of the night's tickets had been reserved for people coming to town for the march. With this in mind, MacKaye introduced the new "Instrument" by saying that "seeing how a lot of you are visiting Washington, I'll tell you about our fair city. We have a lot of young men who are shooting each other every day. This is about how much the consequences might weigh when they affect you and not just them." The stage, now crowded with people, swayed as the song built to its climax.

Prefacing the final song, MacKaye noted softly that the right to abortion "was never theirs to take away. For those who can afford it, there will always be a choice. The issue is . . . the people who can't." MacKaye turned to the band, then suddenly spun back around, screaming, "I've got some skin/You want to look in?/SUGGESTION!" As the song rose, Amy Pickering danced forward from the back of the stage. As she sang the line, "I've got some skin/You want to look in," she lifted her shirt to flash her bra.

After the song's third crescendo, the band dropped away entirely. Pickering broke the hush: "How many of you think you're going to get pregnant?" When someone called out jokingly, she continued, her voice shaking: "Yeah, it's funny, huh? I didn't think I was going to get pregnant—but I did. And you know what? I went and got an abortion, because I had a choice. And for all you people who may or may not get pregnant—and you'd be surprised how many have or will—I'm going to the march." As the crowd applauded, her voice rose: "I'm going to stand up for the fucking people who can't stand up for themselves . . . because I think it's worth it. Why don't you go and stick up for me—I was lucky, I had a choice . . ." She walked offstage, and a subdued Fugazi began the song's soft pulse. After about 30 seconds, the band stopped suddenly and left without a word.

x x x

By mid-1992, news of Riot Grrrl had spread widely, in part because of coverage by *Sassy* and *LA Weekly*, which published a lengthy article that was reprinted in numerous other free weeklies around the country. Hanna later laughed that "I kind of lied to" the *LA Weekly* writer. "I told her that there were all these Riot Grrrls everywhere and this huge thing is happening—which was like an idea in my head—and lo and behold, it happened!" Indeed, chapters of the group had sprung up in several places, many started by DC participants who went off to school in New York, Olympia, LA, and other cities. The group's growth suggested that teenage girls had a genuine hunger for such support.

Riot Grrrl was also increasingly a target, denounced as "separatist" because it didn't allow men to join. One critic was Justine Demetrick, who organized Boston shows with a group called Tools of the Revolution. Demetrick made common cause with Spitboy, an outspoken all-female Bay Area band then on its first US tour. The group had appeared—as had Bikini Kill and Desiderata—on the *Give Me Back* compilation assembled by McClard, Sonia Skindrud, and Kim Carlyle.

When Spitboy played DC for the first time—at a June Positive Force show at the Peace Center—one of the members announced that it was "not a 'foxcore band,' not a 'girl band,' not a 'Riot Grrrl' band." For many in the audience, the equation of a grassroots punk idea like Riot Grrrl with a media tag like "foxcore" seemed a gratuitous insult.

Shortly after Spitboy's Peace Center show, the Supreme Court upheld Pennsylvania's restrictive abortion law, circumscribing *Roe v. Wade*. Positive Force planned a concert/protest in late July near the court building to oppose not only this decision, but the rightward lurch of the Court on many critical topics. Fugazi, just back from a European tour, Bikini Kill, and a folk duo, Egg and Dudley, would join speakers from Riot Grrrl, the DC Student Coalition Against Racism, the Peace Center, and prison reform group Equal Justice.

MacKaye wanted a simple banner that read "30 Years," an oblique reference to the time the country could expect to live with a far-right Supreme Court if the tide was not soon reversed. The banner artist, Riot Grrrl's Von Vacano—and apparently Bikini Kill—favored a more confrontational message, something along the lines of "Keep Your Hands off My Body" or "Abort the Court." The night before the event, a compromise that satisfied no one was reached: The banner would say "Turn off Your TV."

This conflict was further complicated by tensions between Fugazi and Positive Force. The band was tired of being depicted in the mainstream press as Positive Force's musical auxiliary, and MacKaye was not excited by the group's decision to stage a punk percussion protest as the climax of the event. He felt the idea was played out, and encouraged the group to invent a new approach.

By the time Bikini Kill took the stage, the crowd was swelling toward 1000. With the Capitol dome looming scarcely more than a football field's length away, Hanna told the crowd that "if anyone is fucking with you for certain reasons at this show, let us know, come up here on the stage and get away. It shouldn't be just one person's responsibility to deal with fuckers." Then she began the wrenching "Girl Soldier": "Guess you didn't notice/While we were crying /Guess you didn't give a fuck/After all only women were dying/I am screaming/With my hands and my heart/You spread my legs apart . . ."

The band shifted instruments, with Karren taking the drums and Vail coming to the front. Wearing a T-shirt advertising both Madonna and Ignition, she dedicated "Hamster Baby" to Bald, whose face was grotesquely swollen from a pistol-whipping inflicted during a robbery attempt days before while he was going home from work at Ferrando's Logan Circle restaurant, Dante's. When the song ended, Hanna baited the crowd with a "Go Redskins Go" cheer and an a capella rendition of Hall and Oates's "Rich Girl." Then "Jigsaw Youth" began and Hanna exploded into a frenzied go-go

TENSION BETWEEN PF AND FUGAZI
by Mark Andersen

This had been an issue ever since Fugazi's politics began to be equated with the *SOTU* boycott list; shortly before this protest, the *Post* had described Fugazi as "the leading exponents of a musical movement called Positive Force," following that up with an explanation of Positive Force as "Fugazi's street army." Ian had also argued that the percussion protest had become what it initially sought to subvert: "protest as usual." We understood Ian's point, but lacking better ideas—and facing many pressing issues, including disputes with the Capitol Police—PF went forward with the percussion protest.

The day was further complicated by the fact that, in effect, RG and Bikini Kill became partners in approving the mechanics of the event. This only made sense; still, there was a bit of the "too many cooks can spoil the broth" in the air. All of this pre-event wrangling, added to Fugazi's weariness, lent a certain tense undercurrent to the proceedings, especially for me, as I was feeling caught in the middle.

dance: "I can sell my body if I wanna/God knows you already sold your mind/I may sell my body for money sometimes/But you can't stop the fire/That burns inside of me . . ."

The song seemed to be part of the ongoing process of accepting one's self, piecing together an authentic life amid the debris of childhood abuse. The same conflicted yet vibrant spirit animated "Resist Psychic Death"—with Hanna pointing at the Capitol as she sang "Your world not mine/Your world not ours"—"Don't Need You," and "Rebel Girl."

Hanna introduced "Suck My Left One" with a mini-manifesto: "This next song was written because there are all kinds of different ways to resist. You might look at some girl and say, 'Oh, she's not a feminist, she looks like a mall girl,' she wears Limited clothes so she doesn't exist. And that's bullshit because we're all in different places. Then there are poor girls who usually get reputations as sluts a lot easier than rich ones do, and there's all sorts of different stuff to do with race and class and gender . . ." Hanna paused, caught up in emotion. "My sister Mary is here today. When guys used to say stuff to her in Chevy Chase by the Metro she used to reply with this. So, this song is for her, because she wrote it."

Charged by Hanna's palpable love for her sister, this performance of the song carried a sense of triumph while it evoked street harassment and abuse. As the band switched instruments, Hanna pointed to the Capitol. "I don't have to ask my dad for permission anymore when I go out at night, so why should I have to ask them for permission to have an abortion? I think we need to start our own things where we don't have to ask the government for permission anymore. That means starting self-help groups and learning about healthcare and our own bodies and teaching each other about our bodies. We have to get over the polite thing, like 'you don't spread your pussy and stick your fingers in' or 'you don't look at your girlfriend's clit.' We have to learn to do pelvic exams and do menstrual extractions." As the crowd cheered Hanna's advocacy of this illegal procedure, she threw up her hands and said, "So arrest me."

After a few speakers, Fugazi took the stage, looking a bit weary from the long tour. As the band began the instrumental "Sweet and Low," MacKaye pointed into the distance: "That's the Capitol, the Supreme Court is over there. I've lived here my whole life and I've never been in there. I'm not really sure exactly what goes on in there anyway. I used to think that [our rights] were carved in stone. Obviously, I was mistaken. What's next: the right to vote?"

Many women and girls, energized by Bikini Kill, didn't want to relinquish their space at the front of the stage. As Fugazi shifted into "Blueprint," however, a pit began to form, pushing the crowd forward and trapping the girls against the stage. As Fugazi revved up, a fuse blew, interrupting the song. Angered at being crushed, Reinstein climbed up and walked across the stage, flipping off the crowd as she left.

Canty kept the beat going for a while, but it took fifteen minutes to restore power. While the band smoothly finished "Blueprint," the atmosphere had changed. Rough dancing started again, and Picciotto tersely admonished one crowd-surfer to "have a seat, boy." At the song's end, MacKaye pleaded, "Don't push on the stage. And boys: Please stop jumping on people's heads."

Picciotto's desperate voice challenged the occupants of the gleaming white buildings all around: "Why don't you come to my house?/Why don't you drag me right out?" It was the song Picciotto had called "Rend My Body Politic" at the April pro-choice show, and its relevance to the moment was obvious. As the song lurched forward, the crowd appeared to answer MacKaye's plea, abandoning crowd-surfing and easing the frantic dancing.

If the crowd's response was heartening for a band used to far worse in most cities it played, it was still uncomfortably rough for many. Most of the women and girls had been driven from the front of the stage. "We ended up all having to leave because it was just too violent and we were all getting hurt," said Reinstein. "So we were sort of standing on the side of the stage, complaining to each other and getting really mad because this always happened."

What came next was a concrete example of the girls' intention to redefine the punk scene. "We went back, started holding hands, and formed this circle," Reinstein recalled. "We were like, 'No one's coming in this circle, this is a girls-only space.' It was right in the middle of the 'pit' and all these girls started joining it, and it became this really big circle. It was this really powerful thing where something that had been really violent and threatening for a lot of us became a safe space and we were protecting each other."

As the girls moved back into the crowd, Picciotto came to the mic: "When you are in school, if you take civics, you learn that the Supreme Court is the last stop for justice in the land. Well, today's lesson is that if their laws don't reflect our reality, we don't have to fucking obey them." As the crowd roared its approval, Picciotto continued: "So, like Kathleen said, they can take our rights, but they can't take away our action. So do what you got to do." With that, Fugazi threw itself into "Dear Justice Letter."

The band seemed to have found its groove, but the girls' circle was meeting growing resistance. "There were a lot of really ugly confrontations in between songs," Reinstein said. "It was kind of a really big deal that we had 'interfered with the pit.'" Angered by the repeated invasions of the space, Riot Grrrl member Mary Fondriest punched a slamdancer in the face, bloodying his lip.

MacKaye caught sight of the confrontation and asked, "Let's not fight, please." When the girls appeared to take this as a rebuke, he backpedaled: "I'm not saying you, particularly, I'm just saying in general." Nonetheless, his comments were not appreciated. "We were trying to do this really incredibly positive thing," said Reinstein. "We were taking back our space, right in the middle of what used to be this huge violent pit that Fugazi supposedly doesn't even support. I totally felt unsupported by the band."

While the Riot Grrrls considered MacKaye's comments condescending, he thought the audience reasonably well-behaved, given its size, and Fondriest's response excessive. The incident did not noticeably hinder the protest that unfolded after the concert. By the end of Fugazi's set, at least 2000 people were there, and almost half of them marched to the Supreme Court for a raucous demonstration that included—of all things—an impromptu version of Twisted Sister's "We're Not Gonna Take It."

The following week, the Riot Grrrl Convention took place, attended by more than 100 girls—and more than a few boys—from across the

A POWERFUL NEW ENERGY
by Mark Andersen

Over the months, I could see the galvanizing impact of this girl revolution. Long-standing power relations in the scene were clearly being disrupted; if this could bring some discomfort to me or other male punk authority figures, over all, it was inspirational.

The transformation seemed apparent in individual girls and women I had long known in the scene. These words, written by Jasmine Kerns just after the Riot Grrrl Convention, seem to capture a bit of the energy of the moment: "It makes my toes tingle every time I think of a RG meeting where we supported each other through hard times and helped each other deal with the daily subliminal sexism we endure . . . building up our self-esteem and self-love, something I had little to none of a year before. I fucking love you grrrls and will NEVER forget the summer of 1992, the summer of Revolution Grrrl Style Now."

While Jasmine's words might sound a bit over the top, they simply expressed what I had seen blossom over the year. As Jen Smith had written in *Girl Germs* #3, "Motherfucker, I want to FORCE the issue. This injustice has been unsung for too long . . . I don't feel inclined to point the finger but I am willing to give the finger when need be and if that's alienating then tuff shit because some things need to be done . . . For now I take this ardent stand, to stand by my woman, to be for her and then maybe she can be for me. And I hear these girls, girls I don't know, girls I have never met, make these same promises and these same threats. They speak to me and I speak to you and I know our time has come . . ."

Jen had already made the leap from spectator to participant through Bratmobile DC, a new band, Haymaker, and the 'zine *Red Rover* which first appeared at the RG Convention. Numerous others in DC were in the midst of the same process, coming to voice, willing to stand up to longstanding leaders of the scene—including myself—creating something new and challenging of their own . . . something beautiful and hopeful. None of us realized, however, the huge challenge waiting just around the corner.

country. The members of Bratmobile and Heavens to Betsy, a new feminist-punk phenom, had completed their US tour in time to attend. While Bikini Kill did not participate as a band—apparently because of fears that it would be seen as Riot Grrrl's leader—its members were there individually. "It was only seven dollars for three days of housing and events," Hanna exulted. "There was a show every night, including an all-girl dance, and we had workshops on domestic violence and body image and racism and rape."

The workshops were mostly all-female, but other events were open to a mixed audience. Perhaps most important was that the event was organized by girls and women with only minimal input from men. The energy of Bikini Kill, Bratmobile, Toomey and Thomson's Simple Machines, Jen Smith, Christina Billotte, and many others had dramatically altered the DC punk scene. Indeed, RG-related energy would soon surface even in hardcore, through the "Chicks Up Front Posse" initiated by several DC-area girls including PF veterans Daisy and Margaret Rooks.

Revolution Girl Style Now had been first declared by Bikini Kill in early 1991. In barely more than a year, the girl-punk upheaval had taken on a life of its own. But Riot Grrrl's trajectory would soon be impacted by the massive success of Bikini Kill's old ally Nirvana. The ugly noise of the misfit, the rebel, and the fuck-up was about to emerge from its subterranean home into the glare of the mainstream media spotlight.

ISSUE 628 • APRIL 16TH, 1992 • $2.95 • CAN $3.50

RolliStone ®

NEW FACES OF ROCK · 1·9·9·2·

ORPORAT AGAZINE STILL SUCK

NIRVANA

> "Merchandise keeps us in line/Common sense says it's by design
> What could a businessman ever want more/Than to have us sucking in his store?"
> —Fugazi, "Merchandise"

KURT COBAIN, CHRIS NOVOSELIC, AND DAVE GROHL OF NIRVANA (by Mark Seliger)

merchandise

In late 1992, a new ad began airing during teen-oriented TV shows like *Beverly Hills, 90210* and *Star Trek: The Next Generation*. In it, a slightly scruffy young man extolled the virtues of the latest Subaru product by comparing it to . . . punk rock.

The ad soon disappeared, but the phenomenon it represented didn't. With the unexpected ascent of "Smells Like Teen Spirit," punk had been transformed from a contentious outsider into another mainstream pop-music trend.

Fugazi had rebuffed *Rolling Stone*, but DC punk ended up on the magazine's cover anyway, in the form of Dave Grohl. He was pictured next to Kurt Cobain, who had scrawled a paraphrase of an old SST Records slogan onto the plain white T-shirt he wore: "Corporate Magazines Still Suck." The gesture did not change the fact that the band was a DGC recording act on the cover of *Rolling Stone*; Grohl admitted the band had become a "living contradiction."

The same issue featured an article declaring Seattle the "new Liverpool," home to not only Nirvana but also Soundgarden, Alice in Chains, and Pearl Jam. Even "grunge" pioneer Mudhoney had signed to a major label, for which it recorded a song that dismissed the media hoopla over Seattle as "overblown." Dave Grohl laughed that "people are moving to Seattle because that's where they heard the major labels are going to sign bands."

In an interview with *Matrix*, a suburban Virginia high school literary magazine, Grohl noted that "when I got into punk, the attitude was 'kill all the rock stars.' I was never into anything that was in the Top Ten. A lot of the people buying *Nevermind* are the people we're pointing the finger at— the total macho jock scumbags that everybody knows. Everything we have to say about sexism, everything we have to say about racism, it just goes over a lot of people's heads."

As Grohl wrestled with his new band's new audience, his hometown's musical underground appeared to be flourishing, drawing the attention of music moguls and media alike. As one longtime DC punk Scott Crawford noted, "It's hard not to crack a knowing smile when this country's fickle tastemasters herald DC as 'the next Seattle.' Time was, the ones in the know used this city as the barometer for the rest of the US indie lexicon to measure up against."

With new labels, new venues, and a growing network of group houses, DC had become something of the "new youth mecca" the Nation of Ulysses prophesied, attracting outsiders to join the scene. As the *Washington Post* noted, "The new bands are not all that concerned with conventional success. In fact, there's a positively anti-celebrity, anti-success feeling—definitely anti-conventional rock'n'roll."

As the community grew, it inevitably became less unified. It also seemed increasingly a music scene, with explicit politics less pronounced. Still, Positive Force continued to play a central role, and there was the new influence of what Jen Smith termed "revolutionary girl soul force." 'Zines and spoken word performances inspired by Riot Grrrl went beyond sexism, homophobia, and sexual abuse to issues of race, class, and animal rights. Where gay, lesbian, and bisexual punks had once been largely closeted, they now were frequently as open as their heterosexual counterparts.

In the post-*Nevermind* world, a new question became significant: Were DC bands in the underground by choice or by chance? A *Newsweek* article, "Searching for Nirvana II," captured the moment. Illustrated with a picture of Hole's Courtney Love, recently married to Cobain—a Nation of Ulysses poster visible behind her on the wall—the article reported that "the record industry is jumping through hoops to court punk bands. Feeding frenzies of this sort are nothing new to the industry. What's new is that this one is for punk acts, distinguished largely by their stance against the record industry. According to Marc Geiger, an A&R man at Def American Recordings, 'The bands that were worth $5000 a couple years ago are worth $250,000 now.'"

As *Newsweek* noted, "Punk bands remain relatively low-maintenance—they don't need to be promoted to radio, which is the industry's biggest cash drain. And with MTV, they can reach a national audience anyway. The companies are content to lose money on most of the acts (85 percent of all major-label releases lose money) in the hope of making $50 million on one Nirvana."

The *Post* suggested that, besides Fugazi, Washington had a half dozen punk bands worthy of major-label interest: Nation of Ulysses, Shudder to Think, Jawbox, Unrest, Bikini Kill, and Bratmobile. Yet Fugazi's anti-industry stance—supported by bands like Nation of Ulysses and Bikini Kill—suggested that DC punk would not be easily purchased.

"At dinner with Fugazi and Bikini Kill in a ramshackle house called the Embassy in the Mount Pleasant neighborhood of DC," *LA Weekly* recounted, "the talk isn't about taking over society, but remaining outside it. Former underground heroes Nirvana have just made the cover of *Rolling Stone*. Fugazi's Ian MacKaye stares at the cover: Kurt Cobain wearing a 'Corporate Magazines Still Suck' T-shirt. 'Can you believe this?' MacKaye asks. 'This is just so weird.' He riffles through the pages. 'And here's Henry Rollins. Fuck!' As they sit on sprung couches, eating pale orange vegetarian mush and drinking water, the idea of Nirvana hitting the Top 40 makes them lose their appetites. 'Everyone's signing to major labels,' says a bewildered MacKaye, 'except the people in this room.' 'Yeah,' says Hanna, and she's certain they never will."

According to Sub Pop co-owner Jonathan Poneman, "It's not a matter of destroying the music industry, it's a question of being able to be included. Egalitarian revolution—that's what makes Nirvana a punk band." Tobi Vail disagreed: "Now, more than ever, it's the time to forge the underground idea, 'cuz in the face of corporate co-option, us true punks gotta stick together. Some of my best friends are in bands that are on major labels and I respect their choice, but it's not the sound of the revolution."

Tim Yohannon reprinted the *Newsweek* article in *Maximum RockNRoll*, accompanied by fierce commentary: "Punk has absolutely nothing in common with corporate label$, with their $pirit-$ucking opportuni$m, or with their anti-democratic structure . . . or with the fuckhead bands that $ign with them. So, a big FUCK YOU and good riddance to the likes of Butthole Surfers, Flipper, Hole, Nirvana, L7 . . . and to all the 'fans' who, like the hippies, can't see where all this is leading."

Kurt Cobain responded unapologetically: "I should be really guilty about success, I should be living out the old punk rock threat, denying everything commercial, sticking in my own little world, and not really making an impact on anyone other than the people who are already aware of what I am complaining about. It's preaching to the converted." A punk civil war was soon raging full force.

In DC, an angry split erupted at Positive Force House when Simple Machines invited MTV into the building to tape a segment on independent labels without consulting all the other residents. Their label had become so successful that Jenny Toomey and Kristin Thomson were already planning to relocate to its own house, but now the move happened in an atmosphere of anger and recrimination.

After the Riot Grrrl Convention, the press also descended on that group, whose founders soon feared that excessive media scrutiny could create a distorted image. The first condescending salvo was fired by *USA Today*, which warned, "Better watch out, boys. From hundreds of once pink, frilly bedrooms, comes the young feminist revolution. And it's not pretty. But it doesn't wanna be. So there!"

The article did reveal Riot Grrrl's existence to a new audience—including, no doubt, some young girls—but the account of the movement was almost unrecognizable to those who had started it. Even things that were apparently meant to be helpful—like publishing the addresses of 'zines like *Fantastic Fanzine, Gunk*, or *Girl Germs*—backfired when the publications were described as free, burying the publishers with orders they couldn't afford to fill. After calling Riot Grrrls "punkettes," the article ended with a pat on the head: "The more things change, the more they stay the same."

The journalistic pack closed in, having temporarily exhausted topics like Seattle, Nirvana, and Lollapolooza, and fed by a post–*Thelma and Louise* uptick in media interest in feminism. Over the next nine months, it was almost impossible to pick up a magazine without seeing some new—and generally inaccurate, patronizing, or simply dumb—article on Riot Grrrl. Many made simple factual errors, or repeated other stories' mistakes. "Girl riot" originator Jen Smith was confused with Mecca Normal's Jean Smith in one early article, a blunder then parroted by numerous other reporters.

After refusing entreaties from ABC News and Sally Jesse Raphael, Riot Grrrl–DC proposed a press blackout. Most RG chapters—which didn't quite number in "the hundreds" touted by *USA Today*—agreed. In an interview with DC punk Melissa Klein for *off our backs*, a DC-based feminist newspaper, Hanna said, "*Interview* magazine called us yesterday. Maria Shriver wants us on her show. That's scary as shit. I know that we are tokens. I have no fucking illusions that these people give a shit what I have to say for real. I do think that people want to stare at my tits, want to see me put my foot in my mouth, to see us fuck up. They can control what we're doing by labeling it and ghettoizing it and putting it in some weird box. I won't let that happen."

The assumption that the members of Bikini Kill were authorities on or the leaders of

MTV SPARKS A PAINFUL SPLIT
by Mark Andersen

The divisions between Jenny and myself had grown to explosive proportions; the encroachment of the corporate rock world into punk only added to the tension. For me, the final spark came when Simple Machines invited MTV–a company I despised–into the Positive Force House. In our next house meeting, my attack on Jenny led her to a blistering recitation of my own failings within the house; soon we were barely on speaking terms.

Riot Grrrl became ever more grating, and the musicians began refusing virtually all interviews. "Bikini Kill declared the 'Revolution Girl Style Now,'" Vail later wrote. "Riot Grrrl came out of this declaration but has gone on to decide what it meant for themselves."

Ironically, underground opinion-makers were often far more critical of Riot Grrrl than was the mainstream press. Lawrence Livermore dismissed the group arrogantly in a *Lookout!* fanzine article entitled "Riot Frrrumps." Even another punk feminist, Karin Gembus, reported "rumors" in *Maximum RockNRoll* that Riot Grrrl was boycotting not only Spitboy but also Born Against and the Nation of Ulysses as well. These would have been interesting developments, if true—but they weren't, as Gembus could have discovered with one phone call. Nonetheless, the gossip was repeated as fact by *Flipside* the following month.

One article charged that "Kathleen Hanna believes that feminism should exclude men"—even though Hanna was in a band with a male guitarist who she called a "brother in the struggle." The band's decision not to allow men they didn't know to photograph them—adopted after an ugly encounter with a sleazy male photographer—led to reports that Bikini Kill didn't allow any men to take pictures of them. In fact, the cover photo of the band's newly released album had been shot by male DC photographer Pat Graham.

If Bikini Kill was clamorous and confrontational, the band's girl-love slogan "encourage in the face of insecurity" was genuine. Hanna in particular supported other women and girls far beyond the call of duty. Ironically, she was able to do this because of the flexibility provided by working as a stripper.

As she told Klein, "I fucking feed my friends. I take care of my friends when they are sick. I am the one person in this community who gives girls rides home at night. People call me and come to my house when they're sexually abused and talk to me. I can do that because I don't have to get up and go to work at six in the morning. This allows me to be basically a sexual abuse counselor for people when I need to be and to not have to go to work for the Man five days a week and make shit money. I make enough money in two days a week that I can live off it and support other people at certain times."

By the latter half of 1992, disillusionment with the DC scene—as well as general homesickness—had set in. When Bikini Kill began a fall US tour, its return plans were unclear. Meanwhile, Bratmobile was again on hiatus, the members living in three different cities after Neuman's move to the Bay Area.

The new *Pottymouth* was largely recorded with Tim Green in the Embassy basement, but the trio wasn't really around DC much anymore.

Bikini Kill's old ally, the Nation of Ulysses, had continued touring the US and Europe. The band proclaimed that they had seceded from the USA, recognized youth as an oppressed class, and—as a gesture of solidarity with youth—would remain 18 forever. Their stated intent was "the total annihilation of the USA and all of its weak and infernal pawns, until our boundaries are limitless." Their new album announced the Nation of Ulysses' "insurrectional phase" and the end of music itself.

Missing their humor and creativity, some considered the band's image its major selling point, but the music advanced the rhetoric, justifying *Melody Maker*'s judgment that *Plays Pretty for Baby* was a "great punk album." Beneath the twisted syntax, fractured rhythms, grand pronouncements, and references to Mao, Bad Brains, the Beatles, and countless other sources, the band was increasingly accomplished, even visionary.

The Nation's answer to its critics was continual evolution, shedding skins like a snake. By the time the album was released, the band had almost an entire set of new material, which it revealed at a packed Peace Center show with Bratmobile in July 1992. The quintet's solidarity was not as stalwart as its communiqués suggested, however. Soon after the Peace Center show, Steve Kroner—who had been in, out, and back in—left for good.

Even some of the Nation's friends seemed a bit disenchanted. In "Lil' Red Riding Bitch," Bikini Kill charged, "You are not the victim/Tho you'd like to make it that way/Pretty girls all gather round/To hear your side of things/Your s-s-s-s-s-sh-sh-sh-shining path." Jen Smith dissented gently in her 'zine, *Red Rover*: "We prefer to stay in the territory of the familiar and cool, unthreatened, unthreatening, SAFE . . . in that kind of fragmented, exclusive, and easy revolution, an eternal youth agenda seems kind of useless and untrue." Another disillusioned friend remarked that "'revolution' isn't about staying up late and drinking a lot of coffee."

For many of Riot Grrrl's originators, 1991 had been their revolution summer. A year later, the spirit was fading. As Bikini Kill left DC on tour, the Nation of Ulysses—now down to four members—was returning from what would be its final mission. Tim Green deserted just before a 9:30 Club show with Beat Happening, signaling the band's end. Around the same time, Bikini Kill decided to remain in Olympia.

The simultaneous loss of both bands was a major blow to the more militant faction of the DC scene. Yet harDCore and its offshoots was still inspiring people both in Washington and beyond. Sonic Youth's Thurston Moore, who once included Faith and Minor Threat in a *Spin* magazine list of the "Seven Greatest Bands of all Time," explained that a new song, "Youth Against Fascism," was "basically written about some young punk rock kids in DC who protest against the oppression of women and minorities in America." He'd seen "these kids outside the White House banging on pots and pans"—the PF/Fugazi punk percussion protest.

Fugazi remained committed, and in August played another free show at Fort Reno, supporting the ongoing struggle to the keep the Neighborhood Planning Council open—which succeeded when a political compromise saved the group from eviction. Then the band spent two weeks at a house in rural Connecticut, working out new songs. If this retreat suggested that the band's tour schedule was taking a toll, the musicians returned with plenty of new material. After preliminary work in a basement studio, the band traveled to Steve Albini's studio to record a new album.

After these sessions, Fugazi worked with Positive Force on two late-October shows: an inner city benefit at Sanctuary Theater with Britain's Chumbawamba and the Basque band Negu Gorriak, followed by a pro-choice concert with Lungfish and Womyn of Destruction at a Baltimore union hall. At the latter gig, Fugazi debuted "Returning the Screw," which MacKaye described as "a song about fighting back." As the song rose from a hushed yet insistent intro to its roaring crescendo, it seemed a poison pen letter addressed to Reagan and Bush.

A week later, centrist Democrat Bill Clinton was elected president, a transition that did little to change American society or the situation in Washington, where the city's own figures showed there weren't enough beds to accommodate the thousands of homeless. When a battle erupted over the proposed closing of a shelter in Foggy Bottom, the staff rebelled. They and the people who lived there occupied the shelter; among those who joined the protest was Tomas Squip.

Squip's coworker Pete Farina contacted Positive Force, which approached Fugazi to perform at the besieged homeless shelter to focus attention on the situation. The band quickly agreed, but before the plan could be realized the city stormed the shelter and arrested everyone within, including Squip and Farina.

The protest was then relocated to the city government's own front yard: Freedom Plaza, directly across Pennsylvania Avenue from the District Building, Washington's city hall. The protest was scheduled for a Friday afternoon to maximize the disruption of business-as-usual. Hoping to minimize costs, Positive Force decided not to arrange for a backup generator; partly as a result, the show would become the single most confusing and frustrating Positive Force/Fugazi collaboration.

As organizers set up the portable stage, they encountered their first problem. Disregarding a painstakingly negotiated understanding, the on-site staffperson would only allow use of half of the electricity sources promised, arguing that the event should only need that amount of power. After strenuous objections, the staffer promised to be around to help if there were problems.

Following speeches by advocates for the homeless and MacKaye's short explanation of the event's genesis, Fugazi began "Blueprint." As sound technicians Joey P. and Shawn Vitale struggled to adjust the mix, the city staffer instructed organizers to reduce the volume or he would cut the power. As the band went into "Reclamation," its second number, the soundmen agreed to turn the sound down at the song's end. The city employee threatened that if there were noise complaints, the power would be cut. He then disappeared into the crowd—not to be seen again that day.

Unaware of this dialogue, Fugazi went straight into "Walken's Syndrome," only to lose power on part of the stage halfway through the song. Fortunately, it was only an onstage breaker that had flipped. After Vitale got the equipment going again, the band played "Facet Squared" and then "Dear Justice Letter." As that song built to its climax, the power went out again.

One of the two power sources was now gone. Vitale frantically rewired the system to run off the remaining power source, and rumors of city treachery spread through the crowd. This was "about as direct as they were in closing down the Foggy Bottom shelter," MacKaye remarked caustically.

Fugazi made it through "Repeater" only to have the power disappear entirely during the next song. Although by this time organizers had been appealing for help from the stage for most of an hour, the city staffer did not materialize; oddly enough, given past confrontations, no police were apparent at any time during the afternoon.

The homeless advocates present were certain the city was responsible, and proposed an impromptu rush-hour traffic blockade. As the organizers debated what to do, Guy Picciotto grabbed a megaphone, and jokingly told the more than a thousand attendees, "Please, young people, whatever you do, don't cause a disturbance and burn things." MacKaye took the megaphone next and made a mock tearful plea to the building across the street: "Will someone from the city please come turn the power back on? Someone help us please!"

The crowd laughed, but tension was rising. As a last resort, a call went to the city employee who had worked with Positive Force to issue the permit. Horrified to hear what was happening, she rushed to the site to restore the power. In the confusion, the on-site staffer had apparently returned and left, for his van had disappeared. Fortunately, the other city employee was true to her word and the gig was soon underway again.

A stocking cap pulled low over his eyes, Picciotto said, "OK, we're going to play some more and the power's gonna go out and we're gonna trash it all." With that, the band went into "Turnover." The power stayed on, and Picciotto threw off his cap and drove the song home. With the band finally able to establish some momentum, the crowd began to come to life. With lines like "I'm paid to stand around," the new "Public Witness Program" seemed an apt indictment of the city's inaction in the face of the needs of the homeless. At the song's end, the power went out, concluding the afternoon. It had been a tough day for all concerned, but it showed that Fugazi remained willing to attempt harnessing anger with art.

x x x

The band's example was a quiet rebuke to the increasingly businesslike national punk scene. "Fugazi is sending a shock wave through the underground scene," noted Ben Weasel in *Maximum RockNRoll*. "Bands are starting to make more demands on promoters for lower door prices and kinder bouncers. Whether that's because they've finally figured out that they have the power to make such changes or because they're feeling pressured to do so can't be known but it's happening. Most are still taking baby steps, [but] the Fugazi phenomenon is creating a domino effect of sorts."

MacKaye found it "funny as shit how some bands get really irritated at us about this stuff. If they don't like it, they can fuck off." Still, he added, "I don't have problems with bands who do their business differently than us. Punks are way too busy policing how other people operate. Our point is not what other people do, our point is what we do." Having repelled representatives of most of the major labels, Fugazi remained happily on Dischord.

While the members of Fugazi were cautious about criticizing other bands by name, some fans arrived at their own conclusions. When Fugazi played Chicago, it cost five dollars. With the same promoter and venue, Bad Religion tickets were $16. Rap-punk-industrial band Consolidated was known for its radical politics, but faced much criticism of its approach to the business of music; it finally recorded a track listing all the group's inconsistencies and admitting, "We're not Fugazi."

In Ben Weasel's article, the members of Bad Religion noted that two of them had children and one who went to graduate school full time. "We can't do our business like Fugazi," argued bassist Jay Bentley, "even if we wanted to." *Jersey Beat*'s Jim Testa agreed: "Fugazi live like monks. They tour constantly, live in communal houses. Real people don't live like that."

If some viewed the members of Fugazi as so ascetic as to be unreal, they still faced criticism from punk purists. "Fugazi is touring through commercial club land," protested a Belgian punk in a letter to *Maximum RockNRoll*. "They argue that the band draws such large crowds that they have to play these big clubs. Bullshit! They can play a small independent club several times or play in towns not so far away from each other or unannounced or under another name." In the same issue, another correspondent wrote that "Fugazi are getting too damn big for their own good. There is an easy solution for Fugazi to consider if they ever want to get back to their punk roots—change their name. If they became Sperm Whale Patrol or something, they would lose their college crowd and MTV boneheads and attract their true, give-a-damn fans."

The view from *Rolling Stone* was quite different. When Fugazi refused to be interviewed for a proposed article, that magazine's Michael Azerrad settled for a review of the band's packed show at New York's Ritz. He declared Fugazi "one of this country's few truly underground bands," noting the qualities that made the band unique: no major label contract, self-released records, little or no self-promotion, no merchandise, five-dollar all-ages shows, and regular confrontation of any violence.

In addition, he wrote, "the group's rant-anthems relentlessly stump for social justice. [They are] as committed and outspoken as only political rappers seem to be these days. In concert, as well as in theory, Fugazi exists to demolish complacency by confounding expectations. Its unpredictable, stop-and-go arrangements are a musical metaphor. MacKaye is iconoclastic enough to decry slam-dancing, a commonplace of thrash concerts. From both sides of the stage, the Ritz show was a volcanic outpouring of righteous indignation, every bit as cathartic as it was inflammatory. For a measly fin, ticket buyers get intense, impassioned performances that make Fugazi perhaps America's best live band."

Yet the fanzine *Edith*, reviewing the same show, griped that "the last time I felt this far away from the music and the musicians was when I saw U2 in 1987 at a 17,000-seat arena. The song 'Merchandise' made me cry because of the Ritz and the whole atmosphere of the show." While admitting that he might have been "spoiled" by having seen Fugazi in venues like church basements, the writer concluded that "it's time that Fugazi begins to eliminate their dealings with sleazy, shitty, corporate promoters. Even if that does mean playing two weeks straight in the big cities or skipping cities altogether—'cos isn't all this about forsaking convenience for what's right?"

MacKaye was frustrated by such comments. "To some people, we can't seem to do anything right," he said. "People become very suspicious of anybody that sells that many records—'they must have sold out'—whatever the fuck that means. I personally never believed that. I always thought that it could be done."

Weary of the scale of the band's shows, Picciotto admitted that "some days, Fugazi seems like a monster, just too big." After a New Haven gig was marred by violent confrontations with Nazi skins, MacKaye told an interviewer that "I wondered why I was still doing this at 30 years of age"—and then provided his own answer: "We ultimately do the band for ourselves." He later added that "Fugazi is part of a community in DC. That's our primary allegiance. It has supported us and got us to wherever we are. We think that community is very fragile, very precious. It's much more important to us than 'X' amount of 100,000 records sold or whatever. That does not interest us."

A new song that accused "You would make a great cop" evoked a post–Rodney King America and Fugazi's experience with a deceitful *Spin* writer, but it also scorched the self-appointed punk scene police. Otherwise, the band went about its business. Having rejected the album recorded and mixed with Albini, the musicians went and re-recorded the whole thing at Inner Ear with Ted Niceley and Don Zientara. The result was possibly the best representation yet of Fugazi's live fury.

x x x

Elsewhere, the lines between the underground and the corporate world were blurring. Major labels were buying up indies or allying with them, as in Matador Records' distribution deal with Atlantic Records. Several DC acts signed to major labels in this period, including Manifesto, Lucy Brown,

Clutch, and the reunited Obsessed; so did LA's Wool (the Stahl brothers' new outfit) and New York's Gumball (with ex–Velvet Monkeys Don Fleming and later Malcolm Riviera).

Perhaps the most noteworthy of these was a new version of Bad Brains. After firing Chuck Mosley, the band held an open audition for a new singer at the New York club Wetlands. When the new lineup debuted at the 1992 New Music Seminar, it was clear that 22-year-old Israel Joseph I could hold his own. He sang such potent new songs as "Rise," "Coming in Numbers," and "Free" with conviction and skill. Epic soon signed the band, which began work on its first major-label album.

In stark contrast, HR was struggling. Human Rights was barely still together, without a recording contract and unable to tour. For at least part of this period, the singer was homeless. According to ex-manager Paul Cornwell, HR had sold all rights to his songs and the Bad Brains name to pay back debts. After an arrest for vagrancy and a short jail sentence, HR turned up on the doorstep of his old Madams Organ buddy Mic Lowe. He agreed to let HR stay for a few days in a basement room that was vacant between the departure of the old tenant and the arrival of the new one.

When it came time to leave, HR would not. Instead, he informed Lowe that he "lived here now" and that the new tenant should find another place. When tension rose, HR attacked one of Lowe's housemates and barricaded himself in the basement. Such old friends as Russell Braen tried to persuade him to leave, but HR insisted on his claim to the room.

He did eventually leave, moving briefly to his parents', then to his friend Roy Benn's house in Northeast DC. There he got into a wrangle with SST over an advance for a recording called *Peace and Justice* which he had also pitched—unsuccessfully—to Dischord. After leaving Benn's house, HR drifted to the home of longtime friend Sid McCray, the man who first exposed Bad Brains to punk. But when HR insisted on denouncing and threatening Darryl Jenifer—who remained one of McCray's best friends—he was asked to leave there as well.

Benn briefly assumed the role of HR's manager, and set up a show for Human Rights at a Blagden Alley arts space run by a group called the Betapunks. But with poor publicity, bad weather, and competition with other shows, almost no one showed up. Discouraged, the band didn't even play; it dissolved shortly thereafter. At a New York show that Benn booked, HR arrived alone and proceeded to sing along with a tape he presented to the sound engineer.

Many speculated about what was wrong, but Paul Cornwell thought he knew. "Let's just say the word: schizophrenia. Joseph won't go to a doctor, so a total diagnosis is not possible, but that's his problem. Joseph could be counseled, with medication he could be helped to control his behavior, his panic attacks, but he refuses to accept the fact that he's ill. He's got a heart of gold, but he refuses to take help."

x x x

While Riot Grrrl withdrew from the spotlight and Fugazi and Positive Force stayed the course, Simple Machines became Washington's leading punk outreach group. The *Washington Post* credited the label with leading "a recording revolution, an uprising in homemade production, distribution, and consumption of post-punk pop music." Along with Teenbeat and WGNS Studios, the label was "creating the new sound of young America with an equally innocent, alternative approach to the business of music."

The *Post* headline said it all: "Hey Gang, LET'S PUT OUT A RECORD!" Toomey and Thomson not only waved the DIY banner, but provided tools for other aspiring creators. As the article noted, part of their basic operating creed was "to pass on skills and information to avoid reinventing the wheel." From 1989, when Toomey and Thomson helped assemble Positive Force's "You Can Do It!" booklet to their own expanded "Mechanic's Guide to Putting Out Music" booklet in 1991, they had consistently shared their nuts-and-bolts knowledge, helping anyone who called or wrote.

"There is an explosion of small labels," Toomey noted, and Simple Machines was a major cause. The label had already mailed 2000 copies of the booklet, many in response to a mention in *Sassy*. "Now we get at least one [record] a week from someone who says they have used the guide," Toomey said.

Simple Machines was known for playful, elaborate packaging and a personal touch. The label even had a clothing line, Cog Wear, created by silk-screening its sprocket logo on shorts and jackets from thrift stores. "We were a hobby until last year," said Thomson. "Now we have to deal with real-world stuff like taxes and contracts. Luckily, we have a punk-oriented computer software designer, accountant, and travel agent to help us out."

Toomey and Thomson's band, Tsunami, also had a friendly yet independent edge. A characteristic song was "Punk Means Cuddle": After acidly noting that "I'm not your mom," Toomey sang "You say punk means asshole/I say punk means cuddle!" over a dirty-guitar jangle. "I defy anyone to prove we're not a punk band," Toomey said. "Punk means you try and stay independent. We're involved in all levels—we book our own tours, put out our own records, we screen our own T-shirts. We don't believe that punk music can only have one sound. It's about the attitude, not the sound."

While little of Tsunami's politics seeped into its lyrics, there were messages in Simple Machines' packaging. The "Working Holiday" singles club released a two-band 45 every month for a year, spotlighting such anniversaries as the US bombing of Hiroshima or the Stonewall riots, which marked the birth of the gay liberation movement. The label also released *Fortune Cookie Prize*, a Beat Happening tribute album that benefited non-profit groups in inner-city DC.

The musicians faced many questions about Riot Grrrl, to which Toomey replied, "Tsunami are not spokespeople for the movement but I know the Riot Grrrls have a completely valid viewpoint." Some Tsunami songs seemed to address the media onslaught that had largely silenced the group: "She's been had again/She's been had by you/Stabbed in the back by a poison pen/And I feel it too/Girls who do/Girls who dare/Don't sit around and count their lucky stars/Or wait for validation from you," chided "Lucky," while "Waxed" cracked, "So you wake up to find your breasts in one 'zine too many/Makes you think the little boys aren't getting any."

Toomey and Thomson shared a keen interest in alternative capitalism. "There's no reason why business has to be essentially evil," Toomey said. "The more power you have, the more likely it is that you'll be able to make substantial changes. Ben and Jerry's were a total inspiration to us. For instance, they have an outlet that doubles as a skills center for the homeless. They've saved American Indian reservations by buying their fruit. They make concrete changes, which is what we're trying to do.

"As you control capital [and] structures, you are able to wield power for good in a totally helpful way," she argued. "Everyone thinks that Dischord was really punk when they were really small, but I would say that one of punkest, most innovative things they ever did was when they gave their employees health insurance."

For all its owners' disdain for the music biz, Simple Machines was willing to work with MTV,

New Music Seminar, College Music Journal, and other elements of the increasingly mercantile indie-rock world. To Chris Bald, Tsunami and Velocity Girl were "careerist. Just because they are good at making press packs or making connections on the CMJ board—fuck that. If we're supposed to be offended at Van Halen, why can't we be offended by shit like that?"

Tsunami took another step into the mainstream by performing on the second stage at the third annual Lollapalooza, as did Velocity Girl. By this time, there was scarcely anything "alternative" about the festival. In 1991, it attracted 430,000 and grossed $10 million, figures that nearly doubled in 1992 to 800,000 and $19 million.

Tsunami tried to bring its aesthetic to bear on the festival, helping add an indie record store—which failed in the first few weeks. Toomey also criticized the male-heavy band roster. After Babes in Toyland left the tour partway through, she told *Rolling Stone,* "There should have been a stronger commitment to having a strong women-identified band that was going to be there for the whole festival."

Simple Machines aligned with Southern Studios, following the example of Dischord; Velocity Girl signed to Sub Pop, leading drummer Jim Spellman to quit his other band, the High Back Chairs, in which he played guitar. "When we met with Sub Pop, one of the most important things was they were the nicest," said guitarist Kelly Riles. "They were real people. They know how to run a business but there was no industry bullshit."

Despite skepticism, Riles didn't reject major labels outright. "The fact that a 'grunge' record made it to #1 is inspirational," he said. "That's the ultimate punk rock feat. Subvert the masses. People tend to frown on a band if someone they don't like, say Van Halen fans, start buying their band's record. But that avoids the issue. Is it a cool song, is it a good record?"

The quintet's debut album, *Copacetic*, received widespread favorable reviews. Its blurry sound followed the fashion of British bands like My Bloody Valentine, who treated vocals as just another timbre. "The lyrics aren't all that important to the song," explained singer Sarah Shannon. Added guitarist Archie Moore, "The sound and the mood of the song are what we're interested in. If I'm interested in a political issue, I don't turn to pop culture to learn about it."

Fellow pop undergrounders Unrest—now with original Velocity Girl vocalist Bridget Cross playing bass—likewise tended to avoid political topics. Led by Teenbeat impresario Mark E.

Robinson, Unrest was one of DC punk's most enigmatic entities. The band's interviews were often willfully uninformative, with paeans to Kiss, Sammy Davis Jr., obscure British bands like Crispy Ambulance, and kitschy idols of any era.

A full decade after Unrest first played out, the trio began to attract a cult following with its eclecticism, unpredictability, and singles like "Yes, She Is My Skinhead Girl" and "Cherry Cream On," which mixed pop jangle with sexually frank lyrics. Unrest's confrontational, chameleonlike style appealed to Fugazi, who asked the band to open some of its out-of-town gigs. "Fugazi have a pretty hardcore crowd," Robinson later noted. "I thought people would throw things at us—like they threw at Beat Happening when they opened for Fugazi. But it actually went over pretty well."

Like Velocity Girl, Unrest responded to the growing notice by signing to larger indies—first Caroline and then Britain's 4AD. Teenbeat shared Simple Machines' hyper-accessorized approach, and Toomey and Robinson founded a side project, Grenadine. But Robinson replaced Simple Machines' politics with sheer contrariness and absurdism, as when he asked Duran Duran's Simon LeBon to produce Unrest's first 4AD album. The band never had to contend with the major-label dilemma; by the time 4AD was bought by a major, Unrest had broken up.

Shudder to Think was another of Fugazi's incongruous opening acts. The quartet challenged many people's expectations of a "Dischord band" with its neopsychedelic touches and Craig Wedren's un-macho falsetto. At a gig with thoughtful hardcore band 411, "about half the audience really liked it and about half flagrantly, violently booed us," Wedren recalled. "I like to tease them. It's impossible not to tease people who are just so wrapped up in the fucking scene and the fucking 'loud and fast.'

"If punk was something that was saying 'do it yourself,' then I hope that another level would start where anybody can cultivate their own style," he said. "Certainly for me the goal right now is to really find our own voice, which isn't something that can be limited or categorized. I'm into the idea of broadening our audience but also fucking with them, challenging them more and more." After the 1991 EP, *Funeral at the Movies*, the band made the tellingly titled *Get Your Goat* in 1992.

Shudder was not political in any usual sense. "To make something beautiful or to make something ugly, just something that contacts yourself first and then other people is worth as much as any political or social statement," Wedren contended.

By 1993, the band had two new members—former Swiz bassist Nathan Larson replaced guitarist Chris Matthews and ex-Jawboxer Adam Wade took over the drums from Mike Russell—and was hearing the majors' call. "Dischord is a great label, I think it's the best independent label there is, except for maybe Touch and Go," said Wade. "It works for Fugazi but it doesn't always work for us and a lot of the other bands. There's no tour support at all. It's frustrating sometimes when you go to record stores and your records aren't there. I think I'd like to be on a major label. I don't want to be driving around in some little van when I'm 30, sleeping on floors, doubling up in motel rooms, you know?"

Touring was arduous, as indicated by the list of bands that broke up during or right after such treks. The most recent example was Circus Lupus, which made two jagged LPs and a fine Joan Jett–produced single but splintered after a torturous European tour. Word of mouth could carry Fugazi, but for lesser-known bands, Dischord's low-PR, no-tour-support approach seemed a dead end.

Musicians who see signing to a major label as "selling out," Larson said, will "change their tune when they grow up and see what it's like, when they have to pay a few bills and buy their own food." Shudder to Think was about to sign to Epic.

Jawbox found itself at a similar crossroads. Unlike Shudder to Think, Jawbox was still playing Positive Force shows, generally performing one benefit for each paying gig. The band had survived an internal romantic crisis—J. Robbins and Kim Coletta split and the latter linked with new second guitarist, Bill Barbot—and the loss of Wade, replaced by longtime Jawbox fan and DC transplant Zach Barocas. Recorded at Inner Ear with Chicago guitar-brutalist Iain Burgess, the band's new *Novelty* seamlessly combined guitar noise and haunting melody. There was one jarring note, however: the lack of a lyric sheet.

In 1990, Robbins had expressed his pleasure at forming a band with more substance than GI. "To me, lyrics are the most important thing when I listen to a band," he said. "If the lyrics say something, the music doesn't have to be the greatest in the world. Pure musicianship isn't enough for me. I'm not affected by it at all." Times, apparently, had changed.

The message was also less important to Holy Rollers, which seemed never to have fully recovered from the loss of original drummer Maria Jones. The band released a strong self-titled Dischord album in 1993, but something in the band's chemistry had changed, shifting it toward an almost macho, hard-rock vibe. The band continued to play Positive Force benefits, including an AIDS one conceived by Joey Aronstamn himself. But benefits were difficult financially for a band trying to survive, and Aronstamn acknowledged that there was less sympathy for overt politics within the new lineup.

For bands rooted in DC punk, lyrics increasingly seemed to be just part of the sound. While new organizations like Food Not Bombs and the Beehive Collective expanded the scene's political strain, much of the music now seemed apolitical. "It's funny," said Beehive member Brad Sigal, who was formerly involved with both Positive Force and Simple Machines. "The community seems to becoming both more and less political at the same time."

Challenging new bands continued to form. Former members of Admiral, Fine Day, Wind of Change, and Hoonah united to form Hoover, which played moody, emotion-drenched sets. Christine Billotte and Myra Power completed Slant 6's lineup with drummer Marge Marshall, and began playing smart, Wire-y pop-punk. Rain Like the Sound of Trains was a politically pointed new unit with bassist Dug Birdzell, fresh arrival Josh LaRue on drums, and singer-guitarist Pete Chramiec, formerly of Verbal Assault. The band's ranks would soon be augmented by Bobby Sullivan, who returned from Boston after a stint in the reggae-rock Seven League Boots. The band's "Washington Bullets" was a soulful mating of harDCore and the worldbeat-era Clash, and a chilling evocation of the ongoing slaughter on DC's streets.

Still, established bands were becoming increasingly pragmatic. When Coletta noted that Jawbox couldn't afford to change its name after Wade left, because "things were going too well," it made sense—the same sense that it made to Holy Rollers, Shudder to Think, and others as they replaced member after member.

Jawbox still seemed disinclined to sign with a major. "I know what motivates major labels— the bottom line," Robbins noted. "Some market analyst is looking at a percentage of sales and they go, 'Oh look, independents are making money.' To major labels what that means is 'independent labels are taking away money we could be making.' It seems like that happens periodically."

Yet by late 1993, Jawbox had signed to Atlantic. "What happened was an old punk friend named Mike Gitter turned out to be working for Atlantic," Robbins later noted. "We made them a list of what we thought were sort of impossible demands. We wanted creative control over the actual substance of the record, how it sounds, who we're going to record with, where we're recording, what the ads look like, and final approval. Atlantic said yes to everything on the list except the list price of the records. Once we started meeting people at Atlantic, it was really clear that they're going to have some respect for the way we want to do things. It's not at all the cartoon picture of what a major label is all about, you know, 'Let's go find some bar band in Poughkeepsie and turn them into Kiss.'"

Robbins reported "no bad feeling whatsoever from Dischord" about leaving and noted that bands moving to major labels "didn't need to undermine the sense of community." Others, however, perceived a crisis. In a controversial move, *Maximum RockNRoll* decided to ban any music outside the "loud fast rules" mode. The subsequent exclusion of bands like Rain Like the Sound of Trains—one of the era's most militant DC bands—further divided the underground. Meanwhile, MTV had copped part of the Nation of Ulysses concept for a program entitled "Alternative Nation."

In *Jigsaw* #5, a disconsolate Vail called the mass media seizure of Riot Grrrl "enough to make me cry." Referring to their faddish infatuation with the word "grrrl," she called this "just one example of how something which was once mine and genuinely meaningful to me has been taken from me and had been made into something quite else than was initially intended." This was much what had happened with straight edge, but with one significant difference: The struggle for the meaning of straight edge had played out within the underground over the course of a decade, while Riot Grrrl had been claimed by the corporate media scarcely a year and a half after its conception.

The Riot Grrrl label, Vail wrote elsewhere, "seems to be working as a hindrance that women in bands have to contend with whenever they get written about. I personally am not too pleased with being associated with such a phenomenon. I don't consider myself a 'Riot Grrrl' or see much power in the act of calling one's self that anymore although it means different things to different girls."

CAREERS UP; COMMUNITY DOWN
by Mark Andersen

It seemed foolish to be bitter about this shift toward careerism. Some realities were ever harder to ignore, especially as the punk community unraveled. Joey Aronstamn: "You reach this point where it's a lot different than you thought it was going to be. You're sick of sleeping on people's floors, you're tired of getting sick, you're just getting kind of tired after a while. You only have so much time to live, and after you've been touring constantly for three or four months, you go home and you feel like a stranger, really detached from the scene."

In this context, the community seemed illusory and the lure of major label backing was all-too-real. Joey admitted that to live off one's music was most musicians' dream—including punks. Brian Baker had once felt ostracized for arguing just such a point; now most appeared to agree. This new attitude was far from the once-popular DC idea that if one member left, the band had ended. This self-challenging, anti-commercial ethic arguably had helped make DC into perhaps the most creative and influential scene over the past decade. Now DC was becoming much like every other music scene—and it hurt.

In the liner notes to a new Kill Rock Stars compilation, *Stars Kill Rock*, Vail rebutted the claim that "punk is dead" made by—among others—old ally Kurt Cobain: "The mass dissemination of an ideology indicating [that the underground is dead] should be taken for what it is, a desperate plea on the part of those 'alternative nation' co-conspirators who are so busy trying to convince themselves that, simply because they are no longer punk rockers, punk rock must no longer exist."

Vail hailed *Stars Kill Rock*—which included DC bands Slant 6 and Getaway Car, a unit that included Mike Fellows and a dynamic new performer, Kim Thompson—as a testimonial to the continued vibrancy of the underground: "As to encourage you to not wallow in the MTV notion that nothing goes on unless they know about it or whatever, the *Stars Kill Rock* record is important precisely because of how it contradicts all of that."

x x x

Bikini Kill was about to take its struggle for punk's soul into the very heart of rock hype: London. The band had arranged to tour Britain with another band on the compilation, Huggy Bear, a three-woman, two-man band that Vail said "merged an almost Ulyssean-style propaganda with the girl revolution rhetoric."

Shortly before the tour, Huggy Bear performed its anthemic single, "Her Jazz," on the Valentine's Day edition of a live TV show, *The Word*. The band's excitement turned to rage when the program aired a segment on the "Barbi Twins"—identical twin sister models who proudly called themselves "bimbos"—directly after their performance. Huggy Bear guitarist Jo joined some other punks in protesting the item, and chaos resulted. The band, their friends, and many fans were ejected from the studio.

The row effectively shut down the popular show for a few moments, and put Huggy Bear on the cover of *Melody Maker*. The publicity guaranteed that the notoriously sensationalist British music press would cover the upcoming tour intensively.

Bikini Kill accepted *New Musical Express'* offer to write its own article, but found its work sabotaged by the paper. "We were told that we could write our own articles and they would not in any way comment on it or edit it," said Vail. "When the article came out, Kathi's was not included but was rather taken out of context and cited to back up their ideas about us in the introduction that they wrote to my article—everything that to our understanding they weren't going to do. They laid it out in such a way that included catty remarks bigger than our own words."

The band was also not pleased by a *Melody Maker* review of a split Huggy Bear/Bikini Kill album, which further attempted to pit them against other female rockers: "The arrogance of youth—specifically of Riot Grrrls—want to wipe out all musical history, the implications of which suggest that women have waited this long to be saved. Forget about Patti Smith, Janis Joplin, Melanie, Marianne Faithfull, Mo Tucker, punk rock, Crass . . ." This was off-target, for one "Revolution Girl Style Now" aim had always been to rescue past rock heroines from obscurity.

Bikini Kill roared through its first show, at London's Conway Hall, with Billy Karren wearing a gorilla mask in a nod to feminist art activists the Guerrilla Girls. Wrote Sara Kestle, when Bikini Kill "storm[ed] the stage to play 'Suck My Left One', I'm thrown against the wall by the sheer power and emotion."

In Newport, however, violent dancing led Huggy Bear to play a confrontational and abbreviated set. When Bikini Kill came to the stage, Hanna announced that the band would not perform unless men moved back and allowed women and girls to come to the front. Her announcement was met with a chorus of boos. She folded her arms and waited, while the other musicians rested on the floor offstage.

Suddenly, *Melody Maker* recounted, "two girls start chanting Bikini Kill's 'Rebel girl, rebel girl, rebel girl, you are the queen of my world!' And 30, maybe 40 voices pick up the cry. And it's loud and it's hopeful and it's saying fuck off to the wolves in the most perfect possible way. And would you believe it? Men start singing too. I see people start to cry. It's such a release of the violence and tension. The band walk on, plug in, and play."

Four days later in Leeds, Hanna began the show alone with a slow, haunting song apparently inspired by the media insanity. Then the band joined her and played several songs before stopping to note that the crowd near the stage was being pressed forward uncomfortably. When Hanna asked, "Is everything OK?" a angry male voice from the crowd attacked her for encouraging girls to be up front.

After listening to the harangue, Hanna struck back: "Wow, I'm so enlightened now. Did you hear what he said? 'It doesn't matter what gender you are.' I guess the fact that most women in this room get paid a lot less than men for doing the same job, it doesn't matter what gender you are. It doesn't matter that one of four of us will get raped, or that domestic violence exists, or that women are serial-killed or that there aren't many women up front at shows. But I guess it really doesn't matter what gender you are."

Waving her hands dismissively, Hanna spat out, "I've heard it, I've heard it before. It matters to me." When Vail came to the front to sing, Hanna took off her shirt to drum in her bra, sparking a reaction from some men in the crowd. After the songs were over, she put her shirt back on and asked, "How come when Ian MacKaye takes off his shirt, no one gives a shit?" After a short speech by members of the recently formed Riot Grrrl-Leeds, the band went into a new song, "New Radio," followed by "Resist Psychic Death" and a "Rebel Girl" that turned into a rousing singalong.

Several days later, a gig in Derby turned violent when Huggy Bear's Jo was assaulted by an enraged mosher after he was asked to leave. Both Bikini Kill and Huggy Bear were banned from the venue, and the show promoter blamed the trouble on the bands. The attacker got an apology and an invitation to other gigs, and *Melody Maker* ran an article that expressed only the promoter's view: "Bikini Kill inflamed the whole situation to the point where it was obvious something was going to happen. The whole thing became really anti-men." According to some Bikini Kill supporters, however, the promoter didn't even witness the incident.

After the Derby fiasco, Bikini Kill began handing out a flier asking men to respect the girls-up-front idea: "It is not cool or punk in any way for guys to smash into us or rub against us while we are trying to watch a show. I am sick of going to shows where I feel banished to the back cuz I get grossed out by moshing or harassment."

As the tour wound down, *Melody Maker* printed the most fiercely negative commentary yet. It came from Courtney Love, who *Newsweek* had—inaccurately—dubbed "the patron saint of Riot Grrrl." There had long been strained relations and even open dislike between Love (originally from the Portland scene) and many of the crowd in nearby Olympia. This tension increased with Love's romance with Cobain and their shared descent into heroin addiction. Now Love asserted that "Riot Grrrl celebrates the clumsiness and incompetence of femme musicians—that's like giving women high-level corporate jobs even if they can't do the job correctly."

She called Riot Grrrl's handling of the media "fascistic," and claimed that "every musician friend

I have—Jennifer Finch, Donita Sparks, Kat Bjelland, Ian MacKaye, my husband Kurt, Kim Deal—is just as horrified as I am by the antics of the few. Most are fearful to speak out about it, but I've got a kind of big mouth so I don't really care. Most of us aren't rich and spoilt, drinking gourmet coffee with soy milk and dreaming up daily manifestos for the few."

Media relations had become a Riot Grrrl flashpoint. The most famous case was that of Love's friend Jessica Hopper, a 16-year-old Minneapolis Riot Grrrl; she spoke to *Newsweek* and then felt ostracized as a result, although other members of the Minneapolis group insisted that was not their intent. The affair became fodder for another article featuring Hopper, this time in *Seventeen*, which asked, "Will Riot Grrrl refocus feminism or fry in its own fury?"

Love had apparently been angered by Hanna's discussion of differing female punk approaches in *Option*: "What bands like Babes in Toyland, L7, and Hole do is go, 'It's not important that I'm a girl, it's just important that I want to rock.' And that's cool. But that's more of an assimilationist thing. They want to be allowed to join the world as it is; whereas I'm into revolution and radicalism and changing the whole structure."

"I am *not* assimilationist, I am a populist," Love responded. "I believe that everyone, not just people that know Fugazi personally, have a right to revolution. If you want to be in my club you can come and I don't care if you've got that first edition Germs EP. If that's not good enough for you cos you want to be special in my club, then, fine, go just two stops down the freeway to the Loverock Fascist Capital"—that is, Olympia—"and you can press 200 of your singles for all your cool friends and be horrified if any pathetic idiots like me buy it. I'm trying to walk the fine line between benefiting and abetting my culture (West Coast hardcore-No Wave woman/girl) as a woman and following my own chosen true path, all while trying not to be intimidated by three women my age who call themselves girls"—that is, the female members of Bikini Kill—"who act that way just so they can get their stupid, useless 15 minutes [of fame] and feed their egos at the expense of the rest of us."

This assault capped one of most torturous months in Bikini Kill's existence, yet the tour ended with a benediction. When the band declined to let a *Melody Maker* reporter into the tour's final show for free, Sebadoh's Lou Barlow and his friend Kathleen Billus were asked to write a review. "Bikini Kill are a storm of punk rock," they wrote. "They switch instruments constantly, each configuration with a power and charm of its own.

"These bands have already made an impression," the review continued. "Their influence will echo like 1977 punk or 1982 hardcore for years to come. Anyone who believes women do not have some serious inbred barriers to break down is tragically naïve. The strangely personal attacks against [Bikini Kill] and their sister/brother bands only testify to their power and vitality."

x x x

Back in the USA, Bikini Kill braved more confrontations. Playing at a small LA community center, Hanna asked the crowd, "Have you ever heard of cellulite?" Getting little response, she continued, "I'm going to show you mine, you don't see this on TV, this is real." She took off her skirt and turned around to show the crowd. Then, wearing just black underwear and a yellow top, Hanna led the band into "Don't Need You," followed in quick succession by several other songs.

As the band began "Sugar," a male photographer moved behind stage, apparently to photograph Hanna's ass. She put her hand in front of his camera as she sang, but he persisted. After Hanna indicated for him to stop twice more and was still ignored, she finally pushed the camera away. The photographer glared at her through the rest of the song, while Hanna returned the bad vibes by singing directly to him.

When the song ended, an angry Hanna spoke to the photographer and the rest of the crowd: "If I show you that I don't want my picture taken, if I put my hand up three times in a row to show you that and you keep trying to take pictures of me, I'm sorry, but that's not OK. I will not have pictures of my ass being taken by some boy I don't know."

The majority of the crowd applauded, but the exchange showed the band's state of siege. "We just don't know who to trust anymore," Hanna later said. "A short while ago we did an interview with a San Francisco newspaper who promised they'd use photographs we'd okayed. Then it came out with snapshots of us wearing bikinis on the beach. A friend sold them the pictures."

The pressure threatened the band's very existence. After the LA dates and recording a single with producer Joan Jett—a fan since seeing the band at Wetlands in early '92—the band went on hiatus, with Hanna moving to Portland. Although the single as well as an album recorded earlier were set for release on Kill Rock Stars, the band's future was clouded. Vail, Wilcox, and Karren toured the US with Huggy Bear in late summer '93 as members of the Frumpies with Bratmobile's Molly Neuman on drums, but it was not clear that Bikini Kill would ever play again.

As Bikini Kill retreated, Riot Grrrl was nearly buried under media hokum. *Seventeen* tried to counter its rival *Sassy* by distributing little cards that read, "If you like Bratmobile or Bikini Kill or Hole, then you'll like *Seventeen* too."

"You know how there's a rap Barbie doll?" Hanna asked. "I have got this feeling that they're gonna start manufacturing a 'Riot Barbie.' She'll come with a little beat-up guitar, some miniature spray paints that don't work, and a list of dumb revolutionary slogans like 'Riot Coke just for the taste of it.'" One result of all the attention was that, as Vail wrote, "Everybody's talking about what kind of girl, nobody's starting a riot."

This was not entirely true. Encouraged by Hanna, Erika Reinstein and May Summer had started Riot Grrrl Press. As one of their "Six Reasons Why Riot Grrrl Press is Important" noted, "We need to make ourselves visible without using mainstream media as a tool. Under the guise of helping us spread the word, corporate media has co-opted and trivialized a movement of angry girls that could be truly threatening and revolutionary. Besides even that, it has distorted our views of each other and created hostility, tension, and jealousy in a movement supposedly about girl-support and girl-love. In a time when Riot Grrrl has become the next big trend, we need to take back control and find our own voices again."

Infighting continued, however, as the media blackout was enforced by intense peer pressure. Even DC punk-feminist stalwarts Molly Neuman and Lois Maffeo faced intense criticism for talking to mainstream publications about Riot Grrrl.

x x x

Positive Force faced not only the disintegration of the Nation of Ulysses/Bikini Kill axis and the commercialization of many of the better-known Dischord-related bands, but the loss of all its church performance spaces. In the case of St. Stephen's, the residents of the public housing project next door had become so enraged by the continual trashing of their yards by drunk, noisy white kids, that they took up a petition to stop any further shows.

Although it had not been Positive Force shows that had caused the mayhem, St. Stephen's felt it best to accede to its neighbors' wishes without exceptions. It was a bitter development, for Positive Force's aim in opening such spaces had been to increase understanding.

Positive Force found itself largely trapped in the club circuit. Also, there were fewer well-known bands interested in playing benefits. Positive Force shows became less frequent.

The best-known band still available for benefits was almost too large a draw. Given Fugazi's popularity, it was difficult to find a large enough venue. One obvious step was into the college circuit—a move the band had long resisted. IMP Productions, which owned the 9:30 Club, had been pursuing the band for a show at the 2000-capacity University of Maryland Ritchie Coliseum. Lacking other venues, the band was interested. When IMP announced that such a concert would be impossible for a five-dollar door, however, Fugazi declined to sign on.

With Fugazi's approval, Positive Force began negotiating with University of Maryland's concert committee. Once its demands on ticket price, security, and other issues were met, Fugazi agreed to play. The show would be a benefit for the Washington Free Clinic, with Slant 6 and Hoover opening.

CONFUSION, CONTROVERSY, CRASH
by Mark Andersen

Reformist corporate collaboration or revolutionary underground defiance–this was the choice now facing punk. Although it felt a bit lonely, I knew which side I was on.

Or did I? Kurt Cobain had told *Rolling Stone* that "I don't blame the average seventeen-year-old punk kid for calling me a sell-out. I understand that. Maybe when they grow up a bit, they'll realize there's more to life than living out your rock & roll identity so righteously." For all of my critiques of Nirvana, I agreed. The war within punk was scarcely important compared to the larger drama facing America: the potential re-election of Bush and the consolidation of the conservative revolution of the past 12 years.

I couldn't deny the potential importance of Nirvana in this fight. Dave Grohl had attended the April PF/Fugazi pro-choice benefit while back home on vacation. I was then on the Board of Directors of the Washington Free Clinic who, in a very hotly contested vote, had decided to defy the Bush gag rule. Having argued for this stand, I felt responsible to help replace the money and approached Dave to ask if Nirvana would help by playing a benefit concert. He quickly agreed, and put me in touch with John Silva, their manager.

This effort at an alliance between PF and Nirvana for a political protest opened me up to attack. In a delicious (if painful) bit of irony–considering the self-righteous anger I had visited upon Jenny for collaborating with MTV–now I became a target of back-biting even within PF House itself. When some of the residents (who were no longer part of Positive Force as such) overheard me talking with John Silva, they decided that I was sleeping with the enemy. To them, Dave Grohl was just a "rock star"–to me, whatever his mainstream success, he was still a comrade, part of the DC community.

More scorn was directed at me over an article I had written for *Dirt*–a male-oriented spinoff of

The idea was to confront the college "alternative rock" audience with underground punk. While the Clash and the Jam—as well as PiL and Minor Threat—had played the coliseum, it was a massive space for a band used to clubs. Slant 6 and Hoover seemed out of their element.

The crowd was not entirely friendly either, with some booing Riot Grrrl Press speakers Reinstein and Summer. While Riot Grrrl was by now very controversial, such a reaction from a Fugazi crowd was disconcerting. Positive Force tried to subvert the trappings of a "rock concert" by keeping the security guards off on the sides of the stage and freely distributing dozens of backstage passes, but the situation was awkward.

Nonetheless, this was a night with a purpose. Positive Force handed out hundreds of pamphlets detailing the Free Clinic's work and calling for free quality universal healthcare. The Free Clinic had defied the Bush Administration's "gag rule" barring federally funded clinics from providing abortion counseling; now abortion politics had become violent once again with the slaying of Dr. David Gunn by a "pro-life" protester in Florida.

If communicating this to the huge crowd seemed a challenge, Fugazi was undeterred. Midway through the set, MacKaye paused. Asking some body-surfers to "please stop being beach balls for a while," he dedicated "Reclamation" to the slain Dr. Gunn. After a fero-

Sassy–on the history of Positive Force House. Although I had asked all of the then-current residents for their permission before agreeing to do the article, had near-total control over what was printed, and was even paid for, in effect, spreading a radical punk message, the fact that I would cooperate with a mainstream magazine was considered suspicious.

I was already hurting from overwork and a slide back into an addictive problem. I was devastated to discover myself the object of vicious gossip within PF House; it made me want to just say goodbye to the whole punk community, to everything. I knew why Tomas now scoffed at my continued allegiance to punk, which he considered dead. I wouldn't admit that he was right, but I felt ever more alone, like a dinosaur, a joke.

The criticism of the Fugazi/Free Clinic benefit at the University of Maryland was the last straw. In one way, I totally understood the critics' feelings–certainly seeing Fugazi there didn't carry the same punch as at dc space with a hundred people, most of them friends.

Yet, that moment was gone–and by not giving each other room to move, to grow, we were destroying ourselves. In 1990, Henry Rollins had deemed the DC underground "timid." Now I understood. We needed to do more than just play it safe, but, as with straight society, to step outside the accepted bounds of the underground was to risk attack.

My relapse into self-abuse and depression intensified as the center of my world was torn–and tore itself–apart. By the time of the Free Clinic benefit, I had ballooned to 220 pounds, looking and feeling old and beaten down. Thoughts of suicide were common; not surprisingly, since I was already in a slow-motion version of just that.

Fortunately, I still had true friends, who seeing my state, took me aside and expressed their concern. With their encouragement, I left DC in June 1993, returning to Montana to get help. As part of my recovery, I began to finally write the first draft of this book.

cious version of the song, the band raced through its set, playing virtually its entire soon-to-be-released LP.

Except for university-mandated body-searches at the door and one incident with a mosher, security had to be content with shining flashlights on the crowd from the side of the stage. As the set drew to its close, MacKaye joked, "Do you like the light show, the guys with the flashlights? We hired them. We told them, 'This is our crowd. Hug them at the door, embrace them, feel them all over. When they come in, keep a close eye on them, watch them carefully, make sure they know they are loved. And when you feel like you see someone special, put a spotlight on them."

Despite the banter, there were uncomfortable issues underneath. After a feedback-drenched "Shut the Door," MacKaye returned to the theme: "The fact is that we had to put up with a lot of university bureaucracy to do this show—which is OK, because in return the university gave us 100 percent of the door to give to the Free Clinic." As the crowd applauded, MacKaye encouraged everyone to check out the Free Clinic, and Fugazi closed their set with an elegiac "Last Chance for a Slow Dance."

The profit came to almost $8000, the largest amount raised yet at a Positive Force event. Fugazi and Positive Force might have succeeded in bringing punk to a college crowd, yet many erstwhile allies were not impressed. More than a few complained that the night had been a "rock concert," not a punk show. Some had even walked out.

DC punk had come to an odd impasse, where success blended into failure. Punk had become a commodity bought and sold in corporate bidding wars. The underground was deeply, perhaps irredeemably, split. Even Fugazi was now simply too big to be able to please many of its original friends and fans. The realization hurt, but it was unavoidable: the scene might never again feel like home.

riot grrrl

a free weekly mini-zine.

please read and distribute to your pals.

METRO WATCH

The anti-war graffiti was terrible in January and February. So now that the war's over? Don't ask.

On the rise downtown is graffiti most charitably described as anti-male. Some use blunter language.

The most quoted slogan is: DEAD MEN DON'T RAPE. UMBILICAL NOOSE is another. Others: WOMEN FIGHT BACK. GOD IS GAY. ABORT CHRIST. WOMEN REVOLT. And there are lots more, many we can't print in a family newspaper.

For that matter, some of the graffiti doesn't even make sense. One slogan Hutchings says he runs into again and again is: BIKINI KILL. Bikini kill?

Curiouser and curiouser.

Clockwise from top left: 1. COVER OF *RIOT GRRRL* #3, 2. ERIN SMITH, MOLLY NEUMAN, AND ALLISON WOLFE OF BRATMOBILE, RIOT GRRRL CONVENTION, WASHINGTON PEACE CENTER, AUGUST 1992 *(by Pat Graham)*, 3. JEN SMITH OF HAYMAKER, PF WASHINGTON FREE CLINIC BENEFIT, ST. STEPHEN'S CHURCH

Clockwise from top left: 1. JASMINE KERNS, SARAH STOLFA, CORIN TUCKER, KATE COHEN, AND OTHERS FROM RIOT GRRRL ONSTAGE AT PF/FUGAZI/BIKINI KILL SUPREME COURT PROTEST, JULY 25, 1992 *(by Pat Graham)*, 2. PAT MALEY AND LOIS MAFFEO OF COURTNEY LOVE, MUSEUM OF BROADCASTING HISTORY, CHICAGO *(by Allison Stark)*, 3.JENNY TOOMEY AND KRISTIN THOMSON AT SIMPLE MACHINES HOUSE *(by Pat Graham)*, 4. DRAWING BY JASMINE KERNS OF RIOT GRRRL DC, SUMMER 1992

THE REVOLUTION STARTS HERE AND NOW
within each one of us

Recognize that you are not the center of the universe.
Figure out how the idea of winning and losing fits into your
relationships.
Be a dork, tell your friends how you really feel.
Selectively ignore all oppressive laws.
Don't judge other people, only yourself.
Resist the temptation to view those around you as objects and use them.
Acknowledge emotional violence as real.
Close your mind to the propaganda of the status quo by examining it's
effects on you, cell by (artificial) cell.
Resist psychic death.
Be as vulnerable as you possibly can.
Recognize vulnerability and empathy as strengths.
Cry in public.
Don't allow the fact that other people have been assholes to you make
you into a bitter and abusive person.
Burn down the walls that say you can't be connected to other people and
species.
Refute organized religion as a distraction from the revolution.
Resist the internalization of capitalism, the reducing of oneself
and others to commodities, meant to be consumed and discarded.
Commit to the revolution as a method of psychological and physical survival.
Make ammendments to this list and think about why you don't agree with
some of what i've written.
Enjoy sex, food, and the company of other people without having to hoard them
If someone tells you they are in pain, believe them. Help them figure a
way to stop the pain or deal with the pain's existence.
Don't assume people invent pain in order to manipulate you or make you feel
bad.
Decide that you'd rather be truly alive and in a state of constant flux
than to have everything under control (labeled, your identity staid and
unchangeable, you've figured everything out) and lead a dead simulation
of existence.

Top to bottom:
1. "REVOLUTION STARTS NOW" LIST FROM *RIOT GRRRL* #3 *(by Kathleen Hanna)*,
2. JAMES CANTY, IAN SVENONIUS, AND STEVE GAMBOA OF THE NOU AT WASHINGTON PEACE CENTER, 1992 *(by Pat Graham)*

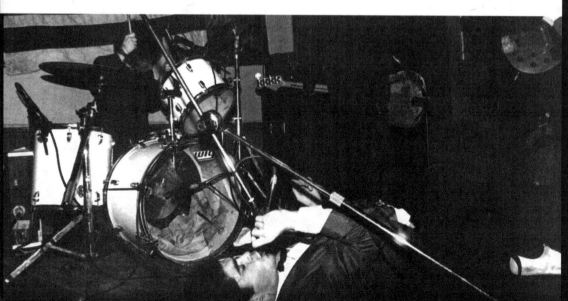

Clockwise from top left: 1. CHRISTINA BILLOTTE, MYRA POWER, AND MARGE MARSHALL OF SLANT 6 *(by Monica Gesue)*,
2. AL DUNHAM AND FRED ERSKINE OF HOOVER, ST. STEPHENS CHURCH *(by Pat Graham)*, 3. SCOTT MCCLOUD, JOHNNY TEMPLE, ALEXIS FLEISIG, AND ELI JANNEY
OF GIRLS AGAINST BOYS *(by Yuri Marder)*, 4. NATHAN LARSON, ADAM WADE, CRAIG WEDREN, AND STUART HILL OF SHUDDER TO THINK *(by John Falls)*

Top to bottom:
1. HR OF BAD BRAINS AT TRACKS, FREE SHOW, 1995 *(by Chris Henderson)*,
2. BRENDAN CANTY AND IAN MACKAYE OF FUGAZI *(by Jim Saah)*

Clockwise from top left: 1. AMY FARINA, ALEC MACKAYE, AND JUAN CARRERA OF WARMERS *(by the Warmers)*, 2. PETE CHRAMIEC
OF RAIN LIKE THE SOUND OF TRAINS *(by Pat Graham)*, 3. JEFF NELSON WORKING ON ANTI-OLIVER NORTH PROJECT
DURING US SENATE CAMPAIGN, 1994 *(by Pat Graham)*, 4. JAMES CANTY, STEVE GAMBOA, IAN SVENONIUS, AND MICHELLE MAE OF THE MAKE-UP
(photography © Glen E. Friedman, reprinted with permission from the Burning Flags Press book, The Idealist)

by Mark Andersen, 1995

"I thought life should be a chance
To defeat statistics
I thought life should be a chance
And if sometimes I don't pursue it
The sea speaks my better half."
—One Last Wish

to defeat statistics

"IMAGINE A BRAVE NEW WORLD . . . where punk rock rules the airwaves, where the revolution already got televised, and now it's old hat. Imagine 1993. . ."

Thus went the introduction of a *Pulse* magazine article written by old school punk scribe Ira Robbins, heralding "The New Mainstream . . . The Lollapalooza Generation." After persisting in America's subterranean nooks and crannies for nearly two decades, punk had at last ascended to the rock pantheon.

Once, to be a punk meant facing potential assault for merely walking down the street. Now it was an accepted, even fashionable part of the landscape; the biggest danger appeared to be tripping over one of the dozens of A&R people scurrying about the scene.

This turnabout was an ambivalent victory. Writing on the eve of the third Lollapalooza tour, Robbins recalled that "way back in the summer of 1991, punk rock was just a recurring dream some of us had, a quixotic fantasy of music as the final chapter in a rebel culture that had already signed on to the antiestablishment establishment. The generation gap that opened four decades back by James Dean closed with the nobody-doesn't-like-Sara-Lee popularity of Michael Jackson . . . Any residual us-vs.-them fantasies were prudently jettisoned to ensure a smoother ride toward the American dream."

After recalling why punk—as "a reminder of how it used to be"—had struck such a chord with an older generation of rock true believers, Robbins noted that "into this pretty picture floated *Nevermind*, a dozen songs that introduced garageland to the wasteland and blasted whatever was left of punk rock straight out of the college radio ghetto into the central social arena . . . Not since the Sex Pistols mouthed off to British TV geek Bill Grundy in 1976 had one group singlehandedly gouged such a deep dent into society's armor."

By the late summer of 1993, the reverberations of Nirvana's breakthrough had brought punk onto the cover of *Time* magazine. The article, "Generation Rage," documented the rise of a new era of raw, angry rock bands epitomized by Nirvana, Pearl Jam, and others. In the aftermath of that story, Henry Rollins told *Rolling Stone*, "In my mind, Nirvana slayed the hair bands. They shot the top off the poodles. All of a sudden, all those bands like Poison, Bon Jovi, and Warrant became like rusty tanks in the desert with no more gas. It's bands like Nirvana, that came along at that time, who are going to be remembered for changing the face of rock."

Yet, if *Nevermind* had catalyzed what could be fairly described as a rock revolution, the outcome was not exactly what many within the movement—including Ira Robbins—had hoped for. Had the system changed—or had the punks?

Robbins was not optimistic: "Money changes everything . . . It's obvious that any traditional beliefs in rock'n'roll as a vehicle for social and cultural progress are obsolete . . . Overwhelming economic synergy has rendered absurd the idea that rock still exists in opposition to anything. Above the lowest grassroots level of independence, everything is for sale and nothing is forbidden. And with any serious political movement in America now 20 years gone, rebellion has become a marketing scam. MTV's promotional tag line aside, Gil Scott Heron was right on: What's being televised is most assuredly not the revolution. Nowadays, when I hear the word rebellion, I reach for my credit card."

In 1968, CBS had boasted "The Man Can't Bust Our Music." In 1994, a new Columbia ad in *Rolling Stone* read, "For Those Who Don't Hang With the Herd." This "alternative rock"–targeted spread featured a hip Holstein cow complete with Walkman amidst selections from Nirvana, Pearl Jam, Sex Pistols, and more. Elsewhere in the same issue were ads for Bud Dry, touted as the "Alternative Beer." Though a vigorous underground remained active in DC, Olympia, and elsewhere, "punk" was becoming a marketing ploy. A rebellion that began nearly two decades before with punks lashing out against the failed radicals of the '60s had come full circle.

Back in the late '70s, Mark Jenkins wrote that "rock had become television," a situation that helped to spark the punk insurrection. In 1993, the ubiquitous power of MTV made this critique truer than ever before. Few artists escaped the seductive grip of "Music Television." Robbins even attacked "that righteous voice of incorruptible independence, Henry Rollins" for "coyly rationalizing the hypocrisy of his off-camera attacks on MTV as the network's red light winked dollar signs at him on Alternative Nation."

Ironically, the *Pulse* article itself represented what Robbins spoke of, for it was written not in Trouser Press or another underground publication, but in the promotional rag of the Tower Records chain. Robbins noted that "punk rock always defined a sound of music that could never—and for countless reasons, should never—be sold in convenience stores." Yet, for good or for ill, that was precisely what had somehow come to pass.

I observed this turn of the wheel from northeast Montana, working on the rough draft of this book, on my way back to health. The "new world" Robbins spoke of confronted me on my return to Service Drug in Williston, the store where I had bought *Rock Scene* and *Creem* publications like *Rock Revolution* in the mid-to-late '70s. Back then, punk artists were rarely noticed outside of the fringes of the rock press.

Now as I shuffled through the racks, the faces of friends, acquaintances, and peers leaped out at me—Henry Rollins on *Details*, Fugazi on *Warp*, Nirvana everywhere. On the cover of *Rolling Stone* was Pearl Jam, with Eddie Vedder paying tribute in the interview to Henry Rollins and Ian MacKaye. Just pages away from a Bad Brains live review in *RIP*, Zack De La Rocha, singer in a militant young band, Rage Against the Machine—who, despite their name and politics, were signed to Epic—spoke of ideals formed by love for DC punk.

De La Rocha's words connected three rock generations: "Music has always been a way of lashing out that goes way beyond whatever talent or sound could offer. There was always something—whether it was Ian MacKaye or Janis Joplin speaking their minds—that spoke to me. It showed me a way to express myself against emotional or political suppression."

Impressed by De La Rocha's vision but troubled by his compromises, I set down *RIP* and picked up *Circus*, the first rock magazine I had ever bought, back in 1973. This was the "History of Rock'N'Roll" issue; next to tributes to the Rolling Stones and Led Zeppelin were sections on the Sex Pistols and Nirvana. As I flipped through the mag, a two-page spread of T-shirts caught my eye. These "rock collectibles" cost $15.50 each, plus shipping and handling. Beside Eric Clapton, Grateful Dead, and Guns'N'Roses shirts was a bootleg "This Is Not a Fugazi Shirt."

Later I walked into a record store a few blocks away. On the wall was a huge poster of my old hero, Jimi Hendrix, hawking the most recent repackaging of his music. On the opposing wall was an even larger poster of Nirvana. As I looked up at the image of Dave Grohl, my mind flashed to meeting him at a Mission Impossible practice in a suburban basement. Then he was a 15-year-old punk with a friendly smile and the most frenzied drumming style I had ever seen. Now Dave was a reluctant rock "god."

Some punks seemed ever more comfortable swimming in the mainstream, liberated from inconvenient moral dilemmas. Billy Corgan, singer and guitarist in another ascendent punk-related band, Smashing Pumpkins, noted in *Rolling Stone* that "I feel less and less like an outsider. Come on, everyone's selling millions of records. Everyone's making videos. The issues of integrity are really blurred. We can pretty much judge things pre-Nirvana and post-Nirvana, at least for my peers . . . that was the absolute turning point."

Punk even appeared in Montana daily newspapers like the *Billings Gazette* in articles headlined, "Punk Music Makes Some Serious Noise Again" or, "Moshers Wear Bruises Like Badges of Honor," assuming a coherent, yet rarely inspiring cultural definition.

"Along with T-shirts and guitar picks, rock fans can add bumps, bruises, and broken bones to the list of things they might bring home from a concert," went the opening of the "moshing" article, noting that a 15-year-old, Jeremy Libby, broke his neck at the Rhode Island Lollapalooza when dropped while crowd-surfing. The *Gazette* reported that "promoters have made no move to stop moshing, saying the bands and fans want it . . . 'I personally think it's good. We're seeing a renaissance in rock music and this is part of it,' said Jim Koplik, president of Montclair, NY–based Metropolitan Entertainment."

This was a bitter pill to swallow. Just as the 1960s left behind a plague of drug damage, the mighty legacy of punk might be, well . . . moshing. It seemed possible that this macho, increasingly brutal style of dancing might well linger on long past the time when punk's creative, subversive spirit had faded beneath the corporate embrace.

Later, while sitting at my computer in the basement of my parents' house, I picked up my tattered copy of *Rock Revolution*. Suddenly I was that lost, lonely kid again, hanging on every word, just beginning to dare to believe in rebel dreams rising dimly in my mind: "The question is what we will do with the future, where we will take it. The carriers of the rock revolution . . . are none other than you out there reading this, right where you are sitting now. Do it and we'll all meet on this same street corner again, an outlaw mob united forever, ready to forge the fire they'll call the rock'n'roll revolution of the '80s."

Then the tears came. In a way, the dream had come true. The music and culture I had given my heart to, somehow believing it could "change the world," was ascendant—but revolution was nowhere to be seen. Was that dream just a lie? It seemed difficult to say. One thing was clear: As 1993 blurred into 1994 and beyond, with bands like Green Day and Offspring also rising into the Top Ten, the erstwhile youth rebels were now perched perilously close to the Establishment. In addition, as most of the big bands fled for greener pastures, the vitality of the underground ebbed.

Even die-hard DC was not immune to this trend. In 1994, both Jawbox and Shudder to Think released their first corporate-backed albums—*For Your Own Special Sweetheart* and *Pony Express Record*—neither noticeably compromised artistically by their new labels. While Shudder to Think had already distanced themselves from punk, Jawbox had not—which put them in the ironic position of facing more abuse. At one show the band was bedeviled by critics in the crowd yelling taunts like, "Get off the stage so a real punk band can play."

In *MRR*, Tim Yohannon attacked Jawbox by name. Comparing the corporate assault to the threat posed to the scene by Nazi skins in the late '80s, Tim wrote that "within the last two years, major labels have bought up at least 50 underground bands, have undermined punk clubs and bought their way into radio programs, have bought off 'zine editors, label owners, and indie distributors. They threaten to stifle and ultimately control this community and little is being done to resist this threat . . . The punk underground scene is under attack. Just as it was then. No difference, except this time the thugs are smarter and richer."

Tim saw little moral complexity in this: "There can be no middle ground when you're under attack by forces alien to the fundamental principles of a community or society. That's easy when a band or label is blatant in their changing behavior, but few are out front like that. It is usually much more difficult when people you thought were your friends and were completely committed start getting chummy with the invaders, whore themselves out, and then rationalize it under a cloak of bullshit. What does it all mean when Green Day is on MTV, or Seaweed signs with Hollywood Records for a million dollars? Or when every corporate 'alternative' band has orange hair? Or when Bono and Madonna appear more threatening to the mainstream by saying 'fuck' on national TV than so-called corporate punkers like Jawbox and Bad Religion who appear as meek 'we're just a band' types?"

For J. Robbins, the issue was not so simple: "Some of the greatest punk rockers of all time were put out on a major label. The whole thing is so gray. Maybe the best way is to do everything yourself and be a total survivalist about it. Or maybe what's more important is getting music out where a lot of people can hear it, where those kinds of subversive ideas get to spread. I wish I could wave a flag and go, 'No, this is the only true path.'"

There was truth in this analysis. Although one UK tabloid claimed in late 1976 that "punk rock—the spitting, swearing, savage pop music of rebellious youth—is sweeping teenage Britain," as *Post* rock writer Richard Harrington noted, "it wasn't, at least not until the media stepped in and made it Topic A in every home in England, in the process recruiting an army of would-be punkers." Sociologist Jeff Goldthorpe argued that "the formula of doom and co-optation is too symmetrical, too neat. Most punks had no access to a 'pure' non-commodified punk experience; the vast majority first learned of punk through the media industry—via the isolated authorship of the Sex Pistols, the Clash, Devo, or Blondie."

Henry Rollins offered his own spin: "I love going into major media holes, slick agencies, taking that money and putting it into my own little art projects. I love spending corporate money on counterculture art. It's a Rambo mission. I'm not doing it to be a rock star. Now that I've got some money, and a lot of people pay attention to me, it's a wonderful opportunity. To me, that is the coup to pull. Go in, do the thing in the marketplace, have the supreme opportunity to be dick—but never sell out."

In *Rolling Stone*, Rollins elaborated: "I don't cuss in songs. It's too easy. I love the idea of coming out with a record that is heavier than NWA but you can't put a sticker on it. Which is the one thing I learned from Jim Morrison, in one interview where he said 'Guns aren't dangerous, minds are dangerous . . . You want a weapon? It's right here,'" Rollins recalled, pointing to his head. "You hear that song 'Five to One'? That's so incendiary . . . My thing has always been: Get up, get into it, get involved. Not drop and tune out. What are you doing slacking? The world's on fire. For me, the '90s are a call to arms."

All of this could be convenient rationalization. However, while the exit of Rollins, Jawbox, Nirvana, and others, in one sense, weakened the underground, their success brought attention as well. Nirvana's popularity had brought massive resources to Sub Pop, just as Green Day brought money to Lookout and Offspring—thanks to the support of MTV—brought profits to Epitaph. While there was no guarantee that those funds would be used to strengthen the underground, it seemed possible. Still, this was cold comfort for punks feeling like victims of a brutal home invasion.

Whether in the underground or the corporate realm, to be creatively vital and financially viable remained a challenge. The new Bad Brains returned to DC to open for Living Color at the WUST Radio Hall—a venue they had headlined in their first return to action in 1985. As if to make amends for past indiscretions, the band came back a few months later for a show at the 9:30 Club that was, in part, a benefit for the Whitman-Walker AIDS Clinic.

Darryl explained the band's decision to go on without HR or Earl by saying that "for me, Bad Brains are not really a band. It engulfed my whole life. When HR left, I could not go, 'Oh my god, there goes the Bad Brains.' We're still Bad Brains . . . If it didn't mean everything to us, we wouldn't still be doing it."

But while their live shows still sold well, many remained unconvinced. Their new Epic album *Rise* appeared in mid-1993 to mixed reviews. Some old fans took the new version of Bad Brains almost as a personal affront. Adolf Kowalksi, who had befriended the band in the late '70s, wrote in *Maryland Musician* that "these pioneers should be ashamed of themselves." Another longtime observer, Mark Jenkins, compared their AOR-friendly ballad "Without You" to '80s hair-band Winger in a critical *Washington Post* review.

Darryl offered this reflection: "There will be a temptation for people who were really into HR to not like the band. I think there will be a lot of that we'll have to overcome. But we were never a band that was all about gaining fans and all that shit. For us, it's about expressing ourselves and our music, that's our mission."

Despite these defiant words, the bottom line still ruled. While far superior to the Mosely-era Brains, the new lineup didn't catch fire like Epic had hoped, with *Rise* selling disappointingly. Multiple personnel changes—the loss of Mackie on drums, replaced by Chuck Treece for a while, followed by the exit of vocalist Israel—left the group floundering. Even though the band soldiered on, by mid-1994, Epic had dropped them.

Just when it seemed that Bad Brains might have finally reached the end of the line, fate revealed another twist. When Chuck Treece left the band, Earl Hudson returned to play drums; within a couple months, he was joined by his brother HR. For the third time, the original Bad Brains were reunited.

Only months before, Darryl had argued that, while HR was "one of the greatest rock and roll frontmen ever," allowing him to determine the band's direction had been a gigantic mistake. Darryl:

"We always had the opportunity to go to a major label but HR would never allow it. He wanted to remain a sufferer who was always struggling. We destroyed ourselves during those years, it was not the industry that did."

Now HR had returned with the understanding that his obstructionism was history. An old friend explained this reversal by saying that "Joseph sees the Bad Brains as his cross to bear . . . It's destiny for him to be in that band." After more than a decade of holding out, HR joined the band in inking a deal with Madonna's label, Maverick, a sudsidiary of Warner Brothers, in the fall of 1994.

Incredibly, Bad Brains were headed for another wall. While the band quickly wrote, recorded, and released a new CD entitled *God of Love* with old ally Ric Ocasek as producer, the results suggested that HR had not eluded his demons. While an occasional song like the sinewy "Justice Keepers" approached the purposeful power of old Bad Brains, HR's lyrics were clichéd at best, incomprehensible at worst. While the band was sharp and explosive, without HR fully engaged, the songs sputtered more than sparked.

When Bad Brains returned to DC in May 1995 for a free homecoming show in SE DC at the dance club Tracks, HR's impairment was obvious. Hitting the stage in dark sunglasses that remained glued to his face the whole evening, the once ferociously focused performer seemed barely present. Several times HR drifted backstage in the middle of songs, singing listlessly. While the trio of Darryl, Gary, and Earl were as impressive as ever live, with HR walking in a haze, this was Bad Brains in name only.

HR's troubles notwithstanding, Bad Brains hit the road opening for their longtime fans, the Beastie Boys. Before the Montreal show, HR refused to go onstage, and then exploded, attacking manager Tony Countey savagely. When Earl and others intervened, HR turned on them as well. Ultimately, he was arrested and taken away in handcuffs.

Although Tony was hospitalized, he declined to press charges, explaining to *Post* reporter Richard Harrington, "Physical things heal. Do you posit one physical experience against 14 years of work?" Upon HR's release, he left the band to return home to Los Angeles—only to be arrested again, this time for possession of marijuana at the Canadian border. After HR was bailed out, the band managed to regroup and finish the Beastie Boys tour, then returned to headlining club dates.

Sadly, the worst was yet to come. A few days later at a show in Lawrence, Kansas, HR flew into a rage, believing that a fan in the crowd was spitting on him—something nobody else observed. HR leaped into the crowd wielding a mic stand. By the time the dust cleared, two fans were in the hospital, HR had been arrested for two felony counts of aggravated battery, and Bad Brains' reputation lay in ruins once again. While HR languished in jail awaiting trial, Bad Brains were dropped by Maverick and quietly disbanded. It was a terrible end for one of the great bands of this generation.

At the same time, other DC expatriates were dealing with the mixed blessing of the post–"Smells Like Teen Spirit" world. Not all had immediately headed for the majors. Girls Against Boys—Soul Side minus Bobby Sullivan, plus Eli Janney on keyboards and second bass, and with Scott McCloud on vocals—had migrated to NYC. Once there, they gained fans and media notice with their driving, industrial-tinged music and powerful live shows. Despite major label interest, when the band left the Adult Swim label in 1993, it was not to hook up with the corporate train, but to work with the exemplary indie label, Touch and Go.

Others cast their lot with the big boys. Manifesto's debut album on Atlantic, long delayed by what Hampton called "ongoing contractual nightmares" with UK indie Fire, was finally released in 1993 to generally favorable reviews, but tepid sales. Not long afterward, they were unceremoniously dropped by Atlantic. Not willing to give in, the band changed its name to Clear, released a DIY 45, and went looking for a new record contract.

As part of Wool, Pete and Franz Stahl had also become major label recording artists. If Wool was a step further into the rock world, songs like "SOS" and "Medication"—delivered live with nearly as much punch as Scream at its best—made it clear that their punk heart was still beating. Again, however, sales were slight. After their second CD failed to break through, Wool also became a casualty.

In the midst of this, Scream resurfaced for a couple of weeks, with its now internationally famous drummer in tow. In mid-1993, Dischord reissued all the past Scream records together with the never-released final album *Fumble* on two CDs. Dave recounted, "When Pete said all this (Scream material) was going to come out on CD, first he just asked me some questions about remixing the stuff. Then it turned into, 'Why not do a show at the 9:30?' Then it turned into a whole tour."

While punk reunions were becoming the order of the day, this one made more sense than most, giving Scream a chance to exit on a better note than the sad on-the-road disintegration of three years before. The Stahl brothers took time out from Wool to rejoin Thompson and Grohl—on break from Nirvana as their new CD *In Utero* neared release—to go on the road in the trusty old Dodge Ram that had taken Scream around the country in the past.

Dave told the *Post's* Eric Brace, "I'm so glad that we're doing this. I think it will throw everything back into perspective. We'll play these clubs and maybe sleep on people's floors like we always did, then in the fall I go out with Nirvana and fly into cities and play in front of 10 or 15 thousand people, go to the nice hotel, and watch TV till I fall asleep. It's not the same as playing on a small stage with guys who are basically my brothers."

By now, Nirvana was the embodiment of the "sell-out" to many underground punks. Nonetheless, the band showed a continuing commitment to punk radicalism. Beyond its rough, angry sound, the new CD also contained a series of post-riot pictures—apparently provided to the band by Jello Biafra—of the burnt-out LA County Republican Party Headquarters. This nasty little valentine was reminiscent of the never realized idea to include what Cobain called "revolutionary debris . . . all kinds of anarchistic, revolutionary essays and diagrams on how to make your own bomb" in *Nevermind*. In the end, *In Utero* was banned by Wal-Mart and other chains due to the "fetus collage" on its back cover.

Cobain had also gotten DGC to release the long-out-of print LPs by the female UK punk band, the Raincoats. Beyond this, and the choice of the Breeders for the tour bill, a distinct theme of support for female rock ran through the new record and its art. In one interview, Cobain argued, "Girls are the future of rock—if it has one."

While detractors argued that Nirvana was hopelessly compromised by their major label status and/or could have done more, the band clearly was trying to use its unexpected fame responsibly. Chris Novoselic—who by this time had begun to use "Krist," the original Slavic spelling of his first name—helped focus attention on the bloody conflict in the former Yugoslavia. He and the band subsequently organized and played a benefit to send aid to hundreds of women who had been raped during a campaign of terror in the Balkan War. Novoselic also lobbied against censorship legislation in the Washington State legislature.

Dave Grohl had not forgotten his old community either. When approached by Dante Ferrando for assistance in building a new club as an alternative to 9:30 (run by the not-always terribly congenial Seth Hurwitz), Dave signed on, plunging thousands of dollars into the project. Owned and operated by harDCore veterans, the Black Cat Club would become a mainstay of the scene, even as it continued a turn toward professionalism.

I knew that the band's commitment was real, for I had been working with Dave and Nirvana's manager John Silva—himself a former shit-worker at *MRR*—to arrange a protest gig in DC, initially plotted as a pro-choice demo shortly before the 1992 election. While scheduling and/or personal difficulties had sabotaged that idea, plans for a future protest to be held on the National Mall were still being worked out.

While our plans became real enough to have permits secured (and to be reported on as a rumor in at least one music magazine), the projected date for the event in early June 1994 had to be reconsidered when it conflicted with Dave's honeymoon. In addition, the band was being pursued to headline the fourth Lollapalooza. Despite the delay, John signaled me that the band was interested in working out a new date, perhaps later in the summer in conjunction with Pearl Jam, as a public reconciliation between the two feuding bands.

On November 13, 1993, Nirvana returned to DC, playing to a packed house in Bender Arena at American University, backed by the Breeders and old-time DC favorites, Half Japanese. Bolstered by ex-Germs guitarist Pat Smear, as well as cellist Lori Goldston during an acoustic mini-set, the band sounded great, performing with skill and conviction. Moreover, they seemed in good spirits, with Cobain and Novoselic engaging in playful onstage repartee, including jabs at "all the pigs" resident in DC, and with Grohl coming to the mic to plug the new Black Cat Club and associated DC underground.

None of this, of course, resolved the tension created by Nirvana's popularity. The band could have played a venue like the Capital Centre but had chosen to play a much smaller place. Even so, with a line of security between band and audience, and most of the other trappings of a "rock concert" (as opposed to a punk show), the night was far removed from their last DC show—at 9:30—or what they probably would have preferred.

At the end of their encore, Cobain embarked on an extended trashing of most of the band's onstage equipment. Although the crowd cheered him on, the display begged a question: Was this real rage or just an entertainment spectacle? Cobain seemed oddly dispassionate as he pursued his mayhem. This costly destruction of gear—apparently repeated frequently—seemed a way to symbolically trash their new-found affluence, to work out unresolved guilt about success.

Charles Aaron captured Nirvana's dilemma in the *Village Voice* shortly after the Bender Arena gig: "On a big stage, bare except for wiry red roses poking up here and there, [Cobain] stood stoically before a sold-out moshing mob, singing song after song, sounding better than ever but looking totally defeated. The room became a free-for-all as the band played 'Smells Like Teen Spirit' and a barrage of debris flew toward the stage—bottles, boots, flannel shirts. Cobain never flinched, screaming as if locked in a trance, a professional punk going through the motions because we wanted him to. The barrier between the audience and the performer"—the initial locus of the punk revolution—"was like a Berlin Wall; he must have felt like an idiot for ever trying to jump over."

It was tempting to toss aside doubts amidst the acclaim being showered on the band after the release of *In Utero*. Many had questioned whether the band would survive to record a new album; Nirvana had pulled it off in an artistically uncompromised fashion. It seemed like almost a redemption, with the rave reviews of the record and the shows suggesting that Nirvana had managed to overcome its struggle with the dark side of mass acceptance.

That was certainly the image the band wished to project. In late January '94, Nirvana were on the cover of *Rolling Stone* again, this time in suits, claiming to have made peace with success. Cobain's interview, however, suggested a more complex reality: "I have to admit that I've found myself doing the same things that a lot of other rock stars do or are forced to do . . . not being able to respond to mail, not being able to keep up on current music, pretty much locked away a lot. The outside world is pretty foreign to me."

Cobain also asserted that "Nirvana is almost exhausted. Things are becoming repetitious. There's not something you can move up toward, there's not something you can look forward to . . . I can barely get through 'Teen Spirit.' I literally want to throw down my guitar and walk away. I can't pretend to have a good time playing it."

All of this would soon gain an awful resonance. The tragic events that transpired in early 1994 must have been reported on by every media outlet on the face of the earth. For anyone who happened to have been engaging in space travel at the time and missed it, here are the basics: Barely a month after *Rolling Stone* broadcast the message "Nirvana: Success Doesn't Suck," Cobain overdosed on pills and alcohol on tour in Europe—a mishap later described as a suicide attempt.

After the European tour was aborted, Cobain returned to the US, apparently relapsing fully into heroin addiction. The month of March turned into a parade of worrisome incidents, including a visit by police to get Cobain out of a room in which he had locked himself with several guns. After the effort was successful, the guns were confiscated.

Amidst intense industry pressure to do otherwise, Nirvana dropped out of Lollapalooza. (Strangely, at the same time, Cobain agreed to allow a change to *In Utero's* back cover to get it into the Wal-Mart chain.) Attempts at intervention by friends, begging him to get help for his drug addiction and depression, did no good. While Cobain briefly agreed to go into treatment, once there he apparently changed his mind and slipped away. For a week, he evaded efforts to locate him. In the end, he apparently saw no way out. Around April 5, 1994, Kurt Cobain died of a self-inflicted shotgun blast to the head.

His suicide note made immediate sense to anyone who had come of age in the punk underground: "All of the warnings from the Punk Rock 101 courses over the years since my first introduction to the—shall we say—ethics of independents and the embracement of your community has proved to be very true. I haven't felt the excitement of listening to as well as creating music for too many years now. I feel guilty beyond words for these things . . . The worst crime I can think of would be to put people off by faking it. Sometimes I feel as if I should have a punch-in time clock before I walk onstage . . ."

The handwritten missive ended with, "It's better to burn out than fade away"—a line written in 1978 by '60s icon Neil Young about the demise of the Sex Pistols. The note seemed to be Cobain's final apology for inadvertently helping to turn punk rebellion into commerce.

In the aftermath of Cobain's death, scores of media commentaries on "slackers" and "Generation X" popped up, analyses with human interest angles, pop psychological theories, fan testimonials, and more. A front page *Washington Post* article proclaimed that Cobain's "fatalism" touched a generation, calling him "an authentic disciple of the punk 'no future' aesthetic"—whatever that meant.

Sadly, this was one of the better articles. Entire forests were felled in order to share the most dubious speculations, written almost invariably by people who had never stepped foot inside the underground. Not surprisingly, virtually none noted what was obvious to veterans of the community that had given birth to Nirvana—Kurt Cobain was a punk rocker, at odds with his generation, not seeking to be its spokesperson.

Connected to this was an anti-star ethic. As Krist Novoselic said in a recorded message for an impromptu post-suicide vigil, held on the site of a free concert Nirvana had given a year before in Seattle, "Kurt's approach to his fans was rooted in the punk rock way of thinking. No musician is royalty. Take a guitar, bang out what you feel inside, and you're the superstar." That this punk idealism must have contributed to Cobain's anguish at suddenly becoming what he disdained was often overlooked.

Of course, there were alternatives to suicide. As Courtney Love tearfully noted while reading his note—also via a tape recording—at the vigil, "If you hated being a rock star, you could just fucking stop." One of Cobain's old punk friends told me, "The note showed that the time in his life he looked toward was while he was in Olympia," adding, with obvious pain, "He could have come back, we never went away."

Her words pointed toward an important fact. While it would have been easy to overlook amidst the hoopla, the underground persisted. In DC, strong new bands like Norman Mayer Group, Mob Action (out of Pitchman), Cupid Car Club (out of the NOU and Getaway Car), Ape House (out of Cupid Car Club), Antimony and Las Mordidas (both out of Circus Lupus), and Kerosene 454 rose and sometimes fell quickly. In a sign of the continuing impact of the girl revolution, most contained females, often in a majority in the band.

The Black Cat quickly became an important venue, especially with the continued absence of new church halls or any real replacement for dc space. While this meant a steady stream of shows, it also tended to shift the focus of the scene into the club/bar circuit, away from the genuinely independent spaces. Politically, groups like the Beehive Collective, Riot Grrrl, Food Not Bombs, prisoner support group Anarchist Black Cross, and Positive Force continued to organize to do service work, benefit concerts, educational events, and protests.

Lois Maffeo had released a strong new record, *Strumpet*, recorded with drummer Molly Neuman for K Records. After touring the UK with Neuman, Maffeo added DC residents Amy Farina and Juan Carrera on drums and bass respectively. At the same time, Tsunami and Velocity Girl both released popular new LPs, leading Mark Jenkins to write in the *Post* that "where a few years ago, DC was known for punk, now pop is making more noise."

The Simple Machines' "Working Holidays" series had been a massive success, ending with a well-attended blow-out at the Black Cat. Simple Machines was featured—complete with a full-color photo of Tsunami—in a *Rolling Stone* piece on indie labels. Although the article soft-pedaled any anti-corporate reason for independent music, it also spread crucial practical knowledge, thanks to Simple Machines' address being printed, together with info on the 1994 edition of their "Mechanic's Guide to Putting Out Music."

Holy Rollers seemed to be back on an upswing with a new female bassist and potent songs like the jagged "Rage Incorporated." While Rain Like the Sound of Trains, Hoover, and Slant 6 all released powerful albums on Dischord over the second half of 1993 and 1994, only Slant 6 was still together by late 1995. In the venerable DC tradition, Sevens and Crown Hate Ruin rose from the ashes of these fallen bands. Forceful singles by Antimony, Norman Mayer Group, Cupid Car Club, and the Suspects were released on Dischord, Kill Rock Stars, and new labels like Torque, the latest entity to incubate in PF House.

Olympia's Kill Rock Stars had developed into perhaps the best independent label in America. Among the outstanding KRS releases in 1994 was an EP from Bratmobile called *The Real Janelle*. Although it was short—six songs, including one cover—the EP showed Bratmobile continuing to grow artistically, in spite of the fact that they now lived in three different places—DC, Olympia, and the Bay Area.

In the liner notes of the CD, Erin, Molly, and Allison tried to to address their media image: "We never set out with a unified agenda about being women/girls making music, although we all agreed that it was cool. We all have different ideas about a lot of things, but because we've been represented and misrepresented so many times, the only way we've been able to represent ourselves is by putting out records (which also unclearly reflect circumstances of money, time, and state of mind) and doing tours whenever we can." The band did some West Coast shows as well as a well-received UK tour.

But if Bratmobile's music seemed stronger than ever, the members of the band—caught in the media pressure cooker—were growing apart. The differences came to a head at a one-off gig in NYC where Bratmobile, in effect, broke up onstage. It was a sad end to an important band—and perhaps to some friendships, for a fifth and final issue of *Girl Germs* was issued by Allison alone. While Erin's and Allison's future plans were unclear, Molly quickly resurfaced, playing drums in the PeeChees, who released a scrappy single on Kill Rock Stars and toured the USA in summer 1994.

As Bratmobile was coming to its end, their old ally Bikini Kill returned, ablaze with renewed vigor. Besides releasing a strong album *(Pussy Whipped)* and an even better single ("New Radio") on Kill Rock Stars, the band did a short East Coast tour in summer 1994 followed by a more lengthy jaunt in the fall. Their shows were becoming huge—600+ in both DC and Berkeley—and the audience reaction was intense. Although the band now faced a bonehead element in their crowd due to their popularity, shows I saw in Santa Cruz, California and St. Paul, Minnesota carried a powerful spirit, with a massive number of girls in attendence. The band itself seemed refreshed, playing better than ever, effectively silencing many of their earlier critics. As Kathleen told me, "They thought that we would go away, that we would shut up, but we didn't."

Bikini Kill also issued its first two EPs on one CD with notes combatting misinformation circulating about the band: "BIKINI KILL IS A BAND MADE UP OF FOUR INDIVIDUALS . . . We have been written about a lot by big magazines who have never talked to us or seen our shows. They write about us authoritatively as if they understand us better than we understand our own ideas, tactics, and significance. They largely miss the point of everything about us because they have no idea what our context is/has been. Their idea of punk rock is not based on anything they have ever experienced directly . . . We want to be an underground band, we don't want to be featured in *Newsweek*."

The band was careful to note that "we recognize that different strategies are totally valid for different situations. We are not trying to set any kind of 'correct' standard, we are just trying to present our views on what our experience with the media has been . . . Think about what you know about us and think about how you got that information, 'cuz in most cases it probably isn't too accurate." Bikini Kill helped to further disarm misunderstanding by playing two big LA shows with Spitboy, who had survived a chancy personnel shift made necessary by original bassist Paula's bout with carpal tunnel syndrome.

Underground sniping against Bikini Kill continued, albeit on a somewhat lower level. Rumors went around that they were going to sign to Warner Brothers or join the next Lollapalooza. Criticism also rose when the band agreed to open a $22.50 show for the reunited Go-Go's, who Bikini Kill respected as punk pioneers—the first all-female band to have a self-written number one record. From the stage at Gilman Street—a six-dollar show two days before the Go-Go's gig— Kathleen acknowledged the controversy unapologetically. Although the band evidenced no intent of leaving the underground, Kathleen defiantly noted the class privilege that could be involved in not signing to majors. This was a courageous statement, sure to be unpopular in a place where graffiti like "Destroy Green Day"—once a regular denizen of the Gilman stage—festooned the walls.

Fugazi also rolled on unbowed. Despite a level of popularity that enabled them to sell out three nights in LA—nearly 12,000 seats total—Fugazi remained unaccomodating to the music business. When friends who now worked for corporate-backed *Dirt* magazine asked for an interview, the band only allowed the magazine to observe one that Ian did with three fanzine writers—an indication of where the band's true loyalty lay.

In the midst of their 1993 tour, *In on the Kill Taker* finally appeared. To me, it was everything a punk record should be—artistically challenging, politically radical, emotionally convincing, and economically independent. Its mere existence on Dischord Records was a triumph within the context of the ascent of corporate punk.

Not everyone agreed. At least a couple old allies found the band now altogether too oblique. Mark Jenkins wrote in the *City Paper* that "*Kill Taker* and its predecessor, *Steady Diet of Nothing*, include some message songs, but with lyrics so cryptic as to resemble code. Today the band sometimes sounds like it cares more about guitar tunings than about injustice." Mark also faulted the band's increasingly abrasive sound: "Nobody expects the band to be cuddly, but a little approachability wouldn't hurt." While Tim Yohannon disliked the album's music for very different reasons, he echoed Mark's critique of its lyrics, calling it so "self-absorbed that it makes me want to take a gun and shoot people."

Others were more sympathetic to the dark, complex vision within Fugazi's words. Witness *Melody Maker's* Cathi Unsworth: "*Kill Taker* scarily evokes all the paranoia, fear, and loathing of an LA summer night that was too hot for anyone to handle, in missives like 'Great Cop' and '23 Beats Off' which ends side one in flames and foul black smoke and the whirring ominous sound of helicopter blades. *In on the Kill Taker* is Fugazi's finest hour . . . Fugazi care a lot. Probably more than is good for their sanity."

Or the Australian magazine *Revue*: "Fugazi's elliptical lyrics may frustrate the listener from unraveling the specific theme of each song, but there's no escaping the collective fear and loathing of their imagery. From the paranoia of 'Great Cop' and 'Public Witness Program' to the foreboding doom of 'Last Chance' and 'Smallpox Champion's' savaging of their country's past and present treatment of Native Americans, the album documents a corrupt and violent society tearing itself apart."

The album showed up in some unusual places as well—like the *Billboard* charts. As *The Music Paper* noted, "If you're unfamiliar with Dischord Records, a huge percentage of the label's sales are through mail order and smaller stores. Even with only about 15 to 25 percent of sales registering with SoundScan, *[Kill Taker]* still managed to chart in the Top 200." With virtually no promotion at all, the album quickly sold more than 200,000 copies, reaching number one in the independent charts of both *NME* and *Melody Maker*. Despite being denied an interview, *Time* ran a laudatory piece on the band entitled "Not For Sale or Lease," complete with a full-color picture.

Kill Taker even managed the near impossible—gaining rave reviews in both *Rolling Stone* and *Maximum RockNRoll*. Ironically, both pieces evoked a common comparison. As *Rolling Stone* wrote, "In 1979, the Clash advertised themselves as 'the only band that matters.' In 1993, that claim belongs to Fugazi. In an era of corporate-sponsored 'alternative' music, Fugazi are the real deal. Remaining staunchly independent, Fugazi manages to sell in the hundreds of thousands while maintaining their incendiary politics and a raw difficult sound born out of the DC hardcore scene."

As the hyperbole grew, Fugazi's insistence on demystifying themselves also became more pronounced. Ian said, "All we do is write music we like and feel challenged by . . . We're human beings. We just don't feel like selling ourselves off as anything other than a band."

Despite such self-effacement, the band's mystique continued to grow. When the *Washington Post* printed a feature article on the band in August 1993, its headline read, "Washington's Fugazi Claims It's Just a Band. So Why Do So Many Kids Think It's God?" Written by veteran writer Eric Brace, the article gave a revealing snapshot of Fugazi in the midst of the chaos generated by punk's breakthrough.

After noting the props given to the band by Kurt Cobain, Courtney Love, Michael Stipe, Eddie Vedder, and others, Brace asked: "Fugazi. It's not on MTV. Not on your radio station. Who are these guys and what is it that brings rock's royalty to their door?"

The initial answer was simply Fugazi's music. Describing a show in Vancouver, BC, Brace wrote, "The dynamic punk-funk music goes from a pin drop to a bomb blast in a beat. It evokes terms like 'visceral' and 'kinetic' and 'empassioned,' adjectives that do nothing to convey the impact of Picciotto onstage, twisting himself like taffy, screaming his lyrics, moving as if he's barefoot on hot coals. They can't explain the emotional explosion in the ampitheater when Joe Lally starts the brutal rhythmic bass notes of 'Waiting Room' . . . MacKaye shouts, a thousand shout along; the connection is made. Two guitars, buzzing with jagged notes and distortion, ride on top of Canty and Lally's funk."

For Brace, this artistic achievement was what made the second element—Fugazi's radical ethics—so significant. Brace: "When Lollapalooza '93 called earlier this year inviting Fugazi to join the traveling road show, the offer was rejected out of hand: the $33 ticket was $28 too high. And if somehow Fugazi had agreed to the offer, it would have been the only band on the main stage without a global corporation behind it." Despite hordes of underground defectors and lavish offers from Atlantic, Geffen, Columbia, EMI, Elektra, Warner, and more, Fugazi remained with Dischord. Brace: "Dischord is now one of the most respected independent rock labels in the world. It has sold nearly 1 1/2 million records, tapes, and CDs mostly by word of mouth, with Fugazi accounting for more than half those sales."

While not denouncing other bands, Fugazi intended to stick to its original community and vision. Later Ian noted, "The moment you sign to a major label, it's an investment where returns are expected. There's nothing necessarily evil or bad about that. But I'm not interested in being manipulated for the sake of someone making money. Sure, we could sign to a major, we've had dozens of offers. But at the end of the day, it's more interesting to have been a punk rock band who stuck to their guns on being super-independent and when they broke up, they're still making their own decisions. Anyway, when you die, money doesn't mean shit."

Although the hoopla surrounding Fugazi—as well as the growing age gap between band and audience—tended to undermine their punk egalitarianism, the band still tried to minimize the distance, as attested to by the regular after-gig conversations that could drag on for an hour or more. When Brace noticed these sessions and suggested that "the audience is curious about a band whose songs seem to offer direction rather than entertainment," his thrust was parried by Guy: "Some people . . . want us to supply some kind of message, but if I wanted to express a message in that way I would have been a politician. I'm not. I'm a musician. It's in the songs. It's there for people to use or not."

Ian added, "Our primary concern is to be ourselves in our own band and never become other people's property. That's why we don't sell our name on T-shirts, that's why we don't go into specifics about what we do in our personal lives, that's why we don't blueprint every song we write."

The band spoke with the whole of its existence, as well as with the PF-organized benefits, free concerts, and protests that continued to make up all of its metro DC shows, as well as more sporadic out-of-town gigs like a gay rights benefit in Colorado after voters approved an anti-gay initiative and an ACT-UP benefit in Catholic-dominated Ireland during which thousands of free condoms were handed out.

At the UM Free Clinic benefit, Ian noted that "the most important thing about benefits is generating fuel for people who are working on the front lines. Or when we played in front of the Capitol, that something like that could happen. To me, that consciousness is crucial, that people can see that things are possible, that you can do things."

Fugazi, more than any other single group to emerge from punk, was breaking new ground, extending the realm of that which was deemed "possible" by conventional wisdom, simply through the quiet, undeniable fact of what they were doing. In a way, not just punk, but rock history was being made. While human and imperfect like all of us, Fugazi nonetheless represented an inspiring example born out of the long years of the punk rebellion.

Nonetheless, the band continued to face stinging rebukes, sometimes from inside their own local underground community. For example, ever since the conflict at the Supreme Court protest, some within Riot Grrrl DC had begun to see Fugazi as less an ally than an enemy.

Erika Reinstein expressed her frustration on Olympia's KAOS-FM: "With Fugazi and a lot of other male punk bands, there is this kind of 'liberal' attitude of sympathizing with the issues but not ever wanting to take any kind of radical action to deal with them—especially when it comes to giving up some of their power. In DC, the boys totally run the scene. Ian MacKaye would have to give up a whole lot of privilege to make for some real equality in that scene. His record label doesn't really encourage women as far as I know."

The irony of this critique was considerable, for Ian had long championed women's empowerment in the scene. To some men and women, RG DC—and Erika and Mary in particular—had become a loose cannon, turning legitimate outcry into purist power-tripping. To sort out who was wrong or right in any given circumstance could be difficult; it was not hard to see the divisions in the scene growing, however.

About the same time, another bone of contention surfaced. Eric Brace had noted in his *Post* article that "one thing earlier Fugazi releases didn't have but that you'll find on *In on the Kill Taker* are UPC bar code stickers. Fugazi now permits the bar codes on the outside of its packaging but refuses to incorporate them into its album artwork as do most record companies . . . a compromise that enables the band to get into the large chain record stores, which do not accept merchandise without the familiar vertical lines."

For some in the underground who despised the chain stores and saw no reason to accomodate their needs, the UPC codes had come to represent the corporate co-optation of punk. Still, even die-hard indies like K and Kill Rock Stars were now incorporating the codes into the artwork on their releases. Fugazi's approach was an artful one, treating the code as simply a fancy adhesive price tag which could be peeled off after purchase. For some, this put them on the wrong side of the latest underground dividing line.

This became obvious when Fugazi gave an unsolicited $500 donation to the Beehive community center. For more militant DC punks, the Beehive was a hopeful element in what otherwise seemed to be an increasingly apolitical and co-opted scene. The band wanted to fuel their work and said so in a friendly note enclosed with the check; grateful members of the Beehive placed the note on their bulletin board.

Shortly thereafter, however, another person from the Beehive tacked a UPC sticker from *In on the Kill Taker* next to the note with the acidic aside: "This is Fugazi's UPC sticker. Isn't it cute?" Since the board was communal space and the note wasn't signed, it appeared that the comment represented the Beehive's general opinion, much to the dismay of Fugazi.

Although some apologies were made over the incident, it further poisoned the atmosphere of the DC underground, as did a subsequent Beehive decision to not work with Jawbox on a benefit concert due to their major label affiliation. Another incident occured when the Beehive was approached by Susan Corrigan of *ID* magazine for an article on the punk group house scene in DC. Led by a couple of members, the collective responded with a savage personal attack on Corrigan, telling her to "fuck off and die."

Ironically, the Beehive itself was soon embroiled in controversy. Once again, Erika and Mary were at the storm's center. The once blighted U Street corridor was now becoming the "New U," a gentrifying "hip" neighborhood. By inserting a punk book/record store with a mostly white, middle-class clientele into this context, Beehive seemed likely to aid this process. When disaffected Beehive members Erika and Mary—together with two non-white friends, Cindy and Akiko, who were affiliated with RG Olympia—pressed the issue, even supporters had to admit that the center had not really dealt with the issue thus far.

While the Beehive's critics had legitimate issues, their approach—which included vandalism, verbal abuse, and unfounded accusations—was scarcely the most constructive. Their insistence that the Beehive immediately leave the neighborhood as the only way to not abet gentrification suggested a moral absolutism now running rampant in punk, largely in a self-defeating response to the corporate threat. In this case, the confrontation catalyzed the Beehive into dealing with gentrification more seriously; overall, crippling splits within the underground were the more common results of such ventures.

The rise of this "punk fundamentalism" seemed nearly as dangerous to the community as the major labels. Honest critique was essential—but it needed to be balanced by reasonable support and flexibility, or the bonds of community would be shredded and potential power blunted, even destroyed. If the underground could not learn to respect differences and find common ground, it might destroy what the corporations could not.

Although African-American lesbian writer/activist Audre Lorde was speaking of schisms within the feminist movement, her essay, "The Master's Tools Will Never Dismantle the Master's House," carried profound relevance for any community of outsiders, including punk. While Lorde's revolutionary commitment was clear, she understood that this process needed to be worked out with an eye toward preserving and not shredding bonds, for "without community, there is no liberation, only the most vulnerable and temporary armistice between an individual and her oppression."

Noting that this "must not mean the shedding of our differences, nor the pathetic pretense that these differences do not exist," Lorde went on to argue for "learning . . . how to make common cause with others identified as outside the structures in order to define and seek a world in which we all can flourish . . . to take our differences and make them strengths."

In words that reflected similar insights, Bratmobile's Molly Neuman noted, "We come to punk rock with our own individual experience, histories, and abuse or, on the other hand, with whatever wonderful situations, wonderful things that have come to us. I'm trying to keep constantly in check with myself, to know that the people who I'm coming in contact with have similar fucked up experiences too, most likely. I'm not going to judge them on every little thing that they do or say because my own history is so fucked up too. Our union is really important. That's one thing I don't want to put in jeopardy."

Molly's words seemed to suggest a hopeful direction for the embattled punk community. In its way, Fugazi's approach also held promise. In late 1986, Ian had told me of his idea for "revolution by example." Formulated out of a distaste for the rhetorical overkill popular with many radicals of the '60s, this concept suggested that any real revolution was not about talking, it was about doing, about speaking with our actions.

The power of such a self-demanding approach in the hyper-critical atmosphere of mid-'90s punk seemed obvious. Amidst so much recrimination and finger-pointing, Fugazi's insistence on pushing forward with their own approach without unduly taking others' inventories seemed a wise corrective. As British band New Model Army put it in their own requiem for the punk movement, the song "Modern Times": "It matters not what you believe in/It matters less what you say/It matters what you are."

In March 1995, I used those words on a flier for a PF show at a reopened Wilson Center with Slant 6 and three powerful new DC bands: the Make Up, the Warmers, and Jury Rig, units who included, respectively, the resurrected remnant of the NOU and Alec and Amanda MacKaye. For me, the show signaled the end of one cycle and the beginning of another. Like all of the best critique, the NMA quote was aimed first and foremost at myself, as a reminder of a path past cynical sell-out on one side and self-righteous purism on the other—a path toward a future that still nourished the promise and possibilities of punk.

The sometimes dreary soap operas described in these pages give insight into a larger drama: the halting, incomplete nature of human progress. "It is not for you to finish the task—but neither can you forsake the work," goes an old Jewish proverb. Punk, for me, has not been about sold-out dreams—it is a story filled with courage and cowardice, with dream and disillusion, yes. But above all, punk is a story of a community that has persisted, imperfectly but powerfully, to raise a vision of a better world that might still be.

The simplistic lines drawn by some falsify reality and undermine transformation. Any sincere effort aimed toward truth-telling or change-making is to be applauded. Having said that, I believe in creating institutions outside the corporate status quo—hence my decision to avoid mainstream publishers in writing this book and to work instead with friends from within the underground. Hopefully, this is not simply a book about punk, but an example of that phenomenon.

For some, punk was just a phase, a momentary interruption in the inexorable march toward a pre-ordained social niche. For others, though, once it had happened, life would never be the same. Guy: "I haven't been to one of those huge Cap Centre shows since I was a midget. I remember thinking that that is what rock'n'roll was about. Then I saw the Cramps playing in front of my face, vomiting and throwing shit through the windows, breaking up the whole joint. And I never went back. *Because you can't go back.*"

I wasn't at the Cramps show, but I know what Guy meant, for in one way or another, I have been there too. Most punks have. Those transparent moments are powerfully intimate brushes with the full magic, beauty, and possibility of life. Indirectly, they energize us to refute the charade that generally passes for "living" in our society, to defeat the statistics that so often rule our lives, to make something that seems real.

What does punk mean; where will it go? That's your question to answer. Labels, in the end, mean little and, for me, that's what punk has been: just the latest label, one among many, for an energy of individuality, compassion, questioning, and creativity that has always fueled the best achievements of humanity, the true progress in our world. That idea, that energy, remains there for anyone who wants to embrace it, to challenge the world, to challenge themselves, to redefine the "possible" by their own sweat, blood, and tears—and, in so doing, maybe even to find happiness and help others in this quest as well.

That last point is crucial, for this is being written in the aftermath of the conservative electoral landslide of November 1994. It is an ugly time, marked by cuts in social programs and the passage of anti-immigrant legislation like California's Proposition 187. Money buys elections—and now no one can run for high office in this country without being rich or in servitude to those who are. The gap between the rich and the poor has grown to its widest since the Great Depression. At 1.5 million, the US prison population has more than tripled in the years covered by this book. [As of 2003, the prison population was over 2 million—four times the number in 1980.] In a sadly adroit summation, Jesse Jackson has noted that we "have declared an end to the war on poverty and declared war on the poor." We are sowing the seeds for suffering—and, ultimately, an explosion—of frightening depth and breadth.

What might punk have to offer to this struggle? Good question, for it is hard to build a movement for broad social change out of moments occuring erratically in subterranean enclaves. According to sociologist Jeff Goldthorpe, "Post-'60s youth subcultures have discovered the possibilities of soldarity in the subcultural arena rather than in political organizations. On the common ground of music clubs, campus assemblies, roving spontaneous marches, blockades, invasions of corporate space, Rock Against Reagan festivals, and gay freedom parades, we have gained the briefest glimpse of life beyond our fragments. But these ecstatic moments pass, and we return to labor in our subdivided cubicles. The 'freedom high' of cultural politics exists in a sea of fear, indifference, and hostility."

Goldthorpe was surely right when he said that "youth subcultures, defined by their marginality, do not offer any direct routes to the promised land." Politically, punk will always be a limited instrument. But, as Goldthorpe noted, "That field is where we start." For years, my work has been increasingly outside of the punk scene. This has not meant an exit from that world. At its best, the punk community is what Dug Birdzell has called "a culture of resistance." It cannot be everything we need, but it can be a touchstone, a home, nourishing us as we join with other communities to work for broader change.

I don't wish to remain in the margins, comfortable in elitist judgment of the mass. I don't want youth revolution, I want bonds of mutual respect reaching across generations, classes, races, sexual orientations, and genders. The politics associated with bands like Los Crudos and Heavens to Betsy as well as phenomena like Riot Grrrl and Beehive (at their best) are hopeful in that they encourage this broader field of concern and action. Punk is where we started—and where we now can hope to go beyond.

This does not mean we should turn away from our vision, unduly compromise ourselves, or deny our individuality—but as Lorde suggests, we have to breach the walls of our all-too-hermetic subcultures, and find a way to embrace our differences with other communities and make them the forge in which a movement for real transformation can be built.

We need not be trapped by old conceptions, by exhausted styles, by limited vision. As I approach middle age, the words of Jen Smith ring true: "The absolute truth is that we will all grow old, we all will die—but we can be the Young Idea manifest in OLD bodies, our lives on the faces of babies, us, in the flesh, the living, living flesh. Couldn't we try?" Or as another friend, Amy Pickering, once gently chided me, "It's easy to be young and idealistic—the trick is to be old and idealistic."

Such open-ended challenges are all that seem real to me today. The past—all these hundreds of pages—is merely prologue. What is truly important remains ahead, bound up in each new moment, right now. The stakes are high, the outcome uncertain . . . and I wouldn't have it any other way.

"Walker, there is no path; you make the path as you walk."
—Antonio Machado

CROWD AT PE MARCH ON WASHINGTON MEMORIAL CONCERT (by Pat Graham)

afterword

by Mark Andersen, November 2000

This is not the end, but this is where I'm stopping. I didn't set out to be DC's "punk historian." I started this project in 1986 simply because I thought this was a story that should be told. That story only grew richer and more challenging as the years passed. By 1993, when I began writing the rough draft, it became a journey into my own struggles, a way, as Rites of Spring once sang, to look back in order to get beyond. Telling this tale was a personal exorcism, an expedition to search the ruins for lesson, for spark in a time of bitter confusion. By 1995 I had found what I needed. As a result, I became focused on the *now* again, on living—hence my disinterest in writing about the last five years of DC punk.

Why did the rough draft sit for five years unfinished? You already know part of the answer. In addition, given all of the vultures circling around the corpse of Kurt Cobain, I didn't desire to publish a book that might appear to be capitalizing on that tragedy. Also, I was simply burnt out on the project, had other priorities, and pursued them. Even when I was refreshed and wished to return to the book, time was hard to come by. I was lucky to find such a sensitive and skilled collaborator as Mark Jenkins; otherwise the rough draft might still be gathering dust.

After all the words, pictures, and emotions, this shared dance comes down to one final point, by far the most important of all: This has been a story about people very much like you. What was done, you could do—or more—in your own context. The past is gone, the future is always just beyond our grasp—all we have is *now*, this moment. *And your story is the one that matters now.*

As the Urban Verbs sang so long ago, history is not over. Find the muscles you've never used yet, speak the languages we've never heard. If you need to, I hope you'll say "fuck you" to me, to everyone in this book, to all our varied ideals and dreams. Find your own ideals, your own dreams. Write your own history/her-story, write it with your passion, with your belief; above all, write it with your actions. Make it a story worthy of being told to others someday, a story worth having lived.

May 2003:

new beginnings

by Mark Andersen

COMING SOON:
THE ARTHUR S. FLEMING CENTER
· EMMAUS SERVICES FOR THE AGING

WOMEN AGAINST THE IRON FIST

"To be old is a glorious thing when one has not unlearned what it means 'to begin!'"
—Martin Buber

POSITIVE FORCE IN FRONT OF THE COMPLETED FLEMMING CENTER, APRIL 2003 *(by Nancy Shia)*

new beginnings

Over the past decade or so, as work on *Dance of Days* dragged on and on, I told more than a few friends that my life seemed likely to consist of roughly three segments: before the book, during the book, and after the book. The discussion invariably ended with the expression of my hope to live long enough to actually get to the third phase!

Well, here it is, kind of . . . only *Dance of Days* still seems to be casting a pretty big shadow. Sometimes "life after" feels like "life during"—just at hyper-speed. Even when the energizing but exhausting book tours were over, I felt buried. All my other work was still there, with more seemingly drawn magnetically to me as a result of meeting new people, entering new arenas . . . all rich, raw material, of course, for new projects.

Not the least of these new vistas is another book, conceived as an activism-focused sequel to this one, extending themes raised at the end of the last chapter. Tentatively titled *All the Power: Radical Illusions and Practical Revolution*, it should be appearing in spring 2004 on AK Press. Those who know me well, of course, will only believe that when they see it. Fair enough—I hope to startle you by doing something on time for once.

Simultaneously, mountains of time and energy have been poured into the Flemming Center. This is a community center that brings together a dozen non-profits involved in radical arts, organizing, education, and service in one 13,000-square-foot structure in the middle of the historic but long-troubled Shaw neighborhood.

As another entire book could be written about this topic, let me settle for simply saying that I consider this, hands-down, the single most important and exciting project in my twenty-plus years of activism. While the Center has finally opened (after eight years of work), it has proven even more arduous to see through to completion than this book.

I realize that I must sound like something of a sourpuss here. Don't get me wrong, I'm not exactly complaining . . . but the past couple of years have been a real challenge. And here I am, still working on this damn book, readying yet another edition!

Perhaps this is just as it should be, given how profoundly important the events and ideas described in this book are—and always will be—to me. It is not just some story I could tell and then leave behind. It is a huge part of what I do, what I believe . . . who I am.

This is not to say that the world is quite the same—but when is it ever? I have been profoundly touched by those who have greeted the book with acclaim. My favorite review was by Peter Scholtes, writing in the Minneapolis *City Pages* that *Dance of Days* was "the DC equivalent of Jon Savage's *England's Dreaming.*" While my pal Mark Jenkins might well disagree, for me, a more flattering comparison would be hard to find.

Of course, we also give thanks for those less impressed, who sometimes had harshly critical perspectives to offer. When those critiques were thoughtful and/or informed, they were an opportunity to learn, to grow, to make ourselves and the book better.

Overall, it seems that this book has been received quite well. In the end, what has impressed me most is not the kudos, however. Rather, it is just how many lives DC punk has touched; indeed— since it is a story still being written—how many lives DC continues to touch, how much its influence continues to reverberate.

This was driven home in a special way while on the road in the UK, during one of several book tours. After the Riot Grrrl frenzy, mass media features about straight edge gangs, and the like, little should surprise me now. So why would detailed explanations in *NME* of that pesky three-letter word (begins with an *e;* ends with an *o)* that we were almost successful in omitting from *Dance of Days?*

Little did I know that the flood had just begun. Before year's end, I had encountered features on the dreaded "emo" in *Time, Rolling Stone,* the *Washington Post* (inexplicably claiming that the progenitor of this odd alleged subset of punk was Minor Threat—shame on you, David Segal!), *Spin,* more. Once again, we found ourselves in the midst of a media storm with roots somehow laid deep in the anti-commercial DC punk bedrock. *Alternative Press* eventually proclaimed 2002 as "The Year Punk Broke . . . Again!"

Of course, the reflection glimpsed in the media's funhouse mirror was hardly recognizable. We were generally treated to a grotesque refracting of an idea that some of us had given our hearts and minds to so long ago, somehow still echoing down the halls of modern consumer culture. Few of the new bands mentioned seemed worthy of being described as "an echo," so diluted, so sold-out and safe was the product. Ah, but that is life, is it not?

This is also not the whole story, however. The most important misconception that I sometimes encountered on the road was that Mark Jenkins or I somehow thought that DC punk had died. Anything but! Even rock industry voice *Billboard* acknowledged the continued vitality of DC and Dischord (together with other indies like Touch and Go, Fat Wreck Chords, and Sub City) on the front page of its May 4, 2002 issue.

Headlined "Punk State of Mind Prevails," the essay somewhat incredulously commented that "the rebellious spirit of punk has been self-maintained during the course of more than two decades." According to writer Chris Morris, this is "thanks in large measure to its do-it-yourself philosophical roots [and] its independent economic approach"—attributes that owe a special debt to DC punk past.

Morris also noted the continued vigor of the underground, regardless of whether punk was "hot" in the pop charts at the moment. In the article, Ian MacKaye explained that punk's ongoing appeal to new generations of teen listeners was "because music is one of the few cultural languages that kids still have access to," adding that "if you are someone who feels disaffected or marginalized by life, then there is a huge aspect of underground music that will provide a perfect soundtrack for that."

Fugazi, together with many other DC bands, obviously continues to fulfill that mission. Other observers, however, have asked a slightly more complicated question: Do Mark Jenkins and I think that DC is still as powerful and creative as it was "back in the day"?

This is an interesting question—and one which I will decline to answer. While I both understand and support groups like the DC Music Revival collective in their efforts to reenergize the local scene, I try really hard not to compare then to now. Although punk (narrowly understood) is hardly as central in my life as in the 1980s or early '90s, I still remain part of that community, if only because it continues to provide inspiration.

So, at the risk of contradicting myself (yet again), I will share just a few of the precious names, places, and moments from my past eight years of DC punk. No doubt many of the deserving will be left out of this extremely subjective mini-tour. I invite you to compose your own version to share (more on this later); meanwhile, here I go . . .

Not surprisingly, many of my prized moments come from PF shows. Perhaps the single most memorable was a Bikini Kill/Team Dresch/Cold Cold Hearts benefit for Helping Individual Prostitutes Survive, held at the GWU Marvin Center, made possible by help above and beyond the call of duty from Liz Ellison.

After the untimely demise of both Cold Cold Hearts and Deep Lust, a startling development occurred: Bratmobile reemerged, better than ever. In 2002, Bratty songs like "United We Don't" and "Shopping for America" provided the perfect post-9/11 dissident soundtrack. Conversely, the passing of Bikini Kill opened the way for a distinctly new voice: Le Tigre. I was astonished by the new unit's power in their first DC show at Black Cat, mixing electronic beats with feminist themes and compelling visuals.

The most striking tribute to the power of reinvention, however, was the Make-Up. I remember the cool defiance of these NOU vets (and their newly adopted comrade, bassist Michelle Mae), reborn resplendent in matching white suits, performing before an uncomprehending and increasingly hostile Fugazi crowd in Philadephia. As shouts of "get off the stage" grew, the band plowed on undeterred, playing their offbeat "Gospel yeh yeh" as an open challenge for all present to stretch their understanding of punk.

It was even more satisfying to see them continue to grow, just as Nation of Ulysses had done in their own way. Eventually, they were near–James Brown tight, creating something not simply brave and visionary, but powerfully realized; at once musically compelling, politically pointed, and just plain fun. Numerous imitators sprang up quickly, testifying to the appeal of this unique new hybrid.

For a time, the Make-Up was as much aligned with PF as any previous band had been, playing more benefits in DC than paying gigs. Shows for Justice for Janitors (held in the Service Employees International Union Hall) and Foundry Housing (held in the church Bill Clinton attended, Foundry Methodist), and a Cuba Libre event—largely designed and conceptualized by the band itself—were as potent as anything PF had ever done.

When the band foundered on the shoals of internal dissension (on the eve of yet another PF benefit, this one with No Lie Relaxer and Dead Meadow), old Mount Pleasant cohort Ted Leo stepped in to fill the drum slot for a couple of final gigs. (The relocated Leo has taken the compelling, but derivative neo-Mod stylings of Chisel into new realms with the brilliant, brainy, politicized pop of the Pharmacists.) Ian Svenonius and Michelle Mae eventually resurfaced in a striking new vehicle, the Scene Creamers, as did James Canty with French Toast.

The Make-Up was hardly the only DC band challenging the bounds of "punk-as-usual." In an equally stirring way, the Warmers challenged DC to turn down the amps while amping up the soul. Bands like the All-Scars, the Crainium, the Vertebrates, El Guapo, Trans Am, and Orthrelm also pushed the experimental envelope.

Some DC punks flirted with other musical styles, from classical (the "Punk Not Rock" project) to jazz (the Sorts) to folk (Homage to Catalonia) to country (Jeff Nelson's Adult Swim label released CDs by Last Train Home and the brilliant Little Pink) and beyond.

Perhaps partly in reaction to such rapprochement with more mainstream forms, Chris Thomson fronted two brittle, brilliantly caustic bands, the Monorchid and Skull Kontrol, that confronted what seemed an increasingly safe, self-satisfied scene. Stocked with venom to spare, Chris asked bluntly, acidly, "Who put out the fire?"

Smart Went Crazy showed that, for some, the fire still burned, surprising observers with a brilliant second CD; I was riveted by their heartbreaking version of "DC Will Do that to You" in the social hall of St. Margaret's Episcopal Church. Most Secret Method was another shining star in DC punk's night sky, as were the jerky, jagged Metamatics and the million-ideas-a-minute punk-rock machine Frodus; rising lights now include Measles, Mumps, and Rubella, Beauty Pill, and Majority Rule.

Dismemberment Plan survived a terrible entanglement with the corporate powers-that-be (ugly enough to make the front page of the *Washington Post)* to remain one of the most fervent and enjoyable exponents of DC punk. I have fond memories of dancing wildly, deliriously to them at a PF benefit in 1998 opposing the crushing sanctions imposed on the Iraqi people. That night at St. Margaret's, the Plan shared a great bill with the (Capitol City) Dusters, Smart-Went-Crazy–descendent Faraquet, and the neo–Riot Grrrl band Princessed.

Old stalwarts like Girls Against Boys and Jawbox—both survivors of challenging corporate hitches—continued to create powerful, uncompromised music (and play PF shows) after going the major-label route. One pleasant by-product of GVSB's tenure with Geffen was Akashic Books; the band itself found a new home with indie Jade Tree. Jilted by Atlantic, Jawbox exited with maximum grace, playing two fiery final benefit shows (rotating the headlining slot with GVSB) at the Black Cat. For a time, Burning Airlines rose from their ashes, a worthy successor to one of DC's great bands—till escalating demand for J. Robbins's production skills also brought this new unit to a halt.

(I am not suggesting, of course, that DC punk-related acts have had entirely negative experiences with the majors. For example, while Henry Rollins has gone from Imago to Dreamworks to BMG-subsidiary Sanctuary, he has been able to continue putting out work seemingly unhindered by the shifts, as well as continuing to release CDs and books through his own independent label and press. Dave Grohl also shifted labels, apparently flourishing at his new roost with his post-Nirvana outfit, Foo Fighters. Shredding the "drummer jinx," Dave has impressed this observer with his skill as a frontman and songwriter, especially on his hard-hitting recent album, *One by One,* recorded at his Virginia home studio. On the other hand, Foo Fighters have hardly aligned themselves with punk, even in the way that Nirvana did; other than his support for the Black Cat, Dave (like Henry) seems barely connected to the DC scene anymore.)

Even as the Black Cat, 9:30, and other clubs gained an increasingly large share of the punk show "market," efforts to keep, develop, and maintain less commercial spaces continued. On the far end of this spectrum, shows kept being held in basements and living rooms of Green House, Disarm House, Earthwell House, Tree Swing House, and more. However, as rents rose, group houses became scarcer, even in old punk havens like Mount Pleasant and Arlington, or were displaced to slightly less gentrified areas such as Columbia Heights. Like many of its contemporaries, PF House was sold. Adding insult to injury, the entire lot was razed to make way for the single most distastefully excessive mansion (complete with stretch limo and sleek sports car in the driveway) imaginable.

As a result, it was ever more important to connect with community institutions that could resist such ominous trends. One of the more significant new sites was a tiny community church/center on Mount Pleasant Street called La Casa. Shows there were initiated by the Stigmatics' Natalie Avery with help from bandmate Amanda Huron and artist/organizer Victoria Reis, many mixing visual arts, cinema, poetry, and music. Some were arranged with participation from neighborhood youths through a pro–immigrant-rights group called "Stand for Our Neighbors" and another Avery innovation, the Youth Research Action Group, made up largely of students from nearby Bell Multicultural School.

Natalie's innovative cross-cultural organizing and other creative endeavors pointed toward another hopeful phenomenon: the growth of punk expression further past the confines of music and narrow conceptions of community. Katy Otto of Bald Rapunzel, Del Cielo, and Exotic Fever Records is another example of a gifted, energetic organizer and artist, freely mixing feminism, punk, and community activism. So are folks like Kirby and Bork of Homes Not Jails, a direct-action outfit that takes over abandoned buildings to turn them into decent housing for the homeless; a chancy proposition, to be sure, especially in a town with as many police as DC. Still, what could be more "punk"?

At the same time, through the Future of Music Coalition, Jenny Toomey and Kristin Thomson have taken punk politics into another treacherous but crucial territory: the fight over artists' rights in the digital age. Thanks to such creative, visionary people as the above, DC punk has flourished on more diverse fronts than ever over the past decade; locking horns directly with the majors, while simultaneously mixing more comfortably with other cultures, especially those of DC's disenfranchised.

Thus, while punk-related institutions like Food for Thought fell victim to the raging-bullish real-estate market, new ones were rising. Amidst the arrival of a massive convention center two blocks to the south that promised to dramatically transform the Shaw community—in ways not friendly to longterm low-income residents—the Flemming Center finally opened its doors in late April 2003. Designed to serve those in danger of being displaced by gentrification, the Center is also my most concerted attempt to help move punk out of its subcultural ghetto into the broader arena necessary to affect social transformation in our time.

This, of course, hasn't meant turning my back on the punk community, even in its more "loud and fast" variants. One such band, in particular, proved itself a powerfully positive force: Crispus Attucks, named for an African-American Revolutionary War hero. Guitarist Matt Moffett was deeply involved with PF, helping to coordinate our work with homeless women at Bethany Women's Center, delivering groceries to neighborhood seniors, etc.

Crispus Attucks played many a benefit, including an anti–police-brutality show at Club Soda in October of 1998 that turned into a near-riot when clueless police—apparently annoyed with the club's past alcohol infractions—raided the show. As the cops brusquely shut it down, they were astonished to face sustained resistance. The image of punks nonviolently blockading that swanky stretch of Connecticut Avenue is not one I will soon forget. The band went out with a touch of class in a carefully crafted final show at Casa del Pueblo, the reopened Sanctuary Theater space that would soon also become a major non-club punk venue.

Casa del Pueblo—a mainline Methodist church transformed by the massive influx of Central American immigrants in the 1980s—also helped house LadyFest DC, which left the city bustling with feminist punk power not seen at least since the heyday of Riot Grrrl a decade before. While there were many great concerts, panels, films, and art shows, I was most touched by the music of the Quails, featuring DC punk vets Jen Smith and Seth Lorinczi. Another one of the highlights of 2002 for me was the dynamite bill of the Quails and Sleater-Kinney that came to the 9:30 Club not long afterward.

Women and girls continued to play key roles in DC-area punk. Few could channel raw rage as skillfully as Womyn of Destruction (a.k.a., Estrojet); the fierce focus of lead singer Andriana during sexual liberation anthem "PVI Is a Lie" was a wonder to behold, as was the infectious sparkle of dreadlocked accordionist Spoon. Nonetheless, diverse bands like Quix*o*tic, Crucial Defect, the Long Goodbye, Cassini Division, No Lie Relaxer, Cry Baby Cry, and Dame Fate each conveyed a potent antidote to the macho buffoonery and prefab style that so often threatens to define punk.

Another dynamic band with a vital female presence is 1905. I first saw them playing at a benefit in my own parish, St. Aloysius, nestled in a potent bill with Virginia Black Lung, Dead Stars, the all-female Four Chambered Heart, and jaggedly powerful two-drummer outfit, Black Eyes. Co–lead singer Jess opened the set with a rippling, melodic solo piano composition, which led seamlessly into gritty guitar crunch. The band's swirling harmonies, vocal interplay, and raw emotion floored me, reminding me once again how seeing a great band for the first time can really rearrange one's brain molecules!

While such benefit concerts continued, PF also diversified, organizing film screenings, art shows, book discussion groups, and other activities. The premiere of the Fugazi/Jem Cohen film *Instrument* at Sidwell Friends School raised funds for the Washington Free Clinic, while other powerful independent films on the history of Shaw, Riot Grrrl, racial issues in punk, Nigerian musician/activist Fela, '60s student radicals SDS, trailblazing feminist writer bell hooks, and more were offered up by PF, often in cooperation with the Black Cat.

My favorite cinematic adventure had to be our unauthorized DC premiere of the Clash documentary, *Westway to the World*. As Sony sat on the film (long available in the UK) for what seemed like an eternity, PF acquired a bootleg copy and screened it on election night 2000. We figured that filmmaker Don Letts and the band would respect the gesture, and were willing to risk legal action by Sony for violating their copyright. In the end, the film sold out both screenings, raising nearly $1000 for the Washington Peace Center.

As DC punk moved into new corners of creation, one of its original havens, the Wilson Center, was reopened. The original wedge was driven in by Fugazi's tenth-anniversary show, with the Stigmatics and dynamic local Latino punk band, Machetres. PF soon developed a fruitful partnership with Lilo Gonzales of Centro de Arte, who coordinated the space. As a result, for about three years, Wilson Center once again became a major underground venue, largely booked by key PFsters Wade and Ryan Fletcher.

After a long, tortuous community battle, the Wilson Center was sold for upscale redevelopment. PF held one last concert, with blistering performances by the likes of Crispus Attucks, Del Cielo, Kill the Man Who Questions, Trial by Fire, Strike Anywhere, and one of DC's great young bands, Q and Not U. Perhaps most memorable of the night was the short, incendiary, audience-challenging set by Virginia Black Lung, which began with a friend of the band initiating an antiwar chant and went confrontationally on from there. If the set seemed sometimes more about the message than the music, the performance was nonetheless electrifying. For me, punk once again seemed like a living challenge to heart, mind, and soul; more protest than safe consumer commodity.

And what is punk without some sense of protest? Sometimes our outcries were somber, even verging on silent, as with the series of memorials we helped organize for slain street sex workers. More often, they were very loud. I hold special affection for one percussion protest at a White Power march. The day ended with the Nazis deciding to not march, and with the counter-demonstrators in control of the street, dancing and drumming deliriously. Even larger, more powerful percussion circles would sometimes rise, such as in a January 2003 march at the Navy Yard in SE DC, protesting the impending war on Iraq.

Equally bracing were various demos that skillfully mixed music, speeches, and dramatic venues: the State of the Union protest with Thievery Corporation, Mr. Lif, and 1905 at the Capitol in frigid winter; Steve Earle on the steps of the Supreme Court in scalding summer, opposing the death penalty; Fugazi at an anti–drug-war rally at Malcolm X Park, against gentrification at the Smithsonian Folk Festival on the National Mall, protesting cuts in programs for the needy at the Washington Monument, or at any of its invariably rain-and-thunder–plagued Fort Reno shows—and many, many more.

As this suggests, Fugazi has soldiered on, doing what it has always done, albeit at a slower pace than in the past—a necessary concession to growing family commitments. Their 2001 album, *The Argument,* was arguably their best recorded effort, continuing their artistic growth while remaining vital, uncompromised, and relevant. The band received perhaps the highest praise imaginable when ex-Clash frontman Joe Strummer singled them out in *Rolling Stone* as the band that most exemplified "the spirit of punk" as he knew it.

During this relative lull, band members have kept busy with other projects. Joe Lally has been playing bass with feisty Frodus-offspring Black Sea. Ian MacKaye has also begun a new musical project, The Evens, with ex-Warmer Amy Farina. The spare, caustic unit debuted in late March with "On the Face of It," a free download available on the Thurston Moore–connected Protest-

Records.com website. The song's low-key music provides a velvet sheath for cold-steel lyrics decrying the frightening political climate of post-9/11 America.

All in all, then, DC punk has remained fertile, multifaceted, and very much alive well into the 21st century. While DC is hardly the same as in pre–"Smells Like Teen Spirit" days, the disruption here has probably been less than in other scenes like Seattle, the Bay Area, or LA. There, key community bands not only signed on with the majors, but then went multi-platinum, thus drawing A&R reps like flies to freshly deposited dung. By contrast, perennial independent stalwart Fugazi has remained the most popular, by far, of the punk-related bands to rise directly from DC.

Or so I thought. Imagine my surprise when I picked up the *Washington Post* in late September 2002 and first learned of the band Good Charlotte.

From what I could glean from Eric Brace's "Night Watch" column, Good Charlotte was a punk band formed in the DC suburb of Waldorf in 1996, shortly after the conclusion of this book's original narrative. Their first album (issued in mid-2000) was about to go gold; a hotly anticipated follow-up record was soon to emerge. In the article, guitarist/singer Benji described the phrase "rock star" as "an insult" within their band and spoke of his abiding love for DC and his desire to remain based here.

While these sentiments rang recognizably with the idealism of DC punk, they nestled uncomfortably next to the reality that Good Charlotte was signed to Epic Records, and that the band's twin-brother frontmen, Benji and Joel, were also VJs on MTV. Beyond the obvious tension in the band's stance, I was a bit flabbergasted to never even have heard of them.

Curious, I sought out their new record, *The Young and the Hopeless.* Immediately, I was struck by the multiple references to harDCore. "The Anthem" paid lyrical tribute to not one, but two Minor Threat songs. "Riot Girl" mentioned the band by name, and a Minor Threat patch was plainly visible on Benji's arm on the CD's back cover photo. Inside the CD booklet, one photo recreated the cover of "Salad Days," while another provided a peek at one of Benji's tattoos: the band's blacksheep graphic, originally drawn by Cynthia Connolly for the cover of the *Out of Step* LP.

With the success of the CD's first single (the scathing "Lifestyles of the Rich and Famous"), Good Charlotte found itself in the Top Ten by early 2003, broadcasting these harDCore samples to a new generation. More important than the references, however lovingly intended, was one simple question: Is Good Charlotte a worthy descendent of the demanding DC punk pedigree?

On one level, this is a question about Good Charlotte's music and its merits; on another, about soul, sincerity, intention. Musically, Good Charlotte is not, as yet, a trailblazer a la Bad Brains, Minor Threat, Fugazi, or other DC greats. Their music mixes sometimes-bristling, sometimes-sweet, always-catchy pop and punk with hip hop, ska, and reggae influences (think Green Day combined with Beastie Boys and the Clash), to an overall winning effect.

On its own, this could seem less than earth-shaking, and it would be easy to dismiss Good Charlotte as "punk posers," as the CD's liner notes suggest many have. Indeed, after the band was featured on the cover of *Alternative Press* with the headline "Punk and Disorderly," one disgruntled reader blistered them as "a prefabricated version of punk with no connection to the punk scene at any point in their existence."

This categorical dismissal is surely inaccurate and unfair. Still, while Good Charlotte has played grassroots venues as central to the late-'90s DC punk scene as the Kaffa House (and as embarrassing as the Grog and Tankard, a bar just up the street from the long-gone initial DC punk dive, the Keg), much of the band's meteoric rise seems due to support from massive industry institutions like MTV, WHFS-FM, and its HFStival—antitheses of punk grassroots networks.

Nonetheless, millions of young people are now learning about Minor Threat, and through them, possibly the entirety of the DC scene, thanks to Good Charlotte. This alone seems worthy of note, even praise. In addition, while tracks like "Festival Song," "The Anthem," "Movin' On," "Little Things," "The Story of My Old Man," and "Waldorf Worldwide" don't exactly break new ground musically or thematically, they touch me deeply, powerfully—and I haven't been a teen since a few months after Sid Vicious died!

Not all of Good Charlotte's songs connect; indeed, some seem a bit paint-by-numbers. But overall the band packs a big punch, animated by a palpable desire to touch an audience in ways that transcend mere entertainment, that give their listeners the hope, direction, and motivation that the punk they grew up with—Minor Threat, Rancid, and beyond—gave to them.

At their best, Good Charlotte not only pay tribute to the past, but continue its mission, hinting at the transformative possibilities that the most potent punk has always harbored. In the end, of course, it doesn't have to speak to me or my generation—not if it speaks to the ones now rising through their teens. Based on the testimony of folks like my 16-year-old PF friend Mandy, it does just that.

In part this is due to the band's outsider stance, a stance made credible by their past struggles. (Benji and Joel have an abusive, alcoholic father who deserted their ailing mother, leaving the family to face eviction and subsist, at times, off welfare.) Indeed, as the *Alternative Press* 2002 Readers Poll showed, Good Charlotte's fans identify deeply with the band in passionate terms that recall the devotion often shown to past DC punk. Amidst jabs at George W. Bush, Avril Lavigne, Eminem, Britney Spears, and Vines/Strokes/Hives–related "Rock Is Back" hype, *AP* readers voted *The Young And The Hopeless* "Best Album of the Year," and Good Charlotte as not only "Best Artist of the Year," but also the "Artist With Most Integrity."

While the band's detractors also made themselves obvious (voting Good Charlotte number three on the "Biggest Sellout" category), the editors of *Alternative Press* chimed in with this assessment: "Yeah, 2002 was the year that punk broke again . . . it was also the year that big business tried to hop the punk bandwagon, throwing anything with liberty spikes against the wall to see if it'd stick. But *AP's* readers saw through the BS, pushing two underdog twins from Maryland [i.e., Benji and Joel] to punk stardom—and the top of this year's Readers Poll."

But if Good Charlotte's impact on their audience is apparent, not yet clear is the answer to a deeper question: Can Good Charlotte continue to grow (and, by extension, help their listeners grow) in ways that will help to realize the artistic/political (rather than simply financial) possibilities implicit in the band's alleged original blueprint: "a combination of Minor Threat and the Backstreet Boys"?

As an increasingly grizzled punk, weary of the subcultural elitism too often prevalent in our circles, I find a certain subversive beauty in that unlikely hybrid. Indeed, while I still give my heart to the underground, I also vehemently endorse any sincere effort to seed the American mainstream with punk's radical ideas and practices—an essential task if we are ever to have something truly worthy of the word "revolution" in this country.

Some might scoff at the idea of Good Charlotte as a conduit for such lofty aims. In reply, I will simply note that these words rest on this indie-publisher page thanks to inspiration by the likes of Patti Smith, the Clash, Sex Pistols, and the Jam—all denizens of major corporate labels. If I can be transformed by such, why not others, why not by Good Charlotte?

Of course, Good Charlotte are not on par with these groundbreaking artists who created a whole new community while often wrestling mightily with the money-make-machine—something I really haven't seen Good Charlotte doing yet. It is easy to understand the appeal of being featured in a Target ad when you once were a lowly shelf-stocker there, as were Joel and Benji. Still, such actions—including having tour sponsors like Honda and MTV—don't smack of resistance, but collaboration.

However, having become acquainted with Benji (a fan of this book, it turns out, and seemingly as much a punk "true believer" as any I have encountered) and begun work on several exciting community-oriented projects with the band, I find it unlikely that Good Charlotte will simply "cash in." Indeed, the band not only agreed to play a special acoustic benefit concert in May 2003 to raise in excess of $20,000 for the Fair Budget Coalition's "From Service to Justice" initiative (a PF/Emmaus-backed effort to help organize and empower DC's needy to ensure that our city's budget puts human needs first); Benji actually took the lead in organizing it!

It surely is true that the standard set by the DC scene is a rigorous one, perhaps likely to be fully attempted by only a hardy few. Good Charlotte could yet walk away from this deeper challenge, leaving a sad, cash-driven coda to the story of DC punk. Time alone will tell. Good Charlotte has come a long way from their embattled pasts and working-class roots in Waldorf; I am certainly curious to see where they will go.

In a way, this all comes back to the gauntlet tossed down in a 1977 Subway Sect song: "Take hold of your life/There's something you've got to prove." The same challenge to "prove it" by our actions, not our words, is true for each of us, every day, all the time.

For me, for Good Charlotte, for all of us, punk remains, as always, about doing what you can, with what you've got, wherever you are right now. Maybe the "young idea" is far less about your age than about never being afraid to feel, to dream; about always being willing to look again, think again, to *begin* again; to try to build/be something real.

So ask yourself: What is "real"? What do I have to give? Where am I going? What do I believe? What do I want? If it is about a chance for everybody (not just a few) to live, to *really* live, not just exist; if it's about an authentic alternative to cookie-cutter/corporate/consumerist conformity, well, then it sounds like "punk" to me.

That's not really the important question, however. What does it sound like to *you?*

Which I guess brings us right around, back to the beginning. Just as some may be horrified that Good Charlotte is included in these pages, others have been angered by what wasn't found here.

Probably the single most consistent criticism of *Dance of Days* is that it wasn't "the whole story" of DC punk.

For such critics, I have a very simple answer: *You are absolutely, undeniably correct.*

Just for the record, neither Mark Jenkins nor I ever thought that *DOD* was the definitive, be-all, end-all book on DC punk. Indeed, given the hundreds of hours of interviews sifted through, the countless fanzines, fliers, audiotapes, and videos ingested as research, we, if anyone, should know that there is SO much more that could be said. Indeed, the rough draft of this book was TWICE the length of what you hold in your hands now—and even then I thought so many crucial stories, people, and ideas were being left out.

This book should also not be seen, in any sense, as having been "authorized" by the people who were so key in helping it come to be. These people—mostly dear friends—trusted me and, later, Mark Jenkins to be true to their stories, without ever asking for control over what was written. I hope we have proven worthy of their trust, worthy of this precious community that gave birth to us as artists in so many ways. I suspect that key figures in this book may yet speak for themselves in print. At the very least, they will continue to do so through their art, interviews, music . . . through their lives.

Thus, we're here to say, "Let a hundred flowers bloom." Why let this book or *Banned in DC* or *Tales of a Punk Rock Nothing,* et. al., stand as the whole of the DC punk story? What is your story, what do you want to tell? Let us know! Please write me at emmausdc@aol.com in order to get your (non-anonymous, non-libelous) submissions posted on our website, www.danceofdays.com. This site has been set up precisely to expand this conversation, to help spread other voices. While more writing by both Mark and me will be included, along with sections of the original draft excised from the final version, most of all, we would like you to be represented there.

We, of course, would humbly suggest that you try, like us, to do some serious research, lest your piece be simply your own opinion/experience; but, in the end, do what you will. In any case, *Dance of Days* is part of your story now. May these words be fuel for other worlds, other visions, other possibilities just waiting for us to have the courage to speak them, to believe them, to live them into reality.

Well, what are you waiting for? Life is short, and you were always the most important piece of this story anyway—the part that remains to be told.

after lives

Strenuous efforts were made to track down key characters from this book. Many could not be located by deadline; sometimes information was sketchy or incomplete. Additions and corrections for future editions are welcomed by Mark Andersen at emmausdc@aol.com.

Joey Aronstamn lives in Washington, working as a private investigator defending the disenfranchised; he is still into music.

Randy Austin performs with several Washington-area bands, including the Throwbacks.

Natalie Avery is singer-guitarist for Scaramouche and works in Mount Pleasant with the Youth Action Research Group and TranZmission, a community radio project.

Bad Brains reunited in 1999 under the name Soul Brains; Darryl Jenifer and Dr. Know continue to do session work and to live in Woodstock, NY with their families; Dr. Know has been a carpenter and a produce manager; Jenifer is working on a solo record. Earl Hudson lives in Atlanta, driving trucks and doing production work, while HR lives in LA.

Brian Baker plays guitar with Bad Religion; he moved back to Washington in 1995.

Chris Bald lives in Louisville, Kentucky, helping to raise his two children while continuing to create art and music.

Bill Barbot runs 3 Spot, a graphic design company.

The Bayou was demolished in 1999 for a luxury hotel-condo-retail development.

The Beehive Autonomous Collective closed in 1995.

Charles Bennington plays with New Wet Kojak.

Bikini Kill broke up in 1998; its final album, *Reject All-American*, was released on Kill Rock Stars.

Christina Billotte is a member of the DC trio Quix*o*tic and operates Ixorstix Records.

Dug Birdzell still plays bass and is raising a child with his partner Susan.

Paul Bishow premiered his latest movie, *It's a Wonderful Horrible Life*, in 2002. He's planning an anthology of his footage of DC punk bands.

Wendel Blow is a father, a songwriter and a carpenter; he lives in Austin, Texas.

Bob Boilen is a director and producer at National Public Radio's *All Things Considered* in Washington.

Ann Bonafede is a special education teacher.

Alec Bourgeois fronts the Dusters and works for Dischord and the Black Cat.

Russell Braen lives in DC's Maryland suburbs and works with computers.

Bratmobile reunited in the fall of 1998 and have released two CDs (*Ladies, Women and Girls* and *Girls Get Busy)* on Lookout! Records; Molly Neuman lives in Oakland, California, is the general manager of Lookout!, has a B.A. from Evergreen State College in feminism and film-making, and has been married since 1996; Erin Smith lives in the East Bay and does radio, video, and tour promotion for Lookout!; Allison Wolfe works for the *Washington Post* and helped to organize LadyFest in Olympia, Washington and Washington, DC.

Myron Bretholz performs and promotes traditional Irish music in the Washington area.

Molly Burnham lives in Massachusetts; she is a writer and also works with children.

Jerry Busher is Fugazi's stage-tech and second drummer. He plays with All-Scars and French Toast (with James Canty).

David Byers passed away suddenly in early 2003.

Keith Campbell plays in two bands, the hard-rock Three on a Match and the blues-rock Going Going Gone, and works part-time at two Northern Virginia music stores.

Sharon Cheslow lives in San Francisco, where she has performed and recorded with the Electrolettes, Red Eye, and members of Deerhoof; she also exhibits sound installations, runs Decomposition, and publishes *Interrobang*.

Leslie Clague is an artist, writer, and independent curator based in Seattle; she is a member of the group the Fuzzy Engine (www.fuzzyengine.com), co-founder of The Redheaded Stepchild, an alternative arts 'zine (www.redheaded.org), and recently the co-owner of Project 416, an alternative art space.

Michelle Cochran has a degree in naturopathic medicine and will soon have another in midwivery; she also is raising two children with husband Brendan Canty.

Kim Coletta is co-owner of DeSoto, an independent DC label, and has completed a Masters degree in library science from Catholic University; she and Bill Barbot recently had their first child.

Cynthia Connolly still works for Dischord

Records, and continues with her art and photography.

Scott Crawford does freelance magazine art direction as well as publishing a new music/culture magazine, *Harp* (www.harpmagazine.com); he is married and has a son, Clay.

Dag Nasty's *Can I Say* lineup released a new album, *Minority of One*, in 2002.

The **DC homicide rate** hit a 13-year low in 2000, declining to 227; it is still higher, however, than before it began its dramatic increase in the late '80s, and has been inching upward over the past two years.

Derek Denckla lives in Brooklyn and is both a lawyer and a musician; he is trying to merge the two worlds by starting a web-based DIY clearing-house for alternative artists.

Pierre DeVeux lives in Washington and manages a movie theater in Alexandria, Virginia.

Don Diego died of alcoholism in the mid-1990s.

Dischord continues to release new records by local artists such as El Guapo, Black Eyes, Lungfish, and Q and Not U; it also distributes many other DC-related bands and labels.

Dischord House is now owned by Ian MacKaye.

Dupont Circle punks have scattered. One of them, Ronnie, died of AIDS; another, Adam, committed suicide; yet another, Scooter, found recovery and subsequent work as an animal protection officer.

Lydia Ely worked for a decade as an advocate for the homeless; she now lives in the Bay Area, developing affordable housing and being a mom.

Jad Fair records and performs as a solo artist and in various collaborations; he lives part time in the Maryland suburbs.

John Falls is a photographer in New York City.

Boyd Farrell continues to live in the DC area, occasionally playing reunion gigs with Black Market Baby.

Jason Farrell lives in New York City, fronts the band Retisonic, and works as a graphic designer.

Dante Ferrando runs Washington underground rock club the Black Cat.

Sean Finnegan currently works as a grip (movie/TV lighting technician) on both coasts.

Food for Thought closed in 1999, replaced by a Parisian-style bistro.

Roddy Frantz works for a redevelopment authority in his native Pittsburgh.

Fugazi continues. Brendan Canty helps to produce other bands, does soundtrack work, and is helping to raise two children with his partner Michelle; Joe Lally is married and a father, operating his own label, Tolotta; Ian MacKaye produces many other bands and remains co-owner of Dischord; Guy Picciotto is also a producer and runs his own label, Peterbilt; all still live in the DC area.

Girls Against Boys is now based in New York, and recently released their sixth album, their first for Jade Tree Records. They continue to regularly play Positive Force benefits. Alexis Fleisig does freelance design work; Eli Janney works as an engineer and remixer; Scott McCloud also plays with New Wet Kojak and Operator; Johnny Temple plays with New Wet Kojak, runs Akashic Books, and writes for *The Nation* and other publications.

George Gelestino, founder and proprietor of Vinyl Ink Records, passed away in 2002 after a long illness.

Robert Goldstein composes music for films and works as a music librarian at National Public Radio in Washington.

Pat Graham splits his time between London and DC while continuing his photography and planning a book of his work.

Tim Green plays guitar in the Fucking Champs, has a solo electronic act called Concentrick, and owns and operates Louder Studios in San Francisco.

Vivien Greene is an assistant curator at the Guggenheim Museum in New York and is working on her PhD dissertation in art history.

Sab Grey plays in a reunited Iron Cross as well as his rockabilly/country band, the Articulate Rednecks; he has three children and is about to become an author.

Skip Groff still runs Yesterday & Today Records, which closed its storefront location in 2002, but continues as a web retailer.

Dave Grohl is the frontman of Foo Fighters and one of the owners of the Black Cat; in recent years he has lived in LA, Northern Virginia, and New York.

Mark Haggerty lives in Oakland, still plays music, and works at a collective vegetarian food store.

Kendall Hall is a UPS delivery person.

Michael Hampton is a music producer and soundtrack composer in New York.

Kathleen Hanna is a member of New York-based multi-media/feminist-punk trio Le Tigre.

Ivor Hanson is a freelance journalist in New York City.

Xyra Harper records and performs goth-art-rock in Washington.

Chris Haskett has played with David Bowie and others since leaving Henry Rollins's band.

Libby Hatch was killed in a motorcycle crash in 1998.

Peter Hayes works at the *Washington Post,* and plays and records with Spoils of NW, a "loud, melodic" rock band that is recording its first album.

Mike Heath lives in San Francisco; besides continuing as a music writer, he has been a courier, radio and club DJ, janitor, used record store lackey, poetry slammer, raver, busker, and market researcher.

Martha Hull and her husband live in Maryland, where she's home-schooling their 10-year-old daughter; she occasionally performs with the Slickee Boys, and hopes someday to complete a half-finished recording project.

Lida Husik's most recent album is 1999's *Mad Flavor.* Her discography and personal reflections are available at www.lidahusik.com.

Danny Ingram has continued to play drums with Swervedriver, Radioblue, and most recently, King Mixer; he has remarried, is a proud father, and lives in the DC area.

Kenny Inouye is a lawyer who runs www.inyoureye.com, a website for musicians who attempt to handle their own business affairs.

Edd Jacobs is a licensed addictions counselor and AIDS educator.

Eddie Janney continues to play music and make art. He and spouse Natalie Avery recently became parents.

Jon Kirschten lives in North Carolina and really likes to bowl.

Kim Kane is concentrating on art, working on MoPar muscle cars, and on a garage-punk LP by his solo group the Grimm Fairys; he still occasionally plays with the Slickee Boys and Date Bait.

Tommy Keene lives in LA and continues to play music. His most recent album, *The Merry-Go-Round Broke Down*, was released by SpinART in 2002.

Donald Keesing lives in Silver Spring, Maryland, raising two sons with his wife Juanita Mendoza; he also works for the Nuclear Information and Resource Service and has released a solo record.

Steve Kiviat is a lawyer, freelance writer, and legal volunteer at the Washington Legal Clinic for the Homeless.

James "Mr. Ott" Kowalski is serving a prison term for sexual child abuse.

Marc Lambiotte lives in the DC area and continues to play music.

Nathan Larson has done film soundtrack work and has just released his first solo CD on the Big Wheel Recreation label.

Andre Lee is an editor for the Washington-based cable channel Animal Planet.

Linda LeSabre was last seen living in LA, playing drums in My Life With the Thrill Kill Kult.

Steve Lorber lives in the DC suburbs, where he runs a mail order business dealing in pop-music collectibles.

Tom Lyle built a home studio and does record production; he also writes for recording and audio equipment magazines.

Lara Lynch is raising her kids in the Southwest.

Alec MacKaye works at the Phillips Collection, a Washington art museum, and is playing music with Eddie Janney and other friends.

Amanda MacKaye still lives in DC and is in a new band, The Deep Six, with old Jury Rig comrades Ryan Nelson and Todd McFarlane.

Michelle Mae plays bass for the Scene Creamers, a DC quartet.

Lois Maffeo lives in Olympia and continues to write and record; her latest album, *The Union Themes*, is a collaboration with Brendan Canty.

Mike Manos is a Washington-area computer consultant.

Roger Marbury is married, lives in Boston, and works as a lighting engineer for film projects.

Marginal Man is reissuing its music through its website, www.marginalman.com.

Michael Marriotte edits the Nuclear Information and Resource Service's *Nuclear Monitor*; he also drums in occasional Tru Fax reunions.

Seth Martin and his partner Christine have two children; he is also a software architect and continues to handle financial matters for Dischord and Fugazi.

Kevin Mattson is a professor of history.

Micro helps to build skate parks through Ramptech, based in Northern Virginia.

Charlie Moats continues to do accounting work and lives with his two dogs in the DC area.

Pete Murray lives in Austin with his wife and

has a degree in electronics; his latest band, Belmont Hall, is named after a street near Wilson Center.

Jeff Nelson is the co-owner of Dischord and also operates another label, Adult Swim, which in recent years has featured alternative country acts like Last Train Home and Little Pink; he lives a few blocks from Dischord House and is working on a coffee table book on Washington's Q Street Bridge.

Ted Niceley is a record producer based in Albuquerque.

Steve Niles is married and lives in LA; with his collaborator Todd McFarland, he writes two monthly comics in the *Spawn* series and has recently finished a pilot for a TV series.

Gordon (Gordon) Ornelas moved to Seattle where he published *Teen Fag Magazine* in the '90s; he sometimes writes for other publications.

The 9:30 Club moved to 815 V Street, NW, formerly WUST Hall, in 1996.

No Business As Usual is long gone, but its spirit lives on in the N30 and A16 protests in Seattle and DC, respectively, and perhaps especially in the Revolutionary Anti-Authoritarian Bloc (a.k.a., "black bloc") faction.

Mark Noone performs with Ruthie and the Wranglers and, occasionally, the Slickee Boys.

Joey P. lives in New York with his wife, helping to raise their two girls; whenever possible, he still does live sound for Fugazi.

Amy Pickering still works at Dischord and continues to play music.

Pirate House and the **Embassy** were both sold as Mount Pleasant gentrified; however, the former is now owned by Faraquet's Jeff Boswell.

Steve Polcari manages the parts department at a Washington-area auto dealership.

Positive Force DC (www.positiveforceDC.org) operates from the Flemming Center, its new home in the Shaw neighborhood. PF House was sold in October 2000 and was demolished to make way for a luxury residence.

Lyle Preslar is an A&R executive at Razor & Tie Records in New York.

Bert Queiroz lives in New York City, where he manages a record store, Other Music, and is working on a book of his photographs.

Diana Quinn performs with the Fabulettes and Honky Tonk Confidential and works at CBS News in Washington.

Andy Rapoport is an actor living in New York City.

Michael Reidy is an artist and sometime renovation worker in Washington; he plays occasional reunion gigs with Razz.

Erika Reinstein graduated from Evergreen State College and has battled health problems while continuing her writing and activism; she now lives in Seattle.

Barbara Anne Rice is a lawyer living and working in the DC area.

Monica Richards lives in Los Angeles, where she was a member of Faith and the Muse.

Riot Grrrl no longer meets in DC or Olympia; however, its energy continues in activist groups like DC's WATTS, bands like Sleater-Kinney, and events like Ladyfest DC.

Malcolm Riviera does web design (www.malco.net) and recording in his home studio in North Carolina, punctuated by occasional live performances with electronic improv combo Bastard Trout.

J. Robbins is a record producer and graphic artist.

Mark Robinson runs Teenbeat, whose operations are now divided between Arlington and Boston; after Unrest, he led Air Miami and Flin Flon, both now defunct.

Henry Rollins is a major-label recording artist based in LA; he continues to do spoken-word gigs and to publish books through 2.13.61.

Jim Saah is a full-time freelance photographer who lives in Siver Spring, Maryland with his wife, Roseann, and his two sons, Jasper and Marco; he can be reached at www.jim-saah.com.

Kate Samworth is an artist in Louisiana.

Kurt Sayenga lives in LA, operating a film production company that has made more than two dozen documentaries, mostly for the Discovery Channel.

Colin Sears has continued to play music in a series of bands including Alloy and the Marshes; he taught as a graduate student at the University of Massachusetts and he now lives in Portland, Oregon, where he works in urban planning and community development.

Brad Sigal is living in St. Paul, and is involved with the antiwar movement as a member of the Twin Cities CISPES Antiwar committee. (www.angelfire.com/mn/cispes)

Simple Machines was closed by Jenny Toomey and Kristin Thomson; its "Mechanic's Guide to Putting Out Music" evolved into a website, themachine.com (www.insound.com/machine) that extends the DIY message to the MP3/Napster age.

Don Smith is a website programmer with Fig Leaf Software.

Jen Smith lives in the San Francisco area, where she does art, writing, and community activist work; she also plays in the Quails.

Jon Spencer fronts the New York-based Jon Spencer Blues Explosion, who record for Matador.

Tomas Squip works at the Everlasting Life food co-op and is a member of the African Hebrew Israelites, a millennial sect.

John Stabb lives in DC with his girlfriend Mika and fronts the Factory Incident, whose latest DIY release is now available; also imminent is his first book, a memoir entitled *Sheer Terror: GI and Other Insanity*.

Franz Stahl lives in LA, helping to raise a family, works as a set-dresser for films and commercials, and still plays guitar.

Pete Stahl lives in LA, continues to play music in bands like earthlings? and Goatsnake, while also doing road work for other bands.

Kent Stax is a carpenter who lives in Northern Virginia with his wife and teenage daughter; he drums with the Spitfires United and the reunited Iron Cross.

Chris Stover lives in the Bay Area with his wife, Sevda, and can be reached at ChrisStover@aol.com.

Straight Edge now appears in the Random House Dictionary, defined as "advocating abstinence from alcohol, cigarettes, drugs, and sex, and sometimes advocating vegetarianism."

Nathan Strejcek is married and works at the Airline Pilots Association in Washington; he is learning to play guitar.

Bobby Sullivan lives in the Smoky Mountains of North Carolina with his partner and their four daughters; he works for a natural foods store.

Mark Sullivan lives in Washington, DC with his wife and two children.

Mo Sussman moved to North Carolina after his restaurant, Joe and Mo's, declared bankruptcy in the '90s.

Ian Svenonius fronts the Scene Creamers.

Jenny Thomas lives in DC, works with youth at risk through Martha's Table, and plays drums in Cry Baby Cry.

Chris Thompson teaches high school English at Georgetown Day School.

Kim Thompson lives in Chicago, is married to Chris Thomson, and has a PhD in clinical psychology, focusing on women victimized by violence, poverty, or other abuse; she continues with music and photography.

Skeeter Thompson lives in Little Rock, Arkansas, helping to raise his three kids, while remaining musically and politically active.

Chris Thomson lives in Chicago and works for an advertising agency. He is married to Kim Thompson.

Kristin Thomson has just completed a Master's degree in urban affairs and public policy; she works with the Future of Music Coalition, is married, and lives in Philadelphia.

Mary Timony now lives in Boston and records for Matador.

Jenny Toomey is on leave from the advertising department of the *Washington Post* while she works as Executive Director of the non-profit Coalition for the Future of Music (www.future-ofmusic.com); she continues to play solo gigs and has recorded a new CD.

Tru Fax and the Insaniacs still perform periodically and are preparing a new CD that will include new and old material (www.muddy-paws.com).

Geoff Turner produces bands and plays with New Wet Kojak. He is married and lives in LA.

Tobi Vail lives in Olympia, does mail order for Kill Rock Stars, and continues to write and play music.

Shawn Vitale retired from Gussound to do sound at the 9:30 Club.

Adam Wade now lives in LA and has continued to play drums with various touring bands, including Krist Novoselic's Sweet 75 and the Lapse; he is also studying sound editing for film and music.

Bernie Wandel is the general manager of the Black Cat Club.

Craig Wedren lives on New York's Lower East Side and composes film soundtrack music; he is working on a new band.

Scott Weinrich plays with Spirit Caravan, a Washington-area band that has released two CDs on Joe Lally's Tolotta label.

WHFS is one of the country's top "modern-rock" stations.

Kathi Wilcox works on film and music projects in DC, and is the *Washington Post* Style section's pop-music copy aide.

The Wilson Center was re-reopened to punk by Positive Force in 1997 for Fugazi's tenth anniversary gig, a benefit for the Latin American Youth Center; it continued to serve as an independent rock venue and community service provider, until being sold for upscale redevelopment.

Howard Wuelfing is a freelance publicist, based in Pennsylvania.

Tim Yohannon died of cancer in spring 1998; *MRR* continues under new coordinators.

Don Zientara continues to operate Inner Ear Studios.

index

Positive Force DC presents:

The ◼ ◼ ◼ ◼
DC Underground
Invitational

with

fugazi
and
The Vertebrates

Monday, Aug. 7 • 7 p.m.
Fort Reno Park

(Wisconsin & Chesapeake Ave. NW near Tenleytown Metro)

All expressions rising out of a grassroots dissident culture of compassion, creativity, and resistance are invited to publicize themselves at this event. This means activist groups, art, fanzines, CD/record/tape labels and probably many other possibilities we haven't even thought of – the more the merrier! Table space will be provided. ONE REQUEST, HOWEVER: Since the selling of merchandise is prohibited on National Park land, please don't sell anything... or do so with a very low profile, and at your own risk.

In other words, *bring it all on,* but leave the checkbook at home!

Thanks... and for more information on this event or on Positive Force, call 703-276-9768. *Spread the word!*

YOU ARE NOT POWERLESS.

N.R.I.D.G.W.B.

ORGANIZE! It's the rest of our lives

CITY PAPER FREE AD BY JIM LYONS AND TINA PLOTTEL WITH GRAPHICS BY JEM COHEN AND JIM SAAH, TEXT BY MARK ANDERSEN, AUGUST 2000; GRAFFITI FROM

to **Chris Bald**, for the use of his words in the title of
this book, and for maximum inspiration over the years.

Much love,
MSA

WE OWE YOU NOTHING:
PUNK PLANET, THE COLLECTED INTERVIEWS
Edited by Daniel Sinker

334 pages, a trade paperback original (6" x 9")

$16.95, ISBN: 1-888451-14-9

"This collection of interviews reflects one of *Punk Planet's* most important qualities: Sinker's willingness to look beyond the small world of punk bands and labels and deal with larger issues. With interview subjects ranging from punk icons Thurston Moore and Ian MacKaye to Noam Chomsky and representatives of the Central Ohio Abortion Access Fund, as well as many other artists, musicians, and activists, this book is not solely for the tattooed, pierced teenage set. All of the interviews are probing and well thought out, the questions going deeper than most magazines would ever dare; and each has a succinct, informative introduction for readers who are unfamiliar with the subject. Required reading for all music fans." *–Library Journal*

IT'S A FREE COUNTRY:
PERSONAL FREEDOM IN AMERICA AFTER SEPTEMBER 11
Edited by Danny Goldberg, Victor Goldberg, and Robert Greenwald

370 pages, hardcover

$19.95, ISBN: 0-9719206-0-5

"A terrific collection of personal stories, legal arguments, and historical reminders about civil liberties in our society. We must never forget that we live in our faith and our many beliefs, but we also live under the law–and those legal rights must never be suspended or curtailed." –Reverend Jesse Jackson

R&B (RHYTHM & BUSINESS):
THE POLITICAL ECONOMY OF BLACK MUSIC
Edited by Norman Kelley

338 pages, hardcover

$24.95, ISBN: 1-888451-26-2

"In this anthology, perhaps the first to deal solely with the business of black music . . . [t]he history of the modern recording industry . . . is dissected in several eye-opening contributions that should be required reading for anyone interested in popular music." *–Library Journal*

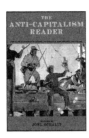

THE ANTI-CAPITALISM READER:
IMAGINING A GEOGRAPHY OF OPPOSITION

Edited by *Punk Planet's* Joel Schalit

336 pages, a trade paperback original

$16.95, ISBN: 1-888451-33-5

A refreshingly non-doctrinaire anthology of writings and interviews covering much of the intellectual geography of the new anti-market left. Featuring Doug Henwood, Naomi Klein, Ali Abunimah, Annalee Newitz, Slavoj Zizek, Toni Negri, Thomas Frank, Wendy Brown, and many others.

NEWS DISSECTOR:
PASSIONS, PIECES, AND POLEMICS; 1960–2000

by Danny Schechter

297 pages, a trade paperback original

$16.95, ISBN: 1-888451-20-3

"Danny Schechter, a kind of journalist without borders, has shaken up public broadcasting, among many other media institutions, in the course of his career as a self-styled 'News Dissector' and human rights advocate . . ." *–The Nation*

FALUN GONG'S CHALLENGE TO CHINA:
SPIRITUAL PRACTICE OR "EVIL CULT"?

A report and reader by Danny Schechter

288 pages, trade paperback

$15.95, ISBN: 1-888451-27-0

The only book-length investigative report on this severe human rights crisis that is affecting the lives of millions.

"[Schechter] offers a persuasive analysis of this strange and still unfolding story . . ." *–New York Times*

These books are available at local bookstores. They can also be purchased with a credit card online through www.akashicbooks.com. To order by mail send a check or money order to:

Akashic Books, PO Box 1456, New York, NY 10009
www.akashicbooks.com, Akashic7@aol.com

(Prices include shipping. Outside the U.S., add $8 to each book ordered.)

MARK ANDERSEN is outreach coordinator for Emmaus Services for the Aging, a small outreach and advocacy group that assists inner-city seniors in DC's Shaw neighborhood. He remains active with Positive Force DC, Helping Individual Prostitutes Survive, and Women's Advocates to Terminate Sexism (WATTS), as well as with the justice and service committee of St. Aloysius Catholic Church. He lives with his beloved, Tulin Ozdeger, and their cat, Demo, in an apartment on the border of the Adams Morgan and Mount Pleasant neighborhoods.

MARK JENKINS writes about music, film, and other topics for the *Washington Post*, *Washington City Paper*, National Public Radio's "All Things Considered," *Time Out New York*, WAMU·FM, and other outlets.

POSITIVE FORCE DC, JUNE 2000, IN FRONT OF PF HOUSE; MARK ANDERSEN IN BLACK T-SHIRT AT FRONT LEFT *(by Darrow Montgomery)*